The Essentials
of Writing
Ten Core Concepts

Second Edition

Robert P. Yagelski
University at Albany, State University of New York

CENGAGE
Learning

Australia • Brazil • Mexico • Singapore • United Kingdom • United States

CENGAGE
Learning

The Essentials of Writing: Ten Core Concepts
Second Edition
Robert P. Yagelski

Product Director: Monica Eckman

Product Manager: Laura Ross

Content Developer: Lynn M. Huddon

Senior Content Developer: Leslie Taggart

Product Assistant: Shelby Nathanson

Marketing Manager: Kina Lara

Content Project Manager: Rebecca Donahue

Senior Art Director: Marissa Falco

Manufacturing Planner: Betsy Donaghey

IP Analyst: Ann Hoffman

IP Project Manager: Erika Mugavin

Production Service and Compositor:
Christian Arsenault, SPi Global

Text Designer: Bill Reuter

Cover Designer: Roycroft Design

Cover Image: Don Mason/Stockbyte/Getty
Images

For product information and technology assistance, contact us at
Cengage Learning Customer & Sales Support, 1-800-354-9706

For permission to use material from this text or product,
submit all requests online at **www.cengage.com/permissions.**

Further permissions questions can be emailed to
permissionrequest@cengage.com.

Library of Congress Control Number: 2016957183

Student Edition:
ISBN: 978-1-337-09173-2

Cengage Learning
20 Channel Center Street
Boston, MA 02210
USA

Cengage Learning is a leading provider of customized learning solutions
with employees residing in nearly 40 different countries and sales in more
than 125 countries around the world. Find your local representative at
www.cengage.com.

Cengage Learning products are represented in Canada by Nelson
Education, Ltd.

To learn more about Cengage Learning Solutions, visit **www.cengage.com.**

Purchase any of our products at your local college store or at our preferred
online store **www.cengagebrain.com.**

Printed at CLDPC, USA, 04-18

Brief Contents

Detailed Contents

Chapter 4   A Student Writer Applies the Core Concepts

Chapter 5   Understanding Analytical Writing

Chapter 6   Understanding Argument

Chapter 7 Working with Ideas and Information

Chapter 10   Evaluating Sources

Chapter 11   Using Source Material

Chapter 12 Citing Sources Using MLA Style

Preface

Writing is a way to understand and participate in the world around us. It is a vehicle for learning, a way to make sense of our experiences and convey what we learn to others. Writing is a powerful means of individual expression and social interaction that has the capacity to change us. As the National Commission on Writing in America's Schools and Colleges put it, "At its best, writing has helped transform the world."

Composition teachers know all this, of course. They understand the power of writing, and they know that writing well is necessary for students to succeed in college and beyond. But instructors also know that a one-semester course is never quite enough to help students develop the sophisticated skills they will need to write effectively in their college classes and in their lives outside school. Research indicates that students need their entire college careers to develop those skills. First-year writing courses can lay the foundation for that process.

To make the most of the composition course, *The Essentials of Writing: Ten Core Concepts* focuses on the most important skills and knowledge that students must develop to be able to write the kind of sophisticated prose expected in college. It teaches the foundational lessons that students need to develop their competence as writers.

A Focus on Important Aspects of Writing

Research underscores what composition instructors well know: most college students tend to have difficulty with a few crucial aspects of writing:

- addressing an audience effectively
- focusing on a main idea and developing it sufficiently
- organizing texts appropriately
- adopting an appropriate register or "voice" in writing
- supporting assertions or arguments
- identifying and using appropriate sources
- revising effectively
- applying the conventions of academic writing

For the most part, these difficulties apply across disciplines and forms of writing. Significantly, research reveals that most of these problems arise from three main sources:

- students' lack of understanding of the rhetorical nature of writing
- students' inexperience with different rhetorical tasks across the college curriculum
- students' misunderstanding of how to manage the process of writing

In other words, these problems arise from a basic misunderstanding of the rhetorical and social nature of writing and inexperience with managing the writing process *in the context of varied rhetorical tasks*, especially the kind of writing tasks typical of academic work in college.

Consequently, *The Essentials of Writing: Ten Core Concepts* rests on three central ideas about writing:

- *Writing is a rhetorical act.* Writing is fundamentally an interaction between a writer and a reader within a specific social context. In this sense, writing is always a social activity, and effective writing connects writers and readers in complex and powerful ways.

- *Writing is a way to participate in the conversations that shape our lives.* Through writing, writers and their readers collaborate in knowledge-making and share information and opinions about issues that matter to them. Writing enables us to take part in the many ongoing conversations about important matters that affect how we live and how we understand ourselves and the world we inhabit. In the most basic way, writing is a way to *construct* the world by participating in these complex conversations.
- *Writing is a means of inquiry.* Writing is an intellectual activity that can lead to a deeper understanding of ideas, experiences, and information. It is a means of understanding ourselves and the world we share. Writing can engage students in careful, critical thinking about themselves and the world around them. Writing is a unique and powerful vehicle for learning.

These ideas inform both the content and structure of *The Essentials of Writing: Ten Core Concepts*. As students are guided through various writing tasks and learn to manage the process of writing efficiently, they also gain a fuller understanding of the nature of writing as rhetoric, conversation, and inquiry. In this way, *The Essentials of Writing: Ten Core Concepts* can help composition instructors meet a central challenge in working with student writers: helping students develop a sophisticated understanding of writing and gain experience as writers acting on that understanding.

The Essentials of Writing: Ten Core Concepts emphasizes what is essential in writing at the college level and guides students as they apply that knowledge to various writing tasks. It trains students to think rhetorically and helps them manage the fundamental characteristics of effective academic writing. In this regard, the Ten Core Concepts serve as a framework for understanding writing and a practical, step-by-step guide for negotiating the demands of academic writing tasks.

Ten Core Concepts

The Ten Core Concepts distinguish this textbook from other writing guides. Most composition textbooks try to cover every conceivable aspect of writing in college and beyond, presenting far more material than students could ever grasp and retain in a single semester. That approach ultimately waters down the most important lessons that student writers must learn. *The Essentials of Writing: Ten Core Concepts* is different. It emphasizes what students must really learn to become effective writers.

These Core Concepts are not basic skills, nor are they procedures for completing specific kinds of writing tasks. Rather, they are fundamental insights into the nature of writing that students must enact as they complete varied writing tasks. These Core Concepts boil down what has been learned through research and practice into key ideas about what writing is and how effective writing works. For example, Core Concept #4—"a writer must have something to say"—emphasizes the need for a piece of writing to convey a clear main point or idea. Studies indicate that college writing instructors identify the lack of a clear main idea as one of the most common weaknesses in student writing. This concept helps students understand why effective writing in most genres is characterized by a focus on a main idea; it also helps them understand how the different expectations in various academic disciplines can shape a writer's main idea and how that main idea is presented and developed in specific kinds of texts. Most importantly, the concept guides students through a process that enables them to identify, refine, and articulate the main idea of any writing project they are working on. In this way, the Core Concepts can deepen students' understanding of key insights about writing at the same time that students practice applying those insights in their own writing.

The Ten Core Concepts are not prescriptive. They are not step-by-step instructions for writing in specific genres. Instead, they are fundamental but flexible guidelines for writing;

they serve as a set of heuristics that students can apply to *any* writing task. *The Essentials of Writing: Ten Core Concepts* is informed by the basic idea that practice is essential in developing writing competence. In a sense, this idea is the 11th Core Concept. Only through sustained, guided practice in writing different kinds of texts for various rhetorical situations can students develop the understanding and ability to write effectively for different purposes. Accordingly, *The Essentials of Writing: Ten Core Concepts* relies in part on the repetition of the Ten Core Concepts to give students the practice they need to make these Concepts part of their repertoire as writers.

The Structure of *The Essentials of Writing: Ten Core Concepts*

The Essentials of Writing: Ten Core Concepts is organized into twelve chapters. Chapters 1 through 4 introduce students to the essential insights into writing that they must acquire if they are to be able to apply their writing skills effectively in different contexts. In these chapters, students explore the fundamental ideas about writing described above: writing as rhetoric, as conversation, and as inquiry. Most important, they learn and practice the Ten Core Concepts that form the heart of this textbook. Chapter 2 explains these concepts, using examples to illustrate the lessons as well as exercises to help students understand how to apply the concepts in their own writing. Chapter 3 is an interactive, visual guide students can use to apply the Ten Core Concepts to any piece of writing. Chapter 4 presents a case study of a first-year student writer as she applies the Ten Core Concepts to complete a writing assignment.

Chapters 5 and 6 are new to this edition and they introduce students to principles of effective analysis writing and argumentative writing. Each chapter concludes with a guide for writing that is based on the Ten Core Concepts and diverse Writing Project assignments.

The remaining chapters provide students with practical advice about working with source material, conducting research for their various writing projects, and mastering and applying the conventions of written English. Chapter 7 focuses on essential intellectual skills that are important to the work that students do throughout college, including summarizing, paraphrasing, and synthesizing texts. Chapter 8 guides students in understanding an increasingly important aspect of effective writing today: document design. Chapters 9, 10, and 11 provide an up-to-date guide for finding, evaluating, and using source material in an interconnected world characterized by access to overwhelming bodies of information. Chapter 12 helps students understand and apply the guidelines for citing sources recommended by MLA.

Throughout *The Essentials of Writing: Ten Core Concepts* students encounter varied examples of effective writing in different genres and different media. They see how other writers, including student writers, meet the challenges of contemporary writing in college and beyond, and they are given varied opportunities to practice what they learn, all the while using the Ten Core Concepts as their framework for writing.

Integrated Coverage of Digital Literacy Practices

The Essentials of Writing: Ten Core Concepts focuses on the contemporary student who lives in an increasingly technological, globalized age. To write well today requires students to manage many different rhetorical tasks using various technologies, including constantly evolving digital media that have become essential tools for communication. Rather than addressing "digital literacy" as a separate skill or topic, *The Essentials of Writing: Ten Core Concepts* incorporates emerging digital technologies and literacy practices into the advice and practice it provides students for all their writing tasks. Throughout this textbook, students encounter examples and exercises that reflect various uses of communications technologies, and they receive advice for taking advantage of these technologies to meet the needs of the rhetorical situations within which they are writing.

New Introductions to Analysis and Argument

New chapters on "Understanding Analytical Writing" (Chapter 5) and "Understanding Argument" (Chapter 6) introduce students to the key features of these two important forms of academic writing. These chapters also include annotated professional readings, step-by-step guides to writing that are based on the Ten Core Concepts, and Writing Project assignments that provide ideas for students' own compositions.

New "Talking About This Reading" Dialogue with Students

The professional readings in Chapters 5 and 6 are accompanied by a unique, new feature called "Talking About This Reading," in which real students comment on challenging or inspiring aspects of the reading and pose questions that the reading raised for them. In response to these comments and questions, I offer advice and strategies to help students understand the reading and meet the challenges it might present to them.

New Student Case Study

Chapter 4 features a new project that enables students to see how a student writer, Chloe Charles, applied the Ten Core Concepts to a real writing assignment. The chapter follows Chloe through the process of composing an essay for an assignment in her college writing course, from generating a timely topic and developing a guiding thesis statement, to revising in response to feedback from her peers and her instructor, to preparing her final submitted essay.

New Research and 2016 MLA Documentation Guidelines

- **Revised Discussion of Finding Digital Sources.** Chapter 9 offers students up-to-date guidance for finding digital source materials when conducting research and developing research projects.

- **Updated MLA Guidelines.** Chapter 12 has been extensively revised to reflect the new 2016 MLA guidelines for documenting sources, including many new model citations and new digital examples to help students cite sources accurately.

Acknowledgments

Writing a textbook can be a daunting undertaking, but it is made less so by the inherently collaborative nature of the work. This book is not mine; rather, it is the result of the sustained efforts of many people, whose ideas, dedication, and hard work helped make *The Essentials of Writing: Ten Core Concepts* a reality. It is impossible to thank them enough.

I am extremely grateful to Lyn Uhl for identifying this project as an important one and providing the support necessary to realize the vision that informed this project from the beginning. Special thanks to Monica Eckman, who provided leadership and support for this project from its very beginnings and whose knowledge and energy helped me manage the pressure of this work.

I am also deeply grateful to Laura Ross, the editor for this project, whose expert guidance in refining it for this new edition has been integral to its success. Laura made this book a better one, and she always made the work fun and fulfilling. I am truly thankful for her dedication to this project and feel fortunate to be able to work with her.

My sincerest gratitude goes to Leslie Taggart, the senior development editor for this project, whose insight, patience, good humor, and constant support not only were essential in keeping the project moving forward but also made it possible for me to find the wherewithal to finish the work. The quality of this textbook is in so many ways a result of Leslie's dedication, expert advice, and exceptional judgment.

I am truly blessed to have had Lynn Huddon as the development editor for this edition. Lynn is as diligent and insightful as any editor I have worked with in more than 15 years of writing textbooks, and there is no doubt that the quality of this new edition is in large part a function of her hard work and keen eye for detail. She kept the project on track in the face of countless unexpected challenges, and she was always ready with excellent suggestions for improvements and refinements. Lynn was also exceedingly patient with this sometimes frustrated author and ever available to solve the many problems, large and small, that arise in the development of a composition textbook. I am extremely grateful to her and consider myself truly fortunate to have had the opportunity to work with her on this project.

My thanks, too, to Andy Fogle, of Bethlehem High School in Bethlehem, New York, who helped with the research for several chapters during the development of the first edition, and Tony Atkins, of the University of North Carolina at Greensboro, who not only provided invaluable insight about the treatment of technology throughout the book but also helped develop the chapter on document design.

I gratefully acknowledge the important role of my terrific colleagues in the Program in Writing and Critical Inquiry at the State University of New York at Albany. Their expertise and dedication as teachers of writing have not only inspired me but also helped deepen my own understanding of effective writing pedadogy. Their influence has shaped this new edition in both subtle and profound ways. In particular, I thank Susan Detwiler and Joe Creamer, superb colleagues and wonderful teachers whose feedback has enriched my thinking about writing instruction in general and about this textbook in particular. Susan and Joe were always willing to help me test ideas and review student writing as I developed this new edition. Also, my sincere thanks to Chloe Charles, a student of Joe Creamer's at SUNY-Albany and the author of the essay that appears in Chapter 4. Chloe is a hard-working, dedicated, and curious student who was cheerfully willing to put in a great deal of time and effort to meet our deadlines for this edition. I am very proud to be able to include her essay in this book, and I am blessed to have had the chance to work with her and learn from her.

I am also deeply grateful to the students who took the time to read and comment on the various selections included in this textbook. Their thoughtful questions and comments have enriched the readings and provided additional avenues of inquiry for their many peers who will eventually read this book.

It should go without saying that my students over the years have been perhaps the most important influence on my work as a teacher and a writer. They have taught me so much of what I know about writing, and they have enriched my life and work. I am grateful to all of them for allowing me to be part of their learning and their lives. They truly do make this work worthwhile.

My colleagues and friends in the Capital District Writing Project (CDWP), including Aaron Thiell, Christopher Mazura, Amy Salamone, Molly Fanning, Alicia Wein, and Christine Dawson, have been my supporters and teachers for many years now. I rely on them much more than they know, and their influence infuses this text. I am especially grateful to Carol Forman-Pemberton, my co-director at CDWP, who has become my most trusted colleague and wonderful friend over the many years we have been working together. I have learned from her more about writing and teaching than I could ever include in a single textbook, and her wisdom as a professional has guided my own work. I am truly fortunate to have her as a colleague and friend.

The many experts at Cengage who helped with the design, production, and marketing of this textbook also deserve a special thanks: Marissa Falco, Rebecca Donahue, Samantha Ross Miller, Kina Lara, Jacqueline Czel and Elizabeth Cranston. I especially wish to acknowledge Erin Parkins, whose tireless work on behalf of this textbook helped make the first edition a success.

I greatly benefited from the advice of many insightful instructors who provided thoughtful reviews and other kinds of feedback that helped shape this edition. My sincerest thanks to all the following instructors: Kevin Allen, Florida Gulf Coast University; Ron Brooks, Oklahoma State University; Neil Connelly, Shippensburg University; Garrett Cummins, University of Cincinnati; Renee DeLong, Minneapolis Community and Technical College; Dana Gregory Griffith, University of Cincinnati; Thomas F. Haffner, Saint Xavier University; Kalissa Hendrickson, Arizona State University; Ferdinand Hunter, GateWay Community College; Kerri Jordan, Mississippi College; Pam Kingsbury, University of North Alabama; Deborah Luoma, Gavilan College; Jeremy P. Meyer, Mesa Community College; Shyam Sharma, Stony Brook University; Tammy Winner, University of North Alabama; and Ivan Wolfe, Arizona State University.

Finally, I am deeply grateful for the support of my family, without whom I could never have completed this work and whose patience with me and confidence in me sustained me through many challenging moments. My parents—Ron and Joan Yagelski—and my siblings—Mary Cooper, Gary Yagelski, and Dianne Yagelski—support me in ways they never really see, and their presence in my life reinforces my belief in myself. My mother-in-law, Charlotte Hafich, is always there to offer encouragement and check in on my progress; I can never thank her enough for her love and support. My sons, Adam and Aaron, who light up my life in ways they can never realize, are always ready to share and debate ideas with me, and I am energized by their pride in what I do; they help me see the world in ways that shape my writing and keep me going. And most of all, Cheryl, my wife of 35 years and the love of my life, is the best partner any writer could ever hope to have. Her love, constant support, and boundless confidence in me are the foundation that make it possible for me to undertake a task as big as a textbook and see it through. I am so deeply blessed to be able to share this work—and my life—with her. She always provides safe harbor.

Robert P. Yagelski

About the Author

Robert P. Yagelski is Associate Vice Provost and Director of the Program in Writing and Critical Inquiry at the State University of New York at Albany, where he is also Professor of English education in the Department of Educational Theory and Practice. He directs the Capital District Writing Project, a site of the National Writing Project, and has worked closely with schools to improve writing instruction at all levels of education. He is the author of numerous articles and books on writing and writing instruction. *The Essentials of Writing: Ten Core Concepts* is his fourth textbook.

In this chapter, you will learn to

1. Identify many purposes for writing both inside and outside of the classroom.

2. Reflect upon your own diverse writing experiences to consider the most appropriate strategies for a specific audience and purpose in future writing situations.

3. Describe new and different ways to think about your own and others' writing.

1950   1970   1990   2010   2030?

Why We Write 1

WRITING IS A POWERFUL MEANS of communicating ideas and information across time and space. It enables us to participate in conversations and events that shape our lives and helps us make sense of the world. In fact, writing can change the world. Consider these examples:

- Adam Smith's economic theories, presented in his 1776 book *The Wealth of Nations*, continue to influence government economic policies today, which in turn affect the lives of almost every person on earth.
- *The Art of War*, believed to have been written in the 6th century B.C.E. by Chinese military strategist Sun Tzu, is still widely read by military leaders, politicians, and business leaders.
- Betty Friedan's *The Feminine Mystique*, published in 1963, is considered by many to have begun the women's rights movement that has reshaped American social, cultural, political, and economic life in the past half century.
- Charles Darwin's *On the Origin of Species*, published in 1859, revolutionized scientific thinking about life on earth and laid the foundation for the modern field of biology.
- *Silent Spring*, by Rachel Carson, which was published in 1962, helped spark the modern environmental movement and influenced the creation of laws to protect wildlife and the environment.
- Al Gore's 2006 book *An Inconvenient Truth* and the film based on it convinced millions of people that global climate change is a grave threat to human life that must be addressed by all nations.
- Messages posted on Facebook and Twitter during the so-called "Arab Spring" in 2011 helped provoke protests in Egypt and Tunisia that led to new governments in those nations.

These are only the most dramatic examples of the capacity of writing to transform our world.

For many college students, however, writing is mostly a requirement. Most students don't seem to mind writing, but few would choose to write the kinds of essays and reports usually assigned in school. Students consider such assignments necessary, but they don't necessarily enjoy them. For many students, writing in school can be tedious and dull. Maybe you feel the same way.

Yet students write all the time, for all kinds of reasons:

- They send text messages, post to Instagram and Facebook, and tweet to stay in touch with friends, share information, let others know what they think, and keep informed about events or issues that matter to them.

- They respond to their favorite blogs or maintain their own blogs.
- They keep journals or diaries.
- They circulate petitions to support causes on their campus or in their town.
- They rap and participate in poetry slams to express their feelings about important issues in their lives.
- They write essays to gain admission to college or graduate school.
- They create resumes to land jobs.

Whether they realize it or not, students regularly use writing to live their lives, to accomplish tasks that they have to do or choose to do, and to participate in their communities.

If these kinds of writing don't seem as important as, say, a book like *An Inconvenient Truth* or *Silent Spring*, they should. For if a book can be said to have changed the world, the same is true of tweets and texts and blogs and essays and letters written by ordinary people, including students. A job application letter can change your life. A petition can change a policy on your campus that affects hundreds or thousands of students (see Sidebar: "How a Student Changed a College Policy on Free Speech"). An essay can inspire your classmates, change their minds about an issue, or move them to take action. A tweet or Facebook post can help spark a social or political movement. In 2013 a young woman from California named Alicia Garza posted a message to her Facebook page about the death of a young black man in Florida named Trayvon Martin. Her message became the hashtag #BlackLivesMatter, which in turn became an important national movement that helped shape discussions about race relations in the United States and even influenced the presidential election in 2016. Sometimes such ordinary kinds of writing can result in even more extraordinary change: in Egypt, in February, 2011, tweets, email messages, texts, blog posts, and Facebook entries from ordinary citizens played a key role in the protest movement that led to the resignation of Egypt's president, who had ruled that nation for more than three decades. In other words, writing by ordinary citizens helped change the government of that country—a change that has touched the life of every Egyptian and many people outside Egypt.

JASON REDMOND/AFP/Getty Images

SIDEBAR HOW A STUDENT CHANGED A COLLEGE POLICY ON FREE SPEECH

In September 2013, a student named Vincenzo Sinapi-Riddle at Citrus College in Glendora, California, was soliciting signatures for a petition about the surveillance of American citizens by the United States government as part of its so-called "war on terror." Sinapi-Riddle was a member of a national student organization called Young Americans for Liberty, whose mission, according to its website, is "to identify, educate, train, and mobilize young people" who are committed to its Libertarian political views. As the following account reveals, Sinapi-Riddle was standing outside the student center on the Citrus College campus talking about his petition with another student when an administrator threatened to remove him from campus for violating the college's policy on free speech. Sinapi-Riddle was told that he was standing outside the designated area for protest and therefore could not continue advocating for his petition. With the help of an organization called the Foundation for Individual Rights in Education, or FIRE, Sinapi-Riddle filed a lawsuit against Citrus College, arguing that the college's free speech policy violated students' constitutional right to free speech. He won his suit, and Citrus College revised its policy. As Sinapi-Riddle wrote on his blog, we "launched our initiative to raise awareness about warrantless government spying with great success. In the end we gathered over 300 signatures for our petition asking student government to denounce NSA spying, but in the process of protesting one egregious violation of our rights we stumbled upon another."

This case provides a compelling example of how students can use writing to effect change. Sinapi-Riddle and his fellow students in Young Americans for Liberty used writing to raise awareness about an issue (government surveillance of citizens) that concerns them, but writing was also an essential tool in his lawsuit against Citrus College. In addition to the various legal documents required in the case, Sinapi-Riddle used blog posts, social media, and news reports to support his position and take action against a policy that he believed was wrong.

Citrus College Stand Up For Speech Lawsuit

On September 17, 2013—Constitution Day—Citrus College (Glendora, California) student Vincenzo Sinapi-Riddle was threatened with removal from campus by an administrator for asking a fellow student to sign a petition protesting NSA surveillance of American citizens. His crime? Sinapi-Riddle was petitioning outside of the college's tiny "free speech area." Sinapi-Riddle is president of the Citrus College chapter of Young Americans for Liberty and is passionate about his political beliefs, but he has curtailed his expressive conduct on campus in light of this incident and Citrus College's speech-repressive policies. . . .

In addition to challenging Citrus College's "free speech area," which comprises just 1.37% of campus, Sinapi-Riddle is challenging two other policies: (1) the college's "verbal harassment policy," which prohibits a wide range of speech protected by the First Amendment, including "inappropriate or offensive remarks"; and (2) the college's elaborate permitting requirements for student group speech, which

Continued

require student groups wishing to express themselves on campus to wait two weeks and obtain the permission of four separate college entities prior to doing so.

College that Suppressed Anti-NSA Petition Settles Lawsuit

LOS ANGELES, December 3, 2014—Today, Citrus College in California agreed to settle a student's free speech lawsuit for $110,000, marking the Foundation for Individual Rights in Education's (FIRE's) second victory for the First Amendment in 24 hours.

Student Vincenzo Sinapi-Riddle filed the federal lawsuit in July as part of FIRE's Stand Up For Speech Litigation Project. Sinapi-Riddle was threatened with removal from campus for soliciting signatures for a petition against domestic surveillance by the National Security Agency (NSA) outside of Citrus's tiny "free speech area."

In addition to the monetary settlement for Sinapi-Riddle's damages and attorneys' fees, Citrus has revised numerous policies, agreed not to impede free expression in all open areas of campus, and adopted a definition of harassment that complies with the First Amendment.

"Citrus College agreed to eliminate its restrictive 'free speech zone' in the face of a FIRE lawsuit back in 2003, but later reinstated its speech quarantine when it thought no one was watching," said FIRE President Greg Lukianoff. "But FIRE was watching, and we'll continue to do so. If the speech codes come back again, so will we."

To hold Citrus to today's settlement, the U.S. District Court for the Central District of California will retain jurisdiction over the case for one year, allowing Sinapi-Riddle to enforce the agreement without filing a new lawsuit.

The incident leading to the lawsuit took place on September 17, 2013—Constitution Day. Sinapi-Riddle had gone to Citrus's designated free speech area to collect signatures for a petition urging the college's student government to condemn the NSA's surveillance program. Then, as Sinapi-Riddle took a break to go to the student center, he began a discussion about the petition with another student. An administrator put a stop to the conversation, claiming that a political discussion could not take place outside of the free speech area and threatening to eject Sinapi-Riddle from campus for violating the policy.

In addition to restricting student free speech to an area comprising just 1.37 percent of the campus, Citrus maintained a lengthy approval process for registered student organizations seeking to engage in expressive activity. Sinapi-Riddle, president of Young Americans for Liberty at Citrus, had given up on organizing events because of a burdensome process that included review by four different college entities and a requirement of 14 days' advance notice. The process was so complex that the Student Handbook had to include a flowchart illustrating it.

The lawsuit against Citrus College was one of four suits filed on July 1, marking the public launch of FIRE's Stand Up For Speech Litigation Project. Attorneys Robert Corn-Revere, Ronald London, and Lisa Zycherman of the law firm Davis Wright Tremaine represented Sinapi-Riddle. FIRE has coordinated seven lawsuits to date, with more on the way. Citrus is the third that has been settled in favor of students' free speech rights; each of the remaining four suits is ongoing.

"I feel that free speech and the ability to express oneself freely is a very important right for all students," said Sinapi-Riddle. "I'm very grateful for FIRE's help in making sure that limitations on free speech are a thing of the past at Citrus College."

Sources: "Citrus College Stand Up For Speech Lawsuit." *Foundation for Individual Rights in Education,* www.thefire.org/cases/citrus-college-stand-up-for-speech/. Accessed 8 May 2016.
"Second Victory in 24 Hours: College that Suppressed Anti-NSA Petition Settles Lawsuit." *Foundation for Individual Rights in Education,* 3 Dec. 2014, www.thefire.org/second-victory-24-hours-college-suppressed-anti-nsa-petition-settles-lawsuit/.

Questions for Discussion

1. Identify the various ways in which writing was used in this case (e.g., petitions, social media). What role did each of these kinds of writing play? (You can visit the website of the Foundation for Individual Rights in Education for more information about the case. Also, search the web for additional news reports.)

2. What do you think the uses of writing in this case reveal about writing as a tool for political action? Do you think Sinapi-Riddle and the other students involved in this case could have accomplished their goals without using writing as they did? Why or why not? What advantages (or disadvantages) do you see in the way students used writing in this situation? What alternatives did the students have?

3. Write a brief essay about a time when you used writing to voice a concern, lodge a complaint, or try to change something. Then, in a group of classmates, share your essays. What similarities and differences do you see in the writing that is described in these essays? What conclusions might you draw from these essays about the role of writing in your lives?

As a college student you will probably do most of your writing for your classes. This textbook will help you learn to manage college writing assignments effectively. But writing well can also help you live your life in ways that extend far beyond the classroom. So in this chapter—and throughout this textbook—we will examine some of the many different situations in which you might be asked to write.

Understanding Writing

This textbook has another important goal: to help you understand what writing is. One reason that so many people struggle with writing is that they don't sufficiently understand the nature of writing. They believe writing is a matter of following arcane rules that are often difficult to remember or grasp. They think writing is a matter of inspiration and creativity, which they believe they lack, or they assume they can't write well because they don't have a large enough vocabulary. These beliefs are based on common misconceptions that can lead to frustration and prevent students from becoming successful writers. Yes, writing well *does* require knowing rules, and having a large vocabulary doesn't hurt. But writing is more than rules or inspiration or vocabulary. Writing should be understood in four important ways:

- Writing is a powerful means of expression and communication.
- Writing is a way to participate in ongoing conversations about ideas, events, and issues that matter in our lives.
- Writing is a unique form of thinking that helps us learn.
- Writing is a way to understand ourselves and the world around us.

For students who come to understand writing in these four ways, learning to write effectively can be a much more satisfying and successful process. *Abandoning common misconceptions and appreciating the complexity, power, and joy of writing are the first steps to learning to write well and feeling confident about writing.* This textbook will introduce you to the most important ideas—the Core Concepts—that you need to know in order to write well. It is also designed to give you practice in the most common forms of writing for a variety of audiences and purposes—in college, in your community, in the workplace, and in your life in general.

FOCUS **THINK DIFFERENTLY ABOUT YOUR WRITING**

What were the most important pieces of writing you have ever done in your life? Under what circumstances did you write them? What form did they take (e.g., were they conventional essays, letters, blog posts, Prezi presentations)? Why were they important? In what ways did they affect your life? What do these pieces of writing suggest about the role of writing in your life? Jot down brief answers to these questions and consider what your answers reveal about the role of writing in your life. You might do many kinds of important writing without really be aware of them.

Writing in College

Let's face it: Students have to write well if they expect to do well in school. Whether it's a lab report in a biology class, a research paper in a sociology course, a proposal in a business class, or a literary analysis essay in an English course, writing effectively means better learning and better grades. In this regard, **writing in college serves three main purposes**:

- It is a way for you to demonstrate what you know.
- It helps you learn.
- It enables you to join important conversations about the subjects you are studying.

Write to Demonstrate What You Know

Writing is a way for you to show your instructors what you have learned. An essay exam in history, for example, helps your instructor decide whether you have understood a particular concept (say, manifest destiny) or learned about historical events that are part of the course syllabus. Similarly, your economics professor might assign an essay requiring you to analyze a market trend, such as the popularity of smartphones, to determine whether you and your classmates have grasped certain economic principles. For this reason, college students are asked to write many different kinds of assignments: reports, research papers, analytical essays, arguments, synopses, creative writing like poems, personal narratives, reflective essays, digital stories, multimedia presentations, and more.

FOCUS | **THINK DIFFERENTLY ABOUT YOUR WRITING**

Think about a recent essay exam or assignment that you wrote for one of your classes. First, describe the writing you did. What was the assignment? What exactly did you write? What do you think was most important about that piece of writing? What did it reveal about what you know about the subject? What do you think it suggests about you as a writer?

When writing essay exams, reports, or research papers for your classes, keep in mind that you are writing to demonstrate what you have learned. Have confidence that your writing reflects what you know. And remember that your writing can also help you identify what you still need to learn.

Write to Learn

Writing an essay exam or a research paper isn't just a way to demonstrate learning; it is also a means of learning in itself. As you will see in the next chapter, writing is a form of intellectual inquiry, and it is essential to student learning, no matter the subject. To write an ethnographic analysis of a culture for an anthropology class, for example, is to learn not only about that culture but also about ethnography as a way of understanding how we live together. It's true that students can learn a great deal by reading, but writing engages the mind in ways that reading does not. Reading about ethnography can help students understand what ethnography is; writing an ethnographic report about a culture enables students to *apply* that understanding, which can lead to a deeper learning of the subject matter.

This idea that writing is learning can be easy to forget when you are trying to meet deadlines and follow detailed guidelines for an assignment. But if you approach your writing assignments as a way to learn about your subject matter, the process of writing can be more satisfying and can lead to more effective essays. And remember that every writing assignment is also an opportunity to learn about writing itself. The more you write, the better you understand the power and joy of writing and the better able you will be to meet the challenges of writing.

And one last point about the power of writing as a way to learn: The more you write, especially when you write as a way to explore your subject matter, the more you learn about *yourself* as a writer and thinker. Knowing your strengths as a writer enables you to take advantage of them; knowing your weaknesses is essential if you are to improve your writing. That understanding will help you become a better writer.

Describe a writing assignment you did for a college or high school class that was especially challenging for you. Explain why you found the assignment challenging. Now consider what you learned by doing the assignment. What did you learn about the subject matter? What did you learn about writing? Did anything surprise you about doing that assignment? What surprises you now as you look back on it? What do you think you learned about yourself as a writer?

If you approach writing assignments as opportunities to discover new information, explore new ideas, and enhance your understanding of your subject, writing can be more satisfying, and you might find you learned more than you think you learned. You might also find that your writing improves.

Write to Join Academic Conversations

Writing is the primary way that experts in all academic disciplines do their work and share their ideas:

- Mathematics professors may work mostly with numbers and formulas, but they also write articles about current problems in mathematics that other mathematicians read.
- Historians study ancient artifacts to help them understand past events, and they share their understanding in the articles and books they write for other historians and for the general public.
- Scientists might spend long hours in their labs, but they test each other's theories by sharing and debating the results of their experiments in papers they write for scientific journals and professional meetings.
- Scholars in all fields regularly share information and debate ideas by posting messages to professional online discussion forums and blogs.

In all these cases, writing is the main vehicle by which scholars discuss the central questions in their fields. They cannot do their work without it.

Writing for a college class, whether it be psychology or business or chemistry, is a way for students to enter these same conversations about the ideas, information, and ways of thinking that define academic fields. Part of what students learn when they write in college, then, is how to use writing as a tool for discovering and sharing knowledge in various academic disciplines. In this sense, writing an assignment for a college class is a process of learning to write like a scholar in that academic discipline. When you are asked to write a research paper in a psychology course or a lab report in a biochemistry class, you are learning to do the kind of intellectual work that psychologists or biochemists do. You are learning to see the world as they do. You are learning to participate in the conversations about important topics in those academic fields. And by doing so you are using writing to expand and deepen your knowledge about those fields as well as about the world in general.

Take two or more assignments you wrote for different college (or high school) classes. For example, take a literary essay you wrote for an English class, a report you did for a biology class, and a research paper for a history class. List the similarities and differences that you notice among them. Look at the writing style you used in each paper, the structure of each paper, and the language you used. What stands out about each paper? In what ways are the papers different or similar? How can you explain the similarities and differences you see in these papers? What do you think the similarities and differences among these papers suggest about the writing you are asked to do in college?

Of course, writing in college also serves another purpose: it gives students genuine practice that helps them become better writers, which can benefit them in their lives outside of school as well.

EXERCISE 1A

Read the three excerpts included here. Each excerpt is taken from an article or book in a different academic subject. The first is from a marketing textbook, the second from an education journal, and the third from a scientific journal. After reading the excerpts, compare them by addressing these questions:

- What do you notice about the writing in these three pieces?
- What do you think are the purposes of the writing in each case?
- What similarities or differences do you see in the writing style, language, and structure of these excerpts? What might these similarities and/or differences suggest about writing in different disciplines?
- What does your comparison of these three excerpts suggest about writing in general?

1. **What Is Marketing?**

What does the term *marketing* mean to you? Many people think it means the same thing as personal selling. Others think marketing is the same as personal selling and advertising. Still others believe marketing has something to do with making products available in stores, arranging displays, and maintaining inventories of products for future sales. Actually, marketing includes all of these activities and more.

Marketing has two facets. First, it is a philosophy, an attitude, a perspective, or a management orientation that stresses customer satisfaction. Second, marketing is activities and processes used to implement this philosophy.

The American Marketing Association's definition of marketing focuses on the second facet. Marketing is the activity, set of institutions, and processes for creating, communicating, delivering, and exchanging offerings that have value for customers, clients, partners, and society at large.

Marketing involves more than just activities performed by a group of people in a defined area or department. In the often-quoted works of David Packard,

(Continued)

cofounder of Hewlett-Packard, "Marketing is too important to be left only to the marketing department." Marketing entails processes that focus on delivering value and benefits to customers, not just selling goods, services, and/or ideas. It uses communication, distribution, and pricing strategies to provide customers and their stakeholders with the goods, services, ideas, values, and benefits they desire when and where they want them. It involves building long-term, mutually rewarding relationships when these benefit all parties concerned. Marketing also entails an understanding that organizations have many connected stakeholder "partners," including employees, suppliers, stockholders, distributors, and society at large.

Source: Lamb, Charles, et al. *Essentials of Marketing*. 7th ed., Cengage Learning, 2012.

2. Brain-Based Teaching Strategies for Improving Students' Memory, Learning, and Test-Taking Success

Decades ago, my high school chemistry teacher slowly released hydrogen sulfide (which produces a smell like rotten eggs) from a hidden container he opened just before we entered his classroom. A few minutes after we took our seats and he began his lecture, a foul odor permeated classroom. We groaned, laughed, looked around for the offending source. To an outside observer entering our class at that time, we would have appeared unfocused and definitely not learning anything. This demonstration, however, literally led me by the nose to follow my teacher's description of the diffusion of gases through other gases. It is likely that during that class I created two or three pathways to the information about gas diffusion that I processed through my senses and ultimately stored in my long-term memory. Since then, that knowledge has been available for me to retrieve by thinking of an egg or by remembering the emotional responses as the class reacted to the odor permeating the room. Once I make the connection, I am able to recall the scientific facts linked to his demonstration.

Event memories, such as the one that was stored that day in chemistry class, are tied to specific emotionally or physically charged events (strong sensory input) and by the emotional intensity of the events to which they are linked. Because the dramatic event powers its way through the neural pathways of the emotionally preactivated limbic system into memory storage, associated scholastic information gets pulled along with it. Recollection of the academic material occurs when the emotionally significant event comes to mind, unconsciously or consciously. To remember the lesson, students can cue up the dramatic event to which it is linked.

Source: Willis, Judy. "Brain-Based Teaching Strategies for Improving Students' Memory, Learning, and Test-Taking Success." *Childhood Education*, vol. 83, no. 5, 2007, p. 310.

3. Screening for Depression

Depression is the second most common chronic disorder seen by primary care physicians.[1] On average, 12 percent of patients seen in primary care settings have major depression.[2] The degrees of suffering and disability associated with depression are comparable to those in most chronic medical conditions.[3] Fortunately, early identification and proper treatment significantly decrease the negative impact of depression in most patients.[4] Most patients with depression can be effectively treated with pharmacotherapeutic and psychotherapeutic modalities.[5]

Depression occurs in children, adolescents, adults, and the elderly. It manifests as a combination of feelings of sadness, loneliness, irritability, worthlessness, hopelessness, agitation, and guilt, accompanied by an array of physical symptoms.[6] Recognizing depression in patients in a primary care setting may be particularly challenging because patients, especially men, rarely spontaneously describe emotional difficulties. To the contrary, patients with depression who present to a primary care physician often describe somatic symptoms such as fatigue, sleep problems, pain, loss of interest in sexual activity, or multiple, persistent vague symptoms.[7]

References

1. Wells KB. Caring for depression. Cambridge, Mass.: Harvard University Press, 1996.

2. Spitzer RL, Kroenke K, Linzer M, Hahn SR, Williams JB, deGruy FV 3d, et al., Health-related quality of life in primary care patients with mental disorders. Results from the PRIME-MD 1000Study. *JAMA*. 1995;274:1511-7.

3. Hays RD, Wells KB, Sherbourne CD, Rogers W, Spritzer K. Functioning and well-being outcomes of patients with depression compared with chronic general medical illnesses. *Arch Gen Psychiatry*. 1995;52:11-9.

4. Coulehan JL, Schulberg HC, Block MR, Madonia MJ, Rodriguez E. Treating depressed primary care patients improves their physical, mental, and social functioning. *Arch Intern Med*. 1997;157:1113-20.

5. Elkin I, Shea MT, Watkins JT, Imber SD, Sotsky SM, Collins JF, et al., National Institute of Mental Health treatment of Depression Collaborative Research Program. General effectiveness of treatments. *Arch Gen Psychiatry*. 1989;46:971-82.

6. Diagnostic and statistical manual of mental disorders: DSM-IV-TR. 4th ed, text rev. Washington, D.C.: American Psychiatric Association, 2000.

7. Suh T, Gallo JJ. Symptom profiles of depression among general medical service users compared with specialty mental health service users. *Psychol Med*. 1997;27:1051-63.

Source: Sharp, Lisa K., and Martin S. Lipsky "Screening for Depression Across the Lifespan: A Review of Measures for Use in Primary Care Settings." *American Family Physician*, vol. 66, no. 6, 15 Sept. 2002, www.aafp.org/afp/2002/0915/p1001.html.

Writing in the Workplace

In almost any job or career you can think of, you will be expected to use writing in some way to do your work. Consider these anecdotes:

- A few years ago a student planning to attend law school asked me what he could do now to prepare himself for law school. I called an old friend who is a lawyer to ask what I should tell my student. My friend offered two bits of advice: (1) get good grades, and (2) take as many writing courses as possible. Writing, my friend said, is the most important thing lawyers do.

- A college friend of mine has worked for many years as a management trainer for a large insurance company. Almost every aspect of her job involves some kind of writing: training materials, memos, reports, multimedia presentations, and formal email messages. Effective writing is a central reason she is an effective manager.
- One of my colleagues teaches nursing. Her students spend a lot of time as interns in hospitals learning how to take a patient's pulse and blood pressure, obtain blood samples, set up IVs, and administer medication. They also learn to write. Writing accurate and thorough reports, my colleague says, is as important as anything else a nurse does. Communicating with doctors and other nurses is one of the most crucial aspects of a nurse's job, and much of it is done through writing. Without good writing skills, she says, nurses could not care for their patients effectively.

These anecdotes underscore the importance of writing in different work environments and illustrate the different ways that writing enables people to do their jobs well. Professionals already recognize this fact. In one recent survey, 97% of business executives listed the ability to write clearly and persuasively as "absolutely essential" or "very important" for success in college and the workplace.[1] And because the modern workplace is changing rapidly, you are more likely than ever to be expected to communicate effectively in writing in a number of different media, including traditional print reports, proposals, letters, and memos as well as email, PowerPoint, blogs, wikis, and other social media and digital formats. This is the nature of the workplace today, one that already places a great premium on communication and especially on writing—and one that is being reshaped by new media. To succeed in the workplace, you must know how to write well.

FOCUS   THINK DIFFERENTLY ABOUT YOUR WRITING

Examine a piece of your own writing that you finished recently. What do you notice about your writing? What strengths or weaknesses do you see? What might this piece of writing suggest about you as a writer? Now think about how you might present yourself as a writer to a potential employer. What would you say to that employer about your writing? What have you learned about writing that might appeal to an employer?

Think of any writing assignment as career training. The better you can write, the more likely you are to succeed in your chosen career. Use your college writing assignments to develop your writing skills in preparation for the writing you will do in your future career. And if you have other kinds of writing experience, such as writing for your school newspaper or developing promotional materials for a student organization, put them on your resume.

---

[1] *The MetLife Survey of the American Teacher: Preparing Students for College and Careers.* Metropolitan Life Insurance Company, 2011, p. 21.

Talk to a few people you know about the writing they do for their jobs. Try to find people who work in different kinds of jobs. For example, maybe you have a relative who is a salesperson, a friend who is a physical therapist, or a neighbor who manages a restaurant. Ask them to describe any writing they do in their jobs and the media they regularly use, such as websites, email, and social media. Ask them about the challenges they face as writers in their workplaces. Also ask them for their advice about preparing for workplace writing. If you have had a job or hold one now, consider asking your co-workers about the writing they do for their jobs and think about any writing you have been asked to do in your job. Then write a brief report for your classmates in which you share what you learned from this exercise about workplace writing—or about writing in general.

Writing as a Citizen

The idea that citizens must be educated in order for democracy to work is deeply embedded in American culture. It is known as the Jeffersonian ideal, which imagines a free and thriving society based on a productive, educated citizenry. Today, "educated" also means "literate," and it's hard to imagine being an active part of society without writing. In fact, we write to participate in our society in many different ways, from political campaigns to consumer advocacy. Consider these examples:

> BECAUSE of a growing budget deficit, your state legislature is considering a tuition increase as well as large cuts in funding for state colleges and universities. Members of your college community, including students, have written letters and emails to legislators urging them to vote against the funding cuts and the tuition hike. Some students have written editorials for the school newspaper expressing opposition to the budget cuts. To organize a rally at the state capitol, students use Twitter, Facebook, email, and blogs, all of which provide information about the rally and background information about the proposed state budget.

Carlo Allegri/REUTERS

❯ A developer has proposed building a giant new retail store in your town. Some local businesspeople are concerned that businesses on the town's main street will suffer if the new store is built. Residents opposed to the new store have organized a citizens' group and created a Facebook page to advocate for their position. They post information about the proposed store and share opinions about its potential impact on the town. They also write letters to the local newspaper and distribute flyers to local businesses. Other residents, concerned about the town's slow economic growth, support the new store and have expressed their support on a blog and in articles and letters they have written for local publications. They also circulate a YouTube video to explain their support for the new store.

. . . .

❯ THE owners of a major league sports team in your city have threatened to leave the city if a new stadium is not built to replace the aging stadium that the team currently plays in. The team is popular and important to the city, and many residents support the proposal for a new stadium. Other residents oppose the plan on the grounds that it will increase taxes without creating new jobs. These residents form a community organization to publicize their concerns. They use social media to explain what they believe will be the impact of a new stadium. They also write letters to government officials and send press releases to local TV stations.

These scenarios illustrate how we can use writing to participate directly in important discussions, decisions, and events that affect our lives. Writing is a way for individual citizens to express their opinions and share information; it is a way for citizens to take action as members of their communities. Through writing, whether in a traditional print form such as a letter to an editor or in emerging new forms of social media, citizens can shape the ideas, opinions, and actions of others involved in the situation at hand. In all these instances, writing helps transform the world.

| FOCUS | THINK DIFFERENTLY ABOUT YOUR WRITING |

Have you ever written a letter to a politician or business leader to express your opinion or voice a concern? Have you ever written a response to a blog or tweeted to share your perspective on an issue or controversy? Have you ever written a letter to the editor of a newspaper or magazine or sent an email message in response to an article or editorial? If so, what prompted you to do so? Why did you choose to write in that situation? To what extent do you think your writing made a difference—to you or to anyone else who might have read what you wrote?

A well-written letter, a carefully crafted blog post, or even a provocative tweet can often be more effective than a phone call to express a concern, request an action, or raise awareness about an issue.

EXERCISE 1C

Think about an issue that concerns you. Maybe there is a controversy on your campus or in your town that affects you somehow. (On my campus, for example, because of concerns about alcohol abuse and vandalism, the university president canceled a popular student picnic, which led to an outcry among students and some faculty.) Or you might have a special interest in an issue in your state or in the nation, such as standardized testing in schools or the creation of wind farms in rural or wilderness areas. Now consider how you might best make your opinion heard in public discussions about this issue. Could you write a letter to someone in authority who is involved in the situation,

Jesus Keller / Shutterstock.com

such as a politician or business leader? What about a letter to the editor of your local paper or school newspaper? A blog post? A Facebook page? A brochure or newsletter? Maybe a formal proposal intended for someone in a position of authority? Decide what kind of writing you think would work best in this situation and explain why. Then write it.

Alternatively, if you have ever written out of concern about an issue that was important to you, write a brief essay describing that situation and explaining what you wrote. To what extent did your writing in that situation make a difference to you or others involved?

Writing to Understand Ourselves

A few years ago my family threw a surprise party to celebrate my father's 70th birthday. Many friends and relatives would attend, and we wanted to do something special to celebrate my father's life. I decided to create a video that would be a kind of documentary about him. With help from my siblings, I spent several months collecting old photographs and memorabilia, gathering facts about my father's childhood and working life, and interviewing friends and relatives about their experiences with him. Using this material, I created a 20-minute video that focused on the important aspects of his life, including his military service and his family. As I composed that video, certain themes began to emerge about my father. I learned a lot about him that I hadn't previously known. More important, I gained a deep appreciation for the impact he had on many other people. Eventually, I screened the video at the surprise party, but composing it gave me a better understanding of my father and the world he grew up in; it also helped me learn about myself and my relationship with him.

My video about my father's life illustrates how writing can help us understand ourselves and the world around us. Here are two other examples:

> A student of mine was a veteran of military service in Iraq during the most intense fighting there between 2004 and 2006. For one assignment, he wrote a graphic and disturbing essay, in which he struggled to understand what he had experienced in Iraq. His essay revealed that he had deeply conflicted feelings about the war, because in the midst of the horror he saw, he also developed very special bonds with his fellow soldiers and witnessed profound acts of love and bravery. His essay was one of the most compelling pieces of writing I have ever received from a student—not because it was about war but because it was such a heartfelt effort by the student to understand some very difficult experiences.

> ONE of my students was hired by the university's office for international students to help write a newsletter. She was a good writer who earned good grades, but she found writing for international students much more challenging than she expected. Her supervisor constantly required her to revise her articles. Little by little, however, she began to see that her problems with these articles had little to do with her writing skill but arose from her lack of familiarity with that audience. The more she learned about the international students and their experiences in the U.S., the better she appreciated their needs as readers of the newsletter. Her articles improved, and in the process of writing them, she learned a great deal about the international students on our campus and the challenges they face as students in the U.S. She also learned something valuable about writing and about herself as a writer—and a person.

Writing is a powerful way not only to describe but also to examine, reflect on, and understand our thoughts, feelings, opinions, ideas, actions, and experiences. This capacity of writing is one of the most important reasons we write. In many college classes, you may be asked to write assignments that are designed to help you understand yourself and the world around you in the same way that my student's essay helped him understand his experiences in Iraq. But all of the writing you do in college, whether or not it is directly about your own experiences, presents opportunities for you to learn about yourself.

FOCUS · THINK DIFFERENTLY ABOUT YOUR WRITING

Think about a time you wrote about an experience or issue that was important to you in some way—in a journal, a letter, or a school essay, or even on Facebook. Why did you choose to write about that experience? Thinking back on it now, what difference did it make to you to write about the experience? What do you think you learned by writing in that situation?

If you approach every writing assignment as an opportunity to learn not only about your subject but also about yourself, you will find that even the most tedious writing assignment can turn out to be a more rewarding experience.

EXERCISE 1D

Write a brief essay about an important experience that helped make you the person you are today. Write the essay for an audience of your classmates, and tell your story in a way that conveys to them why the experience was important to you.

Now reflect on your essay. Did you learn anything—about the experience itself or about yourself—as a result of writing your essay? Did writing about your experience change your view of the experience in any way? What did writing this essay teach you about yourself? What did it teach you about writing?

In this chapter, you will learn to

1. Identify the ten core concepts for effective writing.

2. Apply the ten core concepts to analyze texts written by others.

3. Describe your own beliefs about writing and how that can affect what and how you write.

Ten Core Concepts for Effective Writing

WHEN I FIRST LEARNED to rock climb, an experienced climber gave me some advice: always climb with your eyes. That may sound strange, but it actually makes good sense. The key to climbing a vertical rock face is finding the right holds for your hands and feet, which is not always as straightforward as it sounds. To keep moving safely and efficiently up the cliff, climbers have to link together handholds and footholds. So even before starting up the cliff, climbers examine it carefully and identify a possible route to the top. Climbers call this process "seeing the line" up a cliff or a mountain. Once on the cliff, they are always looking ahead to the next handhold or foothold. That simple statement—"always climb with your eyes"—turned out to be some of the best advice about climbing I ever received. It was a way to boil down the complicated act of climbing into a single, simple, basic idea.

This chapter does the same thing with writing: It boils down the complex, powerful, wonderful, and sometimes challenging activity of writing into ten essential ideas, or Core Concepts. There's much more to learn about writing than these concepts, just as in climbing you have to learn more than how to "climb with your eyes," and Part II of this textbook goes into much more detail so that you can apply these concepts to various writing tasks. But these concepts are fundamental insights that every writer must learn in order to write effectively. Students who incorporate these insights into their writing process will become better writers, no matter what kind of writing they are doing.

Learning to write effectively also requires developing a certain kind of attitude toward writing. Some climbers talk about "conquering" a mountain, but many climbers reject that way of thinking. For them, the point of climbing is not about defeating a mountain but about respecting it, adapting to it, and experiencing it. That attitude influences their decisions about which routes to follow up a mountain, when to start a climb, when to abandon it. It also affects the meaning of climbing: For them, climbing is about appreciating the experience of being in the mountains and meeting their challenges.

In the same way, the experience of writing can depend a great deal on a writer's attitude toward writing. Students who believe that writing is mostly about following certain rules tend to see writing as a process of learning and applying those rules, which can make writing tedious and diminish the joy of writing. If, on the other hand, you think of writing as a process of discovery, then each writing task can become a way to learn—about your subject, about yourself, and about the world around you. Students who approach writing in this way are open to the possibilities of writing and better able to harness its power. For them, writing isn't primarily about applying rules; it's about understanding and engaging the world and communicating effectively with others.

The ten Core Concepts discussed in this chapter, then, are not rules to learn or directions to follow. They are insights into how to write more effectively. Learning these concepts is a matter of experiencing the variety, complexity, and power of writing so that you can harness that power. Learning to write more effectively is partly a process of learning how to think differently about writing and about yourself as a writer.

This chapter asks you to examine your beliefs about writing and adopt a certain attitude about writing—an attitude that might differ from what you have learned about writing in the past. It encourages you to shift your focus as a writer from remembering and applying rules to exploring your subject, addressing your readers, and accomplishing your rhetorical goals. That shift can change your entire experience as a writer. In learning and applying these Core Concepts, you will, I hope, feel more like a rock climber who is fully engaged in the arduous yet exhilarating act of moving toward a mountain summit.

The Ten Core Concepts for Effective Writing

The ten Core Concepts are based on what research and experience tell us about writing effectively. Each concept is based on a fundamental insight that student writers can learn in order to write effectively in a variety of situations—in school, in the workplace, and in the community. Understanding these concepts doesn't guarantee that you will always write effectively, but you cannot learn to write effectively without applying these ten essential insights about writing:

1. Writing is a process of discovery and learning.
2. Good writing fits the context.
3. The medium is part of the message.
4. A writer must have something to say.
5. A writer must support claims and assertions.
6. Purpose determines form, style, and organization in writing.
7. Writing is a social activity.
8. Revision is an essential part of writing.
9. There is always a voice in writing, even when there isn't an I.
10. Good writing means more than good grammar.

Core Concept 1 Writing is a process of discovery and learning.

A few years ago, a student in one of my classes decided to write an essay about her relationship with her parents. Writing that essay turned out to be a much more involved—and important—experience than she expected.

In the first draft of her essay, Chelsea, who was twenty-two years old, described how her relationship with her parents was changing now that she was an adult. Her draft was lighthearted and full of fond memories and funny anecdotes about her parents that revealed how much she enjoyed her new relationship with them. But something was missing from the draft. For one thing, Chelsea mentioned briefly that her parents had recently divorced after more than twenty years of marriage, but she wrote almost nothing about the divorce. That seemed strange to Chelsea's classmates, who asked her about the divorce during a workshop of her draft. The more we discussed her draft, the clearer it became that there was a lot more to the story than Chelsea had revealed in her draft.

As Chelsea revised her draft, her essay began to change. It was no longer a lighthearted story about what it was like to have an adult relationship with her parents; it was now a more complicated essay that revealed Chelsea's conflicted feelings about what had happened to her parents' marriage and how it affected her (see "Changes"). There was still humor in the essay, but it was bittersweet, tempered by her realization that her changing relationship with her parents was accompanied by loss as well as gain.

Chelsea's essay became a journey of discovery through which she learned a lot about herself, her parents, and the experience she was describing in her essay. She also learned a valuable lesson about writing. When she began the essay, she thought it would be a simple narrative about her changing relationship with her parents. But the process of writing took her deeper into her experience and the complexities of human relationships. It helped Chelsea gain insight into an important period in her life and, maybe, understand something important about relationships (and life) in general.

Writing her essay also enabled Chelsea to communicate something interesting about relationships to her readers, but what she communicated was knowledge and insight that she gained *through the act of writing*, which enabled her to examine and reflect deeply on her experience. This capacity of writing to help writers learn about and understand something is part of what makes writing so powerful—and so important.

Changes

I didn't know how to handle the fact that my parents were actually two separate people who had ceased to exist as one entity, two people who had other interests and other desires besides just solely being parents. With three grown children they felt that it was their time to move on and become separate people. The combination "Momanddad" that I had once imagined as this real thing suddenly transformed into a Mom and a Dad who were pursuing their own separate lives and their own interests.

And I had to choose. My brother moved out and found an apartment to hide in, away from the crumbling walls of our family. I was torn—torn between moving out and moving on from the only thing I ever knew, from this Momanddad that was suddenly becoming non-existent. *But we can't leave Dad alone.* And so it was decided that I would live with Mom and my sister would live with Dad. How do you choose? Is who you live with the one you side with, because in that case, it would change everything. Changing. Everything was changing.

—excerpt from "Changes" by Chelsea

As Chelsea discovered, writing is much more than a step-by-step procedure for organizing ideas into a specific form, such as a lab report or a narrative. Writing effectively requires understanding that you are on a journey of discovery that enables you to understand something better and to convey what you discovered to others. That journey sometimes takes you to places that you didn't expect, and it is rarely a straightforward, linear process from start to finish. If you approach a writing task as such a journey, it won't always be easy, but it can be much more satisfying—not to mention more successful.

SIDEBAR   LEARNING BY WRITING

The Irish singer-songwriter Conor O'Brien revealed during an interview that his songwriting has been influenced by post-modern poetry. O'Brien says that he developed a deep appreciation for the poetry of John Ashberry in a college English literature course. "I remember having to write an essay about John Ashberry and I absolutely despised his words," O'Brien said. "I thought they were really elitist. But then by the end of my essay, I actually fell in love with it and I thought the complete opposite about it. . . . It was very rhythmic and very beautiful."

Redferns/Getty Images

Any writing task can be a surprising journey that leads to new learning and insight, no matter what your topic is or what kind of assignment you're working on:

- When you write a narrative about an experience, as Chelsea did, you might understand that experience more fully.
- When you write an analysis of someone else's words or ideas, as singer-songwriter Conor O'Brien did (see Sidebar: "Learning by Writing"), you can develop a deeper appreciation for those words or ideas.
- When you write a blog post about a political campaign, you engage the ideas of others who might disagree with you, which can help you examine the basis for disagreement.
- When you write an argument about a problem, you might understand that problem better so that you are able to see solutions that were invisible to you before you began writing.
- When you write a lab report about an experiment you did for a chemistry class, you might gain a better grasp of the experimental process and the specific research question you were examining.

This kind of discovery and learning is possible because writing engages your intellect in a way that goes beyond reading or listening. If you have ever been so immersed in a writing task that the time seems to fly by, then you have experienced this capacity of writing to engage your mind fully.

What This Means for You as a Writer

- **Approach every writing task with curiosity.** Don't assume you already know exactly what you want to say or where your writing will end up, even when you're writing about something you know very well. Don't expect to know at the beginning exactly how everything will turn out in the finished text. Be open to unexpected possibilities as you work through an assignment. Even when your assignment is very specific and has rigid rules to follow (for example, a chemistry lab report with explicit directions for format or a persuasive essay in which you're required to provide exactly three arguments for and against your position), remember that you can't know everything at the start. That's why you're writing in the first place: to learn something new or deepen your understanding of something you thought you knew.

- **Be patient.** Because writing is rarely straightforward, it shouldn't be reduced to a step-by-step procedure. You can't do everything in a single draft. To engage in writing as a process of discovery and learning almost always involves working through several drafts as you explore your subject, gather information, develop ideas, consider your audience, learn more about your subject, and refine what you thought you wanted to say. This process can be messy and even frustrating at times, but it can also be illuminating. Forcing this process into a step-by-step procedure will not only make it more difficult (as you probably already know) but also prevent it from becoming a worthwhile journey of discovery. And it will usually result in less effective writing. If, on the other hand, you have a little patience as you engage in this process of discovery and learning, you might be surprised by where your writing can take you.

- **Don't try to make your writing perfect as you work through an assignment.** Early drafts of any assignment are opportunities to explore your subject and learn more about it. Avoid the impulse to make everything perfect the first time. Rough drafts are just that: drafts. They can be changed and improved. Sometimes you have to allow yourself to write messy drafts, especially in the early stages of an assignment. You can even temporarily ignore rules of usage and style in your early drafts and focus instead on exploring your subject matter and discovering what you want to say in your piece, as Chelsea did. You will go back later to correct errors, tighten up your sentences, develop ideas, or clarify a point. (See Core Concept #10.)

- **Allow yourself sufficient time to write.** Writing at the last minute forces students to rush, which undercuts the process of discovery and learning that writing should be. It is also stressful and less enjoyable. Allowing sufficient time to move through the process deliberately and patiently will result not only in greater learning but also greater enjoyment—and more effective writing.

PRACTICE THIS LESSON

Keep an informal journal or a private blog as you work on your next piece of writing. Each time you work on your writing, describe in your journal or blog what you did. If you read something and take notes for your writing, describe that. If you make an outline or jot down some ideas for your introduction, describe that. If you get an idea while taking a shower or riding a bus, describe that. If you share a draft with a friend or roommate, describe that. Also record any questions, concerns, or problems that arise as you work on this piece of writing, and explain how you addressed those questions, concerns, or problems. Describe how you feel as you work on the piece. What seems to be going well and what doesn't? Keep a record of *everything* you did and thought as you completed the writing task. Once you're finished with the writing task, go back and review your journal or blog. What does it reveal about how you write? What does it suggest about writing in general? What surprises you about your descriptions of what you did to complete your writing task? What do you think you can learn from this journal about writing? About yourself as a writer?

If possible, interview someone who is a professional writer or who writes regularly in his or her work, and ask that person what he or she does when writing. What steps or activities does the person engage in when completing a writing task? How does this person explain what he or she does when writing? After you finish your interview, describe in a paragraph or two what you learned about writing from this writer and compare what he or she does to what you do.

Core Concept 2 Good writing fits the context.

If writing is a journey of discovery, how do we know when that journey produces writing that is good? The answer is, It depends.

Consider the expression, "Today was a very good day." People say this all the time, but what exactly does it mean? A student who earned a good grade on a test could say it was a good day. Someone receiving a raise at work might consider that a good day, but quitting a job could also make for a good day. Winning the lottery would be a very good day for most people. So would getting married. But getting divorced might also be considered a good day. You get the point: What counts as a good day depends on the person and the circumstances.

The same goes for writing. Students generally believe they know what an instructor means by "good writing," but **what counts as good writing can only be determined by examining the specific context of the writing.**

When it comes to writing, *context* is often understood as the *rhetorical situation*, which traditionally includes the writer, the subject of the writing, and the audience (see Focus: "The Rhetorical Situation"). These components determine what constitutes effective writing in a given situation. For example, a lab report that earns an A in a biology class might not qualify as a good report in a pharmaceutical company, because the biology instructor and the lab supervisor in a pharmacy might have different expectations for lab reports; moreover, the purpose of the writing differs in each case. Writers have to determine the expectations for each writing situation. They must consider their audience and make decisions about content, form, and style that they believe will most effectively meet the expectations of that audience. Good writing is writing that meets the needs of the rhetorical situation—which often means meeting the specific criteria for an assignment (see Sidebar: "Grades vs. Good Writing" on page 30).

FOCUS   **THE RHETORICAL SITUATION**

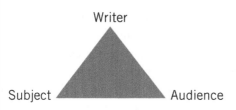

Writer

Subject   Audience

In classical rhetorical theory, the rhetorical situation is represented as a triangle:

The metaphor of a triangle illuminates the relationships among the writer, reader, and subject matter in a particular act of writing. The writer and the audience have a specific relationship to the subject matter in the form of their shared knowledge about the subject, their opinions about it, their respective experiences with it, their stake in it, and so on. In addition, the writer has some kind of relationship to the audience, even if he or she doesn't actually know that audience. For example, a historian writing an article for a

(Continued)

professional journal assumes that she is writing as a member of the community of professional historians, with whom she will share certain values, knowledge, and expectations when it comes to the subject of the article and to history in general. To write well requires understanding your audience and its relationship to your subject—and to you—so that you can adapt your writing appropriately to achieve your goals in that rhetorical situation.

The rhetorical situation is an essential concept that helps writers better understand the social nature of writing and thus create more effective texts. Most instructors use the term to highlight the observable elements of the writing situation, especially the intended audience and the writer's purpose in addressing that audience. (In this textbook, I generally use the term in this basic way.) Some theorists, however, have illuminated how other factors can influence writing within a rhetorical situation. These factors might include the writer's identity (including race, gender, ethnicity, and so on), the cultural context of the writing, the historical moment, and the reader's background, among other such factors. These factors can shape not only what and how a writer writes but also how the writer's text is given meaning within the rhetorical situation.

To write effectively, then, requires assessing the rhetorical situation. Writers should consider **four key dimensions of the rhetorical situation** to guide their decisions as they complete a writing task:

- **Purpose.** *Why* you are writing helps determine *what* to write and whether your writing is appropriate and effective in a particular context. A high school guidance counselor might praise your college admissions essay because it is clear and well organized, but can that essay really be considered "good" writing if it does not convince the college admissions officer to admit you to the college? And what if you are rejected by one college but accepted by another? Does that make your essay "good writing" or not? Writing can never really be evaluated without considering the writer's purpose: Are you trying to persuade an admissions officer that you are a good student? Are you attempting to solve a problem by analyzing it carefully? Do you want to share an insight about love by telling the story of a relationship? Good writing accomplishes the writer's goals in a specific rhetorical situation.

- **Form or genre.** Each rhetorical situation demands a specific form or genre—that is, a specific kind of text: an argument, a report, a blog post, a multimedia presentation, a poem. And each form is governed by specific criteria regarding structure and style. A lab report will usually be written in a formal, objective style, whereas a blog post might have a less formal, more provocative style. Writers select the appropriate form for the rhetorical situation and adapt their writing to that form. Certain forms of writing are appropriate for specific rhetorical situations, and no one style is appropriate for every kind of writing.

Understanding and using various forms for different rhetorical situations is essential for effective writing.

- **Audience.** Good writing meets the expectations of the intended audience. That college admissions essay is "good" if it resonates with the college admissions officer who reads it. To write effectively, then, requires anticipating the expectations of your audience and adapting your text to those expectations in that rhetorical situation. Sometimes that's a straightforward task: In a job application letter, you adopt a formal writing style and avoid irrelevant personal tidbits, knowing that such language and information would be considered inappropriate by the person reviewing job applications. Usually, though, analyzing your audience is more complicated, even when you know the audience. That's because there is always a subjective element to writing. Readers can agree on the general characteristics of good writing but disagree on whether a specific piece of writing is good. For example, they might agree that an editorial is well organized and clearly written—characteristics usually associated with good writing—but disagree about whether that editorial is "good" because one reader finds the writer's style too glib whereas another finds it engaging. Readers react to a piece of writing on the basis of their backgrounds, age, gender, experiences, and personal preferences as well as their reasons for reading that piece. So different audiences might judge the same piece of writing very differently. Writers must understand the challenge of anticipating such differences and adapt their writing as best they can to achieve their purposes with their intended audience.

- **Culture.** The dimensions of context described so far are all shaped by the broader cultural context. *Culture* can be defined as your sense of identity as it relates to your racial and ethnic backgrounds, your religious upbringing (if any), your membership in a particular social class (working class, for example), and the region where you live (for example, central Phoenix versus rural Minnesota or suburban Long Island). Not only does culture shape how readers might react to a text but it also shapes basic aspects of a rhetorical situation such as the subject matter and language. An important issue (for example, gender equality) might be understood very differently by people from different cultural backgrounds. Writers can't be expected to address all the complex nuances of culture that might influence a specific rhetorical situation, but to write effectively requires being sensitive to these nuances and understanding how a factor such as religious background or ethnic identity might shape readers' reactions.

In addition, the rhetorical context for any writing task includes **the medium**, which can significantly affect what and how a writer writes in a given situation (see Core Concept #3).

So the question of whether the writing is "good" is really beside the point. What matters is whether the writer accomplished his or her purposes with a specific audience in a specific rhetorical situation. The important question, then, is not whether a piece of writing is "good" but whether the writing is appropriate and effective for the rhetorical situation.

Most students understand that producing good writing and getting good grades on writing assignments aren't always the same thing. Usually, instructors have specific criteria for grading student writing based on course goals and their own views about effective writing. Different instructors can have different expectations for writing even in the same course and for the same writing assignments. So getting an A on a specific assignment doesn't necessarily mean that the student is a "good writer"; it means that the student's writing successfully met the criteria for that assignment in the view of the instructor. By the same token, getting a poor grade on an assignment doesn't mean that the student is a poor writer. Students who regularly get good grades in one subject—English, say—are sometimes frustrated when they get lower grades in another—say, psychology. But usually the lower grades mean that the student has not adjusted to the demands of writing in a different subject.

What This Means for You as a Writer

- **Consider your purpose.** What do you hope to accomplish with a specific piece of writing? Answering that question, even in a general way, can guide your writing and make it more likely that your text is effective for your rhetorical situation. For college writing assignments, avoid the temptation to think of your purpose as simply getting a good grade. Instead, identify your purpose in terms of the specific characteristics of the assignment and what the instructor expects you to learn or do. If your instructor doesn't provide such information, try to obtain it so that you have a clearer idea of the expectations or guidelines that will help determine what counts as good writing for that assignment. Have a clear sense of purpose that matches the expectations for the assignment.

- **Consider your audience.** The decisions writers make about matters like content, form, and style should be driven by their sense of what will work best for their intended audience. Even when writing for a general audience (for example, when writing a letter to the editor of a newspaper read by thousands of people with very different backgrounds and expectations), try to identify basic characteristics of your audience and their likely expectations about a given subject (for example, readers of a regional newspaper are likely to be familiar with a local political controversy or be generally supportive of a local industry). One of the first things you should always do when you begin a piece of writing is think carefully about your audience.

- **Consider the form of the writing.** Form does matter when it comes to determining whether a piece of writing is effective. A research paper for a sociology class will be very different from a letter to the editor of your campus newspaper, yet both pieces of writing might be considered "good." The form of your writing will shape your decisions about style, organization, and length as well as the content of a piece. For each writing task, use an appropriate form and identify the standards for organization, style, length, etc., for whatever form of writing you are using.

- **Study good writing.** Although there is no single definition of "good writing," students can learn a lot by paying attention to what others—including their instructors—consider good writing. What counts as good writing in each of your classes? What is different or similar about how different instructors evaluate their students' writing? What is it about a specific piece of writing that certain readers like or dislike? Exploring such questions can lead to insights into what features of writing readers value in different situations.

PRACTICE THIS LESSON

Find a short piece of writing that you think is good. (You might select one of the readings included in this textbook.) Share that piece of writing with two or three friends or classmates and ask them their opinion of it. What do they like or dislike about the piece of writing? What did they find especially effective or ineffective about it? Ask them to explain their opinions as clearly as they can. Then write a brief reflection on what you learned about "good" writing from this activity. In your essay, compare the reactions of your friends or classmates to the piece of writing you chose, and draw your own conclusions about the role of audience in writing.

Core Concept 3 The medium is part of the message.

Good writing depends on context, and that context includes the medium—that is, the tools or technology the writer uses. Writing a blog entry about a controversial parking policy on your campus will be different from writing an analysis of that parking policy for a business course or a letter of complaint to the campus parking office. Different media place different demands on writers. Effective writing means adjusting to the medium.

Students today are fortunate to be living in an age of astonishing technological developments that open up countless opportunities for writers. Using widely available technologies, students exchange ideas and information in ways that were unimaginable even a few years ago. They can communicate easily and widely through social media. They can use cell phones to send text messages, take and share photos, update websites, or download music and videos. They can participate in online discussions with their professors and classmates without leaving home. They can use computers to produce sophisticated documents that only a decade ago would have required a professional printing service. They can easily create multimedia presentations incorporating sound, image, and text.

These technologies are dramatically changing how we communicate and may be changing the very act of writing itself. When I create a website for one of my classes, I write differently than when I create a printed syllabus for the same class, even though most of the content is the same. I organize the website differently, because students will use it differently from the syllabus. I change some of the content, because my students don't access content on the website in the same way they find it on the syllabus. I include images as well as links to other online resources. Even my writing style changes a bit. In short, the medium changes my writing.

Think about creating a Prezi presentation as compared to, say, writing a report for an economics class. The audience and purpose might be the same, but the form and the content will differ. More to the point, the tools for composing are different. Prezi enables you to create documents that include much more than text. All these factors can influence both *what* and *how* writers write. For example, you will probably use less text in a Prezi presentation, which will affect your decisions about the content of your presentation. In addition, you will likely incorporate images and even audio and video clips into your Prezi document but not in your report. You also adjust your writing style: for the report you will use a formal academic style and probably complex sentences and lengthy paragraphs, whereas the Prezi presentation will require more concise language, bulleted lists, and titles for most slides. All these differences might seem obvious, but because writers today often have several choices for the medium they will use, they need to be aware of the ways in which the medium shapes what they write and how they write in that medium to accomplish a specific purpose.

iStockphoto.com/Cameron Whitman

Although most essays, reports, and research papers assigned in college courses still require students to write in conventional formats, increasingly students are asked or choose to write in other media. More and more students are asked by their instructors to participate in online discussions about course topics and use multimedia programs to make presentations, sometimes in place of traditional papers. In each case, the medium can shape the writing task in important ways. The medium can also affect your relationship to your audience (see Sidebar: "Blogging vs. Writing a Newspaper Column"). Part of your task as a writer, then, is to understand how different media might affect your writing and to adapt to the medium you're using.

SIDEBAR BLOGGING VS. WRITING A NEWSPAPER COLUMN

Political writer Andrew Sullivan, a columnist for the *Sunday Times of London*, has written numerous books on politics and culture as well as articles for magazines and newspapers, including *Time*, the *New Republic*, and the *Atlantic*. In 2000 he began writing a blog called *The Dish*. These different media, he says, influence his writing style, choice of subject matter, and interactions with his readers. According to Sullivan, blogging "is instantly public. It transforms this most personal and retrospective of forms into a painfully public and immediate one." It also calls for "a colloquial, unfinished tone." Here's part of how he describes the differences between these two kinds of writing:

> A blogger will air a variety of thoughts or facts on any subject in no particular order other than that dictated by the passing of time. A writer will instead use time, synthesizing these thoughts, ordering them, weighing which points count

more than others, seeing how his views evolved in the writing process itself, and responding to an editor's perusal of a draft or two. The result is almost always more measured, more satisfying, and more enduring than a blizzard of [blog] posts.

Source: Sullivan, Andrew. "The Years of Writing Dangerously." *The Dish,* 6 Feb. 2015, dish. andrewsullivan.com/2015/02/06/the-years-of-writing-dangerously/.

Although Sullivan was one of the earliest proponents of blogging and helped popularize the medium among political writers, he stopped blogging in 2015 in part because of health concerns. In a post on his blog in which he announced his retirement from blogging, Sullivan described blogging as "a genuinely new mode of writing" and identified its essential characteristics: "its provisionality, its conversational essence, its essential errors, its ephemeral core, its nature as the mode in which writing comes as close as it can to speaking extemporaneously."

What This Means for You as a Writer

- **Know the medium.** For most college writing assignments, student use computers to write conventional papers or reports. Such assignments place familiar demands on writers when it comes to organization, style, etc. Other media, such as blogs, wikis, or Prezi, call for different strategies regarding organization, style, and even content. In many cases, what and how you write may be similar in different media, but not always. Be familiar with the characteristics of the medium in order to use it effectively for the task at hand.

- **Choose an appropriate medium.** If given a choice, consider which medium would enable you to create the most effective document for that rhetorical situation. A Prezi presentation with embedded audio and video clips might be the best choice for an assignment in which your audience will be your classmates or students attending a presentation about extracurricular activities on your campus. For other writing situations, a blog or even a Facebook page might be more effective, depending upon the your message and the audience you hope to reach. Consider the medium carefully as you decide how best to achieve your intended purpose with your intended audience.

- **Adjust your writing process to the medium.** All writing tasks require planning, developing ideas, drafting, revising, and editing. But those activities can differ depending upon the medium, so effective writers adjust their writing process accordingly. Obviously, you will organize a research paper for a history course differently than you would a blog entry or video script, but sometimes the differences between one medium and another aren't so obvious. For example, many students make the mistake of writing a PowerPoint or Prezi presentation as if it were a conventional report. As a result, they include too much text in the presentation and use too few visual elements. The outcome can be an ineffective document that may be tedious for an audience to follow. It is better to consider the characteristics of the medium *as you are creating your document* and move through the writing process with the medium in mind.

Review several text messages or tweets that you recently sent or received. Then write a brief style guide for text messaging and/or tweeting. In your style guide, include what you believe are the main rules for writing text messages or tweets to specific audiences and for specific purposes. Include any advice that you think writers should heed when writing texts or tweets. Also include common abbreviations that writers of text messages use. Consider the different ways that people might use texts and tweets. Now compare your style guide to standard academic writing. What are the main differences and similarities between the two? What might the differences suggest about the role of the medium in writing? (Alternatively, write a brief style guide for another medium, such as Facebook or Prezi.)

Core Concept 4 · A writer must have something to say.

Having a clear, valid main point or idea is an essential element of effective writing—not only in college but also in the workplace and other settings. In most cases, college instructors expect students to have a clearly defined main point or idea that is appropriate for the assignment, no matter what kind of writing the assignment calls for. (Research shows that college instructors identify the lack of a clearly defined main idea as one of the biggest problems they see in their students' writing.) If you describe a favorite book or movie to a friend, you will very likely be explaining what you see as its main idea or point. In the same way, readers expect writers to have something to say; as a writer, you should oblige them. (See Focus: "So What?" on page 35)

This is not to say that the main point or idea is always simple or easily boiled down to a one-sentence summary or thesis statement. Much college writing is about complex subjects, and students are often required to delve into several ideas or bodies of information in a single assignment. A 20-page research paper for an information science course about how new digital technologies are affecting the music industry will include many complicated points, kinds of information, and key ideas. So will a critique of the major arguments about the existence of God for a philosophy course. But even such involved pieces of writing, if they are to be effective, will be focused on a main idea and will convey a clear main point. That critique of major philosophical arguments about the existence of God, for example, might focus on the central point that all those arguments reflect the human desire to understand why we exist or that most philosophers equivocate when it comes to this basic question.

Remember, though, that you when you're beginning a writing assignment, you won't always know exactly what your main point will be. Sometimes, the assignment will determine your main idea or point. For example, in an anthropology class you may be asked to write an essay defining *culture* as anthropologists generally understand that concept. In such a case, you will be expected to convey a main point based on what you are learning in the course about how anthropologists

©iStockphoto.com/MsLightBox

understand culture. Sometimes, however, identifying your main point or idea will be more complicated. A student of mine once wrote a research paper about being a vegetarian. She started out thinking that she would write about the pros and cons of being a vegetarian to show that vegetarianism is not practical for most people. But as she wrote, she learned more about the subject and began to shift her focus to the environmental destruction caused by eating meat. In the end, her main point changed: she argued in favor of a vegetarian diet as an ethical response to the environmental destruction caused by the standard American diet. As she explored her subject, she was guided by a sense of her main idea, which evolved as she wrote. Her final paper had a clearly articulated main point but not the one she started with.

One useful way to help identify and refine your central idea or the main point in a piece of writing is to ask, So what? Suppose you've written a personal narrative about your first job. So what? Why should readers care about that experience? What's in it for them? What will you say *about* that experience that might matter to others? Answering such questions can help ensure that you are telling your story in a way that conveys a *relevant* main idea or point to your readers. The same applies to just about any kind of writing you will do in college. For an economics class you might write an analysis of tax cuts as a way to generate jobs. So what? To answer that question requires you to decide whether your analysis is relevant in the field of economics. Why analyze tax cuts now? What makes that topic something that will interest others in the field? Is your main point something that economists would consider relevant and important? Asking this question about your topic also ensures that you are thinking about your audience and connecting your main point or idea to their interests as well.

What This Means for You as a Writer

- **Identify your main idea.** Every kind of writing—even the most formulaic lab report in a biology or chemistry class—should have a main point. But it is important to distinguish between your *subject* and your main idea or point. The subject of a biology lab report might be osmosis, but the main point might be that osmosis doesn't occur with a certain type of membrane. Similarly, for an American history course you might write an analysis of the impact of the Civil Rights movement on race relations in the U.S. Your subject would be the impact of the Civil Rights movement on race relations, but your main point would be what you have to say *about* that impact on the basis of your analysis—for example, that race relations were changed in specific ways as a result of the Civil Rights movement.

- **Have something relevant to say.** Having something to say is one thing; having something *relevant* to say is another. Whenever you write, you are participating in a conversation (see Core Concept #7), and what counts as relevant or appropriate depends on the nature of that conversation. In college, what counts as relevant usually depends on the academic subject. For example, in an analysis of the social importance of Hip Hop music for a sociology class, you might conclude that Hip Hop became popular because it expressed the discontent young people of certain social and racial groups felt. For a paper in a music appreciation class, by contrast, you might argue that certain musical qualities, such as rhythm, account for Hip Hop's popularity, an argument that might be considered irrelevant in a sociology course. Part of what makes writing effective is not only having something to say but also knowing what is relevant or appropriate to say in a specific context.

- **Make sure that your main idea or point is clear to your readers.** Don't assume that because something is clear to you, it will also be clear to your readers. Sometimes, students can become so deeply immersed in their writing that they lose perspective. They think they have made their points clearly, but their readers may have trouble seeing the main idea. This is especially true when the assignment is complicated and lengthy. So it's important to share your drafts to get a sense of whether readers are understanding your main idea (see Core Concept #7) and then to revise with your audience in mind to make sure your main idea comes through clearly (see Core Concept #8).

- **Don't try to say too much.** A clear main point is partly a result of what the writer *doesn't* say. Including too many ideas or too much information in a piece of writing can obscure the main point, even if the ideas and information are relevant. Because most college writing assignments address complicated subjects, it can sometimes be a challenge for students to decide what to include in their writing. So it's important to decide whether an idea or piece of information is *essential* in an assignment. If not, consider removing it.

PRACTICE THIS LESSON

Post a draft of an assignment you are working on to your Facebook page or to an online forum for sharing documents, such as GoogleDocs. Ask your friends to summarize the main idea of your paper. Compare their summaries to your own sense of your main idea. Do their summaries match your idea? If not, consider revising your draft so that your main idea is clear to other readers.

Alternatively, reread an assignment you wrote for a previous class and see whether you can identify the main point.

Core Concept 5 — A writer must support claims and assertions.

"Winters are warmer than they used to be around here."

"Most people would rather text than talk face-to-face."

"The average person doesn't pay attention to politics."

In casual conversation we usually don't expect people making statements like these to provide supporting arguments or facts to prove the point. In most college writing, however, appropriate support for claims and assertions is essential.

As we saw in Chapter 1, a central purpose of writing in college is to understand and participate in conversations about the topics and questions that define each academic discipline. To participate in those conversations requires knowing how to make a case for a particular point of view and support conclusions about a relevant topic. In other words, not only must writers have something relevant to say, but they must also be able to back up what they say.

Students sometimes fail to support their ideas or assertions effectively because they are unfamiliar with the expectations for doing so in a specific academic subject. The important point to remember is that *all* academic disciplines have such standards, though different disciplines might have different conventions regarding what counts as appropriate support or evidence for a claim or assertion:

- In an English literature class, you might cite passages from a poem or quote from critical reviews of that poem to support a claim about the work of a particular poet. Your claim would be more or less persuasive depending upon whether readers consider those passages or quotations to be sufficient support for your claim.

- In economics, some kinds of statistical information carry more weight than other kinds when drawing conclusions about economic trends or developments.

- In a biochemistry lab, data from experiments might be the main evidence for conclusions or claims.

In each case, an important element of effective writing is using evidence that is considered appropriate and persuasive by readers familiar with that discipline. The same holds true outside of school, though the standards for supporting your statements tend to be less well-defined and less rigorous in most popular writing than in academic or workplace writing (see Focus: "Supporting a Claim").

FOCUS   SUPPORTING A CLAIM

The need for writers to support their claims or assertions applies to any kind of writing, including newspaper and magazine articles, business proposals, legal documents, government reports, petitions, blogs, and many other kinds of documents. The following examples are taken from various sources: a government report on higher education, an excerpt from a

(Continued)

book on women and careers, and a newspaper column about fair pay for baseball stadium vendors. As you read them, notice how each writer backs up his or her statements and consider how that support affects your reaction as a reader:

There is a troubling and persistent gap between the college attendance and graduation rates of low-income Americans and their more affluent peers. Similar gaps characterize the college attendance rates—and especially the college completion rates—of the nation's growing population of racial and ethnic minorities. While about one-third of whites have obtained bachelor's degrees by age 25–29, for example, just 18 percent of blacks and 10 percent of Latinos in the same age cohort have earned degrees by that time.

Source: *A Test of Leadership: Charting the Future of Higher Education.* United States Department of Education, 2006, p. 11.

. . . .

When I arrived at college in the fall of 1987, my classmates of both genders seemed equally focused on academics. I don't remember thinking about my future career differently from the male students. I also don't remember any conversations about someday balancing work and children. My friends and I assumed that we would have both. Men and women competed openly and aggressively with one another in classes, activities, and job interviews. Just two generations removed from my grandmother, the playing field seemed to be level.

But more than twenty years after my college generation, the world has not evolved nearly as much as I believed it would. Almost all of my male classmates work in professional settings. Some of my female classmates work full-time or part-time outside the home, and just as many are stay-at-home mothers and volunteers like my mom. This mirrors the national trend. In comparison to their male counterparts, highly trained women are scaling back and dropping out of the workforce in record numbers. In turn, these diverging numbers teach institutions and mentors to invest more in men, who are statistically more likely to stay.

Source: Sandberg, Cheryl. *Lean In: Women, Work, and the Will to Lead.* Alfred A. Knopf, 2013, p. 1414.

. . . .

The Angels are one of the richest and most successful franchises in Major League Baseball—in fact, in all pro sports.

They're valued by Forbes at $554 million (up 6% from a year ago), carry the fourth-largest player payroll in the major leagues, and at this point in the season rank fifth in per-game attendance. As they're very much in the hunt for their division lead, it's quite possible that lucrative post-season games will be added to the schedule.

So why are they trying to nickel-and-dime their stadium ushers, ticket sellers and janitors? . . .

The Angel Stadium employees are the worst paid among all California ballpark workers in their job classifications, the SEIU says. Here are some comparisons provided by the union, which also represents some of the workers at the other parks:

Angel Stadium ushers (the lowest paid among the affected employees) earn $11.21 an hour. At Dodger Stadium the rate is $12.77, and at the Oakland Coliseum it's $14.03. Janitors in Anaheim receive $11.50 an hour; at Chavez Ravine it's $12.31, in Oakland $17.50 and at the San Francisco Giants' AT&T Park $15.15. Ticket sellers at Angel Stadium get $13.65 an hour, but at the San Diego Padres' Petco Park they get $16.43.

Source: Hiltzik, Michael. "Angel Baseball, Paying the Little Guy Peanuts." *Los Angeles Times*, 7 Aug. 2011, articles.latimes.com/2011/aug/07/business/la-fi-hiltzik-20110807.

What This Means for You as a Writer

- **Provide sufficient support.** First and foremost, make sure you have adequately supported your main points, claims, and assertions. Regardless of your subject or the kind of writing you are doing, readers expect that you make a case for what you have to say. Review your drafts to be sure you have provided the necessary support for your ideas.

- **Provide relevant and appropriate support.** What counts as appropriate and effective support for a claim depends upon the subject, the academic discipline, and the rhetorical situation. The kind of evidence used to support a claim in a history course, for example, won't necessarily work in a psychology course; similarly, readers of newspaper editorials have different expectations for relevant support than, say, economists who read professional journals. As a writer, part of your task is to understand the expectations for evidence and support for the kind of writing you're doing. You should be able to anticipate readers' expectations so that the support you provide for your claims will be persuasive and appropriate for the rhetorical situation.

- **Evaluate your sources.** Citing relevant sources to support or illustrate a point is a crucial part of effective academic writing, but not all sources are created equal. A self-help blog might not suffice as an appropriate source in an essay about teen depression for a psychology course, whereas a study published in a professional journal would. Having information from a source to support a claim or assertion is not the same as having information from a credible source. Make sure the sources you cite are not only appropriate for the writing task at hand, the course, and the rhetorical situation but also trustworthy. (Chapters 9 and 10 provide detailed discussions of finding and evaluating sources.)

Compare how the authors of the following two passages support their statements or arguments. The first passage is from a report by an economist examining the impact of poverty on educational achievement. The second is an excerpt from an analysis by an economist about how the American public's misconceptions about economics affect their voting habits. First, write a brief summary of each passage, identifying its main assertions or points. Then identify the supporting evidence or arguments for each main point. What kinds of evidence or support does each author use? What sources do they use to support their points? Finally, discuss the differences and similarities in how these authors support their points. What are the main similarities and differences? How might you explain these similarities and differences?

1. The impact of education on earnings and thus on poverty works largely through the labour market, though education can also contribute to productivity in other areas, such as peasant farming (Orazem, Glewwe & Patrinos, 2007: 5). In the labour market, higher wages for more educated people may result from higher productivity, but also perhaps from the fact that education may act as a signal of ability to employers, enabling the better educated to obtain more lucrative jobs. Middle-income countries—which frequently have well developed markets for more educated labour—are particularly likely to see the benefits of education translated into better jobs and higher wages. In Chile, for instance, between one quarter and one third of household income differences can be explained by the level of education of household heads (Ferreira & Litchfield, 1998, p. 32).

Source: van der Berg, Servaas. *Poverty and Education*. UNESCO / International Institute for Educational Planning, 2008, p. 3.

2. Consider the case of immigration policy. Economists are vastly more optimistic about its economic effects than the general public. The Survey of Americans and Economists on the Economy asks respondents to say whether "too many immigrants" is a major, minor, or non-reason why the economy is not doing better than it is. 47% of non-economists think it is a major reason; 80% of economists think it is not a reason at all. Economists have many reasons for their contrarian position: they know that specialization and trade enrich Americans and immigrants alike; there is little evidence that immigration noticeably reduces even the wages of low-skilled Americans; and, since immigrants are largely young males, and most government programs support the old, women, and children, immigrants wind up paying more in taxes than they take in benefits.

Given what the average voter thinks about the effects of immigration, it is easy to understand why virtually every survey finds that a solid majority of

Americans wants to reduce immigration, and almost no one wants to increase immigration. Unfortunately for both Americans and potential immigrants, there is ample reason to believe that the average voter is mistaken. If policy were based on the facts, we would be debating how much to increase immigration, rather than trying to "get tough" on immigrants who are already here.

Source: Caplan, Brian. "The Myth of the Rational Voter." *Cato Unbound*, 6 Nov. 2006, www.cato-unbound.org/2006/11/05/bryan-caplan/myth-rational-voter.

Core Concept 6 — Purpose determines form, style, and organization in writing.

A resume is a carefully structured record of the writer's work history and qualifications; a cover letter for a job application is a statement of the writer's suitability for the job. Each document has familiar conventions regarding content, organization, and style, which the reader (usually a person involved in hiring for the job) expects the writer to follow. A resume shouldn't be organized in the narrative format that might be used for a report on an internship, nor should a cover letter be written in the informal style and tone of a text message or Facebook post.

The conventional forms of a resume and cover letter serve very specific purposes for both reader and writer. These forms convey relevant information efficiently within the rhetorical situation. They are functional. That's one reason that they have become standard. Writing an effective resume and cover letter, then, is partly a matter of knowing how to use a well-established *form* to accomplish a specific purpose (to get a job interview) within a specific rhetorical situation (the job application process). The same is true of *any* kind of writing, including academic writing. Every kind of text—a lab report, a research paper, a personal narrative, a blog entry, a proposal, a review—

vicky/Fotolia LLC

is governed by expectations regarding form. For some forms, such as resumes, these expectations can be very specific and rigid; for others, such as personal narratives, the expectations tend to be much more flexible. (See Focus: "What Is *Form* in Writing?") A writer must be familiar with expectations of the form in which he or she is writing if the text is to be rhetorically effective.

You have probably heard teachers refer to *form* when discussing writing assignments, but what exactly is *form*? Generally, *form* refers to the way a piece of writing is organized as well as to any features that determine the shape or structure of the document, such as subheadings or footnotes. *Form* also includes the introductory and concluding sections of a piece of writing. *Form* is often used interchangeably with *genre*; for example, you might hear an instructor refer to *narrative* as both a form and a genre of writing. But *genre* generally refers to a type of writing, such as narrative or short story, rather than to the form of the writing. *The Merriam-Webster Dictionary* defines *genre* as "a category of artistic, musical, or literary composition characterized by a particular style, form, or content." In other words, a specific genre can appear in several different forms.

Often, terms such as *design* and *layout* are used to describe features of documents that include visual elements, such as graphs or photographs; design and layout can therefore be considered part of the *form* of a document. In many kinds of digital texts—including multimedia documents and online media such as web pages—design, layout, and related components can be as important as the text itself. The alignment of the text or the contrast in font sizes and colors can influence how the text is received by an audience (see Chapter 8).

For most traditional college writing assignments, *form* is generally used in two ways: (1) to refer to the general kind of writing expected for that assignment (research paper, narrative, argument, etc.); and (2) to describe the relevant conventions regarding the style and structure of the document for a specific kind of writing.

Notice that *purpose* drives *form*. For example, a writer structures a narrative in a certain way to tell a story effectively. In this sense, it is helpful to think of the form of a piece of writing as a tool to help you achieve your purpose in a specific rhetorical situation.

For many students, the problem isn't learning rules or guidelines for specific kinds of writing, such as lab reports or books reports; the problem is that they learn *only* rules and guidelines for specific kinds of texts without understanding the *purposes* of those rules and guidelines and without considering the rhetorical situation—that is, how their intended readers will likely read that text. As a result, students often approach writing as a matter of creating a certain kind of document rather than adopting a specific form that serves a specific purpose for a specific rhetorical situation. Think again about a resume. An effective resume requires more than proper format. It must also include appropriate information about the job applicant that is presented in carefully chosen language. An employer reviews a resume quickly, looking for specific information to determine whether the writer is a suitable candidate for the job. A resume is designed to present that information clearly and efficiently. Knowing that, the applicant must select and present relevant information strategically so that the qualifications match the requirements of the job. A successful resume is one in which the writer uses the form to present his or her qualifications effectively to an employer. Form follows function.

The same principle applies to the writing that students commonly do in college. The format of a lab report in chemistry, for example, enables a reader (the course instructor, other students, or perhaps other chemists) to find relevant information about a lab experiment quickly and easily. A literary analysis essay has less rigid guidelines for form, but readers still expect the writer to follow a generally recognizable pattern when presenting an analysis of a poem or novel. The same is true of analytical writing in philosophy or psychology. The specific forms might differ, but in each case, the form serves certain purposes within the academic discipline. Writers in each discipline learn to use the form to achieve their rhetorical purposes.

Many students focus only on *form* (on the rules and guidelines for a specific kind of text) and neglect *function* (the purpose of the text within the rhetorical situation). Good writers learn the rules and guidelines for the forms of writing they do, whether those forms are business letters or lab reports or blog posts, but they also understand the *purposes* of those forms of writing and apply the rules to accomplish their purposes.

What This Means for You as a Writer

- **Determine the appropriate form for the rhetorical situation.** In many situations, the form will be obvious: a resume and cover letter for a job application; a lab report for a chemistry class. For most college writing assignments, instructors will specify the genre (argument, analysis, review, report, etc.) and provide guidelines for the form (organization, style, length, and so on). When the form of writing isn't clear or specified, assess the rhetorical situation to determine which form would be most appropriate and effective. What is the purpose of the writing? Who is the intended audience? What form of writing would mostly likely reach that audience and communicate your message effectively? Answering these questions will help you decide on the best form of writing for the task at hand. Remember that the form is a rhetorical choice: select the form that will enable you to accomplish your purpose with your intended audience.

- **Become familiar with the conventions of the form of writing you are doing.** Writers should follow the conventions governing form for well-established genres (e.g., lab reports) to meet their readers' expectations. But *there are no universal rules governing either forms or genres of writing that apply to all situations*. In many instances, writers have a great deal of choice regarding organization, style, length, and similar features of a document. Digital texts such as web pages and social media offer writers great flexibility, and even very specialized kinds of writing, such as resumes and cover letters, can appear in many acceptable variations of format, style, and even content. As a writer, your task is not only to learn the basic expectations for a specific kind of writing but also *to adjust your style and tone according to the specific rhetorical situation and to organize your text accordingly*. In most academic disciplines, there are established conventions for form, style, etc., but sometimes instructors do not make those conventions clear. If you're not sure about those conventions—for example, how to organize an assignment, whether the style must be formal, and so on—ask your instructor.

- **Pay attention to organization.** How a document is organized is one of the most important elements of form in writing. It is also one of the most challenging for many students. Studies show that college instructors consider the inability to organize texts appropriately to be one of the biggest problems in their students' writing. So it's important to learn how to organize an essay or report or digital document appropriately for the specific academic subject. In some cases, the general structure will be provided. For example, lab reports usually require specific sections in a specific sequence. Following the guidelines for such assignments will essentially organize the report for you. However, other forms allow for more flexibility in organizing the text. Ask your instructor about the expectations for organizing writing assignments, and if possible, find examples of that form or genre to see how they are organized.

PRACTICE THIS LESSON

Visit a job search website, such as Monster.com, and read several advertisements for jobs that interest you. Then write a resume and cover letter for two or three such advertisements. (For this exercise, you might write a "fictional" resume and cover letter, inventing appropriate job experiences and relevant background information. Or you can use your own work experience and background.) Alter your resume and cover letter for each job. Then consider the differences in your resumes and letters. What changes did you make? What remained the same? Why did you make those changes? Now consider what this exercise might suggest about the conventions for the form and style of resumes and cover letters.

Monster.com

Core Concept 7 — Writing is a social activity.

We tend to think of writing as a solitary activity. The image of the writer working alone in a quiet room is a popular one. But this image is incomplete and even misleading. In fact, **writing is an inherently social act in at least three ways:**

- **First, writers write for an audience.** Unless you are writing an entry in a personal diary that you plan never to share with anyone or a note to remind yourself to take out the trash, your writing is almost always intended to be read by someone else. And as we saw earlier, your audience significantly influences what you write, how you write, and even *whether* you write. Whether the audience is a course instructor, classmates, a friend, co-workers, or a larger audience, writers write with their reader or readers in mind, even if they're not always aware of it. In this sense, writing is always a social transaction between writer and reader, a way to connect writers and readers. In addition, the reason for writing something usually arises from a social situation: a paper assigned in a college class; a problem in your town that prompts you to write a post to an online discussion board; an essay commemorating an important anniversary; a blog post about a current controversy. Writing happens because our interactions with others give us reasons to write. (See Focus: "The Rhetorical Situation" on page 27.)

- **Second, writers often involve others in the process of writing.** Writers regularly receive advice or suggestions from trusted readers as they develop a piece of writing. In class, students often engage in peer review—that is, sharing drafts with classmates and commenting on their classmates' writing. College instructors offer their students suggestions for improving their drafts. Digital media such as blogs enable writers to receive feedback from their readers. Wikis allow writers to collaborate directly. In these ways, the act of writing is social rather than solitary. In fact, in business settings and in many other situations outside of school, collaborative writing is the norm, not the exception.

- **Third, the rules, conventions, and forms of writing are socially constructed.** These rules, conventions, and forms have evolved over time as a result of the way people have used writing to communicate, to share ideas and information, to learn, and to accomplish a variety of other purposes. Familiar forms of writing, such as narratives and business letters and research reports, have developed because people needed these forms in order to accomplish specific purposes in writing. Research reports, for example, help make it easier for scientists to share the results of their experiments and to collaborate in answering important scientific questions. Resumes are efficient forms for conveying information about a job candidate's qualifications. By the same token, certain rules for writing style, such as the rule that you shouldn't use the first person in scientific writing, have evolved to fit the purposes of that kind of writing. Even *what* writers choose to write about is shaped by what others have written. The topics considered relevant in, say, a course on business ethics are determined in large part by what others in that field are saying. So both *what* and *how* we write are shaped by social factors.

The notion that writing is social is important because it undercuts the myth that writing ability is innate or exclusively the result of individual effort. This myth leads many students to believe that they don't have the ability to write well or that writing is something that they have to figure out exclusively on their own. Neither belief is true. In fact, many social factors shape an act of writing. Individual skill and experience along with effort and motivation do matter, but many other influences outside a writer's individual control affect writing. In this sense, writing ability is as much a function of how writers respond to specific rhetorical situations, which are inherently social, as it is a result of individual effort. So your effectiveness as a writer depends not only on the effort you put into a writing task but also on the way you fit in and respond to the social situations in which you are completing that task. Learning to respond to those situations effectively begins with understanding the social nature of writing.

What This Means for You as a Writer

- **Place your writing in context.** As we saw earlier (Core Concept #2), all writing takes place in a rhetorical context, which shapes what and how the writer writes. Make it a habit to analyze the rhetorical situation for *every* writing task. Students tend to think of writing assignments as a matter of producing a certain kind of text rather than responding to the rhetorical situation. That kind of thinking can lead to ineffective writing because it tends to focus only on the *what* (the subject matter and form) rather than the *why* (the rhetorical purpose) of the writing task. Focusing instead on the rhetorical situation, which is inherently social in nature, can help you adapt successfully to the different kinds of writing tasks you are likely to face as a college student; moreover, emphasizing the *purpose* (that is, the *why*) of your writing rather than focusing only on creating a specific kind of text (the *what*) is more likely to engage you in inquiry and learning about your subject (see Core Concept #1).

- **Remember the larger context.** Even when you write for a college course, you are part of larger conversations about important issues in specific academic fields and in the society at large. For example, an analysis of U.S. involvement in the Vietnam War for a history course can be shaped by current debates about the U.S. military efforts in Afghanistan and Iraq. Broader social, cultural, and historical factors can influence what you write, giving it a sense of immediacy and significance. Being aware of these larger contextual forces can lend a sense of relevance to your writing.

- **Seek the input of others.** Even if you do most of your writing by yourself, at some point it will be helpful to get advice or feedback from others. In your writing course you may be required to engage in peer review and share your writing with your classmates or to revise in response to your instructor's feedback. But even if you aren't, you can benefit by asking a trusted friend, classmate, or co-worker to read your work-in-progress and consider their reactions to what you've written. Many online sites enable writers to share drafts and ideas and seek advice about their writing. Listening carefully to what others say about your writing can help you decide how to revise to make your writing more effective. (Much more discussion about getting and using feedback appears later in this textbook.)

- **Write for your readers.** When you're in the midst of creating a document and perhaps struggling with matters such as organization or style, you can easily forget that you are writing for a reader. Reminding yourself that your text is being created for an audience can often help make the task clearer. Instead of focusing on whether a sentence is correct, for example, consider how a reader might respond to it. That shift in perspective can help you keep the purpose of your writing in view and avoid getting bogged down in rules and procedures. The rules and conventions are important, but following rules and conventions doesn't result in good writing if the writing does not effectively address the intended audience and meet the needs of the rhetorical situation (see Core Concept #10).

PRACTICE THIS LESSON

Take a piece of writing you did recently and, in a brief paragraph or two, explore the social aspects of that text:

1. Consider the topic. What made you decide to write about that topic? Was your decision influenced in any way by others? Is the topic of interest to others?

2. Think about your audience. What do you know about that audience? What was your purpose in writing to that audience? What kind of reaction did you hope your writing would provoke?

3. Describe any advice or input you received as you completed this piece of writing. Did you share your drafts with anyone? Did you consult an instructor or post a draft on social media?

4. Examine the broader relevance of what you wrote. For example, if you wrote an analysis of a poem or short story, consider what might make that analysis relevant beyond the course and the assignment. Does the analysis focus on subjects that concern people other than your classmates in that course? If so, in what ways? What makes the analysis relevant to your life outside that course? What might make it relevant to others?

5. Consider what your experience with this piece of writing suggests about the social nature of writing.

Core Concept 8 Revision is an essential part of writing.

The famous American writer Ernest Hemingway once told an interviewer that he revised the ending of his novel *A Farewell to Arms* 39 times. The interviewer asked, "Was there some technical problem there? What was it that had stumped you?" Hemingway replied, "Getting the words right."

"Getting the words right" doesn't mean fixing a "technical problem." It means writing and rewriting until the meaning is clear and the message comes through for the audience. Sometimes, that requires tinkering with words and phrases, but often it means much larger changes: adding new material, deleting sentences or paragraphs, moving them from one place to another in the draft, or completely rewriting entire passages. Such rewriting is an integral part of the writing process.

Creating an effective text is rarely so simple that a writer can move from beginning to end in a straight line and then go back to "fix" things. Writing is more often a circuitous, recursive process in which the writer stops and starts, goes back, jumps ahead, changes something, adds or deletes something, starts over, and maybe even writes the ending first (as the best-selling novelist John Irving says he does). It is through this process that writers explore their subjects and make meaning for their readers. Rarely does a writer know at the beginning exactly what his or her text will finally look like or what it will say. The shape of the text and its meaning emerge from the process of writing, and revising is central to that process.

Inexperienced writers often make the mistake of believing they can get everything right in a single draft, which they can quickly review to correct minor errors. This belief arises from a lack of practice with the various kinds of sophisticated writing required in college. Eventually students learn that writing an effective text can't be squeezed into a single draft. In most college writing assignments (and most other kinds of writing as well), there are simply too many things going on for a writer to attend to all of them at once. For example, if you are struggling to describe a complicated concept in an analytical essay for a political science course, you are probably not going to be thinking much about spelling and punctuation. By the same token, if you are focused on spelling and punctuation, you are probably not thinking in depth about how to explain that concept.

So most experienced writers divide each writing assignment into manageable tasks. When writing rough drafts, they mostly ignore matters like spelling and punctuation, knowing they can address those matters later, and focus instead on larger matters: Is my paper complete? Are the ideas clearly presented? Are there unnecessary passages that can be eliminated? Is the piece well organized? Have I addressed my intended audience appropriately? Does this piece achieve my rhetorical goals? As they revise each draft, they don't just "fix" mistakes; rather, they pay attention to how well they've explored their subject, how effectively they've addressed their audience, and how successfully they've accomplished their purpose. And they "listen" to their draft to see what meaning begins to emerge from it, learning more about their subject as they write and revising accordingly. Only after they have addressed these larger issues do they focus on improving sentences and correcting errors. (See Focus: "Revising versus Editing.") Writers who understand revising in this way usually find writing easier—and their writing becomes more effective.

FOCUS   REVISING VS. EDITING

Inexperienced writers tend to confuse revising with editing. Revising is the process of working with a draft to make sure it explores the subject adequately, addresses the intended audience effectively, and meets the needs of the rhetorical situation. It is not simply correcting spelling or punctuation errors, adjusting capitalization, and eliminating usage problems. Those activities are *editing*. Editing means making sure that your writing is correct and that you've followed the appropriate rules for form and usage. It is usually the very last step before a piece of writing is finished. (See Core Concept #10.)

What This Means for You as a Writer

■ **Understand revision as a process of discovery and meaning-making.** The British writer E. M. Forster is reputed to have said, "How do I know what I think until I see what I say?" I take that to mean that Forster never began a piece of writing knowing exactly what he was thinking or what he wanted to say. He found out through the process of writing. His statement can serve as advice for all writers. If you believe that writing is simply a matter of putting down on paper what's already in your head, you'll be frustrated and your writing will never feel right. But approaching writing as a process of discovery opens up possibilities, and revising is how writers find and realize those possibilities. It is the process of making the meaning of writing clear—both to the writer and to readers. (In this sense, this Core Concept is an extension of Core Concept #1.)

■ **Don't try to do everything at once.** Approach every writing task as a series of smaller tasks, each of which is more manageable than the whole. Write a *first* draft without trying to make it a *final* draft. Once you have a first draft, work on it in stages, focusing on specific issues or problems in each stage. Start with larger issues, such as whether you have developed your main idea sufficiently or supported your main argument adequately, and then revise for organization or structure. Later, revise to make sure your tone is right for your intended audience, and then attend to your word choice and sentence structure to make sure your sentences are clear. Finally, edit for correctness. Working through a draft in this way will make revision easier and more effective.

■ **Leave the editing for last.** Focusing on matters like spelling and punctuation while you're writing a first draft will divert your attention away from your subject and make it harder to focus on the ideas you are trying to convey to your readers. The best way to avoid this problem is to ignore minor errors of spelling, punctuation, grammar, and usage until you are just about finished with your text. At that point, after you have worked through your drafts and developed your ideas sufficiently, you can run your spellchecker, look for punctuation mistakes, attend to usage or grammar problems, and make sure that you have followed the basic rules of standard English. Leaving the editing for last will make your writing go more smoothly.

PRACTICE THIS LESSON

Using a wiki or a site like GoogleDocs, share a draft of your writing with two or three classmates or friends. Be sure to explain the assignment and purpose of your draft. Ask each person to identify the strengths and weaknesses of your draft and suggest at least one revision for each weakness. Then compare the suggestions for revision provided by your classmates or friends. In what ways do their suggestions overlap? Do they disagree about what needs to be changed in your draft? How might their suggestions help you revise so that your text will achieve your rhetorical purpose? Now consider what their various suggestions might indicate about the process of revision. (You can do this exercise without using a wiki or GoogleDocs by simply having your readers comment on the same copy of your draft.)

There is always a voice in writing, even when there isn't an I.

When I was in graduate school I took a course in sociolinguistics. As someone who knew little about sociolinguistics, I found the assigned readings slow and difficult. But one book by a famous anthropologist named Clifford Geertz stood out. Geertz pioneered a research technique called "thick description," by which he would describe in very rich detail the rituals and common beliefs of a culture in order to understand the culture from an insider's perspective. His research profoundly influenced the fields of anthropology and sociolinguistics. What really struck me about Geertz's work, though, was his writing style. Although his work was scholarly, specialized, and theoretical, it was also engaging to read, even for someone who knew little about anthropology and sociolinguistics. When I praised Geertz's writing during a discussion with my professor, he smiled and acknowledged that students often reacted as I did to Geertz. Geertz's writing, he said, was seductive. His comment surprised me, because I had never heard anyone describe academic writing as "seductive." (You can judge for yourself: An excerpt from an essay by Geertz appears in Focus: "The Voice of a Scholar.")

My professor was really talking about *voice* in writing. Voice is difficult to define, but it has to do with what we "hear" when we read a text, how the writing "sounds." Voice is partly a technical matter of word choice and sentence structure, but it is also a function of the writer's confidence and authority (or lack of it). It is that nebulous quality that makes a piece of writing distinctive. It's what enables a reader to say, "That sounds like Stephen King." Or Clifford Geertz. As I learned in my sociolinguistics course, it isn't only popular writers like Stephen King whose writing can be said to have a distinctive voice. Even the most conventional scientific research report or philosophical treatise can have a distinctive voice. In fact, a strong, distinctive voice is one of the key elements of effective writing.

FOCUS THE VOICE OF A SCHOLAR

Here are the opening two paragraphs from "Thick Description: Toward an Interpretive Theory of Culture," by Clifford Geertz, one of the most influential essays ever written in the field of anthropology. As you read, consider which features of Geertz's writing contribute to his voice:

In her book, *Philosophy in a New Key*, Susanne Langer remarks that certain ideas burst upon the intellectual landscape with a tremendous force. They resolve so many fundamental problems at once that they seem also to promise that they will resolve all fundamental problems, clarify all obscure issues. Everyone snaps them up as the open sesame of some new positive science, the conceptual center-point around which a comprehensive system of analysis can be built. The sudden vogue of such a *grande ideé*, crowding out almost everything else for a while, is due, she says, "to the fact that all sensitive and active minds turn at once to exploiting it. We try it in every connection, for every purpose, experiment with possible stretches of its strict meaning, with generalizations and derivatives."

After we have become familiar with the new idea, however, after it has become part of our general stock of theoretical concepts, our expectations are brought more into balance with its actual uses, and its excessive popularity is ended. A few zealots persist in the old key-to-the-universe view of it; but less driven thinkers settle down after a while to the problems the idea has really generated. They try to apply it and extend it where it applies and where it is capable of extension; and they desist where it does not apply or cannot be extended. It becomes, if it was, in truth, a seminal idea in the first place, a permanent and enduring part of our intellectual armory. But it no longer has the grandiose, all-promising scope, the infinite versatility of apparent application, it once had.

Source: Geertz, Clifford. "Thick Description: Toward an Interpretive Theory of Culture." *The Interpretation of Cultures: Selected Essays*, Basic Books, 1973, p. 3.

Many students believe that academic writing is supposed to be dull and "voice-less." But they're confusing voice with style or tone (see Focus: "Voice vs. Tone"). A scientific paper might be written in an objective style, but that doesn't mean it will have no voice. Moreover, college instructors usually expect students' writing to have voice, even when they don't allow students to use the first person in course writing assignments. Being aware that you always have a voice in your writing and that voice is an element of effective writing is an important step toward developing your voice in your writing.

FOCUS   VOICE VS. TONE

Trying to define voice in writing is like trying to describe the color blue: You can't quite say exactly what it is, but you know it when you see it. Still, it's important to be able to talk about voice, because it is a key element of effective writing. It's also important to understand how voice differs from other aspects of writing, especially *tone*. If *voice* is the writer's personality that a reader "hears" in a text, then *tone* might be described as the writer's attitude in a text. The tone of a text might be emotional (angry, enthusiastic, melancholy), measured (such as in an essay in which the author wants to seem reasonable on a controversial topic), or objective or neutral (as in a scientific report). Tone is kind of like your tone of voice when speaking: you can be upset, sad, happy, uncertain, or concerned, and the tone of your voice (how loud or soft it is, how you inflect your speech, how you emphasize certain words—for example, stretching out *told* in a statement like this: "I *told* you not to go outside in the rain!") reflects your mood. In writing, tone is created through word choice, sentence structure, imagery, and

(Continued)

similar devices that convey to a reader the writer's attitude. Voice in writing, by contrast, is like the sound of your spoken voice: deep, high-pitched, nasal, etc. It is the quality that makes your voice distinctly your own, no matter what tone you might take. In some ways, tone and voice overlap, but voice is a more fundamental characteristic of a writer, whereas tone changes depending upon the subject and the writer's feelings about it. Consider, for example, how you would describe Clifford Geertz's voice as compared to his tone (see Focus: "The Voice of a Scholar" on page 50).

What This Means for You as a Writer

- **Recognize and develop your own writerly voice.** Part of every writer's challenge is to refine his or her voice and use it effectively. The first step is to recognize that you always have voice in writing, even in academic writing. Many of the exercises in this textbook will help you develop and strengthen your voice. It takes practice. Listen for the voice in the assigned texts in your classes. Try to get a sense of what makes them distinctive. Listen for your voice in your own writing as well. When revising a draft, pay attention to the "sound" of the writing—not only to make sure your writing is clear and understandable but also to give it the "sound" of confidence and authority. Adjust your style and tone so that they are appropriate for the kind of writing you are doing (for example, avoiding vivid descriptive language in a lab report but using description to convey emotion in a narrative or argument), but always strive to write with a strong voice. A strong voice is more likely to make your writing effective.

- **Remember that *all* writing has voice.** Although you might have been taught that some kinds of academic writing, such as lab reports or science research papers, should be "objective" and therefore do not have a voice, the truth is that good writing will always have voice. That does not mean you should use "creative" language in every kind of writing you do. It *does* mean that you should follow the appropriate conventions for style and tone and use them as effectively as you can to bring out your own distinctive voice.

- **Don't fake it.** If you are unsure of your main idea or if you are confused about the assignment you are working on, your writerly voice is likely to reflect that. Often when students are unfamiliar with a subject or learning something for the first time, they try to "sound" academic by writing convoluted sentences, using inflated language, or substituting wordy phrases for more common words (for example, using "due to the fact that" instead of "because"). Such strategies usually make the writing less clear and weaken the writer's voice. And it's usually easy for an instructor to see that students are "padding" their writing because they aren't sure they have anything valid to say or they're confused about the assignment or subject (as Calvin does in the comic strip). So one way to have a strong, effective voice is to explore your subject sufficiently (Core Concept #1), do appropriate research if necessary (Core Concept #5), and have a clear sense of your main idea or argument (Core Concept #4). These can lead to confidence, which is an essential element of voice.

I USED TO HATE WRITING ASSIGNMENTS, BUT NOW I ENJOY THEM.

I REALIZED THAT THE PURPOSE OF WRITING IS TO INFLATE WEAK IDEAS, OBSCURE POOR REASONING, AND INHIBIT CLARITY.

WITH A LITTLE PRACTICE, WRITING CAN BE AN INTIMIDATING AND IMPENETRABLE FOG! WANT TO SEE MY BOOK REPORT?

"THE DYNAMICS OF INTERBEING AND MONOLOGICAL IMPERATIVES IN *DICK AND JANE* : A STUDY IN PSYCHIC TRANSRELATIONAL GENDER MODES."

ACADEMIA, HERE I COME!

PRACTICE THIS LESSON

Compare the three excerpts below. Each excerpt is the introductory passage from an academic article published in a scholarly journal. How would you describe the voice in each passage? What differences and similarities do you see in the voices of these passages? What specific features of the writing do you think accounts for the voice in each passage (e.g. word choice, sentence structure, use of first or third person, etc.)? Which do you like best? Why? What do you think your reaction to these passages suggests about voice in writing?

1. Writing represents a unique mode of learning—not merely valuable, not merely special, but unique. That will be my contention in this paper. The thesis is straightforward. Writing serves learning uniquely because writing as process-and-product possesses a cluster of attributes that correspond uniquely to certain powerful learning strategies.

   Although the notion is clearly debatable, it is scarcely a private belief. Some of the most distinguished contemporary psychologists have at least implied such a role for writing as heuristic. Lev Vygotsky, A. R. Luria, and Jerome Bruner, for example, have all pointed out that higher cognitive functions, such as analysis and synthesis, seem to develop most fully only with the support system of verbal language—particularly, it seems, of written language. Some of their arguments and evidence will be incorporated here.

   Here I have a prior purpose: to describe as tellingly as possible how writing uniquely corresponds to certain powerful learning strategies. Making such a case for the uniqueness of writing should logically and theoretically involve establishing many contrasts, distinctions between (1) writing and all other verbal languaging processes—listening, reading, and especially talking; (2) writing and all other forms of composing, such as composing a painting, a symphony, a dance, a film, a building; and (3) composing in words and composing in the two other major graphic symbol systems of mathematical equations and scientific formulae. For

   (*Continued*)

the purposes of this paper, the task is simpler, since most students are not permitted by most curricula to discover the values of composing, say, in dance, or even in film; and most students are not sophisticated enough to create, to originate formulations, using the highly abstruse symbol system of equations and formulae.

Source: Emig, Janet. "Writing as a Mode of Learning." *College Composition and Communication*, vol. 28, no. 2, May 1977, p. 122.

2. Over the past two decades, the presence of computers in schools has increased rapidly. While schools had one computer for every 125 students in 1983, they had one for every 9 students in 1995, one for every 6 students in 1998, and one for every 4.2 students in 2001 (Glennan & Melmed, 1996; Market Data Retrieval, 1999, 2001). Today, some states, such as South Dakota, report a student to computer ratio of 2:1 (Bennett, 2002).

Just as the availability of computers in schools has increased, their use has also increased. A national survey of teachers indicates that in 1998, 50 percent of K–12 teachers had students use word processors, 36 percent had them use CD ROMS, and 29 percent had them use the World Wide Web (Becker, 1999). More recent national data indicates that 75 percent of elementary school-aged students and 85 percent of middle and high school-aged students use a computer in school (U.S. Department of Commerce, 2002). Today, the most common educational use of computers by students is for word processing (Becker, 1999; inTASC, 2003). Given that, it is logical to ask: Do computers have a positive effect on students' writing process and quality of writing they produce?

As is described more fully below, the study presented here employs meta-analytic techniques, commonly used in fields of medicine and economics, to integrate the findings of studies conducted between 1992–2002. This research synthesis allows educators, administrators, policymakers, and others to more fully capitalize on the most recent findings regarding the impact of word processing on students' writing.

Source: Goldberg, Amie, et al. "The Effect of Computers on Student Writing: A Meta-analysis of Studies from 1992 to 2002." *The Journal of Technology, Learning, and Assessment*, vol. 2, no. 1, 2003, p. 3.

3. Cognitive, or executive, control refers to the ability to coordinate thought and action and direct it toward obtaining goals. It is needed to overcome local considerations, plan and orchestrate complex sequences of behavior, and prioritize goals and subgoals. Simply stated, you do not need executive control to grab a beer, but you will need it to finish college.

Executive control contrasts with automatic forms of brain processing. Many of our behaviors are direct reactions to our immediate environment that do not tax executive control. If someone throws a baseball toward our face, we reflexively duck out of the way. We have not necessarily willed this behavior; it seems as if our body reacts and then our mind "catches up" and realizes what has happened. Evolution has wired many of these reflexive, automatic processes into our nervous systems. However, others can be acquired through practice because learning mechanisms gradually and thoroughly stamp in highly familiar behaviors.

For example, consider a daily walk to work. If the route is highly familiar and if traffic is light, our mind can wander. Before we know it, we may have gone a considerable distance and negotiated street crossings and turns with little awareness of having done so. In these cases, the control of our behavior occurs in a "bottom-up" fashion: it is determined largely by the nature of the sensory stimuli and their strong associations with certain behavioral responses. In neural terms, they are dependent on the correct sensory conditions triggering activity in well-established neural pathways.

Source: Miller, E. K., and J. D. Wallis. "Executive Function and Higher Order Cognition: Definition and Neural Substrates." *Encyclopedia of Neuroscience*, edited by Larry R. Squire, vol. 4, Academic Press, 2009.

Core Concept 10 — Good writing means more than good grammar.

When I was a brand-new professor of English, I submitted a grant proposal in which I misspelled the name of Christopher Columbus in the very first sentence. (I spelled it "Columbis.") I learned of the error only after one of the members of the review committee told me about it. It was extremely embarrassing, but it wasn't disastrous. My proposal was selected as a finalist for the grant competition. The reviewers obviously saw the error, but they nevertheless selected my proposal. Why? Despite such a blatant error, they considered the proposal good enough to make the first cut in the grant competition. The error didn't mean that the writing was poor.

I sometimes tell this story to illustrate the point that a correct paper isn't necessarily an effective one—or that an incorrect paper isn't necessarily *ineffective*. Following the rules and conventions of standard written English is important, but good writing is much more than good grammar. A perfectly correct essay can also be a perfectly lousy piece of writing if it does not fulfill the expectations of the intended audience and meet the needs of the rhetorical situation. An error-free history paper won't earn a good grade if it does not meet the instructor's guidelines for historical analysis or if it includes erroneous information, superficial analysis, and unsupported assertions. By the same token, a brilliant historical analysis that also includes numerous misspelled words, punctuation errors, inappropriate word choice, and convoluted sentences is not likely to earn an A+. Those errors will probably distract your instructor and might even suggest that you were unwilling to devote adequate time and attention to the assignment. For better or worse, "grammar," good or bad, makes an impression upon readers, even if it is only one element of effective writing.

Student writers tend to make the same errors, and for most students, errors of spelling, punctuation, and usage are not a very serious problem. Sometimes, these kinds of errors *do* constitute a serious challenge for a student writer and require time, attention, and effort to overcome. Nevertheless, many students spend too much time worrying about correctness and far too little time attending to larger issues that make writing effective. As this chapter makes clear, effective writing encompasses many things, "good grammar" among them. It is essential that you apply the rules of usage and follow the conventions of written English, because those rules are part of what makes writing effective. However, if you learn the rules and conventions of standard written English but little else about writing, you will most likely not be a very good writer.

What This Means for You as a Writer

- **Learn and apply the appropriate rules for standard written English.** By the time they reach college, most students know most of what they need to know about the rules for correct writing. They may not always be able to explain those rules, but they have learned many of them intuitively. So recognize that you already know a great deal about the rules for correct writing, but also be aware of what you don't know. When you're unsure about a matter of usage or punctuation, consult your instructor, your campus writing center, an online writing resource, or a textbook such as this one.

- **Recognize that few rules apply in every instance.** Many of the rules for correct writing are clear and well established, but some aren't. There is often disagreement among grammarians and writing teachers about specific points of usage and style. As a writer, you have to be aware that such differences occur and that the rhetorical context determines what rules apply. So learn the accepted conventions for the kind of writing you are doing. Remember, too, that these conventions can change from one academic subject to another, so make it a point to become familiar with the conventions for writing in the different courses you take.

- **Always edit your writing for correctness.** Don't be obsessive about minor errors as you're working through early drafts of a piece of writing (see Core Concept #8), but make sure you edit carefully and thoroughly before submitting your work. It usually doesn't take very long to review a finished draft for minor errors, to reread it for clarity, and to make corrections to words or sentences, and it doesn't take much effort to run the spell check on your word processing program. Editing for minor problems and ensuring that you have followed the conventions of standard English should become a regular part of your writing process.

- **Focus on the errors you regularly make.** Identify the mistakes you regularly make and review the appropriate rule for each one. For example, maybe you often forget to include a comma after an introductory clause (e.g., "When he woke up the next morning, his wallet and keys were missing."). If you're not sure about the rule, talk to your writing instructor or someone at your campus writing center. Studies show that most students tend to make the same kinds of minor errors. If you focus attention on the errors you tend to make, you will learn to look for these errors when you edit your assignments. Eventually, most of those errors will disappear from your writing.

PRACTICE THIS LESSON

Make a list of the five most common errors of spelling, punctuation, or usage that you tend to make. For each one, consult a handbook or an online resource like the Purdue OWL to identify the appropriate rule. (You may have to review several past writing assignments to develop this list of common errors.) Use this list when you edit your writing future assignments.

In this chapter, you will learn to

1. Apply the ten core concepts in your own writing to create effective texts.

2. Engage in writing as a process of inquiry.

The Ten Core Concepts in Action

WRITING GROWS OUT OF A NEED to answer a question, make a decision, or solve a problem. For college students, that need is usually created by course assignments—but not always. Sometimes it grows out of a situation that calls for writing of some kind:

- a problem on your campus that affects you;
- a tweet or news editorial that you want to respond to;
- an event that raises questions for members of your community;
- an important anniversary that evokes memories you want to share with others;
- a controversial online video that you want to comment on;
- a project that you believe might improve your workplace.

In each of these examples, circumstances prompt you to create a document intended for a specific audience for a specific purpose. In other words, the need to write grows out of a rhetorical situation (see page 27 in Chapter 2). Sometimes, too, writing grows out of a writer's simple desire to understand something better.

Whatever your motivation for writing, this chapter takes you through the process of creating an effective text for your specific rhetorical situation:

- *If your assignment specifies a topic and genre*, then follow the guidelines your instructor has provided and adjust each of the following steps to fit those guidelines.
- *If your assignment doesn't specify a topic and genre and gives you free choice about what to write*, then develop a project that enables you to answer a question, make a decision, or solve a problem on an issue that interests you; develop your project so that it fits your specific rhetorical situation.

This chapter uses the Ten Core Concepts described in Chapter 2 to help you identify a relevant topic, explore that topic thoroughly, and write an effective document on that topic that is appropriate for your rhetorical situation.

Think of this chapter as a guide rather than a set of step-by-step instructions for completing a writing project. Parts II, III, and IV of this textbook provide specific guidance for analytical, argumentative, and narrative writing. Those later chapters examine different genres in detail; this chapter shows how to put the Ten Core Concepts in action. Use this chapter in conjunction with the chapters in Parts II, III, and IV to guide you through the process of effective writing for a specific kind of text.

The ten steps in this chapter correspond to the Ten Core Concepts described in Chapter 2. As you work through this chapter, you might find that you do not need to complete each step or that you need to repeat a step. You might also move through the steps out of sequence. Some steps may take a few moments to complete; others will take much longer. That's OK. Writing is a process of exploration that can lead to insights into complicated issues that matter for you and your readers, and the process will not be exactly the same for every writer or writing task. So use this chapter to learn about your topic and create a project that engages your readers.

Step 1 Discover and explore a topic.

Begin with a Question

Identify something you are wondering about, something that intrigues or puzzles you, something that calls for a decision or solution.

If your assignment specifies a topic	If your assignment does not specify a topic
↓	↓
Review the guidelines to get a sense of appropriate topics.	Think about problems, issues, or questions that you have been puzzling about.
↓	↓
What intrigues or puzzles you about the subject of this assignment?	Is there a question or issue that you want to address for some reason?
↓	↓
What questions or issues might be appropriate for this assignment?	Are you facing a situation that requires you to understand something better?
↓	↓
Make a list of three or four **questions** that most interest you.	Make a list of three or four **questions** that most interest you.

Explore Your Questions

Write a brief paragraph for each question, explaining why it might be worth exploring for this project. In each paragraph:

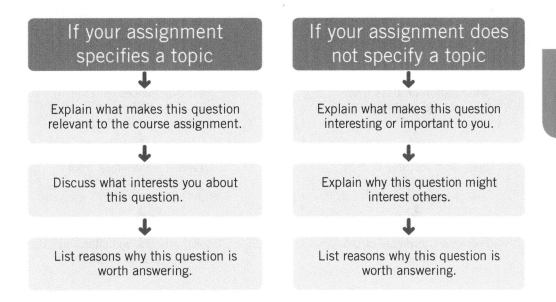

Select a Working Topic

Review your paragraphs and select one of the questions from your list as your working topic for your project. (This question might change as you learn more about your topic, but for now it is the question that will serve as your working topic.)

Identify What You Know about Your Topic

Jot down what you already know about your working topic, including:

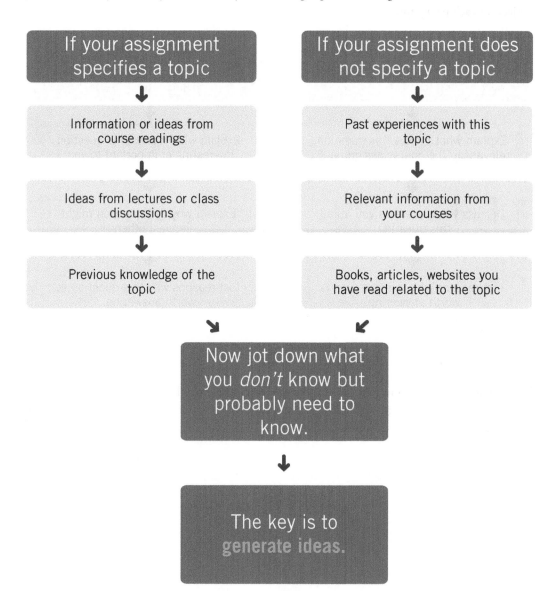

If your assignment specifies a topic

↓

Information or ideas from course readings

↓

Ideas from lectures or class discussions

↓

Previous knowledge of the topic

If your assignment does not specify a topic

↓

Past experiences with this topic

↓

Relevant information from your courses

↓

Books, articles, websites you have read related to the topic

↘ ↙

Now jot down what you *don't* know but probably need to know.

↓

The key is to generate ideas.

Adjust Your Question

Review your notes to determine whether you should amend your question and working topic.

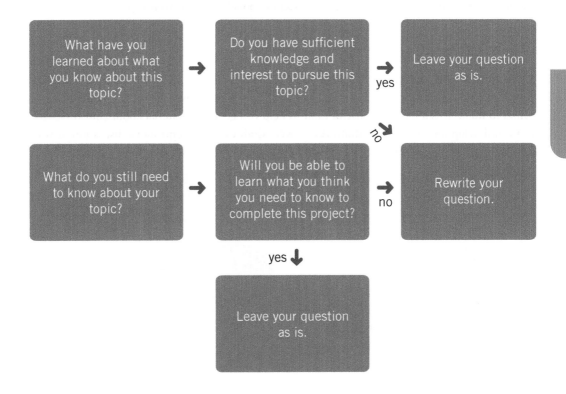

Use Technology to Generate Ideas and Gather Information

Explore your question with digital tools:

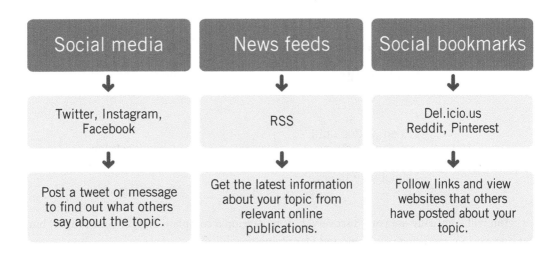

Hearing what others say or think about a topic can help you generate ideas and identify questions you will need to address. These tools provide a fast and easy way to tap into ideas, information, and conversations about your topic. Keep in mind that you are not looking for source material; rather, you are generating ideas and seeking possibilities for your topic.

Write a Discovery Draft

A discovery draft is focused but informal and open-ended writing intended to help you explore your topic. It is not a first or rough draft, nor is it freewriting, in which you just write whatever comes to mind. It is a more purposeful draft to help you generate material about your topic that you can develop into a complete draft. A discovery draft can be a continuous discussion of your topic or it can be pieces and fragments, some of which are more developed than others.

To write a discovery draft

Do
- Begin writing, using ideas and information you have.
- Write as much as you can about your topic.
- Make notes about questions to be explored later.
- Keep writing until you have nothing more to write about your topic.

Don't
- Try to write a finished essay.
- Focus on organization or coherence.
- Worry about the quality of your writing.
- Leave anything out at this stage.

You will eventually use your discovery draft to develop a complete draft of your project, but for now you are exploring your topic and identifying possibilities.

Step 2   Examine the rhetorical context.

Identify Your Audience

Briefly describe your intended audience for your project:

Describe who you expect or hope will read your project.

If your assignment specifies an audience, describe that audience.	If you have no assignment, identify the audience you would most like to reach.

Be as specific as possible.

If your assignment does not specify an audience, assume that your instructor and/or your classmates are your audience.	If your intended audience is general (e.g., readers of a national newspaper like *USA Today* or people interested in politics), say so. If you are writing for a more specialized audience (e.g., students on your campus, people who snowboard, or video gamers), identify that audience as clearly as you can.

Explore your audience.

Jot down your sense of your instructor's expectations for this assignment. Refer to the assignment guidelines to understand additional audience expectations for the assignment.	Anticipate what your intended audience might know about your topic. Write down what you think they will expect from your project. Consider relevant special circumstances (e.g., video gamers will likely be familiar with online gaming sites).

Consider the Context

Examine how the specific circumstances under which you are writing might influence your project:

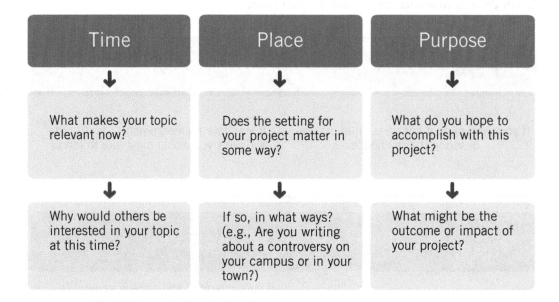

Review Your Question

Adjust the question you developed for Step #1 in view of what you have learned about your audience and the context for your project:

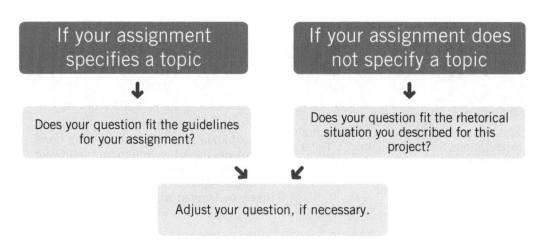

Develop Your Discovery Draft

Review your discovery draft in light of what you have learned so far about your audience and your rhetorical situation:

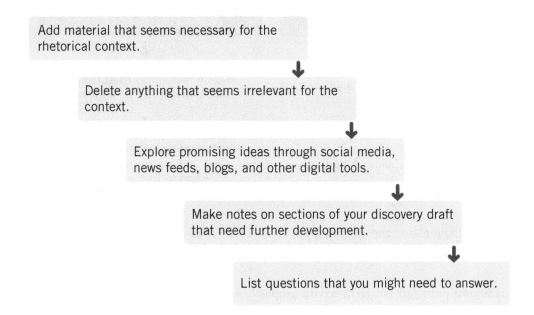

Add material that seems necessary for the rhetorical context.

Delete anything that seems irrelevant for the context.

Explore promising ideas through social media, news feeds, blogs, and other digital tools.

Make notes on sections of your discovery draft that need further development.

List questions that you might need to answer.

Remember that at this point you are still exploring your topic in a way that will make it effective for your intended audience.

Step 3   Select an appropriate medium.

Most college assignments call for conventional academic essays, which are usually submitted either electronically (as a Word or PDF file) or in hard copy. In such cases, the medium is traditional print text, and you should follow appropriate conventions for standard academic writing. (Assignments that call for conventional writing for non-academic forums, such as newspapers, magazines, or newsletters, might follow slightly different conventions but are still print texts.) However, writers today have access to many different media, including digital and online media.

Select a Medium

Identify a medium that would be appropriate for your rhetorical context:

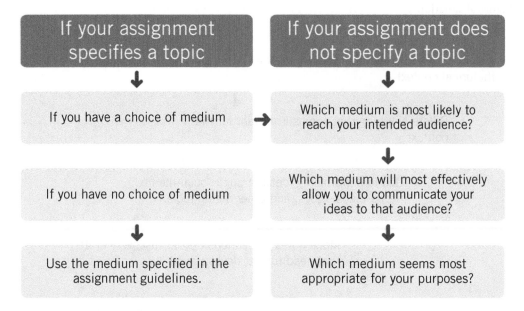

A traditional print text (an essay, report, proposal, research paper) might be the best way to achieve your rhetorical purpose and adhere to the guidelines of the assignment, but consider other media through which you can present your ideas:

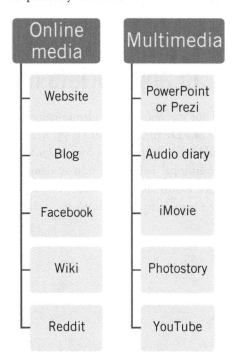

Consider How the Medium Might Shape Your Project

Your choice of medium can significantly affect the way you present your ideas to your audience:

Structure	• Does this medium require you to organize your project in a specific way? • What options for structuring your project does this medium provide?
Length	• Does this medium place any length restrictions on your project? (For example, an essay written to be read as part of an audio diary may need to be shorter than a traditional print essay.) • If so, how will these restrictions affect the depth of your exploration of your topic?
Image and sound	• Does this medium enable you to incorporate sound and/or visual elements? • If so, what kinds of images and/or sound are appropriate? • How will you incorporate these elements?
Style	• What are the expectations for writing style in this medium? • Will you have to adopt any specific stylistic conventions for this medium? (For example, blogs usually call for shorter sections, or "chunks," of texts to help readers scroll more easily through the post.)

3

Return to Your Discovery Draft

Make notes about how the medium you have chosen might affect the development of your project.

Consider whether the medium will make it necessary to eliminate, add, or change material you have already generated.

Revise your main question to fit the medium, if necessary.

Step 4 | Have something to say.

At this point you have a topic, but you must determine what you will *say* about that topic. What will the main point of your project be?

Revisit Your Main Question

Reread your Discovery Draft and then return to the question you developed for Step #1:

If your assignment specifies a topic	If your assignment does not specify a topic
How does your main question relate to the subject of the course? (E.g., if you are analyzing the causes of high rates of suicide among teens in the U.S. for a psychology class, consider what makes this question relevant in the field of psychology.)	**How does your question relate to larger conversations about your subject?** (E.g., a question about whether charter schools help minority students improve their chances of going to college is part of a longstanding debate about education reform in the U.S.)
Consider these questions: • In what ways is your topic important in this academic field? • How will your project contribute to an understanding of this topic? • What will your project say to your readers about this topic? • What do you think you want to say about the topic, based on what you know at this point?	**Consider these questions:** • Why is your topic important? What makes it relevant now? • What might your project contribute to ongoing discussions about this issue? • Why would your intended audience find your topic interesting or important? • What do you have to say, based on what you know at this point, that will be interesting and relevant to your audience?

Write a Guiding Thesis Statement

On the basis of your notes from Step #1 and your revised Discovery Draft, write a brief paragraph explaining your main point and the purpose of your project as you understand it at this point. Include your main question and a brief explanation of why it is important to your intended audience.

This paragraph is your Guiding Thesis Statement, a working summary of the main idea for your project. Your Guiding Thesis Statement may change as you develop your project, but you can use it to guide your work as you explore your topic. Revise your Guiding Thesis Statement as often as necessary as you gain a clearer sense of the main point of your project.

Review Your Discovery Draft

Use your Guiding Thesis Statement to review your discovery draft:

Identify ideas, issues, or questions that seem important to your main point as described in your Guiding Thesis Statement:
- Which sections of your discovery draft seem especially important to your main point?
- Which sections need more development, given your main point?

Identify gaps in your Discovery Draft:
- Does anything seem to be missing that is relevant to your main point?
- What questions about your topic remain to be addressed?
- What more do you need to know about this topic to address the main point described in your Guiding Thesis Statement?

Consider the Rhetorical Situation:
- Is your main point relevant to your intended audience?
- Does your Discovery Draft clearly present your main point in a way that addresses your intended audience?
- What might be missing from your draft that your audience will expect?

Revise Your Guiding Thesis Statement

On the basis of your review of your Discovery Draft, revise your Guiding Thesis Statement so that it clearly explains the nature and purpose of your project and accounts for audience expectations. You now have a working statement of the main point of your project.

Step 5   Back up what you say.

Most college writing assignments require students to support their claims, assertions, and positions. Even in narrative writing, writers provide support (often in the form of anecdotes or descriptions rather than factual evidence) for the ideas they want to convey to readers. As you develop your project and learn about your topic, be sure to support your main points or claims.

Remember that at this point in the process you are still exploring your topic, developing your ideas, and gathering information. "Backing up what you say" is as much a process of learning and exploring as it is a matter of identifying evidence or support, so be open to possibilities.

Begin by referring back to your Guiding Thesis Statement to remind yourself of your main question and the main purpose of your project.

Identify Your Main Claims or Assertions

On the basis of your Guiding Thesis Statement identify and explore the major points you will make in support of your main point:

List your major claims or assertions.

List any claims or assertions that seem relevant at this stage.	Be as specific as possible, knowing you will adjust your list as you explore your topic.

↓

Explore each claim or assertion.

Write a sentence explaining why each claim is relevant to your main point.	Write a sentence describing what you need to know to support each claim or assertion.

↓

Prioritize your list of claims or assertions.

Which claims or assertions seem most important?	Which claims or assertions might be secondary to other claims or assertions?

↓

Identify potential sources.

What kinds of information or evidence do you need to support your claims or assertions?	Where might you find the information or evidence you need? (See Chapter 9.)

↓

Begin exploring each claim.

Develop your ideas for each major claim or assertion.	Find information or evidence to support each claim or assertion.

Review Your Discovery Draft

Return to your Discovery Draft and be sure it includes the major claims and assertions you identified in Step #1.

Write a Complete Draft

At this point, you should be ready to write a draft of your project. If so, write as complete a draft as you can based on what you have learned so far about your topic and using the information you have gathered for this exercise. Use your Discovery Draft as the basis for your Complete Draft, or simply refer to your Discovery Draft for ideas to be included in your Complete Draft.

If you are ready to write a draft

Keep in mind that this is a rough draft.

Make your draft as complete as possible but don't worry about making it polished.

If you are not ready to write a draft

Write whatever portions of your draft that you feel ready to write.

Continue exploring your topic and move on to Step #6.

Step 6 | Establish a form and structure for your project.

The form of your project should present your ideas and information clearly and effectively to your readers. In deciding on an appropriate form for your project, consider:

Genre	• Follow the conventions governing form for the genre (argument, analysis, narrative) in which you are writing. • Parts II, III, and IV of this textbook will guide you in developing a proper form for specific genres (e.g., proposals, public argument, etc.).
Medium	• The medium can shape the form and even the content of your project. • Multimedia and online projects will influence how you structure your project.
Rhetorical situation	• The form of a project will be shaped in part by your sense of your intended audience. • The form will also be influenced by your sense of the purpose of your project.

If you have already written your rough draft, use this exercise to determine whether your draft is organized effectively.

Identify the Main Parts of Your Project

Review your rough draft or use your Discovery Draft as well as your notes to make a list of the main sections or components of your project.

Develop an Outline

Use your list to create a basic outline for your project (refer to chapters in Parts II, III, and IV for more detailed guidance on organizing specific kinds of texts):

If you have written a rough draft

Create an outline on the basis of your draft.

Make sure to include the main sections from your list.

If you have not yet written a rough draft

Use your Discovery Draft and your list to develop an outline.

Make your outline as detailed or general as is helpful at this point.

Refine Your Outline

Review your outline to determine whether it effectively meets the needs of your rhetorical situation:

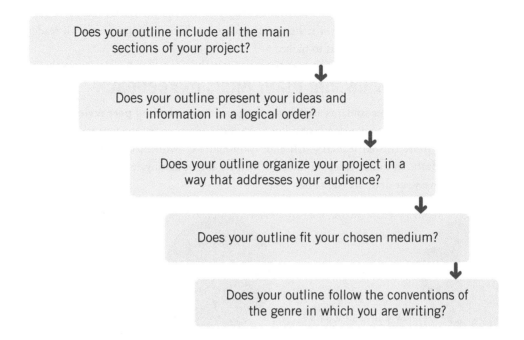

Does your outline include all the main sections of your project?

Does your outline present your ideas and information in a logical order?

Does your outline organize your project in a way that addresses your audience?

Does your outline fit your chosen medium?

Does your outline follow the conventions of the genre in which you are writing?

Write or Revise Your Draft

Using your outline as a guide, write a rough draft of your project or revise the rough draft you have already written so that you have strengthened the structure of your project.

Step 7 | Get feedback.

At this point it makes sense to involve others in the process of developing your project to help you determine whether your draft is effective and to identify potential problems to address in your revisions. The goal is to get a sense of whether your project is achieving its purpose with readers and to help you decide which revisions to make.

Consider Peer Review and Other Kinds of Feedback

In most college writing classes students are asked to engage in some kind of **peer review** of drafts with classmates. If your instructor does not ask you to engage in peer review, you can seek feedback from one or more trusted readers—a friend, roommate, co-worker, or relative—who can respond to your draft. In either case, the main principles for obtaining, evaluating, and using feedback to improve your draft are the same.

If you have peer review in your class

- Follow your instructor's procedure for providing and receiving feedback on drafts.
- Be sure you understand what you are expected to do during peer review.
- Listen carefully to your classmates' feedback on your draft.
- Take your classmates' comments seriously.
- Ask questions to clarify their comments or to encourage them to give you feedback on specific questions or concerns you have about your draft.
- Use the lists of questions below to guide your readers and evaluate their feedback.

If you seek feedback on your own

- Identify one or more readers whom you trust to read your draft thoughtfully.
- Consider finding readers online through a discussion forum for writers or a writing center, or post your draft on Facebook to share it with friends.
- Make sure your readers understand the nature of your assignment or project.
- Explain your rhetorical situation (especially your intended audience and your purpose for this project).
- Use the lists of questions below to help guide your readers and evaluate their feedback.

Remember that it takes practice to learn how to give and receive useful feedback on writing-in-progress. Think of it as part of the process of inquiring more deeply into your subject and making your project more effective.

Ask Your Readers to Respond to Your Draft

Use the following sets of questions to guide your readers' responses:

3

Topic	• How interesting and relevant is the topic? • Is the purpose of the project clear? Is it worthwhile? • Is the main point or idea clear? Does the writer have something to say? • How well does the draft explore the topic? Is anything missing or unnecessary? • What are the main claims or assertions? Are they adequately supported? • What questions are left unanswered for readers?
Medium and Form	• Does the medium work for this topic? Does it address the intended audience effectively? How does the writer take advantage of the capabilities of the medium? • How is the project organized? In what ways can the writer organize it more effectively? • How well does the introduction introduce the topic and main ideas? How well does it draw readers into the project? How can it be more engaging or focused? • How well does the conclusion sum up the project? Does it emphasize the writer's main ideas?
Style	• Is the writing generally clear and readable? Is the prose engaging? • Which passages are confusing or difficult to follow? How can they be improved? • Where in the draft do problems with usage or grammar impede meaning? How can those problems be corrected? • Does the writer's voice come through clearly and effectively?

In addition, ask your readers to jot down any other questions or comments they might have about your draft.

Remember that the more specific your readers' comments, the more useful they are likely to be. So ask your readers to elaborate on their responses to specific sections of your draft.

Identify Common Themes in Your Readers' Responses

If you engaged in peer review with several classmates or you had more than one person outside of class read your draft, you will need to consider their feedback carefully and evaluate the usefulness of their responses as you consider the need for specific revisions. (If you had only one reader respond to your draft, pay special attention to that reader's strongest reactions.)

First, look for similarities in your readers' responses.

If your readers agree that something in your draft is working well, →	That part of your draft likely needs little (if any) revision.
If your readers all cite the same problems, →	You should probably address those problems in your revisions.

Consider Conflicting Advice in Your Readers' Responses

Different readers might have different reactions to your project. Such disagreements might indicate sections of your draft that need revision, though not always. Sometimes disagreements can simply be matters of personal preferences among your readers. Nevertheless, carefully consider disagreements among your readers as you decide upon specific revisions:

If your readers disagree about specific aspects of your draft	• Review the readers' comments to understand their disagreements. • Consider each reader's perspective about that part of your draft. • As you review disagreements among your readers' responses to your draft, consider which feedback seems to take your rhetorical situation into account.
If you agree with one reader and disagree with others	• Consider why you agree or disagree. • Review the relevant sections of your draft to see whether your readers' comments might have changed your mind. • If possible, ask readers to explain or clarify their reactions. • Keep in mind that not all feedback will necessarily be relevant or helpful.

Identify Possible Revisions on the Basis of Your Readers' Feedback

On the basis of your review of your readers' responses to your draft, make notes about possible revisions you should make:

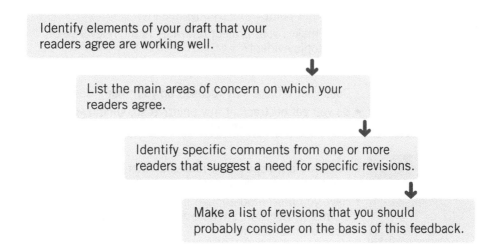

Identify elements of your draft that your readers agree are working well.

List the main areas of concern on which your readers agree.

Identify specific comments from one or more readers that suggest a need for specific revisions.

Make a list of revisions that you should probably consider on the basis of this feedback.

Remember that *you* must decide which revisions are best, based on your assessment of the rhetorical situation and your own purposes for your project.

Step 8 Revise.

Revision is part of the process of discovery and learning. It is also a rhetorical process by which you craft your project so that it effectively reaches your intended audience and achieves your rhetorical purposes. As you revise, keep in mind that you will continue to learn about your topic even as you improve your draft.

As you proceed, refer to your list from Step #7 as well as to your Guiding Thesis Statement to decide on specific revisions.

Focus First on Content

Review your draft to determine whether you have sufficiently developed your ideas and effectively made your main point:

Main idea	• What is your main point in this project? • Does that point come through clearly? • What makes your project relevant? Is the relevance of your topic evident?

Focus	• Does your project stay focused on your main idea? • Do you get off track at any point? If so, should you rewrite or eliminate those sections?

Development	• Have you developed your ideas sufficiently? Which sections need further development? • Have you presented enough information to support your claims or assertions? Where are your claims or evidence weak or insufficient? • Have you gone into too much detail in any sections? If so, should you condense or eliminate those sections?

Consult your list of potential revisions from Step #7 to make sure it includes any issues related to content that you have identified. If necessary, add to or revise that list.

Focus Next on Form

Reread your revised draft from beginning to end to determine whether you need to reorganize it or strengthen its form or structure (refer to your outline and your notes from Step #6):

Organization	• Have you presented your ideas in a sensible order? • Which sections should be moved so that your ideas are more logically presented to your readers? • Which sections might be combined to make your project tighter?
Transitions	• What are the main sections of your project? Do you make clear transitions between these sections? Where might transitions be missing? • Do your transitions help your readers follow your discussion? • Which transitions might confuse readers?
Medium	• Have you followed the conventions for your medium? • If you are working in a digital medium, have you structured your project so that readers/viewers can follow it easily? • For multimedia projects, have you placed visual or audio elements effectively?

Consult your list of potential revisions from Step #7 to make sure it includes any issues related to form that you have identified. If necessary, add to or revise that list.

Consider Your Rhetorical Situation

Review your revised draft to be sure you have addressed your intended audience effectively and fulfilled the needs of your rhetorical situation:

Use the questions from Step #2 to review your draft in view of the rhetorical situation.

Consult your list from Step #7 to identify potential revisions related to your rhetorical situation.

If necessary, add to or revise that list to include revisions that will help your draft better meet the expectations of your intended audience.

Revisit Your Introduction and Conclusion

Return to your introduction and conclusion to make sure they effectively introduce and conclude your project in view of your rhetorical situation:

Introduction
- How clearly does your introduction describe your topic?
- How well does it draw your readers into your project?
- What compelling reason does your introduction give your intended audience for reading your project?
- Does it convey the purpose of your project?

Conclusion
- What main ideas are emphasized in your conclusions? Is this the appropriate emphasis in view of your rhetorical purpose?
- Does your conclusion do more than simply restate your main idea?
- How does it leave your readers with a sense that you have fulfilled the purpose of your project?

Return to your list of potential revisions from Step #7 to make sure it includes any revisions you now think you should make to your introduction or conclusion.

Prioritize Your List of Potential Revisions

Now review the list of potential revisions that you developed for Step #7. No matter how long or short that list is, you will need to decide which revisions are most important and which might be most challenging. Organize your list of potential revisions according to the following four broad categories:

1. List revisions related to content

Do you need to develop any sections of your draft? Do you need to do additional research or develop additional ideas?

Do you need to condense or eliminate sections that are too lengthy or unnecessary?

2. List revisions related to form and medium

Does your project need to be reorganized in any way?

Which sections of your project need to be moved? Which transitions need to be revised, added, or eliminated?

3. List revisions related to your introduction and conclusion

Do you need to make any revisions to your introduction?

Do you need to revise your conclusion?

4. List any changes needed to address your rhetorical situation

Do you need to make changes to your draft to address your readers' expectations more effectively?

Do you need revisions to make sure your project fits your rhetorical situation?

Your list of potential revisions amounts to a **revision plan**. Begin revising your draft according to this plan, moving from the first item on your list to the last. Keep in mind that this process might take more than one sitting, and you might find a need to write new sections of your draft and then revise again. That's OK. As we noted earlier, revision is a recursive, sometimes circuitous process, and the goal is to explore your subject fully while you bring your draft into line with the expectations of your rhetorical situation.

Once you work through your revision plan, you should have a revised draft that is close to finished. All the main pieces should be in place: a focused, sufficiently developed project that presents your main ideas effectively and clearly to your intended audience; a sound structure; an engaging introduction; and an effective conclusion.

Step 9 | Strengthen your voice.

No matter the rhetorical situation, effective writing has a strong voice that reflects the writer's command of his or her subject matter. Your voice will give your readers confidence that your project is worth reading.

Consider Your Rhetorical Context

Review the rhetorical context for your project to gain a better sense of how your voice might meet the expectations of your readers and help you achieve your purpose:

Are there any specific expectations or restrictions regarding voice, tone, and writing style in this rhetorical context? (For example, a business proposal should not be written in a conversational style.)

Do your voice, tone, and writing style fit the form or genre of your project? (For example, a lab report should have an objective voice and formal writing style.)

Does your draft speak with a voice that fits your rhetorical context? If not, what changes should you make so that your voice and writing style fit the rhetorical context?

Consider Whether You Should Use the First Person

Determine whether the use of first person is appropriate for this project:

| If first person is appropriate | Decide whether using the first person will make your project more effective. | If so, revise accordingly. |

| If first person is inappropriate | Review your draft to eliminate any uses of "I." |

Strengthen Your Voice

Reread your draft out loud to "listen to" your voice and consider the following questions to guide your revisions:

> Does your voice sound authoritative and confident? Does it convey a sense that your project is valid and worthwhile?

> Is your voice consistent throughout your project? If not, where is it weakest? What changes might make it stronger in those sections?

At this stage, assume that your project is complete and appropriately structured and try to ignore those aspects of your project as you review your draft for voice and style.

Step 10   Make it correct.

Edit your draft for clarity and correctness.

Make your sentences clear	• Revise sentences that are unclear. • Eliminate wordiness. • Restructure sentences that are difficult to follow. • Refer to Chapter 7 for advice on style.
Use sources correctly	• Integrate source material smoothly into your prose. • Check quotations for accuracy. • Make sure sources are cited correctly (see Chapter 12). • Format your bibliography correctly (if appropriate).
Correct errors	• Correct errors of usage and punctuation. • Refer to a handbook or an online resource like the Purdue OWL for guidance in correcting errors.

In this chapter, you will learn to

1. Apply the Ten Core Concepts to a specific writing assignment.

2. Demonstrate how an idea for a piece of writing develops through the use of the Ten Core Concepts.

A Student Writer Applies the Core Concepts

4

CHLOE CHARLES was a first-year student at the State University of New York at Albany when she wrote the following essay for her introductory writing course. As a psychology major and someone who had taken advanced English courses in high school, Chloe well understood the importance of writing. When she received an assignment requiring her "to develop an in-depth, informed argument that reflects an understanding of an issue," she was already exploring an issue that mattered to her.

Chloe Charles

Step 1   Discover and explore a topic.

Begin with a Question

Chloe's idea for her essay began to take shape a few months before she received the assignment to write an argument. For an earlier assignment, Chloe had written an essay describing her stepfather's struggles to find work after losing his job during the Great Recession that began in 2007. Although her stepfather had a college degree and many years of work experience, he was unable to find a new job in his field. After many months of trying and failing to find work, he decided to change careers, and at the age of 36 he returned to college to earn a certificate that would enable him to become a high school teacher.

Writing about her stepfather's experience raised questions for Chloe about the widespread belief in American society that college is the best choice for every student. Her essay about her stepfather suggested that the issue is more complicated than she had previously thought. So when her writing instructor gave an assignment asking students "to examine a question related to the purpose of college," Chloe already had a question:

Is college for everyone?

Chloe had always believed it is, but her stepfather's experience made her wonder. Her great-grandfather had never gone to college, yet he had become a successful businessman and led a comfortable life. Her stepfather, by contrast, had gone to college—twice—and was struggling to make ends meet. As a new college student herself committed to pursuing a career as a lawyer, Chloe wanted to understand the implications of her own choice and learn more about why Americans seem to place such a high value on attending college. She needed to examine these issues more carefully if she was going to make "an in-depth informed argument," as her assignment required.

Explore the Question

Chloe's instructor, Joe, had given his students several assignments that encouraged them to explore the question of the purpose of education. One of those assignments required students to read and interpret several essays about education. One of those essays was "Knowledge Its Own End," written in 1852 by the influential 19th Century thinker John Henry Newman. Chloe was intrigued by Newman's claim that higher learning is a basic human need. In a draft for the assignment she wrote,

> Newman states that knowledge is not good or bad but depends on how we treat it. Even in ancient Greece and Rome, he says, most people had the will to look outside their own perceptions to find out what was happening around them. Newman acknowledges that some people are better suited for manual labor or serving in the military, but they still need knowledge to do their jobs well. He knows that people everywhere in the world, not just a few, want to know and understand what is going on in the world.

Reading and writing about Newman acquainted Chloe with important philosophical ideas about the role of knowledge in human society. She also read more recent scholarly essays, including one published in 2015 by Charles Murray, a controversial political thinker, who argued that not everyone is suited for college. Although Chloe believed she disagreed with Murray, she found some of his arguments persuasive, especially in view of her stepfather's and grandfather's experiences. Wrestling with these scholarly perspectives began to inform Chloe's own thinking about whether college is for everyone, and when Joe finally assigned the argument essay, Chloe was immersed in this topic.

Select a Working Topic

Chloe knew she would focus her essay on the broad question of whether college is appropriate for everyone, but at this early stage of her assignment she wasn't entirely sure what specific direction her project would take. Joe asked his students to submit a one-page proposal in which they described their topics, stated the main research question they would address, and identified an appropriate audience for their arguments. As a result of her preliminary exploration, Chloe began to wonder how college had become such a powerful expectation in American society and how that expectation affects young people today. In her proposal she wrote, "Not everyone gets the opportunity to go to college, and I want to look at the history of higher education in the U.S.

and its importance in American society." At this point, her primary interest was in examining the history of higher education in the U.S. to understand why college has become such an important expectation.

Identify What You Know About Your Topic

Because Chloe had been writing about her topic for most of the semester, she already had a lot of relevant material and she knew some important things about her topic. For example, writing about her stepfather gave her insight into some of the factors, such as the economic situation, that can affect one's career choices and success. Chloe also began to understand how complicated her topic was. For example, the lack of a college degree didn't seem to be a disadvantage for her great-grandfather, who established his business in very different economic circumstances from those her stepfather faced. But a college degree seemed to be a mixed bag for her stepfather: His degree in English helped him establish a career in journalism, but when he lost his job as a journalist, his degree didn't seem to help him find a new job. These cases suggested that there are no easy answers to the question of whether college is a good choice for everyone and helped Chloe understand that she needed to examine the historical context in order to address the issue sufficiently.

Chloe's reading of scholarly essays, such as those by John Henry Newman and Charles Murray, also helped her become familiar with longstanding philosophical questions about the purpose of education and the ongoing debates about education in Western culture. At the same time, Chloe was aware of extensive coverage in the mass media about the high rates of college loan debt among American students today, a problem that is often cited in debates about the value of college.

Chloe's efforts to explore the question of the purpose of college encouraged her to learn more about the history of higher education in the U.S. and about the advantages and disadvantages of a college degree in contemporary American society. As a new college student herself, the question she was trying to answer was directly relevant to her own life as well as to that of her classmates.

Adjust Your Question

On the basis of her exploration, Chloe felt confident in focusing her project on the following questions, which she included in the proposal she submitted to her instructor:

Why is it expected in American society that everyone should pursue a college education? Where does this expectation come from?

Use Technology to Generate Ideas and Gather Information

Chloe was working on her essay at a time (in 2015) when the question of whether college is worthwhile was getting a great deal of attention in the press and on social media. One of the candidates running for U.S. president at the time, Senator Bernie Sanders, had proposed making college free for all students, a proposal that provoked much debate. Concerns about high levels of student debt prompted many Americans to question whether college was really worth the seemingly high cost. Chloe could follow these debates online to learn more about the various perspectives on these issues, and she could use social media platforms like Twitter to follow key figures in these debates and to share ideas with her peers.

Write a Discovery Draft

Because Chloe had already been writing about her topic by the time her instructor assigned the argument essay, she had a lot of material to work with. So instead of writing a Discovery Draft from scratch, she pulled together material from her essay about her stepfather and her essay about the assigned readings by John Henry Newman and Charles Murray. These various writings, which focused on different aspects of her topic, amounted to a Discovery Draft that included key ideas and information that Chloe could use to build her argument in her new essay. Here's part of what she wrote in her essay about her stepfather:

> Most people think of college as a resource to obtain a degree so that later on when they are entering the job force, they will receive a higher paying job. However, this is not true for everyone, especially in my family. When I was young, my stepfather had a job at my hometown news station. He was a journalist and an editor. He loved his job and was one of the most qualified people there, having earned a Bachelor's degree in English with a minor in communications. But all of this was not enough for him to keep his job during the recession in 2007. After many months with no success finding a job, he had to go back to school to get a new degree, so he could get a new job to support our family—one he could keep.

In this excerpt Chloe examines her own family's experience in a way that raises important questions about the value of a college degree today. She continued to explore these questions in her essay about John Henry Newman and Charles Murray:

> Many Americans in past decades could live relatively successful lives without earning college degrees, but now times have changed. Many people today question the value of a college degree and wonder why college has become the expected path for high school graduates. One reason is that college became much more accessible after World War I. Before that war, there was little fluctuation in college attendance rates, but after the Great Depression ended in the 1940s, more Americans began to go to college. This increase happened partly because many people believed that they could earn more money in the long run if they obtained a college degree. That was true. In 1975, a person with a bachelor's degree earned about 1.5 times more in yearly pay than

did someone with only a high school diploma (Brock 111). There are also many social and intellectual benefits of attending college that students can take advantage of to create successful careers. Having a college education can lead to better health, living arrangements, and lifestyle (Brock 110).

Another important factor that helps explain the increase in the number of Americans attending college was changing societal norms in the United States. Prior to 1965 mostly white men, usually from upper-middle or upper classes, were seen and welcomed on college campuses (Brock 111). African Americans and women were not encouraged to attend college. College was also a financial hardship for many families. Then in 1965 Congress passed the Higher Education Act, which helped the general population obtain financial aid to attend the college of their choice. As well, federal aid for higher education increased from $655 million in 1955 to $3.5 billion in 1965 (Brock 111). This increase in funding made tuition prices affordable for many. And as societal norms began to change, so did the demographics in college populations. Many universities were more open to diversity due to the Civil Rights Act, which was passed in 1964, and attitudes about gender began to change as well. Colleges all over the country began to welcome students of any race, culture, gender, etc. (Brock 111). This made attending "an institution of higher learning for virtually anyone who possessed a high school diploma and the necessary financial resources" possible (Campbell and Siegel 488).

In these excerpts Chloe is not only continuing to explore her main questions about the value of college but also strengthening her own understanding of her topic. In addition to writing about her own experience, she is drawing on materials she found through her search of scholarly articles. (Some of this material ended up in the final version of her argument. See page 117.)

In her proposal for her argument assignment, Chloe pursued these ideas that she had been writing about for her previous assignments. Here's an excerpt from her proposal:

For my argument I want to look at what happened historically that made acquiring a higher education a necessity in the U.S. I want to learn when and why this became the norm since historically most people did not need a college degree to live a successful life. I want to see what national events shaped this view. Understanding what makes people believe that college is so important will help me answer the question that we have been asked frequently in our class: Is college worth it for me?

Chloe's Discovery Draft, then, included materials from previous assignments as well as new ideas, and writing the draft gave her a clearer sense of her topic. At this stage, she still had a lot of research to do, but her main idea for her argument was already beginning to take shape.

Step 2 Examine the rhetorical context.

Identify Your Audience

Chloe's immediate audience for her essay was her writing class. She had shared her previous assignments with some of her classmates, all of whom were also writing about topics related to education. In this way, the class became a community of scholars who were working together on their writing to gain a better understanding of important questions, issues, and problems in education. Chloe also knew that her topic was relevant to her classmates, because, like her, they all had to make the decision to attend college and would therefore likely be interested in understanding the implications of that decision. In her proposal for this assignment, she wrote,

> Students will be interested in my topic because I'm sure they want to know why there is a societal expectation that everyone should attend college. I can assume that students might want to know their own role in the history of higher education. How have we, as college students, affected the institutions we attend, and how have we ourselves benefited from attending those institutions?

In posing such questions, Chloe was trying to anticipate the expectations of her primary audience, which could ultimately help her make her argument more relevant and therefore more persuasive.

Chloe's assignment also called for her to write an argument that would be relevant to a broader audience, including scholars and experts interested in education. She believed her questions were relevant to such an audience because colleges have had to make adjustments as the number of Americans who attend college has increased. And although Chloe's assignment called for an academic paper, she selected a topic that actually had wide appeal outside academic settings. At the time she was writing in 2015, questions about the value of college were being intensely debated not only by college students and their families but also by politicians and educators. So although Chloe was writing most directly to an audience of her classmates and other college students, her argument was also relevant to an audience that went beyond her class.

Consider the Context

Time: As already noted, Chloe's topic was timely because of recent economic and political developments that potentially affected the decisions of many Americans about whether or not to attend college. These developments helped intensify the debates about the high cost of college, student loan debt, and related issues that were occurring at the time Chloe was writing. In fact, though, Chloe was addressing questions that Americans have been wrestling with for many decades—questions that had taken on a new urgency because of these recent developments.

Place: In New York state, where Chloe was a college student, the tuition increases at state universities stirred controversy at the time Chloe was writing her essay. And what was happening in New York was happening in many other states as well. So Chloe was addressing issues that were relevant to college students and others throughout the U.S.

Purpose: As she indicated in her proposal, Chloe wanted to gain a better understanding of American attitudes about higher education so that she would have a more informed perspective on her own decisions. But she also saw her essay as part of a larger conversation about higher education in the U.S., and she believed that other students would benefit from understanding how American attitudes about college had changed over time.

Review Your Question

In thinking about the rhetorical context, Chloe felt confident that her topic was relevant to her intended audience, but her preliminary work on her essay prompted her to adjust her working question slightly:

> *Is college worthwhile for everyone?*

This version of her question encompassed the current debates about college as well as the larger issue of the purpose of college better than her earlier version ("Is college for everyone?").

Develop Your Discovery Draft

After reviewing the rhetorical context, Chloe could now return to her Discovery Draft to identify important ideas that she needed to explore further. She knew that her historical analysis might be unfamiliar to some readers, and she wanted to make sure she explained key historical developments clearly and thoroughly. For her earlier essay about the assigned readings by John Henry Newman and Charles Murray, she learned about important scholarly perspectives on the purpose and value of college, and she had done some research on federal policies, such as the Higher Education Act of 1965, and social movements, such as the Civil Rights movement, that helped increase the number of Americans attending college. Now she wanted to learn more about the current debate surrounding the value of college and the economic and social pressures facing students today as they decide whether college is the right choice for them. She also wondered whether there were other government policies that she should consider in her effort to understand how college came to be so valued in American society.

Step 3 Select an appropriate medium.

Select a Medium

Like most college assignments, Chloe's called for a conventional academic essay to be submitted electronically (as a Word or PDF file) or in hard copy. So she did not have to select a medium for her project. However, she knew that she would have to follow the conventions for academic writing, and part of the purpose of the assignment was to help her learn how to take advantage of those conventions to make an effective argument.

Consider How the Medium Might Shape Your Project

The structure and style of Chloe's paper would be shaped by the conventions of academic writing, as you'll see later. As a student who had taken advanced English classes in high school, she was generally familiar with these conventions and kept them in mind as she proceeded with her project. In addition, Joe, Chloe's instructor, had certain expectations for how his students would use source material in making their arguments. For example, he wanted to make sure that students consulted scholarly sources in addition to sources from popular media so that they might gain a broader perspective on their topics. Chloe had already found several scholarly articles, and she would supplement her research with other kinds of sources as well, such as statistical data from the U.S. Department of Education. In this way, the conventions for an academic essay influenced not only the form of her essay but also her decisions about the kind of material she should look for as she explored her topic.

Step 4   Have something to say.

As you can probably tell, Chloe had a genuine interest in her topic and wanted to learn more about it. As she wrote in her proposal, "This topic matters to me because I have always been taught how important it is to receive a college education so that I can be successful in the rest of my life." So she had a stake in answering her question, "Is college worthwhile for everyone?" She also knew that her question mattered to thousands of other students. Moreover, because of her work on her previous essays and her preliminary research for this essay, she already had a strong sense that college has value beyond a career—all of which gave Chloe a good start on a main point or claim.

Revisit Your Main Question

Here is Chloe's main question after she adjusted it in Step #2:

> *Is college worthwhile for everyone?*

For her proposal she had already begun to identify how this question is both timely and relevant to her intended audience—which included her classmates, other college students, and a much larger audience interested in issues related to higher education—and she had already begun to formulate a main point or thesis.

Write a Guiding Thesis Statement

Here is the Guiding Thesis Statement that Chloe developed as a result of her work on her proposal and Discovery Draft:

> Various social and economic developments along with government policies in the past century have resulted in a dramatic increase in the number of Americans who attend college, and today many students feel pressure to go to college. However, many students might be attending college because of this societal pressure rather than pursue other career paths that would be right for them.

Review Your Discovery Draft

After reviewing her Discovery Draft and other materials she had gathered through her preliminary research, Chloe realized that her Guiding Thesis Statement did not really encompass the larger question of the value of college, a question she explored in her essay on John Henry Newman and Charles Murray and one that is central to the ongoing debates about college in the U.S.

Revise Your Guiding Thesis Statement

Here is Chloe's revised Guiding Thesis Statement:

> Various social and economic developments along with government policies in the past century have resulted in a dramatic increase in the number of Americans who attend college. Today many students feel pressure to go to college rather than pursue other career paths that would be right for them, believing that college will lead to a better-paying job. However, in view of a challenging job market, some students are questioning whether college is worth the increasing tuition and high rates of student debt. But the question of whether college is worthwhile is more than a matter of money; college has value that goes beyond the salary a college graduate might earn.

This statement captured the main point Chloe expected to make in her essay. However, as she conducted research, learned more about her topic, and developed her argument, she would find that she had to refine this statement.

Step 5   Back up what you say.

As we have seen, Chloe had begun her research for this assignment long before developing her Discovery Draft. Previously, she had written essays on related topics and had already identified some relevant sources. But she knew she had more to learn about her topic. In other words, Chloe wasn't just finding relevant sources to support her thesis or back up her claims; she was delving more deeply into her topic to understand it better so that she could make a more informed, compelling argument. That's the process of inquiry that writing should be, and she was fully engaged in that process.

Identify Your Main Claims or Assertions

Using her Guiding Thesis Statement as a starting point, Chloe could begin identifying some of the claims she expected to make in her essay:

- College has become an expectation for many students today.
- Federal education policies as well as social and political developments over the past century have led to an increase in the number of Americans who attend college.
- The pressure to attend college might prevent some students from pursuing other career opportunities that are right for them.

- Recent economic developments have made attending college much more challenging for many students.
- College generally leads to better jobs.
- College has value that goes beyond getting a better job.

Reviewing this list, Chloe realized that she could reorganize the list into two main claims and several supporting claims:

1. College has become an expectation for many students in the U.S.

   a) Federal education policies as well as social and political developments over the past century have led to an increase in the number of Americans who attend college.

   b) The pressure to attend college might prevent some students from pursuing other career opportunities that are right for them.

   c) Recent economic developments have made attending college much more challenging for many students.

2. College is worthwhile in several different ways.

   a) College generally leads to better jobs.

   b) College has value that goes beyond getting a better job.

Obviously, Chloe had already been exploring some of these claims for her previous assignments and her proposal, and as a result of Step #4 she identified questions and subtopics that she needed to learn more about. Her ongoing research led her to some new information, including a scholarly study that examined how the demand for access to college in the U.S. changed between 1919 and 1964. This material related directly to the first main claim listed above.

Through this process, Chloe continued to find supporting evidence for her claims, which deepened her understanding of her topic. In fact, what she was learning about the history of higher education in the U.S. was beginning to influence her own opinion about whether college is the best choice for everyone.

Review Your Discovery Draft

Chloe's Discovery Draft already included some of her key claims, and her ongoing research generated additional material to support those claims as well as new ideas about her main point. She now had a lot of relevant material for her historical analysis, a rough idea for organizing her essay, and a clear sense of the direction of her argument. She felt confident that she was ready to write a complete rough draft.

Write a Complete Draft

Here's Chloe's first full draft of her essay. As you read, you'll notice that Chloe incorporated into this draft much of the material she included in her Discovery Draft. In addition, her main idea is essentially the same as in the Discovery Draft. She includes an in-depth and complicated historical analysis to explain the rise in college attendance over the past 100 years and to provide some insight into why students today feel such pressure to attend college. But you might also notice that Chloe's main argument isn't always clear and that she doesn't fully address all the main claims she identified in Step #5. There are other problems in the draft as well. That's OK. This is a rough draft on a complex topic, and Chloe was still developing her argument. The goal at this stage was to write as complete a draft as possible; Chloe would develop and refine that draft in subsequent steps.

DRAFT

The Ever-Changing Norms About College in the United States

My great-grandfather never attended college and he led what I believe is a very successful life. He owned a sports shop in Syracuse, New York where many high school and even some college athletes bought their equipment. My great-grandfather only had a high school education. He never once took a business course, or had to even take a general education course, so why do I? Today, it is very common for students graduating high school to receive a higher education. "In the fall of 2015 some 20.2 million students are expected to attend American colleges and universities" ("Back to School Statistics"). So what changed? Why have so many people in the past five or six decades lived a nice life without any form of college education, but today those who don't are struggling to make ends meet. Today, students that are thinking about attending college or a university are asking many why questions. Why were they so influenced to attend college when they can go into many other careers, some their recent ancestors have taken? Why has our society decided that a higher education is needed for the majority of United States citizens? Many factors have caused a change in our nation's attitudes about the acceptability of going to college. These factors include social movements, laws, even the availability of jobs over time. Since the World Wars, and specifically World War I, the social norm among Americans has changed from a view that a college degree was not needed to succeed to a view that people needed one to survive in our fragile economic infrastructure.

One of the main reasons it is so common for people to attend college today is that it is a lot more accessible than it was before World War I. Before WWI there was no actual fluctuation in the number of individuals attending a college or university in the United States. After the war the rate of students attending college actually declines, but this was due to the Great Depression, when many people had to focus on making money instead of spending it on college tuition. However, after World War II the economy righted itself, and college attendance increased rapidly (Campbell and Siegel 487). This increase was due to two main reasons: the approach to investment in education and household income. After WWII many individuals believed that they would be able to make more money in the long run if they obtained a college degree. In 1975, a person who had a bachelor's degree earned about 1.5 times more in yearly pay than did someone with only a high school diploma (Brock 111). There are also many social and intellectual benefits of attending college that a student can use to create a successful career for themselves and/or their families, after they graduate from college. Having a higher education can lead to better health, living arrangements, life style choices, etc. (Brock 110). The second reason was the wealth of families of students wanting to pursue a degree. Years ago it was hard for someone in the working or lower-middle class to go to college because the family could not pay tuition in full (Campbell and Siegel 484). Today, many families can afford to send their children to college because of the financing opportunities colleges now have to offer.

Another important factor to help explain the increase in population size at colleges was the changing societal norms in the United States. Prior to 1965 only white men, usually from the upper or middle class, were seen and welcome on college campuses (Brock 111). African Americans and women were not seen as candidates for attending college due to their status in society and because of the hardship in receiving financial aid from universities. Then in 1965, the "Higher Education Act of 1965" was passed which helped the general population to receive federal aid to attend any college of their choosing. As well, federal aid for higher education increased from $655 million in 1955 to $3.5 billion in 1965 (Brock 111). This helped colleges budget more of their money towards scholarships, so more students from lower income households, many of whom were Black or Hispanic, had a higher chance of attending. Later on in 1972, the Pell Grant program was initiated to "focus on the circumstances and needs of recent high school graduates from low-income families" (Baum 24). Even though the amount of students attending a higher education institution was growing, the United States numbers were still low compared to other nations' averages. This program was intended to increase those numbers so it targeted people who could not attend college. Along with these new and growing programs, the government started to target more community colleges. These institutions were seen as "developing institutions"; if the government could focus on making this form of higher education better, then more students could be put into classrooms for slightly lower prices than that of a four-year private or public university. This overall increase in funding also made tuition prices affordable for many, especially those who had a lower income.

The government overall ended up changing the mind sets of many individuals; they made people believe that "young people should not have to be born to affluent or educated parents in order to be able to expect a college education" (Baum 23). With this new mind set, more and more students of many different backgrounds were able to attend the college of their choice. This gave people who did not think they were right for college an incentive to work hard, since they now had more to look forward to in the future. Since the norms of society started to change, the demographics in colleges started to change as well. Many universities were now more open to diversity because of the Civil Rights Act, and views about women in society were changing. Colleges all over the country started to welcome those of any race, culture, gender, etc. (Brock 111). This made attending "an institution of higher education for virtually anyone who possessed a high school diploma and the necessary financial resources" possible because of this national view of acceptance to others, no matter who they are (Campbell and Siegel 488). This long-awaited access was just what people were looking for to obtain a degree, which in turn bettered their lives.

Even though technology is a smaller factor that led to the increase of college students, and did not come around until later on, it has played a tangible role. Today, more colleges are able to reach out to high school graduates or people seeking to go back to school who are looking for information on that certain college. Many campuses have even changed their curriculum to better fit the newest advancements that have come out over the past forty years. One of those is online courses. The University of Phoenix in 2005 enrolled more than 117,000 students, many of whom need to have flexible schedules and cannot attend an actual campus (Brock 113). Numerous community colleges have reached out to students looking to stay close to home. A community college is a safe decision for those who have many specific needs and are looking for an affordable higher education. Over the years community colleges, through the help of the media, have targeted the "non-traditional" college student, the one who may have a job, want to save money, or is not quite ready to take the big step to attend a large private or public university (Brock 114). Whatever the reason, community colleges and online courses have expanded and become popular to many seeking a higher education due to what technology has given them.

All of these factors have positively encouraged more and more United States citizens to believe that a degree is what they must receive in order to do well throughout their lives, especially in today's society. So many people seem to grow up thinking after they graduate they must go to college. This is not a bad concept to believe. However, many students are still asking the question: Why must I go to college when there are other jobs out there for me? This question has been answered as the U.S. has grown over the past decades.

The norm in the 1960's was that women stayed at home, African Americans worked lower-end jobs, white men with a high school diploma got trade/labor jobs, and those with a college degree landed jobs that enabled them to enter the comfortable middle and upper classes. However, things have changed since then. Now many of the jobs that get you into the middle class require a college degree. Even in the 1990's, the *Chicago Tribune's* listing of the 100 best jobs included accountant, engineer, computer programmer, teacher, dentist, paramedic, and pilot (Kleiman). Today some of the top jobs are "dentist, nurse practitioner, software developer." All of these jobs have one thing in common: They all require a college degree, whether it is an associates, bachelors, masters, or even a doctorate. The lower ranking jobs, including social worker, preschool teacher, and architect, also require some form of schooling ("100 Best Jobs"). This is one of the reasons that so many people have gone to college: There are barely any jobs that allow a person to live comfortably today, or even in the past twenty years, that do not require a college degree. In an earlier economy people could "make it" without a degree, but many economic factors, such as job security and fluctuating job markets, have caused this to change.

As our nation has changed socially, economically, and even politically, one of the major views that have changed is our basic ideas about receiving a college degree or higher education. Before the World Wars the number of students attending college was low and only encompassed one primary group of people. Many believed that they did not need to attend college after high school, and some who wanted to were not allowed. As the years have gone by, many programs have been established, grants have been proposed, and systems have changed on campuses. Each of these factors has helped to change the bias about those who can attend a college or a university. Today, people cannot live the life they want without having a good-paying job, which they cannot have without a degree. This is why it is of dire importance that everyone be eligible and have the resources to attend college. We still have not accomplished as much as other nations have, but as a country we are doing the best we can to help fulfill the needs of students, so they can live a full and comfortable life.

Works Cited

"Back to School Statistics." *Fast Facts*, National Center for Educational Statistics / Institute of Educational Science, nces.ed.gov/fastfacts/display.asp?id=372. Accessed 30 Nov. 2015.

Baum, Sandy. "The Federal Pell Grant Program and Reauthorization of the Higher Education Act." *Journal of Student Financial Aid*, vol. 45, 2015, pp. 23-34.

Brock, Thomas. "Young Adults and Higher Education: Barriers and Breakthroughs to Success." *The Future of Children*, vol. 20, no. 1, Spring 2010, futureofchildren.org/futureofchildren/publications/docs/20_01_06.pdf.

Campbell, Robert, and Barry M. Siegel, "The Demand for Higher Education in the United States, 1919-1964." *The American Economic Review*, vol. 57, no. 3, June 1967, pp. 482-494. *JSTOR*, www.jstor.org/stable/1812115.

Kleiman, Carol. "Best Jobs for the 90's: From Cook to Cop." *Chicago Tribune*, 31 May 1992, articles.chicagotribune.com/1992-05-31/news/9202180452_1_new-jobs-carol-kleiman-career-counselors.

"The 100 Best Jobs." *US News & World Report*, money.usnews.com/careers/best-jobs/rankings/the-100-best-jobs. Accessed 30 Nov. 2015.

Step 6: Establish a form and structure for your project.

Chloe's assignment called for a conventional academic paper, but the guidelines for organizing the paper were vague. Like many college instructors, Chloe's instructor did not impose a specific structure but left it up to students to decide how to organize their individual projects. For Chloe, deciding how to organize her essay was not straightforward, since her argument included a complicated historical analysis and several subclaims. In reviewing her draft, she considered the following:

Genre: Chloe's assignment called for "an in-depth, informed argument that reflects your understanding of the issue." Those instructions didn't give Chloe much to go on, but she decided her best strategy was to organize her paper according to the two main claims she identified in Step #5, incorporating her analysis and evidence into her discussion of each claim. (See Chapter 5 for advice about organizing an analytical essay and Chapter 6 for advice about organizing arguments.)

Medium: Chloe would follow the conventions for writing an academic paper, which meant that she would present supporting evidence for each claim and cite her sources using MLA style (which her instructor required). However, there is no standard method for organizing an academic essay, so she had to rely on her sense of her rhetorical situation in making her decisions about the structure of her essay.

Rhetorical Situation: Chloe had two primary concerns: (1) informing her audience about why college has become such a powerful expectation in American society, and (2) persuading her audience that college is worthwhile though not necessarily the best choice for every student today. She decided to retain the structure of her rough draft, which was organized roughly around these two main purposes.

Chloe determined that her draft was generally well organized, with the first half devoted to her historical analysis of American attitudes about college and the second half focused on her main argument about whether college is appropriate for everyone. However, each of these two main sections of her essay was not as clearly focused and well organized as they could be, and the transition between them was weak. Part of her challenge was to clarify her argument and integrate her analysis (the first half of her essay) more effectively into that argument (the second half of her essay). So her task at this point was to improve the organization of each section so that her analysis supported her argument and her main claims were clear to her audience.

Identify the Main Parts of Your Project

As we have seen, Chloe began her draft with a clear sense of her main claims. She was making two central claims and several supporting claims. So the basic organization of her draft around her two central claims was sound. Now she could focus on clarifying and organizing her supporting claims in each of those two main sections.

Develop an Outline

Chloe learned to use outlines in high school, and she continued to use a basic outline format for most of her college assignments. However, for this assignment she did not create an outline before completing her rough draft. She found that working on an outline at this stage of her project distracted her from exploring her ideas and developing her analysis. Instead, she made notes to herself about the main ideas she would incorporate into her essay. She also had her list of claims from Step #5, which functioned as a kind of outline for her essay. This approach made sense, because Chloe was still trying to understand some of the reasons for the increase in college attendance and the developments that helped make college such a highly valued experience in American society. But now she had to improve the organization of her draft so that her claims were more clearly conveyed to her audience.

The basic organization of her draft looked like this:

I. Introduction.

   A. Great-grandfather's experience

   B. Main question: How did attending college become a norm in American society?

II. College Attendance in the U.S. Increased after WWI.

   A. A college degree brought financial, social, and intellectual benefits.

   B. College became more affordable for many families.

   C. Changing societal norms meant that more women and minorities were able to attend college after 1965.

   D. Government policies also helped increase college attendance.

      1. Higher Education Act of 1965

      2. Pell Grants

      3. Support for community colleges

III. Attitudes Toward College in the U.S. Changed after WWII.

   A. Government policies made colleges more accessible to more Americans.

   B. College welcomed a more diverse student population.

IV. Technology Played a Role in Increased College Attendance.

   A. Online courses gave many people access to college.

   B. Community colleges used media to increase student access.

V. Is College Right for Every Student?

   A. Societal norms encourage more people to attend college.

   B. Many of the most sought-after jobs require a college degree.

   C. It is difficult to make it in society today without a college degree.

If you compare this outline of Chloe's rough draft with her list of claims from Step #5, you can easily see that her draft was out of balance. Most of her essay is devoted to her analysis of how attending college has become a norm in the U.S., and she did not focus sufficient attention on making her argument about whether college is worthwhile for everyone; only her second-to-last paragraph directly takes up her argument (which is reflected in Part V of her outline).

This outline also reveals that some sections of Chloe's essay might not be necessary. For example, Part IV is devoted to a discussion of technology, which her instructor suggested might not strengthen her analysis (see below under Step #7). So in addition to developing Part V, she might need to condense or even eliminate some of Part IV.

Write or Revise Your Draft

Reviewing her draft, Chloe identified some weaknesses in its structure, but before revising it, she decided to wait and see what her peer reviewers and her instructor would have to say about the essay's structure.

Step 7 Get feedback.

Ask Your Readers to Respond to Your Draft

Chloe received both written and verbal feedback on her draft from classmates during in-class peer review. Her instructor provided students with specific questions to address as they reviewed each other's drafts, but Chloe was also eager to see whether her argument was convincing to her peers. Later, she met with her instructor to discuss possible revisions to her draft.

Identify Common Themes in Your Readers' Responses

Chloe's classmates identified two main strengths of her draft: (1) they generally found her topic interesting and relevant, and (2) they found her anecdote about her great-grandfather engaging and effective. Several classmates offered their own perspectives on Chloe's main question of whether college is worthwhile. One classmate wrote that although many careers require a college degree, he could "off the top of my head think of many stories of people I know who didn't need a degree" to be successful. So Chloe knew that the question of whether college is worthwhile resonated with her audience.

But her classmates also identified two main concerns: (1) her analysis was sometimes hard to follow, and (2) she didn't adequately represent alternative perspectives on the value of college. Chloe's instructor, Joe, agreed with those concerns and added a third one: a lack of complexity in her discussion of some of her key points. He noted that her draft "sometimes explores the topic in depth and sometimes oversimplifies the issues." Specifically, he felt that her discussion of women and minority students in her third paragraph was oversimplified, in part because she neglected to mention the existence of all-women's colleges and Historically Black Colleges (HBCs). Similarly, he felt that her discussion of jobs in her second-to-last paragraph did not sufficiently account for the significant changes that have occurred in the American economy in the past several years.

Despite these concerns, Joe felt that Chloe's draft was generally strong:

- He noted that her topic was especially relevant to her audience.
- He described her historical analysis as "excellent."
- He praised her use of source material.

To address these concerns, Joe suggested that Chloe find alternative perspectives on the value of college; specifically, he noted that Charles Murray, about whom she had written for a previous assignment, represented an alternative viewpoint that she could incorporate into her argument. He also wondered why she did not incorporate into her essay the ideas of John Henry Newman, whom she also wrote about for her previous assignment. Finally, he encouraged Chloe to bring out her own voice more clearly rather than rely so heavily on source material; doing so would likely make her argument more persuasive to her audience.

Here are sections of Chloe's draft with comments by her instructor, Joe, and three of her classmates (Ashley, Bart, and Bethany):

My great-grandfather never attended college and he led what I believe is a very successful life. He owned a sports shop in Syracuse, New York where many high school and even some college athletes bought their equipment. My great-grandfather only had a high school education. He never once took a business course, or had to even take a general education course, so why do I? Today, it is very common for students graduating high school to receive a higher education. "In the fall of 2015 some 20.2 million students are expected to attend American colleges and universities" ("Back to School Statistics"). So what changed? Why have so many people in the past five or six decades lived a nice life without any form of college education, but today those who don't are struggling to make ends meet. Today, students that are thinking about attending college or a university are asking many why questions. Why were they so influenced to attend college when they can go into many other careers, some their recent ancestors have taken? Why has our society decided that a higher education is needed for the majority of United States citizens? Many factors have caused a change in our nation's attitudes about the acceptability of going to college. These factors include social movements, laws, even the availability of jobs over time. Since the World Wars, and specifically World War I, the social norm among

Bart: I like the way you start your essay with your great-grandfather's successful experiences and then move to the question of why you should attend college.

Bethany: I especially like how you begin with the anecdote about your great-grandfather. It makes the topic seem more personal and more real.

Joe: Is this your thesis?

Americans has changed from a view that a college degree was not needed to succeed to a view that people needed one to survive in our fragile economic infrastructure.

One of the main reasons it is so common for people to attend college today is that it is a lot more accessible than it was before World War I. Before WWI there was no actual fluctuation in the number of individuals attending a college or university in the United States. After the war the rate of students attending college actually declines, but this was due to the Great Depression, when many people had to focus on making money instead of spending it on college tuition. However, after World War II the economy righted itself, and college attendance increased rapidly (Campbell and Siegel 487). This increase was due to two main reasons: the approach to investment in education and household income. After WWII many individuals believed that they would be able to make more money in the long run if they obtained a college degree. In 1975, a person who had a bachelor's degree earned about 1.5 times more in yearly pay than did someone with only a high school diploma (Brock 111). There are also many social and intellectual benefits of attending college that a student can use to create a successful career for themselves and/or their families, after they graduate from college. Having a higher education can lead to better health, living arrangements, life style choices, etc. (Brock 110). The second reason was the wealth of families of students wanting to pursue a degree. Years ago it was hard for someone in the working or lower-middle class to go to college because the family could not pay tuition in full (Campbell and Siegel 484). Today, many families can afford to send their children to college because of the financing opportunities colleges now have to offer.

Another important factor to help explain the increase in population size at colleges was the changing societal norms in the United States. Prior to 1965 only white men, usually from the upper or middle class, were seen and welcome on college campuses (Brock 111). African Americans and women were not seen as candidates for attending college due to their status in society and because of the hardship in receiving financial aid from universities. Then in 1965, the "Higher Education Act of 1965" was passed which helped the general population to receive federal aid to attend any college of their choosing. As well, federal aid for higher education increased from

Joe: Chloe, I'm having a little trouble following your discussion here. Is this paragraph really about access to higher education? You seem to have several key points to make here, but your discussion could be more coherent.

Bart: I think your historical approach helps us understand the issue. I like the fact that you look at how norms are changing, and I think it's good that you look back into the early 1900's.

4

Joe: But my mom graduated from college in 1960.

Joe: Yes, that's true. But what about women's colleges and Historically Black Colleges? Women and African Americans could attend those, right? Your statements here oversimplify the situation at the time.

$655 million in 1955 to $3.5 billion in 1965 (Brock 111). This helped colleges budget more of their money towards scholarships, so more students from lower income households, many of whom were Black or Hispanic, had a higher chance of attending. Later on in 1972, the Pell Grant program was initiated to "focus on the circumstances and needs of recent high school graduates from low-income families" (Baum 24). . . .

The government overall ended up changing the mind sets of many individuals; they made people believe that "young people should not have to be born to affluent or educated parents in order to be able to expect a college education" (Baum 23). With this new mind set, more and more students of many different backgrounds were able to attend the college of their choice. This gave people who did not think they were right for college an incentive to work hard, since the now had more to look forward to in the future. . . .

Even though technology is a smaller factor that led to the increase of college students, and did not come around until later on, it has played a tangible role. Today, more colleges are able to reach out to high school graduates or people seeking to go back to school who are looking for information on that certain college. Many campuses have even changed their curriculum to better fit the newest advancements that have come out over the past forty years. One of those is online courses. The University of Phoenix in 2005 enrolled more than 117,000 students, many of whom need to have flexible schedules and cannot attend an actual campus (Brock 113). Numerous community colleges have reached out to students looking to stay close to home. A community college is a safe decision for those who have many specific needs and are looking for an affordable higher education. Over the years community colleges, through the help of the media, have targeted the "non-traditional" college student, the one who may have a job, want to save money, or is not quite ready to take the big step to attend a large private or public university (Brock 114). Whatever the reason, community colleges and online courses have expanded and become popular to many seeking a higher education due to what technology has given them.

All of these factors have positively encouraged more and more United States citizens to believe that a degree is what they must receive in order to do well throughout their lives, especially

Joe: Good! These two important government programs affected college attendance. But were there others that were as important? I know the G.I. Bill helped many Americans go to college after WWII.

Joe: Yes. Good point. And you use the quotation very effectively to make your point.

Ashley: I found this point a little hard to follow. Specifically, why exactly would lowering the cost of college make people work harder? And what are they looking forward to in the future? I think I get what's you're trying to say, but your point will be stronger if you are a bit clearer here.

Joe: It's true that technology might increase access to college, but this does not add much to your analysis, since by the time online courses were developed, the main trends you discuss earlier in your essay had already resulted in higher college attendance. Do you need this material?

Joe: Yes, community colleges have targeted non-traditional students, but they have not expanded only because of technology, as you suggest in this paragraph. You're oversimplifying matters.

in today's society. So many people seem to grow up thinking after they graduate they must go to college. This is not a bad concept to believe. However, many students are still asking the question: Why must I go to college when there are other jobs out there for me? This question has been answered as the U.S. has grown over the past decades.

Joe: How? you need to explain.

Consider Conflicting Advice in Your Readers' Responses

The students who reviewed Chloe's draft generally agreed on the main strengths and weaknesses in the draft, and their feedback was consistent with some of Joe's comments. There were no significant disagreements among her reviewers, and their comments helped Chloe see that her main argument was not getting through to her readers. She also could see that her historical analysis was strong but needed to be clarified and more fully developed in some sections; moreover, she needed to integrate that analysis more effectively into her main argument.

4

Step 8 Revise.

Using her classmates' and instructor's comments as a guide, Chloe had a clear plan for revision, and she worked through several drafts, each time addressing more specific issues to strengthen her essay. In addition, she was still exploring her topic, refining her analysis, and strengthening her argument.

Focus First on Content

Chloe focused her revisions on two main areas: developing her main argument and integrating her analysis more effectively into that argument. These two main areas included the following related concerns:

- **Clarify the main argument.** During their conference about her rough draft, Chloe's instructor described her thesis as "squishy," and her classmates told her that they weren't always clear on the main point of her essay.
- **Include alternative viewpoints.** Her instructor and several classmates suggested that Chloe could add depth and complexity to her argument by incorporating the ideas of John Henry Newman as well as alternative viewpoints about the value of college, especially the arguments of Charles Murray.
- **Clarify the historical analysis.** Chloe realized from her classmates' comments that she needed to explain several key points in her analysis more clearly.

- **Avoid oversimplifying.** Chloe's instructor pointed out several places in her drafts where she seemed to oversimplify important developments, such as the increase in the numbers of women and minorities who attend college.

Here are some of the revisions Chloe made to address these concerns:

- She revised her opening paragraph to establish her focus more clearly and introduce her main point:

Draft: My great-grandfather never attended college and he led what I believe is a very successful life. He owned a sports shop in Syracuse, New York where many high school and even some college athletes bought their equipment. My great-grandfather only had a high school education. He never once took a business course, or had to even take a general education course, so why do I? Today, it is very common for students graduating high school to receive a higher education. "In the fall of 2015 some 20.2 million students are expected to attend American colleges and universities" ("Back to School Statistics"). So what changed? Why have so many people in the past five or six decades lived a nice life without any form of college education, but today those who don't are struggling to make ends meet. Today, students that are thinking about attending college or a university are asking many why questions. Why were they so influenced to attend college when they can go into many other careers, some their recent ancestors have taken? Why has our society decided that a higher education is needed for the majority of United States citizens? Many factors have caused a change in our nation's attitudes about the acceptability of going to college. These factors include social movements, laws, even the availability of jobs over time. Since the World Wars, and specifically World War I, the social norm among Americans has changed from a view that a college degree was not needed to succeed to a view that people needed one to survive in our fragile economic infrastructure.

> The latter half of this paragraph poses an important question about why college has become such a powerful expectation for American students, but it does not convey a sense of Chloe's main argument about the value of college today.

Revised version: My great-grandfather never attended college, and he led what I believe is a very successful life. He owned a sports shop in Syracuse, New York, where many high school and even some college athletes bought their equipment. He never once took a business course to learn how to run a business or even a general education course, so why do I? Today, it is common for students graduating high school to pursue a

> Chloe kept her reference to her great-grandfather, which her readers found engaging and effective.

higher education. 20.2 million students were expected to attend American colleges and universities in the 2015-2016 academic year ("Back to School Statistics"). In the 1940's only 8% of men and 5% of women between the ages of 20 and 24 attended college. By 1991 almost 31% of men and 29% of women attended college (Snyder 16-17). So what changed? Why did so many people in my great-grandfather's generation live a nice life without any form of college education, yet today those without college degrees can struggle to make ends meet?

Students today face very different challenges from those my great-grandfather faced. Even with a college degree, many people entering the job market cannot find the jobs in their majors. My stepfather is a good example. Even with a college degree, he struggled to find work in his field of study. And the average student now leaves college with more than $35,000 in loan debt (Sparshott). Not surprisingly, many students now question whether college is worth the time, effort, and cost. They wonder whether they really need a degree to be successful, despite the pressure they feel to go to college. Although many people see numerous benefits to college, many others argue that a college degree is no longer the best path to being successful. The decision about whether to attend college is not a simple one, but I still believe college offers great benefits in addition to a possible career path. And everyone should at least have the opportunity to go to college if they choose to.

- She revised passages in which her claims were oversimplified:

Draft: Another important factor to help explain the increase in population size at colleges was the changing societal norms in the United States. Prior to 1965 only white men, usually from the upper or middle class, were seen and welcome on college campuses (Brock 111). African Americans and women were not seen as candidates for attending college due to their status in society and because of the hardship in receiving financial aid from universities.

Revised version: Prior to the 1940's usually white men from the upper or middle class populated college campuses (Brock 111). Fewer African Americans and women attended college partly due to social norms and also because of the difficulty of obtaining financial aid. Although there were all-black and all-women colleges, those institutions often did not have the resources that the larger universities had.

Chloe added facts to help support her claim about how common attending college has become.

Chloe divided her original introductory paragraph into two, making it easier for readers to follow her discussion and also enabling her to give emphasis to her questions about how things have changed by ending the paragraph with them (highlighted in blue).

Chloe expanded her discussion of the situation facing students today. She also added new material about her stepfather to illustrate that situation.

The paragraph now ends with a clear statement of Chloe's main argument (highlighted in orange).

Chloe's instructor questioned her claim about the lack of access to college among African Americans and women, noting that there were women's colleges and Historically Black Colleges that they could attend.

Chloe revised this sentence to make her point clearer.

This new sentence (highlighted in orange) adds complexity to Chloe's point by acknowledging women's and Historically Black Colleges but noting an important limitation facing those institutions.

- She incorporated new material to address alternative perspectives on the value of college and to add depth to her argument:

Draft: The norm in the 1960's was that women stayed at home, African Americans worked lower-end jobs, white men with a high school diploma got trade/labor jobs, and those with a college degree landed jobs that enabled them to enter the comfortable middle and upper classes. However, things have changed since then. Now many of the jobs that get you into the middle class require a college degree. Even in the 1990's, the *Chicago Tribune's* listing of the 100 best jobs included "accountant, engineer, computer programmer, teacher, dentist, paramedic, pilot" (Kleiman). Today some of the top jobs are "dentist, nurse practitioner, software developer." All of these jobs have one thing in common: They all require a college degree, whether it is an associates, bachelors, masters, or even a doctorate. The lower ranking jobs, including social worker, preschool teacher, and architect, also require some form of schooling ("100 Best Jobs"). This is one of the reasons that so many people have gone to college: There are barely any jobs that allow a person to live comfortably today, or even in the past twenty years, that do not require a college degree. In an earlier economy people could "make it" without a degree, but many economic factors, such as job security and fluctuating job markets, have caused this to change.

In this passage Chloe uses source material to support the claim that college is necessary today for having a successful career. She offers no additional supporting arguments, nor does she acknowledge counter-arguments.

Revised version: As time went on, more and more people in American society realized the economic benefits of a degree. In 1975, a person who had a bachelor's degree earned about 1.5 times more in yearly pay than did someone with only a high school diploma (Brock 111). In 2013 median annual earnings for young adults (ages 25-34) with a bachelor's degree were $48,500 as compared to $30,000 for those with a high school diploma ("Income"). There are also many social and intellectual benefits of attending college. Having a higher education can lead to better health, living arrangements, life style choices, etc. (Brock 110). Before World War I few people would have believed that statement, because people could do okay without a degree. Today, so many people grow up thinking that they must go to college to have a successful life. But does a college degree guarantee success? Are too many students going to college because of societal expectations when college might not be the right path for them? . . .

Charles Murray, author of *Are Too Many People Going to College?*, believes that college is not worth it for everyone.

Chloe retains some material from her rough draft (orange) and adds new material (blue) to show how a college degree can affect income.

Chloe retains her point about the connection between college and a successful life (orange), but she adds important questions (blue) that complicate her point.

He states that not everyone is prepared for the strenuous intellectual challenge of a liberal education (Murray 237). One study Murray cites shows that only 10% of high school students who take the SAT score in the percentile that would lead them to get at least a 2.7 GPA in college (Murray 238). If students are not going to do well, then what? Many drop out and attempt to find a full-time job; others return home to figure out a new plan, but overall this is affecting graduation rates. Murray points out that only those who are interested in getting a liberal education should attend school (Murray 240). Many who do not want to go to college can do well in other fields, such as trade jobs.

> This new paragraph introduces an alternative perspective on whether college is worthwhile and adds complexity to Chloe's discussion. Acknowledging important counter-arguments not only reflects a better understanding of the issue but also strengthens her own position.

Chloe made many other revisions to

- elaborate on, develop and refine her analysis,
- clarify important points,
- support her claims, and
- strengthen her main argument about the value of college.

You can see these revisions in her finished version on page 117.

Focus Next on Form

Reviewing her instructor's and classmates' comments as well as her outline helped Chloe recognize the need for the following revisions:

- Reorganize the supporting claims in her analysis about why Americans have come to place such a high value on attending college.
- Eliminate unnecessary material.
- Add or strengthen transitions, especially from her introduction into her analysis.

These revisions, which addressed problems with how Chloe's rough draft was organized, also helped integrate her analysis into her main argument, which was one of the two main concerns she needed to address (see Step #8). In other words, strengthening the structure of her essay also strengthened her main argument.

Here are some of her revisions to strengthen the form and structure of her essay:

Draft: One of the main reasons it is so common for people to attend college today is that it is a lot more accessible than it was before World War I. Before WWI there was no actual fluctuation in the number of individuals attending a college or university in the United States. After the war the rate of students attending college actually declines, but this was due to the Great Depression, when many people had to focus on making money instead

> The second paragraph of Chloe's rough draft jumped directly into her analysis of how college attendance increased in the U.S. after the World Wars without explaining why that analysis is important.

of spending it on college tuition. However, after World War II the economy righted itself, and college attendance increased rapidly (Campbell and Siegel 487). This increase was due to two main reasons: the approach to investment in education and household income. After WWII many individuals believed that they would be able to make more money in the long run if they obtained a college degree. In 1975, a person who had a bachelor's degree earned about 1.5 times more in yearly pay than did someone with only a high school diploma (Brock 111). There are also many social and intellectual benefits of attending college that a student can use to create a successful career for themselves and/or their families, after they graduate from college. Having a higher education can lead to better health, living arrangements, life style choices, etc. (Brock 110). The second reason was the wealth of families of students wanting to pursue a degree. Years ago it was hard for someone in the working or lower-middle class to go to college because the family could not pay tuition in full (Campbell and Siegel 484). Today, many families can afford to send their children to college because of the financing opportunities colleges now have to offer.

Chloe moved most of the material in this second paragraph to paragraph 6 in her revised essay, where it fit more logically. This move was part of her effort to reorganize her analysis so that it was clearer to her readers.

Revised version: To understand the situation facing students today, it helps to know how we got here. As my great-grandfather knew, it wasn't always the case that young people were expected to go to college. During the 20th Century a number of important developments helped make attending college a societal norm and influenced how Americans think about the importance of a college degree. One of those developments was increased government financial aid. Prior to the 1960's it was hard for someone in the working or lower-middle class to afford college tuition (Campbell and Siegel 484). Today, many families can afford to send their children to college because of numerous government programs. For example, the Higher Education Act of 1965 helped the general population receive federal aid to attend any college of their choosing. Federal aid for higher education increased from $655 million in 1955 to $3.5 billion in 1965 (Brock 111), which enabled colleges to budget more money for scholarships. As a result, more students from lower income households had a better chance of attending college. One of the most important government programs was the Servicemen's Readjustment Act of 1944, commonly known as the GI Bill, which helped soldiers returning from World War II pay for college. By the end of 1947 almost half

These two new sentences (blue highlight) provide a transition from the introductory paragraphs to the historical analysis and explain the reason for that analysis.

Chloe retained these sentences (orange) from her rough draft but she replaced the vague phrase "years ago" with the more specific phrase "prior to the 1960's."

This material (green) was moved from paragraph 2 of her rough draft to this paragraph in her revised draft, where it helped her tell the story of the impact of government programs on college attendance in the U.S.

Chloe added information about the GI Bill (blue) to provide more support for her claim about the government role in increasing college attendance.

of the students attending colleges in the U.S. were benefitting from this bill ("History and Timeline"). **Later programs such as the Pell Grant program, which was initiated in 1972, would "focus on the circumstances and needs of recent high school graduates from low-income families" (Baum 24).** All these programs affected not only how many Americans attended college but also which Americans could attend.

The final sentence (orange) sums up the main point of the paragraph and sets up the transition to the next paragraph.

These are careful revisions that not only strengthen Chloe's analysis but also make it easier for her readers to understand.

Consider Your Rhetorical Situation

All the revisions described so far were intended to clarify key points or develop Chloe's main ideas in response to feedback from classmates and her instructor. She interpreted that feedback not only as suggestions for improving her essay but also as clues to how her essay was being received by readers and how well she was reaching her intended audience.

For example, Chloe knew that her readers reacted positively to her references to her great-grandfather in her opening paragraph, so she not only retained those references but she also added references to him later in her essay. In addition, because her use of her family's experience seemed effective in conveying her ideas to her readers, she added a brief reference to her stepfather's experience. These revisions were undertaken specifically with her audience in mind.

Chloe also considered her larger rhetorical purpose. As noted earlier, she understood her essay as part of a much larger, ongoing conversation about education in the U.S., and her historical analysis reinforced the idea that the issues she was writing about have long interested Americans. But she also knew that these issues had special relevance to her classmates. She wanted her essay to resonate with readers who shared her concerns about access to college and who, like her, might have wondered about their own decision to attend college.

With this in mind, in her revised essay Chloe decided to add more up-to-date facts and figures to convey a better sense of the situation facing students today. She also incorporated the perspectives of experts who had more recently been writing about the question of the value of college, something she had not included in her rough draft. These revisions, she felt, gave her essay currency as well as greater relevance to other college students.

Revisit Your Introduction and Conclusion

We have already seen the significant revisions Chloe made to her introduction (page 108), which were part of her effort to clarify the focus of her essay and establish her main argument. In addition to the new material she added to that introduction, she made careful changes to strengthen successful elements that her readers had identified in their comments. For example, in the opening paragraph of her rough draft she posed several questions, which didn't clearly establish her focus; her revised version, by contrast, includes a more carefully worded question that points more clearly to the main issue she will address in her essay, which is whether college is worthwhile today:

> **Draft:** So what changed? Why have so many people in the past five or six decades lived a nice life without any form of college education, but today those who don't are struggling to make ends meet? Today, students that are thinking about attending college or a university are asking many why questions. Why were they so influenced to attend college when they can go into many other careers, some their recent ancestors have taken? Why has our society decided that a higher education is needed for the majority of United States citizens?

This passage from the rough draft actually poses three related but separate questions. Chloe will address all these questions in her essay, but the way they are introduced here is confusing.

> **Revised version:** . . . So what changed? Why did so many people in my great-grandfather's generation live a nice life without any form of college education, yet today those without college degrees can struggle to make ends meet?

This question, placed at the end of the first paragraph, leads effectively into the second paragraph.

> Students today face very different challenges from those my great-grandfather faced. Even with a college degree, many people entering the job market cannot find jobs in their majors. My stepfather is a good example. Even with a college degree, he struggled to find work in his field of study. And the average student now leaves college with more than $35,000 in loan debt (Sparshott). Not surprisingly, many students now question whether college is worth the time, effort, and cost. They wonder whether they really need a degree to be successful, despite the pressure they feel to go to college. Although many people see numerous benefits to college, many others argue that a college degree is no longer the best path to being successful. The decision about whether to attend college is not a simple one, but I still believe college offers great benefits in addition to a possible career path. And everyone should at least have the opportunity to go to college if they choose to.

This new material about Chloe's stepfather (green) helps establish the contrast between the situation facing students prior to WWI and the one facing students today.

Chloe has turned the questions from her previous draft into statements (orange) that clearly identify the problem she will address in her essay.

Chloe has added two sentences (blue) that clearly state her main argument (her thesis), which was missing from her rough draft.

Chloe also substantially revised her conclusion. Her original version unnecessarily restated several main points and did not convey a clear sense of what she was advocating. Her revised version, however, is more succinct and ends with a more forceful statement about the need to make college available to Americans:

> **Draft:** As our nation has changed socially, economically, and even politically, one of the major views that have changed is our basic ideas about receiving a college degree or higher education.

Before the World Wars the number of students attending college was low and only encompassed one primary group of people. Many believed that they did not need to attend college after high school, and some who wanted to were not allowed. As the years have gone by, many programs have been established, grants have been proposed, and systems have changed on campuses. Each of these factors has helped to change the bias about those who can attend a college or a university. Today, people cannot live the life they want without having a good-paying job, which they cannot have without a degree. This is why it is of dire importance that everyone be eligible and have the resources to attend college. We still have not accomplished as much as other nations have, but as a country we are doing the best we can to help fulfill the needs of students, so they can live a full and comfortable life.

These three sentences (orange) unnecessarily restate main points from the essay.

The last two sentences (blue) are a weak ending that seem to contradict one another and don't clearly state Chloe's position.

Revised version: As our nation has changed throughout the years, attitudes about college have changed as well. Today, people cannot live a comfortable lifestyle without having a well paying job, which can be difficult to receive until they get a degree. This is why it is of such great importance that everyone be eligible and have the resources to attend college. Charles Murray stated that "we should not restrict the availability of a liberal education to a rarefied intellectual elite" (Murray 234). We still need universities that are available to the majority of students who want to attend and who are willing to put in the work to succeed. Our country and our universities have done a lot for their students, but now they need to do more.

Chloe retains her point that college can lead to a good job (orange), but she adds three new sentences (blue) that reinforce her main argument and leave her readers with a strong statement of her position.

4

Chloe did not make all these revisions at once. Rather, she worked through multiple drafts, beginning with the larger issues and eventually focusing on more minor issues until she was satisfied that her essay was adequately developed and her argument well supported.

Step 9 Strengthen your voice.

Chloe felt that the revisions she made to strengthen her argument also strengthened her voice. Specifically, her use of her own family's experience and her effort to keep her classmates in mind as she revised helped make her voice more personal without losing a sense of authority.

Consider Your Rhetorical Context

Chloe's main goal was to write an essay that conveyed her analysis and argument clearly to her readers, who, she hoped, shared her interest in her topic. In fact, Chloe's own intense curiosity about the questions she addressed in her essay energized her research as well as her writing, and her voice in her essay reflects that. She developed a serious, informed, yet engaging voice that, she hoped, contributed to the effectiveness of her argument. She wanted her readers to sense her genuine interest in the topic and to see her as a credible writer with something worthwhile to say about a topic that was timely and of great interest to many Americans, including her classmates. In this sense, her voice emerged from her constant attention to the rhetorical context.

Consider Whether You Should Use the First Person

Chloe used the first person in the earliest draft of her essay and retained it in the final version. She did so partly because her instructor did not prohibit its use. The assignment guidelines stated that students should write in an appropriate academic style but that doing so "does not mean that you cannot use the first person (you can) or create a voice that engages your readers (you should)." Chloe took those instructions to heart and believed that using the first person was a good rhetorical strategy for her essay, given the nature of the assignment and her own sense of her purpose.

Strengthen Your Voice

We've already seen some of the most important revisions that Chloe made to strengthen her voice:

- adding material about her own family's experiences
- using the first person strategically
- clarifying confusing passages in language that was more straightforward
- strengthening her conclusion by emphasizing her own heartfelt and informed perspective

With these revisions, her voice in the final version of her essay was much stronger than in her rough draft.

Step 10 Make it correct.

Chloe's early drafts had numerous minor errors of punctuation, spelling, and usage, and in those drafts she also failed to cite some sources properly. Chloe addressed these problems in her final set of revisions, editing carefully to correct errors and make her prose clearer and more concise.

Here's Chloe's finished essay:

Chloe Charles

Prof. Joseph Creamer

Seminar in Writing and Critical Inquiry

1 March 2016

Why Is College So Important in the United States?

My great-grandfather never attended college and he led what I believe is a very successful life. He owned a sports shop in Syracuse, New York, where many high school and even some college athletes bought their equipment. He never once took a business course to learn how to run a business or even a general education course, so why do I? Today, it is common for students graduating high school to pursue a higher education. 20.2 million students were expected to attend American colleges and universities in the 2015-2016 academic year ("Back to School"). In the 1940's only 8% of men and 5% of women between the ages of 20 and 24 attended college. By 1991 almost 31% of men and 29% of women attended college (Snyder 16-17). So what changed? Why did so many people in my great-grandfather's generation live a nice life without any form of college education, yet today those without college degrees can struggle to make ends meet?

Students today face very different challenges from those my great-grandfather faced. Even with a college degree, many people entering the job market cannot find the jobs in their majors. My stepfather is a good example. Even with a college degree, he struggled to find work in his field of study. And the average student now leaves college with more than $35,000 in loan debt (Sparshott). Not surprisingly, many students now question whether college is worth the time, effort, and cost. They wonder whether they really need a degree to be successful, despite the pressure they feel to go to college. Although many people see numerous benefits to college, many others argue that a college degree is no longer the best path to being successful. The decision about whether to attend college is not a simple one, but I still believe college offers great benefits in addition to a possible career path. And everyone should at least have the opportunity to go to college if they choose to.

To understand the situation facing students today, it helps to know how we got here. As my great-grandfather knew, it wasn't always the case that young people were expected to go to college. During the 20th Century, a number of important developments helped make attending college a societal norm and influenced how Americans think about the importance of a college degree. One of those developments was increased government financial aid. Prior to the 1960's, it was hard for someone in the working or lower-middle class to afford college tuition (Campbell and Siegel 484). Today, many families can afford to send their children to college because of numerous government programs. For example, the Higher Education Act of 1965 helped the general population receive federal aid to attend any college of their choosing. Federal aid for higher education increased from $655 million in 1955 to $3.5 billion in 1965 (Brock 111), which enabled colleges to budget more money for scholarships. As a result, more students from lower income households had a better chance of attending college. One of the most important government programs was the Servicemen's Readjustment Act of 1944, commonly known as the GI Bill, which helped soldiers returning from World War II pay for college. By the end of 1947, almost half of the students attending colleges in the U.S. were benefitting from this bill ("History and Timeline"). Later programs such as the Pell Grant program, which was initiated in 1972, would "focus on the circumstances and needs of recent high school graduates from low-income families" (Baum 24). All these programs affected not only how many Americans attended college but also which Americans could attend.

These government programs also influenced American attitudes about higher education and encouraged the belief that "young people should not have to be born to affluent or educated parents in order to be able to expect a college education" (Baum 23). As a result, students of many different backgrounds were able to attend the college of their choice. Prior to the 1940's, usually white men from the upper or middle class populated college campuses (Brock 111). Fewer African Americans and women attended college partly due to social norms and also because of the difficulty of obtaining financial aid. Although there were all-black and all-women colleges, those institutions often did not have the resources that the larger universities had. But that began to change as a result of the Civil Rights and Women's Movements in the 1960's and 1970's. Many universities were now more open to diversity due to these movements, and colleges began to welcome students of any race, culture, gender, etc. (Brock 111). This growing national acceptance of diverse groups made attending "an institution of higher education [possible] for virtually anyone who possessed a high school diploma and the necessary financial resources" (Campbell and Siegel 488).

In addition to these earlier programs, the government began supporting community colleges as far back as the 1990's. A community college can be a safe decision for students with specific needs who are looking for an affordable education. Over the years, community colleges, through the use of media, have targeted the "non-traditional" college student: the one who may hold a job, cannot afford the tuition at a university, or is not quite ready to attend a large private or public university (Brock 114). These benefits of a community college are what interested government policymakers most. If community college could improve and grow, then more students could attend college for a lower price than that of a four-year private or public university. This option was appealing to many students, especially those who had financial troubles but still wanted to get a degree, and helped increase overall college attendance.

These various factors all contributed to the idea that college is a path to a better life. After the U.S. pulled out of the Great Depression and World War II ended, college attendance increased rapidly (Campbell and Siegal 487). As time went on, more and more people in American society realized the economic benefits of a degree. In 1975, a person who had a bachelor's degree earned about 1.5 times more in yearly pay than did someone with only a high school diploma (Brock 111). In 2013, median annual earnings for young adults (ages 25-34) with a bachelor's degree were $48,500 as compared to $30,000 for those with a high school diploma ("Income"). There are also many social and intellectual benefits of attending college. Having a higher education can lead to better health, living arrangements, life style choices, etc. (Brock 110). Before World War I, few people would have believed that statement, because people could do okay without a degree. Today, so many people grow up thinking that they must go to college to have a successful life.

But does a college degree guarantee success? Are too many students going to college because of societal expectations when college might not be the right path for them? My stepfather earned a college degree in English and then landed a job as a journalist. He did everything society expected him to do, but it wasn't enough. In 2007, during the Great Recession, he lost his job like many others in the country, and after months of trying, he couldn't find work in his field. Because of that, he returned to college to try to find a new career. He is not alone. According to the Economic Policy Institute, "Unemployment of young graduates is extremely high today," 7.2% as compared to 5.5% in 2007; in addition, "wages of young high school and college graduates have failed to reach their pre-recession levels, and have in fact stagnated or declined for almost every group since 2000" (Davis et al.). So now many college graduates are asking, Was my degree even worth it in the first place?

Charles Murray, author of *Are Too Many People Going to College?*, believes that college is not worth it for everyone. He states that not everyone is prepared for the strenuous intellectual challenge of a liberal education (Murray 237). One study Murray cites shows that only 10% of high school students who take the SAT score in the percentile that would lead them to get at least a 2.7 GPA in college (Murray 238). If students are not going to do well, then what? Many drop out and attempt to find a full-time job; others return home to figure out a new plan, but overall this is affecting graduation rates. Murray points out that only those who are interested in getting a liberal education should attend school (Murray 240). Many who do not want to go to college can do well in other fields, such as trade jobs.

The other major factor students must consider when deciding whether to go to college is the cost. In the United States many top ranked public universities cost $20,000 to $30,000 per year in tuition, fees, room and board, and additional personal costs, while at most private colleges a student pays from $50,000 to $65,000. In an article titled "College Calculus: What's the Real Value of Higher Education?" John Cassidy quotes Professor Peter Cappelli, who discusses the burden many families face when attempting to send their children to school. Cappelli reveals that students in college are paying almost four times as much as other students around the world (Cassidy). With the help of financial aid some or most of these costs can be taken care of, but that is just for the select few. Everyone else must either hope to receive local/private scholarships or take out loans. If you are a person from a lower income family, it is nearly impossible to pay for college by yourself. In 2013 the average debt college students graduated with was $27,670 (Snider), and in 2015 it was more than $35,000, the highest ever (Sparshott). If graduates cannot find a job, this serious debt cannot be paid off, which leaves them in more debt due to the interest (Snider). It is a deadly cycle that students do not want to get sucked into.

Even though the cost of college and student debt are major concerns, college has much more to offer than just a degree. In a response to Charles Murray, Kevin Carey argues that college not only exposes students to the skills they will need for the workplace but also helps them better understand the world we live in and how they will fit into it. Carey states that "higher education exposes students to our intellectual and cultural inheritance, to hard-won wisdom and works of surpassing beauty" (Carey). College is grueling for many students, but the benefits of getting a degree today are extremely rewarding. Especially when students can reflect on how much effort they put into learning and see how it helped them become successful. Also, students benefit from many valuable opportunities to grow intellectually that they can only receive by going to a university. The influential 19th Century education philosopher John Henry Newman believed that after our basic human needs are covered, we are destined to go out and seek a higher form of knowledge. We have to discover the beauty of knowledge and how it affects our own world. Since everyone has this God-given capability, we just need the motivation to act on it.

The high cost of college and the high rates of student loan debt should not prevent students from taking advantage of these many benefits of attending college. Government policies can be adopted to help students pay for college and reduce student debt. Programs like the Higher Education Act and Pell Grants, which helped millions of Americans attend college during the 20th Century, can be implemented today to make sure that college remains an option for any student who chooses to attend.

As our nation has changed throughout the years, attitudes about college have changed as well. Today, people cannot live a comfortable lifestyle without having a well paying job, which can be difficult to receive until they get a degree. This is why it is of such great importance that everyone be eligible and have the resources to attend college. Charles Murray stated that "we should not restrict the availability of a liberal education to a rarefied intellectual elite" (Murray 234). We still need universities that are available to the majority of students who want to attend and who are willing to put in the work to succeed. Our country and our universities have done a lot for their students, but now they need to do more.

4
MLA

Works Cited

"Back to School Statistics." *Fast Facts*, National Center for Educational
Statistics / Institute of Educational Sciences, nces.ed.gov/fastfacts/
display.asp?id=372. Accessed 15 Feb. 2016.

Baum, Sandy. "The Federal Pell Grant Program and Reauthorization of
the Higher Education Act." *Journal of Student Financial Aid*, vol. 45,
2015, pp. 23-34.

Brock, Thomas. "Young Adults and Higher Education: Barriers and
Breakthroughs to Success." *The Future of Children*, vol. 20, no. 1,
Spring 2010, futureofchildren.org/futureofchildren/publications/
docs/20_01_06.pdf.

Campbell, Robert, and Barry M. Siegel. "The Demand for Higher
Education in the United States, 1919–1964." *The American Economic
Review*, vol. 57, no. 3, June 1967, pp. 482-494. *JSTOR*, www.jstor.org/
stable/1812115.

Carey, Kevin. "The Best of American Opportunity." *Cato Unbound*, 13 Oct.
2008, www.cato-unbound.org/2008/10/13/kevin-carey/best-american-
opportunity.

Cassidy, John. "College Calculus: What's the Real Value of Higher
Education?" *The New Yorker*, 7 Sept. 2015, www.newyorker.com/
magazine/2015/09/07/college-calculus.

Davis, Alyssa, et al. *The Class of 2015*. Economic Policy Institute, 27 May
2015, www.epi.org/files/2015/the-class-of-2015-revised.pdf.

"History and Timeline." *U.S. Department of Veterans Affairs*, www.ben-
efits.va.gov/gibill/history.asp. Accessed 14 Feb. 2016.

"Income of Young Adults." *Fast Facts*. National Center for Education
Statistics / Institute of Education Sciences, nces.ed.gov/fastfacts/
display.asp?id=77. Accessed 15 Feb. 2016.

Murray, Charles. "Are Too Many People Going to College?" *"They Say/I Say": The Moves That Matter in Academic Writing, with Readings*, edited by Gerald Graff and Cathy Birkenstein, 3rd ed., W. W. Norton, 2015, pp. 234-53.

Newman, John Henry. "Knowledge Its Own End." *Reading the World: Ideas That Matter*, edited by Michael Austin, 2nd ed., W. W. Norton, 2010, pp. 53-59.

Snider, Susannah. "10 Colleges That Leave Graduates with the Most Student Loan Debt." *US News & World Report*, 17 Feb. 2015, www.usnews.com/education/best-colleges/the-short-list-college/articles/2015/02/17/10-colleges-that-leave-graduates-with-the-most-student-loan-debt.

Snyder, Thomas D., editor. *120 Years of American Education: A Statistical Portrait*. National Center for Educational Statistics, 1993, nces.ed.gov/pubs93/93442.pdf.

Sparshott, Jeffrey. "Congratulations, Class of 2015. You're the Most Indebted Ever (For Now)." *The Wall Street Journal*, 8 May 2015, blogs.wsj.com/economics/2015/05/08/congratulations-class-of-2015-youre-the-most-indebted-ever-for-now/.

4

MLA

In this chapter, you will learn to

1. Understand the nature of analytical writing as an important means of inquiry.

2. Recognize appropriate rhetorical opportunities for analytical writing.

3. Identify the three elements of effective analytical writing.

4. Apply the elements of analytical writing to the reading of sample texts.

5. Identify the four main features of effective analytical writing.

Understanding Analytical Writing

FOR MANY YEARS *Car Talk* was one of the most popular shows on American radio. Each week listeners would call in for help solving problems with their cars. Usually, after listening to a caller's description of the problem—say, the car stalls unexpectedly—the *Car Talk* hosts, Tom and Ray, would ask questions: What kind of car is it? How old is it? How many miles are on it? How long has it been stalling? When exactly does it stall? When you're idling at a traffic light? When you first start it up? After you've been driving it for a while? Does it stall in all kinds of weather? Does anyone else drive it? Then Tom and Ray would propose an explanation for the problem. Sometimes they would disagree on the reasons for the problem, and each would present his own explanation based on how he interpreted the information provided by the caller. Their back-and-forth was usually funny, and their efforts to solve their listeners' car troubles were intended to be entertaining. But Tom and Ray didn't just make jokes about car problems to keep their audience engaged; they also used sophisticated analysis to solve problems that matter to their audience. That is, they tried to understand how or why something was happening by carefully examining the situation and considering relevant information.

We use analysis every day to make decisions and solve problems. Even something as mundane as deciding which roads to drive home from school or which bus route to take to campus involves analysis. In making such a decision, we consider many factors, such as time, weather, cost, and circumstances like road construction or traffic. More complicated matters—for example, deciding which college to attend or whether to borrow money to buy a car—might require more sophisticated analysis. But all analysis involves carefully examining an issue, phenomenon, or situation so that you can understand it sufficiently to decide on an appropriate action or draw reasonable conclusions about it. Analysis is an important part of how we live in a complicated world, and it is central to college studies.

Occasions for Analytical Writing

Analytical writing grows out of a writer's need to understand something better. Effective analytical writing communicates clearly to readers who share the writer's interest in the question or problem being analyzed. A main purpose of all analytical writing is to help interested readers better understand the topic at hand. In a sense, then, analytical writing is a kind of collaborative problem solving by which writers and readers explore questions or problems in their quest for answers or solutions. Consider the following scenarios, in which circumstances prompted students to engage in analytical writing:

> AFTER learning in an environmental policy class about the potentially harmful environmental and health impacts of large-scale agriculture, a few students at a college near a large city became concerned about the campus policy to purchase foods from large distributors that transport produce hundreds of miles. When the students approached the food service coordinator about the possibility of buying produce from farms located just outside the city, they were told that such a policy would be too expensive and difficult to implement. The students understood these objections, but they were not convinced that buying food from local farms was not feasible. So they decided to investigate. If such a policy did not save money, would it nevertheless help make the campus "greener"? Would it help the local economy? Would local food be healthier or taste better? Would students be unhappy with changes to the dining hall menus? The students discussed these questions with their instructor and did some research; they also talked to other students about the issue. Their investigation eventually led them to write a letter to their college president proposing a new policy to purchase more locally produced foods for the campus dining hall. Their letter included an analysis of the advantages and disadvantages of such a policy, including a breakdown of potential costs and a discussion of how other students on the campus felt about such a policy.

....

> JIM, a student at a large state university, began following a discussion on Facebook about the value of college after a classmate informed his Facebook friends that he was leaving college because he could no longer afford it. Jim's classmate did not think borrowing more money to pay for his final few semesters was a good idea. His comment provoked a debate about whether a college degree is worth the cost. Some students wondered whether their degrees would lead to good-paying jobs, which prompted other students to argue that the purpose of college isn't just to prepare students for careers but to educate them as citizens as well. A few students posted links to articles about the rising costs of college tuition as well as average salaries of college graduates compared with those of workers without degrees. Jim followed the discussion closely because of his own concerns about paying for college. To save money, Jim enrolled in a less-expensive community college for two years before transferring to a four-year university. After he posted a message about his decision, someone asked whether Jim received the same quality of education at the community college as he would have had he enrolled for all four years at the university. Jim wasn't sure. As he followed the discussion, he

also read the articles that others had posted, found more information about the advantages and disadvantages of two-year college degrees, and posted links to relevant articles on his social media accounts. Eventually, his investigation helped him understand some benefits and costs of attending a two-year college, which he shared on his Facebook page. One of his friends suggested that Jim write an essay about the issue for his old high school newspaper, which Jim did, using his Facebook post as his starting point.

❯ AMBER, a part-time college student who serves in the National Guard, took a leave of absence from classes because her unit was deployed to Afghanistan for six months. Part of the unit's mission was to build roads and an irrigation system for farmers in a remote region of Afghanistan. Amber was excited about this mission, which she believed would improve the lives of Afghans and relations between Afghans and Americans. However, during her months there, Amber began to realize that the situation was more complicated than she first believed. Many residents feared reprisals from insurgents if they accepted American help. Others worried that new roads would mean more military vehicle traffic. Also, the new irrigation system didn't reach some of the smaller farmers. Cultural and religious differences between Afghans and Americans exacerbated misunderstandings about these projects. All these problems caused Amber to wonder whether the Americans' humanitarian efforts created more problems than they solved. Amber talked to other soldiers about these concerns. She read articles and online discussions to learn more about the complexities of humanitarian aid in Afghanistan. When she returned to the United States, she continued writing a blog that she began in Afghanistan, focusing on her own analysis of the difficulties faced by American units engaged in humanitarian efforts. Her blog attracted many readers, some who shared her concerns and others who challenged her conclusions.

In each of these situations, complex questions prompted students to investigate further. In each case,

- **the need to understand an important issue** motivated the students to engage in analysis
- **the desire to communicate what they learned** through their analysis with others motivated the students to write up their analysis in some form

All three of these scenarios illustrate the importance of the rhetorical situation not only in creating a reason for analytical writing but also in shaping the writing itself. The most effective analytical writing addresses the needs of a particular rhetorical situation and communicates to an interested audience what the writer learned as a result of his or her analysis (see Sidebar: "One Writer's Motives for Analytical Writing " on page 128).

Charles C. Mann's award-winning book *1491* examines the state of scientific knowledge about the people who were living in the Americas before Christopher Columbus arrived in 1492. Mann's curiosity about the history of indigenous cultures in North and South America led him to explore a complicated, ongoing controversy about how many people inhabited these continents before Columbus arrived, who they were, and the civilizations they created. His book is an extended analysis of that controversy and how scientists use available archaeological evidence to understand life in the Americas before 1492. In the preface to his book, Mann explains how he came to his subject:

> My interest in the peoples who walked the Americas before Columbus only snapped into anything resembling focus in the fall of 1992. By chance one Sunday afternoon I came across a display in a college library of the special Columbian quincentenary issue of the *Annals of the Association of American Geographers*. Curious, I picked up the journal, sank into an armchair, and began to read an article by William Denevan, a geographer at the University of Wisconsin. The article opened with the question, "What was the New World like at the time of Columbus?" Yes, I thought, what *was* it like? Who lived here and what could have passed through their minds when European sails first appeared on the horizon? I finished Denevan's article and went on to others and didn't stop reading until the librarian flicked the lights to signify closing time.

Source: Mann, Charles C. *1491*. Vintage Books, 2006, p. x.

EXERCISE 5A EXPLORING OCCASIONS FOR ANALYTICAL WRITING

1. Think about a decision you had to make about an important situation or problem in your life. For example, perhaps you had to decide whether to renew the lease on your apartment or move to a less expensive apartment with new roommates. Or maybe you decided to change your major or take a semester off to volunteer for an organization like Habitat for Humanity. Write a brief essay in which you describe the situation and explain how you came to your decision. Discuss the factors you considered as you arrived at your decision. Did you do any research—for example, by talking to others for advice or by looking for information on the Internet? What information did you gather? How did you use this information? In other

© Helga Esteb/Shutterstock.com

words, what did you do to analyze this situation? On the basis of this experience, draw conclusions about how you use analysis in your life.

2. Examine an article or essay in a publication you like to read (online or in print) that analyzes a problem or issue of interest to you. Why do you think the writer chose the topic? What kind of analysis did he or she conduct to understand the question or problem at hand? In what ways does the writer address his or her readers with this analysis? Draw conclusions about how useful the analysis is in this case. What makes it worthwhile? What problems do you see?

3. Think about an issue or problem on your campus that interests you. What do you know about the issue or problem? What do you need to know? Now imagine that you were to write an analysis to address that issue or problem. Who would be your audience? What outcome would you hope for if you were to write such an analysis? Write a paragraph describing the problem, the analysis you would write about it, and the audience for that analysis.

Understanding Analytical Writing in College

Analytical writing is perhaps the most common kind of writing assigned in college classes. The familiar *research paper* is usually an analytical project in which the writer examines an issue or problem and, using appropriate sources, analyzes that issue or problem in a way that is appropriate for that course. For instance, in a psychology course, you might write a paper about gender differences in interpersonal relationships, and part of your task would be to analyze the role of gender in relationships, much as a psychology researcher might do. Your analysis would involve reviewing appropriate sources, such as relevant psychological studies, to understand better how gender plays a role in relationships; it would also involve using psychological concepts or theories to help make sense of interpersonal relationships. Ideally, your paper would demonstrate that you understand those concepts and can apply them to your topic. In this sense, analytical writing is an effective way to learn because, in analyzing a subject like interpersonal relationships, you are likely to think more carefully (and perhaps differently) about that subject and understand it better.

Effective analytical writing in college begins with the desire to understand. Usually, this desire is focused on a complex issue or problem involving a number of different considerations. Analytical writing requires delving into the complexity of a topic by examining available evidence carefully, looking for patterns or trends in that evidence, and drawing reasonable, well-supported conclusions on the basis of the evidence.

In the following sections, we will examine three examples of analytical writing to illustrate these **three elements of effective analytical writing:**

- a desire to understand
- a careful examination of the evidence
- well-reasoned conclusions

All three readings focus on the same general subject—education—but the specific topics are different.

A Desire to Understand

This first example is from an essay by a distinguished professor who examines the impact of the increasing competition that American students face as they try to get accepted to college. In this excerpt from the beginning of his essay, Mark C. Taylor notices a problem with his students that leads him to a question, which in turn leads to the beginnings of an analysis of the problem:

> Several years ago I was teaching a course on the philosophical assumptions and cultural impact of massive multi-user online games at Williams College. The students in the course were very intelligent and obviously interested in the topic.
>
> But as the semester progressed, I began to detect a problem with the class. The students were working hard and performing well but there was no energy in our discussions and no passion in the students. They were hesitant to express their ideas and often seemed to be going through the motions. I tried to encourage them to be more venturesome with tactics I had used successfully in the past but nothing worked.
>
> One day I asked them what was or, perhaps better, was not going on. Why were they so cautious and where was their enthusiasm for learning? They seemed relieved to talk about it and their response surprised me. Since pre-kindergarten, they explained, they had been programmed to perform well so they could get to the next level. They had been taught the downside of risk and encouraged to play it safe. What mattered most was getting into a good elementary school, middle school and high school so that they would finally be admitted to a top college. Having succeeded beyond their parents' wildest expectations, they did not know why they were in college and had no idea what to do after graduation.
>
> In today's market-driven economy we constantly hear that choice is the highest good and that competition fuels innovation. But this is not always true. Choice provokes anxiety and competition can quell the imagination and discourage the spirit of experimentation that is necessary for creativity. In a world obsessed with ratings, well-meaning parents all too often train their children to jump through the hoops they think will lead to success.

Source: Taylor, Mark C. "The Perils of Being Perfect." *The New York Times*, 12 Sept. 2010, www.nytimes.com/roomfordebate/2010/09/12/why-are-colleges-so-selective/the-perils-of-being-a-perfect-student.

This excerpt reveals that Taylor's analysis of his students' lack of motivation began with his desire to understand something he noticed in his class.

We all have these moments of wondering, driven by a desire to understand something that interests, puzzles, or concerns us:

- Why do my friends prefer Snapchat to Facebook?
- How can parking be made more convenient on campus?
- What makes my dog so afraid of thunder but not of loud noises from the street?
- Why do more students seem to have trouble with math than with history or English?

Such wondering can lead to a kind of informal analysis: talking with friends, reading relevant newspaper articles, seeking information online. In academic writing, however, such wondering is usually shaped by the academic subject being studied, so that certain questions are considered important or relevant and certain ways of exploring those questions are expected. Psychologists, for example, are interested in certain questions about human behavior (Why are some people shy while others are not? How do children learn concepts? What is depression, and what causes it?), while economists are interested in others (Why do some people buy things they don't need? What factors affect the decisions people make about whether to save or spend money? How does family income influence investment decisions?). In this sense, Taylor's question about his students can be viewed as part of a larger conversation among scholars and policymakers in the field of education, and his analysis of that question will be influenced by what others in his field have said about the topic.

A Careful Examination of the Evidence

The next example also begins with a desire to understand something. Authors Michael McPherson and Morton Schapiro want to know why some Americans are more likely to attend college than others. This question of access to education has been widely studied in the United States, and experts know that several factors, such as family income, affect the ability of different groups of Americans to go to college. Therefore, McPherson and Schapiro can assume that readers of their report, who are likely to be other education researchers or policymakers, are familiar with the idea that family income affects access to college. But because this issue is so complicated, they also know that one factor, such as family income, can't entirely explain the problem, so they have to look more closely at the issue. Here's part of their analysis:

> There are certainly significant financing constraints that contribute to differential higher education access. But there are equally important differences in pre-college preparation. Table 5 looks at college enrollment by family income and mathematics test scores. It shows that students scoring in the top third in math are quite likely to go on to college, especially if they come from families above the 25th percentile in income. Even for students in the lowest quartile, the enrollment rate is 82 percent. However, as test score performance declines, enrollment rates plummet. The decrease is especially large for students from lower income backgrounds—for example, the 82 percent rate for

TABLE 5 Postsecondary enrollment rates of 1992 high school graduates by family income and math test scores				
Math Test Scores	Lowest Income	Second Quartile	Third Quartile	Highest Income
Lowest Third	48	50	64	73
Middle Third	67	75	83	89
Top Third	82	90	95	96

Source for table: *Education Pays 2004*, p. 30

those with the highest test scores mentioned above falls to 48 percent when math test scores are in the lowest third. Income clearly plays a role here, but scholastic performance also contributes to explaining college entry.

Source: McPherson, Michael S., and Morton Owen Schapiro. "Opportunity in Higher Education." *Reflections on College Access and Persistence*, Advisory Committee on Student Financial Assistance, 2006, www.ed.gov/acsfa.

In this excerpt, McPherson and Schapiro carefully review math test scores of high school graduates from different family income levels, looking for patterns in the scores to explain why some students are more likely to attend college than others. But they don't jump to easy conclusions. Although they acknowledge that family income is a key factor, their analysis indicates that even low-income students who have high math scores are likely to attend college. Obviously, the issue is more complicated than just a matter of family income. Most questions worth analyzing are more complicated than they seem at first glance.

Well-Reasoned Conclusions

In this next example, education researchers Linda Darling-Hammond and George Wood examine another complicated education issue: determining which government policies are likely to improve education in the United States. They draw conclusions from test scores and other statistical information about students. Like McPherson and Schapiro, Darling-Hammond and Wood also review test scores and family income, but in this case, they compare U.S. students to students from other nations, using scores from the Programme for International Student Assessment (PISA). Notice how they move from an examination of their data to conclusions about the most effective government policies:

> Of nations participating in PISA, the U.S. is among those where two students of different socio-economic backgrounds have the largest difference in expected scores. On this measure of equity, the U.S. ranked 45th out of 55 total countries, right above Brazil and Mexico. On the PISA assessments in reading, math, and science, for example, the distance between the average score for Asian and white students, on the one hand, and Hispanic and Latino students, on the other, is equal to the distance between the United States average and that of the highest scoring countries.
>
> In all these content areas, U.S. students from all groups do least well on the measures of problem-solving. These data suggest, first, that the United States' poor standing is substantially a product of unequal access to the kind of intellectually challenging learning measured on these international assessments. In addition, U.S. students in general, and historically underserved groups in particular, are not getting sufficient access to the problem-solving and critical thinking skills needed to apply this knowledge in a meaningful way.
>
> The reason for these disparities is not a mystery. The United States not only has the highest poverty rates for children among advanced nations with the fewest social

supports, it also provides fewer resources for them at school. America is still at risk in large measure because we have failed to ensure access to education and basic family supports for all of our children.

Source: *Democracy at Risk: The Need for a New Federal Policy in Education*. Forum for Education and Democracy, 2008, www.forumforeducation.org/sites/default/files/u48/FED%20FINAL%20 REPORT.pdf.

In the first paragraph of this excerpt, the authors review data that reveal inequities in test performance among U.S. students of different socio-economic and racial backgrounds. In the second and third paragraphs, they conclude from their analysis that many American students do poorly on international tests because their family income prevents them from having access to high-quality education.

Because most topics for analysis in academic subjects are so complex, writers rarely offer easy answers or simple solutions. Instead, they reach conclusions that are well supported by their analysis of available data—and sometimes they raise new questions.

Doing Analysis

So far we have explored reasons for conducting an analysis, and we have looked at examples of analysis in academic work. But what exactly does it mean to analyze something? This section gives you practice in three important kinds of intellectual tasks that are usually part of the process of analysis:

- using a framework to analyze something
- making reasonable claims on the basis of available data or information
- supporting claims

Using a Framework to Analyze Something

Analysis often involves applying some kind of framework—a theory, a principle, or a set of criteria—to help explain or understand a problem, event, trend, or idea. For example, in psychology a writer might use the theory of behaviorism to explain the actions of children in a school lunchroom. An economist might use the principle of supply and demand to analyze prices of iPhones. For a theater arts class, students might use specific technical criteria to analyze the cinematography of chase scenes in action films. (See the flowchart on the next page.)

The use of a framework helps illuminate what is being analyzed by focusing attention on specific elements, questions, or issues. For example, using technical criteria to analyze chase scenes in action films can help us understand how a director used camera angles, lighting, and editing to provoke certain reactions in viewers.

To be effective, frameworks must be applied appropriately. Students sometimes simply refer to a theory or principle rather than actually use it for analysis. For example, in this excerpt from an

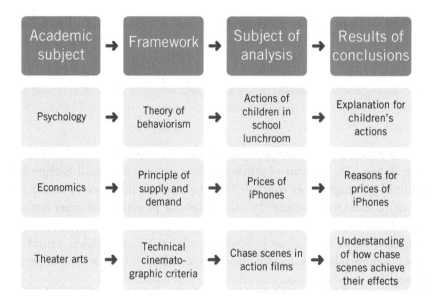

Academic subject		Framework		Subject of analysis		Results of conclusions
Psychology	→	Theory of behaviorism	→	Actions of children in school lunchroom	→	Explanation for children's actions
Economics	→	Principle of supply and demand	→	Prices of iPhones	→	Reasons for prices of iPhones
Theater arts	→	Technical cinemato-graphic criteria	→	Chase scenes in action films	→	Understanding of how chase scenes achieve their effects

essay about teaching philosophies, the student attempts to apply a theory of teaching (proposed by education scholars Gerald Grant and Christine Murray) to explain the philosophy of a specific teacher (Ms. Jones):

> Ms. Jones' teaching philosophy stresses the importance of being connected with her students and the community. "When I first started teaching, I didn't understand my students' behavior or home life. I still don't," she said. "The more I learn about my students, the better idea I have of how I can relate to them." Living in the urban community where her school is located has given Ms. Jones certain insights about her students. For example, she is aware that her students are regularly exposed to gangs, drugs, and violence as well as rich cultural traditions. Her first-hand experience with the community has given Ms. Jones an opportunity to learn about her students. "Teachers must be part detective and part researcher, shifting clues children leave, collecting data, testing hypothesis and looking unblinkingly at the way children really are . . . in order to fill out and make credible the story of their growth and development." (Grant & Murray, 1999, p. 35)

In this case, the student refers to Grant and Murray's theory of effective teaching but does not use it to help readers understand Ms. Jones' teaching philosophy. To *apply* Grant and Murray's theory, the student writer should have used each of the key ideas of that theory (e.g., the teacher as detective and the teacher as researcher) to explain why Ms. Jones teaches as she does. To be helpful, a theory should be used as a "lens" to help readers see more clearly whatever is being analyzed.

Here's an example in which a student analyzes a writer's experience as a biracial woman by using a psychological theory. In an article published in a scholarly journal in psychology, Carmen Braun Williams describes her struggles with her own sense of identity as a woman whose mother is white and whose father is African American. In the following excerpt, the student uses a theory of racial identity development developed by a scholar named W. S. Carlos Poston to explain part of Williams' experience:

> In her article, Carmen Braun Williams suggests that race is a socially constructed category that has been misconstrued as biological (Williams 34). She explains how a biracial person such as herself is confronted by the problem of not fitting neatly into the socially constructed racial categories of "White" and "Black." Williams describes her experience as a child, when she was unself-conscious and unaware of these racial categories, after her family moved to the U.S. in the 1950s: "I was around eight years old when I first started noticing that my parents were often subjected to intense scrutiny by passers-by. I started hearing ugly words kids shouted at us from their porches as we walked past" (33). These incidents led to Williams realizing that her "entire being was reduced to one thing: 'not White'" (33).
>
> Williams' experience is consistent with W. S. Carlos Poston's first stage in his model of racial identity development. According to Poston, during this first stage, which he calls "Personal Identity," "The child will tend to have a sense of self that is somewhat independent of his or her ethnic background" (Poston 153). This was the case for Williams. "As a child," she writes, "I was blissfully unaware of my difference"; however, her "innocence . . . was shattered by racism" (Williams 33). As Poston notes, "Individuals at this stage are often very young, and membership in any particular ethnic group is just becoming salient" (Poston 153). Accordingly, Williams' awareness of her own biracial identity was "just becoming salient" as a result of her experiences after her family moved to the U.S.

Notice how this student applies the framework—in this case, Poston's theory of racial identity development—directly to Carmen Braun Williams' experiences as a biracial woman in order to explain those experiences. Poston's theory becomes a way for us to better understand Williams' experiences, which is what a framework should do.

EXERCISE 5B **USING FRAMEWORKS FOR ANALYSIS**

The following passage is an excerpt from a 2015 report titled "Social Media Usage: 2005–2015" from the Pew Research Center:

> Across demographic groups, a number of trends emerge in this analysis of social media usage:
>
> - **Age differences: Seniors make strides**. Young adults (ages 18 to 29) are the most likely to use social media—fully 90% do. Still, usage among those 65 and older has more than tripled since 2010 when 11% used social media. Today, 35% of all those 65 and older report using social media, compared with just 2% in 2005.
> - **Gender differences: Women and men use social media at similar rates**. Women were more likely than men to use social networking sites for a number of years, although since 2014 these differences have been modest. Today, 68% of all women use social media, compared with 62% of all men.

(Continued)

- **Socio-economic differences: Those with higher education levels and household income lead the way**. Over the past decade, it has consistently been the case that those in higher-income households were more likely to use social media. More than half (56%) of those living in the lowest-income households now use social media, though growth has leveled off in the past few years. Turning to educational attainment, a similar pattern is observed. Those with at least some college experience have been consistently more likely than those with a high school degree or less to use social media over the past decade. 2013 was the first year that more than half of those with a high school diploma or less used social media.

- **Racial and ethnic similarities:** There are no notable differences by racial or ethnic group: 65% of whites, 65% of Hispanics and 56% of African-Americans use social media today.

Source: Perrin, Andrew. *Social Media Usage: 2005-2015*. Pew Research Center, 8 Oct. 2015, www.pewinternet.org/2015/10/08/social-networking-usage-2005-2015/.

Using this report as a framework, analyze the way a specific group of people—for example, your family members, students who live in your dormitory, or members of a club to which you belong—use social media. Try to explain their uses of social media in terms of the research on different demographic groups that is cited in this article.

Making Reasonable Claims on the Basis of Available Information

Analysis requires examining and interpreting information in a way that leads to reasonable claims or assertions. One of the most common mistakes students make in analysis is going too far in making claims on the basis of available information—that is, making assertions that are not supported by the evidence at hand. Here's one example of a student making that mistake:

> According to one study, boys tend to associate their academic performance with skills and effort while girls associate it with luck (Grossman and Grossman, 1994). My concern is with the implications of such research. Other studies suggest that American students attribute academic success to ability and intelligence, whereas in other nations, such as Japan, students attribute academic success to effort (Kitayama and Cohen, 2007). Therefore, either there was a paradigm shift in the effort by American boys and girls or the data are false.

In this excerpt, the writer reviews two bodies of research that seem to contradict each other. The student draws two possible conclusions from this apparent contradiction: (1) that there must have been a change (a "paradigm shift") in the way American boys and girls perceive the role of effort in academic success, or (2) that the data are somehow incorrect. Neither conclusion is necessarily supported by the available information. It is possible that the attitudes of American students did change, but we can't know for certain on the basis of the two studies cited. Nor does it follow that the apparent contradiction in the two studies means that the results of the studies were incorrect. In fact, there are many possible explanations for the contradiction between the studies. For example, the studies might have examined very different student populations, or they might have used different methods (surveys, interviews, and so on). In addition, the studies might have treated gender differences differently. Given the information provided in this excerpt, we have no way of knowing whether the two studies were even examining the same thing. (For example, one study might have focused on gender differences in a specific subject area such as math, whereas the other study might have investigated student attitudes in general.)

All these possibilities suggest that the matter is too complex and the available information too limited for the claims the student makes. Given the limited information provided, the student should revise these claims. For example, it is reasonable to claim that student attitudes about the reasons for academic success seem to vary by gender as well as by nation. Such a limited claim is supported by the information provided.

The point is that you should make only those claims that reasonably emerge from your information or that can be clearly supported by your data. Here's an example of a writer doing just that. In this excerpt from a book about diet and health, the author reviews the evidence for the widespread belief that a lack of fiber in one's diet can be a factor in developing diseases of the digestive tract, including colon cancer:

> Over the past quarter-century . . . there has been a steady accumulation of evidence refuting the notion that a fiber-deficient diet causes colon cancer, polyps, or diverticulitis, let alone any other disease of civilization. The pattern is precisely what would be expected of a hypothesis that simply isn't true: the larger and more rigorous the trials set up to test it, the more consistently negative the evidence. Between 1994 and 2000, two observational studies—of forty-seven thousand male health professionals and the eighty-nine thousand women of the Nurses Health Study, both run out of the Harvard School of Public Health—and a half-dozen randomized control trials concluded that fiber consumption is unrelated to the risk of colon cancer, as is, apparently, the consumption of fruits and vegetables. The results of the forty-nine-thousand-women Dietary Modification Trial of Women's Health Initiative, published in 2006, confirmed that increasing the fiber in the diet (by eating more whole grains, fruits, and vegetables) had no beneficial effect on colon cancer, nor did it prevent heart disease or breast cancer or induce weight loss.

Source: Taubes, Gary. *Good Calories, Bad Calories: Challenging the Conventional Wisdom on Diet, Weight Control, and Disease.* Alfred E. Knopf, 2007, pp. 132–33.

The author's purpose is to determine whether a high-fiber diet has specific health benefits, as many health care professionals and researchers have long claimed. Notice that he emphasizes that the best available studies do not support prevailing conclusions about the health benefits of eating fiber; moreover, he limits his claim to what he can reasonably support on the basis of the few available studies, asserting only that the hypothesis about specific health benefits of a high-fiber diet, such as lower rates of colon cancer, is not borne out by these studies. He does not say that eating fiber isn't beneficial; rather, he concludes that eating fiber does not lead to lower colon cancer rates and similar health benefits.

Remember to say only what your information allows you to say. Make sure your claims and assertions are reasonable given the information you have.

EXERCISE 5C **MAKING REASONABLE CLAIMS**

These charts present data on income and wealth distribution in the United States. For each of the following claims, determine whether the claim can be made on the basis of the data reflected in the charts; if not, revise the claim so that it is supported by the data in the charts:

1. In the past three decades, the rich have become richer while the poor have become poorer.

2. Since 1980, the incomes of the wealthiest Americans have risen more rapidly than those of other Americans.

3. College has become less affordable for all but the wealthiest Americans.

4. Economic recessions don't significantly affect income growth in the United States.

Income gains at the top dwarf those of low- and middle-income households

Percent change in real after-tax income since 1979

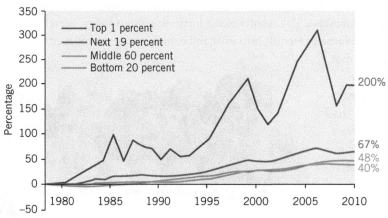

Source: Center on Budget and Policy Priorities, www.cbpp.org/income-gains-at-the-top-dwarf-those-of-low-and-middle-income-households-0.

(Continued)

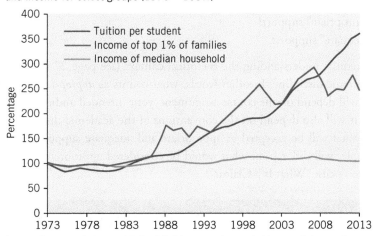

Tuition growth has vastly outpaced income gains

Inflation-adjusted average tuition and fees at public four-year institutions and income for select groups (1973 = 100%)

Legend:
- Tuition per student
- Income of top 1% of families
- Income of median household

Source: Center on Budget and Policy Priorities, www.cbpp.org/tuition-growth-has-vastly-outpaced-income-gains.

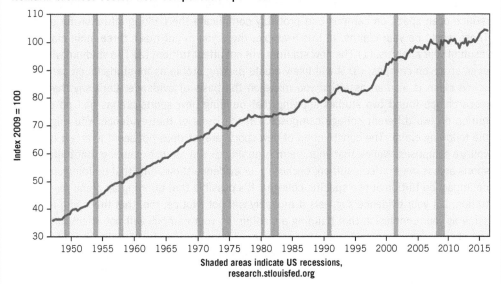

Nonfarm business sector: Real compensation per hour

Shaded areas indicate US recessions,
research.stlouisfed.org

Source: United States, Bureau of Labor Statistics. *Nonfarm Business Sector: Real Compensation Per Hour* [COMPRNFB]. FRED, Federal Reserve Bank of St. Louis, research.stlouisfed.org/fred2/series/COMPRNFB. Accessed March 4, 2016.

5

Supporting Claims

When it comes to supporting claims in analytical writing, writers must consider two important questions:

- What is "appropriate" support?
- What is "adequate" support?

Both questions require understanding the rhetorical context (see page 27 in Chapter 2), which includes the academic discipline. In other words, what counts as *appropriate* and *adequate* support for a claim will depend on the course assignment, your intended audience, and the purpose of your project; it will also depend on the conventions of the academic discipline within which you're writing. What will be accepted as appropriate and adequate support in a chemistry lab report, for example, will differ from what would be considered appropriate and adequate for a history paper (see Focus: "What Is a Claim?").

FOCUS   WHAT IS A CLAIM?

A claim in analytical writing is a statement or assertion you make as a result of your analysis. For example, if you are analyzing the impact of a proposed new football stadium on your campus, you might examine whether the cost of the new facility will affect tuition, increase traffic on campus, complicate parking, or reduce open space that students currently use for various activities. Your research might reveal that a new stadium will not likely affect tuition but will reduce open space on campus and probably complicate the parking situation for students. Those would be your claims. In this example, then, you might make three main claims as a result of your analysis: (1) The new stadium will not affect tuition; (2) The stadium will reduce open space on campus; (3) It will likely create parking problems for students on campus.

A claim is also an assertion you make on the basis of evidence. Let's say that in your research you found two studies showing that building new sports arenas had no effect on tuition on two different college campuses. On the basis of that evidence, you might make the following claim: The construction of new sports arenas does not seem to affect tuition on college campuses. Notice that your claim is qualified: You are not claiming that building new sports arenas *never* affects tuition, because your evidence shows only that building arenas had no impact on tuition at two specific colleges. It's possible that building an arena *might* affect tuition, but your evidence suggests it probably will not. Notice, too, that this claim is not the same as your conclusion that building a stadium on your campus will not affect tuition. The two claims are related, but one is based on your interpretation of a specific body of evidence (two studies) and the other is based on your overall analysis of various kinds of evidence.

One last point: A claim is not the same thing as an opinion. In this case, you are making a *claim* about the possible impact of building a sports stadium on tuition at your college. Your *opinion* might be that building the stadium is a bad idea, but for this analysis, that opinion might not be relevant. What matters is what your analysis reveals as you try to address the research question about what effect building the stadium might have on your campus in general. You make your claims on the basis of that analysis. Although your analysis might influence your opinion, your claims and your opinion are not the same thing.

Consider the following criteria as you decide whether your support for a claim is appropriate and adequate:

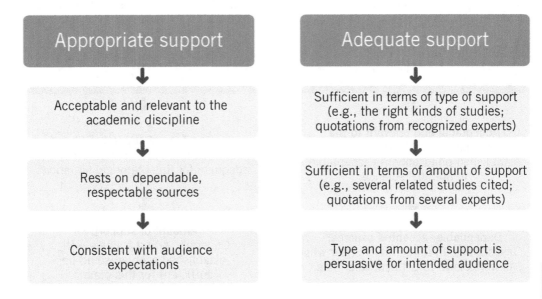

To some extent, the decision about whether support for a claim is appropriate and adequate is subjective. Not all readers will agree that a writer has sufficiently supported a claim, even when those readers have similar backgrounds and expectations, but you can try to anticipate whether your support is sufficient by considering the expectations your audience is likely to have for your rhetorical situation.

Let's look at a political scientist supporting a claim effectively in an essay, written for a scholarly journal, about the value of civility in modern society:

> Because we are all members of the same political community, interacting on grounds of civic equality, we have an obligation to be polite in our everyday interactions with our fellow citizens. In the linguistic analogy developed by the philosopher Michael Oakeshott, civility is a kind of "adverbial" restraint on the civic language we speak with one another. In the same way that one is enjoined to speak politely, modestly or temperately, the adverbial condition of civility modifies and qualifies conduct without specifying its content. We can communicate our wishes or injunctions to fellow citizens—whatever those wishes may be—so long as we agree to subscribe to common conditions on the means we may legitimately use in the pursuit of those self-chosen ends (Oakeshott, 1990, pp. 120–121, 126 and 128; see also Boyd, 2004a). Membership is defined in terms of this common moral relationship and it is this relationship that in turn gives rise to our responsibility to be civil to others.

Source: Boyd, Richard. "The Value of Civility?" *Urban Studies*, vol. 43, no. 5–6, May 2006, p. 864.

The author, Richard Boyd, states his claim in the first sentence of this excerpt. To support his claim, he refers to an analogy by an influential philosopher (Michael Oakeshott). To what extent is Boyd's support *appropriate* and *adequate* for his academic discipline and rhetorical situation?

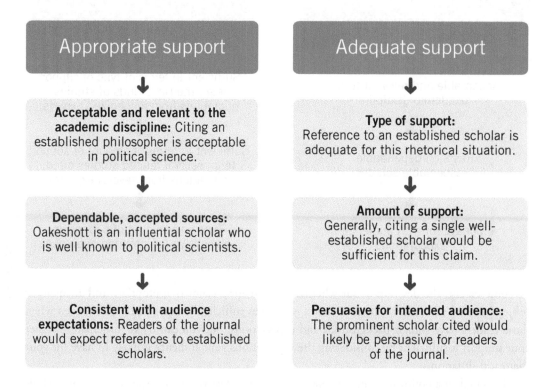

This example illustrates the importance of the rhetorical context in supporting claims. Although some readers might disagree, it is likely that most readers in Boyd's discipline (political science) would find his support for his claim reasonable.

Deciding what kind of information you need to support a claim and how much support is enough can be confusing. In the following excerpt from an essay written for a general writing course, the student tries to make a claim about the reasons for a certain community's economic struggles. In the beginning of the paragraph the student provides statistical data to support a claim that the community's economic status might be the result of its "low educational achievement." But then she makes a further claim about additional causes of the community's economic struggle. The assignment called for an analysis that would be appropriate for a general audience (for example, readers of the local newspaper):

> One could argue that because of the low educational achievement in this community, the socioeconomic status is relatively low. Thirty-two percent of the adults in the area did not complete secondary education. Twenty-three percent of the population in this district are below poverty level and 35.7% make under $25,000 (the per capita income is $15,272, according to the U.S. Census Bureau, 2000). However, other factors cause this village to struggle economically. First, there are not many high-paying job opportunities.

This area's industry consists primarily of manufacturing (17.2%); education, health and social services (19.9%); and recreation and accommodation (16.6%) (U.S. Census Bureau, 2000). There are four main institutions that provide jobs for this community: the Big Mountain Resort, a state prison, the school district, and a regional hospital. A small percentage of the population (3.6%) owns private businesses (U.S. Census Bureau, 2000).

The statistical evidence the student provides in the second and third sentences of this paragraph is insufficient to support the claim in the first sentence (that low educational achievement is the cause of the community's low economic status). That statistical evidence indicates that significant percentages of the residents have not finished high school and have low incomes, but the evidence does not show that the high rate of high school incompletion explains or causes low income. So the writer looks to other statistical evidence to try to explain the community's economic struggles—for example, the kinds of jobs available there and the percentage of the population that own private businesses. But do the figures actually support her claim about the likely causes of the community's economic status? For one thing, the percentage of specific kinds of jobs (manufacturing, service, and so on) tells us nothing about the number of "high-paying" jobs. For another, the small percentage of people who own private businesses does not necessarily mean low-paying jobs. Jobs in a private business can be low-paying or high-paying, and jobs in the public sector, such as in education, can also be both. In the end, although the writer provides a lot of statistical information that seems appropriate, it is not exactly relevant to her claim nor is it sufficient to support that claim:

5

Appropriate support	Adequate support
Acceptable and relevant to the academic discipline: The kind of support seems acceptable for the rhetorical situation but not relevant to the claim.	**Type of support:** Statistical information on jobs, income, and education is appropriate, but the specific information is inadequate for the claim.
Dependable, accepted sources: Census Bureau is a dependable source.	**Amount of support:** Too little support that is directly relevant to the claim is provided.
Consistent with audience expectations: A general audience would likely expect more relevant information for the specific claim.	**Persuasive for intended audience:** Although the kind of data is likely persuasive for a general audience, readers might not find the data sufficient to support the claims.

SUPPORTING A CLAIM WITH APPROPRIATE AND ADEQUATE INFORMATION

Use the criteria described in this section to identify sufficient support for each of the following claims. For each claim, list two or three kinds of evidence or information that you think would provide appropriate support (for example, a specific kind of statistical information, a certain kind of study, the views of a certain kind of expert, etc.). The basic rhetorical situation is described in parentheses after each claim.

1. The economic benefits of a college degree outweigh the costs of tuition. (letter to the editor of the campus newspaper)

2. Religion is an important component of American politics. (analytical paper for a political science course)

3. Popular films suggest that racist attitudes persist in the United States. (review for a film class)

Features of Analytical Writing

The examples earlier in this chapter illustrate **four main features of effective analytical writing:**

1. **A relevant topic worthy of analysis.** Academic fields are defined by certain bodies of knowledge (for example, the periodic table in chemistry, the nature of human emotion in psychology) and by the kinds of questions or problems that experts in those fields examine (What happens when two substances from the periodic table are combined? Why are some people more likely to suffer from depression than others?). So identifying a worthy topic for analysis requires knowing what kinds of questions are relevant in a specific field and what is known about those questions. The best analytical writing grows out of questions that are genuinely interesting to the writer and relevant to readers. Considering whether your topic might interest other students in your class or other readers familiar with that academic subject is an important step toward determining whether the topic is worthy of analysis.

2. **Complexity.** Rarely are interesting questions or problems as straightforward as they might seem. Good analysis, therefore, is about exploring complexity and trying to understand a question, problem, trend, event, or idea more fully by examining it in depth. Good analytical writing requires a measure of objectivity and even skepticism to avoid oversimplified explanations. It should help readers appreciate and grasp the complexity of a topic.

3. **Sufficient and appropriate evidence and support.** Effective analytical writing involves finding sufficient information about a topic and gathering appropriate evidence to support claims and conclusions. How much information is *sufficient* depends on the topic, the rhetorical situation, and the depth of analysis. Similarly, what counts as *appropriate* evidence

depends on the subject, the expectations of the audience, the purpose of the analysis, and the field of study. The right kind of information and evidence can lead to more effective analysis.

4. **Reasonable conclusions.** Because most topics in academic writing are complex, writers must interpret the information they find and draw reasonable conclusions supported by relevant evidence. In good analytical writing, writers resist the temptation to settle on seemingly obvious conclusions. Instead, they examine possibilities and draw conclusions that their readers should find reasonable on the basis of available information and evidence.

All good analytical writing shares these characteristics. Let's look at how one writer employs these features of analysis effectively.

In the following essay, well-known sociolinguist Deborah Tannen examines why hairstyles seem to be such a point of contention among mothers and their daughters. Tannen's essay was published in 2015 in *The American Prospect*, a magazine devoted to politics and culture. It demonstrates strategies that are widely used in any analytical writing.

. . . .

Talking About This Reading

Mark Fenlon (student): This essay includes many concepts and definitions from linguistics and other fields. It's hard to make sense of the main point when I'm struggling to keep up with all this new information. How can I keep track of the analysis and the terms being defined?

Bob Yagelski: Mark, you have begun to answer your own question. Your challenge is following the author's analysis at the same time you are learning unfamiliar terms and concepts. So separate your reading into steps. First, try to get an overall sense of the author's main point by skimming the article. Second, identify and define unfamiliar terms. (Take notes for both steps.) Once you have done so, reread the article more carefully.

. . . .

Why Mothers and Daughters Tangle Over Hair
by Deborah Tannen

1   "Do you like your hair that long?" my mother asked soon after I arrived for a visit. I laughed. Looking slightly hurt, she asked why I was laughing. "I've been interviewing women for the book I'm writing about mothers and daughters," I explained, "and so many tell me that their mothers criticize their hair." "I wasn't criticizing," my mother said, and I let it drop. Later in my visit I asked, "So Mom, what do you think of my hair?" Without missing a beat, she replied, "I think it's a little too long."

2   I wasn't surprised by any of this, because my mother always thought my hair was too long. I'd taken to getting a haircut shortly before visiting my parents, sometimes the very morning before I boarded a plane to Florida. But that never made a difference. I could count on her telling me my hair was too long.

3   While talking to women for the book *You're Wearing THAT?: Understanding Mothers and Daughters in Conversation*, I collected a cornucopia of mothers' remarks on their daughters' hair. Many of these comments were more overtly critical than my mother's, such as "Comb your hair. The birds will make a nest in it." Some were both overt and indirect: "You did that on purpose?" Sometimes the wolf of criticism came dressed in the sheep's clothing of a compliment: "I love your hair when it's pushed back off your face," said when her daughter's hair was falling forward onto her face, or "I'm so glad you're not wearing your hair in that frumpy way anymore."

4   Sometimes it wasn't criticism that frustrated women so much as the focus on hair instead of matters the daughters thought more important. During a presidential campaign season, a journalist interviewed both candidates for president. When her mother asked, "How did it go?" she began an enthusiastic account of the interviews. "No," her mother interrupted, "I mean at the hair salon. What style did you settle on? Did you put it up or leave it down?" Another woman told me that after she appeared on television standing behind the president of the United States in a bill-signing ceremony, her mother's comment was, "I could see you didn't have time to cut your bangs."

5   I came to think of the subjects about which mothers (and daughters) were critical as the big three: hair, clothes, and weight. I always thought of them in that order, because hair was the subject of the largest number of remarks repeated to me, and, it seemed, the most unnerving.

6   Why? Why so much preoccupation with hair? I first asked myself this question years ago, while taking part in a small academic conference at which each participant—eight men and four women—gave a brief presentation. As I listened to one of the women give her talk, I was distracted by her hair, which seemed intentionally styled to render her half-blind. When she looked down to read her paper, thanks to a side part and no bangs, a curtain of hair fell clear across her face, completely covering one eye. As she read aloud, she kept reaching up to push the hair off her face, but it immediately fell right back, a result she ensured by stopping short of hooking it behind her ear. She must have believed that pinning her hair behind her ear would spoil its style.

7   After catching myself concentrating on the speaker's hair rather than her talk, I scanned the room to check out the other two women's

> **A Relevant Topic Worthy of Analysis**
> In the opening paragraphs, Tannen poses a question that she believes her readers will find worth analyzing: Why is there such preoccupation with women's hair? Her question, which grows out of her own experience as well as her observations of other women, leads to her analysis, which can be seen as part of a larger conversation about the role of gender in contemporary life.

hairstyles. One, the youngest among us, had long, frosted blond hair that cascaded over her shoulders—an effect she enhanced by frequently tossing her head. The third woman had dark brown hair in a classic style that, I thought to myself, was a cross between Cleopatra and Plain Jane.

8   Then I wondered why I was scrutinizing only the women; what about the men? A glance around the room made the answer obvious: Every one of the men had his hair cut short, in no particular style. There could have been a man with a ponytail or a thick wavy mane or long hair falling below his ears. But there wasn't. All the men had chosen neutral hairstyles. What, I asked myself, would be a comparably neutral hairstyle for a woman? Then I realized: There's no such thing.

9   I came to think of this contrast in terms of a concept from linguistics, my academic field: The men's choices were "unmarked," but any choice a woman makes is "marked"; that is, it says something about her. Here's how linguistic markedness works. The "unmarked" forms of most verbs in English communicate present tense. To communicate past tense, a speaker "marks" a verb by adding something. For example, you can take the verb *visit* and mark it for *past* by adding -ed to make *visited*. Similarly, the unmarked forms of most nouns in English are singular, such as *toy*. To make the word plural, you add -s to get *toys*. Like a present-tense verb or a singular noun, a man can have a hairstyle that is "unmarked"—that is, neutral; it doesn't tell you anything about him except that he's male. But any choice a woman makes carries extra meaning: It leads observers to conclude something about the type of person she is. That's why I titled an essay on this subject "There Is No Unmarked Woman."

10   The concept of markedness helps explain many mothers' seemingly excessive concern with so apparently superficial a topic as their daughters' hair. They are thinking of how others will interpret their daughters' character. That concern was explicit in one mother's warning that no one would take her daughter seriously if she didn't style her hair more carefully: "If they see someone with loose ends in their hair, they'll think you have loose ends in your life."

11   Mothers aren't the only ones who are inclined to be critical of women's hair (as well as their clothes and weight). Because the range of hairstyles from which a woman must

Complexity
In **paragraphs 7, 8, and 9**, Tannen begins to delve into the complexity of her seemingly straightforward question about hairstyles, indicating that the question really has to do with gender. She also introduces the concept of "linguistic markedness," which she uses as a framework for her analysis.

5

Sufficient and Appropriate Evidence and Support
In **paragraph 10** and elsewhere in her essay, Tannen relies on experiences that we all share to explore and support her main assertion. She is essentially asking her readers to think carefully about their own experiences with and views about hairstyles as evidence for her claims. Using experience in this way is not unusual in analytical writing and can be an effective way for a writer to help readers understand the analysis and to persuade them of the validity of the writer's claims.

choose is vast, the chances that anyone—especially another woman—will think she made the best choice are pretty slim. How often do you look at a woman and think, She would look better if her hair were longer, shorter, curlier, straighter, pushed back, pulled forward, colored, not colored, dyed a different color, highlighted or not, more fashionably styled, just differently styled? We think these things but we don't say them. A mother, however, often feels that she has a right if not an obligation to say something, because it's her job to ensure that things go as well as possible for her daughter.

12   There is yet another layer to all this: Women's and girls' hair (as well as clothes and weight)—indeed, the preoccupation with women's appearance more generally—is inextricably intertwined with sex. Our very notion of "woman" entails sexuality in a way that our notion of "man" does not. A woman who is not attractive is dismissed, and being deemed attractive requires being sexy—but not too sexy, because that would lead to her being dismissed in a different way. Furthermore, the line between too sexy and not sexy enough is a fine one and is located differently by different observers, so there is no way a woman can be certain of getting it just right. This criterion drives many, if not all, fashion choices: how short or long a skirt or dress should be; how tight-fitting and shape-showing slacks, tops, or dresses should be; how much skin is revealed, what body parts are glimpsed or displayed. And hair is an essential element in this sexual equation.

> **Complexity**
> In **paragraphs 11 and 12**, Tannen adds "another layer" to her analysis of our preoccupation with hairstyles: the role of sex, which complicates how people react to women's hairstyles. In this way, Tannen explores her subject's complexity and avoids oversimplified explanations.

> **Sufficient and Appropriate Evidence and Support**
> In **paragraph 12**, Tannen uses an example from the Orthodox Jewish tradition (and her own family history) to support her claim about "the connection between exposing hair and seeking to attract men."

13   Hair, in short, is a secondary sex characteristic: Like breasts and the distribution of body fat that gives women a curvy shape, more head hair (and less facial hair) is one of the physical features distinguishing the sexes that begin to appear during puberty, signaling sexual maturity. Enhancing and drawing attention to secondary sex characteristics can be a way of emphasizing sexual attractiveness. Thus, hair so abundant that it partially covers a woman's face can be sexy, and more hair can be sexier than less. That is the aesthetic that drives "big hair," and the anxiety that underlies the concept of a "bad-hair day." And that is the reason why many societies require women to cover, hide, or remove their hair. The connection between exposing hair and seeking to attract men is explicit in the Orthodox Jewish tradition by which women cut off their hair when they marry, as my grandmother did in the early 1900s Hasidic Jewish community of Warsaw. (My father was told that when his mother was having her head shaved in preparation for her wedding, her younger sisters, who had abandoned orthodoxy, pounded on the door, begging her not to let them do it; she later regretted having acquiesced and let it grow back.)

14 This tradition came to mind when I asked an Arab woman whether mothers in her country comment on their daughters' appearance. She replied that a common mother-to-daughter remonstrance would be, "I can see hair"—a way to admonish a daughter to tighten her headscarf. Though the requirement to wear headscarves might seem at first very different from the "freedom" to expose hair, these seemingly opposite customs are really two sides of the same coin, divergent ways of managing men's responses to this secondary sex characteristic: on one hand, precluding it by hiding hair; on the other, capitalizing on it by displaying hair in as alluring a style as possible.

Sufficient and Appropriate Evidence and Support
In **paragraphs 14 through to 17**, Tannen uses an anecdote support her claims about the importance women place on their hair. Anecdotes can be appropriate evidence in academic writing, but usually academic audiences expect other kinds of evidence, such as statistical data or quotations from scholarly texts (see "Supporting Claims" on pages 140–144). In this case, however, because Tannen was writing for a more general audience, she did not cite scholarly sources, which would be expected for a scholarly journal.

15 While I was working on this essay, my phone rang. It was my cousin Elaine calling. "I'm visiting my mother," she began. I was concerned, because I knew that her mother had recently been discharged from the hospital after a life-threatening illness. Elaine continued, "'What do you think was the first thing she asked me?" Still living in this essay, I offered, half-joking, "Was it about your hair?" "Yes!" she exclaimed. "That is what she asked! I had been here maybe ten minutes when she said, 'Don't you think you need a haircut?'"

16 "You won't believe this," I said, and then read her the first paragraph of this essay.

17 After we both laughed at the uncanny similarity, Elaine continued, "I'm trying to assert myself now that I'm 60, so I told her, 'I just had it cut!'" She explained that she'd made sure to do that because her mother always thinks her hair is too long. At that I read her the second paragraph of this essay.

18 After more shared laughter, Elaine resumed her account. Her mother kept returning to the topic: "Are you sure you don't think it would be better shorter?" and "We have to go to my hairdresser." Elaine capitulated: "I was in her house for less than half an hour before she was whisking me off, walker and all, to her hair salon!" But Elaine drew the line at cutting her hair; she submitted only to having it blow-dried. Then she questioned her own sanity when, upon hearing her mother say, "Now you're a pleasure to look at," she heard herself say: "Maybe it would have been better shorter."

Reasonable Conclusions
In **paragraph 18**, Tannen interprets what she has learned through her analysis. She concludes that the desire for acceptance is an important part of the reason for women's preoccupation with their hair. In analytical writing, conclusions and interpretations must be supported by available evidence.

5

19   After we laughed together, our conversation turned serious. Wondering aloud why her mother's concern with her hair bothered her so much, Elaine said, "It's a symbol of lack of acceptance." Without doubt, that's part of why we all react so strongly to perceived criticism, no matter how subtle, from our mothers—and why many of us are so quick to perceive criticism in any comment or, for that matter, gesture (like reaching out to brush hair off our faces) or facial expression ("I didn't say anything"; "But you had that look"). There is an exquisite irony—a perfect relationship storm, you might say—between daughters and mothers. Because girls and women are judged by appearance, mothers want their daughters to look as attractive as possible. But any suggestion for improvement implies criticism. And therein lies the irony: For mothers, the person to whom you most want to offer helpful suggestions is the one most likely to resist and resent them; for daughters, the person you most want to think you're perfect is the one most likely to see your flaws—and tell you about them.

20   My cousin then told me something I hadn't known: Her mother hated her own hair, because her mother had told her it was ugly. Indeed, Elaine's mother had gone to medical school to ensure she'd be able to support herself, because her mother had led her to believe she was too unattractive to count on getting married. How, Elaine wondered, could her mother not see that she was doing to her daughter just what her own mother had done to her? There are many ways to answer that question. One is that Elaine's mother wanted to make sure her daughter didn't suffer the same fate, by making sure she was attractive. Another is that she was doing what many women do: Both mothers and daughters often regard each other as reflections of themselves and consequently look at each other with a level of scrutiny that they otherwise reserve for themselves. For mothers, especially, that isn't entirely irrational: They are held responsible for their daughters in a way that fathers are not. Someone who disapproves of a girl's appearance will often think, Why did her mother let her go out looking like that?

Complexity
Tannen's analysis focuses on how gender norms influence attitudes about appearance in general and hairstyles in particular. In **paragraph 19** she examines another factor: relationships between mothers and daughters. By showing that mothers "are held responsible for their daughters in a way that fathers are not" Tannen avoids oversimplifying her analysis and shows that differences in how men and women think about hairstyles have to do with gender roles, sexuality, and familial relationships.

Reasonable Conclusions
In her final three paragraphs Tannen concludes her essay with speculation about what her analysis means for women. Notice that although she offers some advice, she qualifies it by using adverbs such as "maybe" (paragraph 20) and "perhaps" (paragraph 21), and in her brief concluding paragraph (paragraph 22) she leaves her readers with a somewhat ambiguous statement regarding her mother's criticisms of her own hairstyle (which she relates in her opening paragraph). Such ambiguity can result when a writer has carefully analyzed a complex topic and has reached no straightforward conclusions.

21　Maybe it doesn't matter what mothers' motives are. The challenge for daughters is deciding how to respond. I always chuckle when recalling the woman who told me she silenced her mother by saying, "My lifetime interest in the topic of my hair has been exhausted."

22　Or perhaps more important than figuring out what to say in response to perceived criticism is how to stop feeling bad about it. Women tell me it helps to realize that criticizing and caring are expressed in the same words. That way, a daughter can shift her focus from the criticizing to the caring. This often happens automatically after our mothers are gone, or when we fear losing them. One woman told me of getting a call that her mother had been hospitalized. Full of worry and fear, she caught a plane and rushed to the hospital right from the airport. Distressed to see her mother with an IV bag attached to her arm and an oxygen tube in her nose, she approached the bedside and leaned over to give her a kiss. Her mother looked up at her and said, "When's the last time you did your roots?" Rather than reacting with her usual annoyance, the daughter heaved a sigh of relief: Her mother was OK.

23　As for me, it is now nearly a decade since my mother died. Several years ago, I began getting my hair cut shorter. My mother was right: It does look better this way.

5

Questions to Consider:

1. How well do you think Tannen's analysis answers her main question about why women are preoccupied with hairstyles? What main factors does she identify in her analysis to help explain this preoccupation? Does her analysis sufficiently explain it, in your view? Why or why not? What might your answer to these questions suggest about you as an audience for this essay?

2. Assess Tannen's use of evidence in this essay. What kinds of evidence does she use to examine women's preoccupation with hairstyles? Why do you think she chose these specific kinds of evidence? Do you find her use of evidence persuasive? Why or why not? What other kinds of evidence might she have cited to support her claims and further her analysis?

3. What conclusions does Tannen draw from her analysis about the importance of hairstyles among women? Do you think her analysis sufficiently leads to these conclusions? Explain, citing specific passages from her essay to support your answer.

4. Tannen uses the concept of "linguistic markedness" as a framework for her analysis (see paragraph 9). What advantages do you think this framework offers her in her analysis? What conclusions about hairstyles does she draw from her use of this framework? How effective do you find her use of this framework in explaining our preoccupation with hairstyles?

MindTap
Reflect on your understanding of analytical writing.

Writing Analysis

Analysis is really a function of our curiosity about the world around us—and about ourselves. It is a means to fulfill our inherent desire to understand; to ask why; and to explain a phenomenon, trend, development, problem, or event. This section will help you develop an analytical writing project that arises from your own curiosity about something important to you. It will take you through the Ten Core Concepts to help you use analysis to answer a relevant question. Each step described here corresponds to a step described in Chapter 3.

As you develop your project, keep in mind **the four main features of effective analytical writing:**

1. **A relevant topic worthy of analysis.** Establish why it is important to understand the subject of your analysis:
   - Why would readers want to understand this event, trend, problem, or phenomenon?
   - What's at stake for them—and for you—in trying to explain this event, trend, problem, or phenomenon?
   - What makes this topic worthy of analysis now?

2. **Complexity.** Explore possible explanations and avoid settling for easy or obvious explanations:
   - What claims do you make about your subject on the basis of your analysis? How reasonable are these claims?
   - How well does your analysis explain the event, trend, problem, or phenomenon you are examining?
   - To what extent does your analysis illuminate the complexity of your subject and avoid oversimplified explanations?

3. **Sufficient information and appropriate evidence.** Gather enough information to explain the event, trend, problem, or phenomenon you are analyzing and to rule out other possible explanations:
   - Does your analysis go into sufficient depth to explain the event, trend, problem, or phenomenon you are examining?
   - What evidence do you present to support your claims? To what extent is this evidence sufficient to support your claims? What makes it appropriate for your rhetorical situation?
   - How valid and trustworthy are the sources for the evidence you provide to support your claims?

4. **Reasonable conclusions.** Present well-reasoned and persuasive conclusions on the basis of your analysis:
   - What conclusions do you draw from your analysis?
   - Do your conclusions grow logically out of your analysis?
   - To what extent do your conclusions reflect the complexity of your subject?

Step 1 Identify a topic for analysis.

Begin with a question that interests or puzzles you about something you would like to understand better. If your assignment calls for a specific topic for analysis, follow your instructor's guidelines. Otherwise, consider something that happened in your life, an important trend, or a controversial issue:

Something happening in your life	• What impact will a proposed tuition plan at your college have on student loan debt? • Why is soccer so popular among people your age? • How will your major affect your prospects in the job market?
An important trend	• How do social media affect voting habits among college students? • What are the advantages and disadvantages of online classes? • How should people manage their online identities on social media?
A controversial issue	• Should the minimum wage be raised? • Does illegal immigration hurt the U.S. economy? • Are trigger warnings a violation of free speech rights?

Develop this question using Step #1 in Chapter 3.

Step 2 Place your topic in rhetorical context.

Your question should be interesting to you but also be relevant for your intended audience or your course assignment. Consult your assignment guidelines for information about the specified audience for your assignment. If no audience is specified, address the following questions:

- Who would be interested in this topic? Why would they be interested in it?

- What makes this topic important now? What would an analysis that addresses this topic mean for this audience?

- What purpose would be served by analyzing this issue, trend, phenomenon, or problem? What can be learned from such an analysis?

Using your answers to these questions as a guide, follow the steps for Step #2 in Chapter 3.

Step 3 Select a medium.

An effective analysis can be presented in any medium, although most academic analyses will be presented in the form of a conventional essay.

If your assignment specifies a medium	Use the medium specified in the assignment guidelines.	Focus on how this medium enables you to present your analysis effectively.
If you have a choice of medium	Consider which medium best addresses your intended audience.	Focus on how your choice of medium best accomplishes your rhetorical goals.

For example, imagine that you want to analyze the advantages and disadvantages of online classes, which are growing in popularity. Consider how your intended audience and rhetorical purpose might influence your selection of a medium for your analysis:

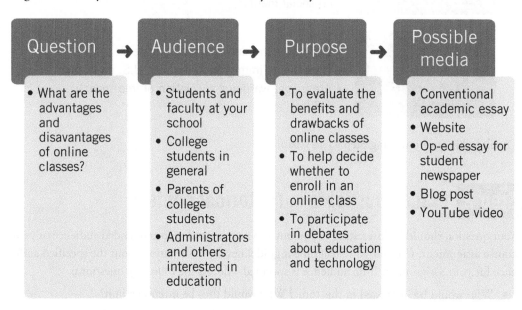

Question	Audience	Purpose	Possible media
• What are the advantages and disavantages of online classes?	• Students and faculty at your school • College students in general • Parents of college students • Administrators and others interested in education	• To evaluate the benefits and drawbacks of online classes • To help decide whether to enroll in an online class • To participate in debates about education and technology	• Conventional academic essay • Website • Op-ed essay for student newspaper • Blog post • YouTube video

Consider the advantages and drawbacks of each possible medium in light of your intended audience and purpose: Which medium will most effectively present your analysis to your intended audience?

Step #3 in Chapter 3 provides additional advice to help you decide on an appropriate medium for your analysis.

Step 4 Identify your main claim.

Your analysis should lead to one or more claims about whatever you're analyzing—claims that address your main question from Step #1. For example,

Question: What are the advantages and disadvantages of online classes?

Analysis: Online classes provide flexibility and access to college for some students; some students excel in self-paced learning environments, whereas others struggle; students with certain learning styles benefit from traditional face-to-face classes.

Claim: Online classes provide effective learning opportunities for many students but might not be the best choice for students with certain learning styles.

Question: Should the minimum wage be raised?

Analysis: Workers in certain low-wage jobs will benefit; small businesses might be hurt; some low-wage workers could lose their jobs; living wage can improve social conditions for many workers; social service costs can be reduced.

Claim: Increasing the minimum wage will likely affect workers differently, depending upon the nature of their jobs, but might benefit more workers in the long run.

5

In each of these examples the writer's task is to analyze the topic to try to answer the main question. To put it differently, the writer develops an analysis that leads to a main claim about his or her subject.

At this point, you probably won't know exactly what your main claim (or claims) will be because you are still investigating your topic and don't yet know what your analysis will reveal. As you research your topic and better understand the subject you are analyzing, your claim(s) might evolve. But at this point, your main question should suggest possible claims, and you probably have some idea of what you might find as you continue to research your topic. So begin there:

- What claims do you expect to make about your main question?

- What do you expect to find as you investigate your topic?

- What are the possible answers to your main question, based on what you know at this point?

Complete Step #4 in Chapter 3 to develop a Guiding Thesis Statement, which is essentially a statement of the main claim(s) you expect to make in your analysis. As you develop your Guiding Thesis Statement, address the following questions:

How does your claim address the question you identified for Step #1?

Why will this claim matter to your intended audience? How will it contribute to ongoing discussions about the trend, problem, phenomenon, or issue you are analyzing?

How will your claim help your audience understand the problem, phenomenon, trend, or event you are analyzing?

Step 5 Support your claim(s).

At this point, you should be well into your research. As you explore your topic, keep in mind that you are trying to understand what you are analyzing so that you can address your main question and achieve your rhetorical purpose. Your claims and support will develop through this process of inquiry. In addition to your main claim, your analysis will likely result in several supporting claims. These claims might change as you learn more about your topic.

Let's return to the question we posed earlier,

What are the advantages and disadvantages of online classes?

On the basis of your research so far, you develop your main claim:

Online classes provide effective learning opportunities for many students but might not be the best choice for students with specific learning styles.

This claim is based on what you have learned so far through your research about online classes. This research would likely lead to several supporting claims:

- *Online classes offer students flexibility in scheduling.*
- *Online classes are convenient and don't require a student's physical presence on campus, making it easier for some students to attend college.*
- *Some students thrive in the self-paced learning environment of an online class.*
- *Some students' learning styles make online learning less effective for them.*

- *Face-to-face classes offer some advantages, such as instantaneous feedback from an instructor and multiple opportunities for student-to-student interactions, that are not necessarily available in online classes.*
- *Colleges can save costs by offering more online classes.*

These supporting claims essentially build your case for and elaborate on your main claim. For each of these claims, you will need to provide evidence or reasoning. To do so, complete Step #5 in Chapter 3, supplementing it with the following steps:

1. List what you have learned about your topic.	• Online classes offer flexibility in scheduling. • Online classes don't require travel to campus. • Some students thrive in a self-paced learning environment. • Students with certain learning styles struggle in online classes. • Colleges can save money by offering online classes.
2. Determine whether each item on your list helps support your main claim(s); eliminate items that don't.	• Bulleted items 1-4 in #1 support the main claim. • The last bulleted item in #1 is not necessarily relevant to the focus of this project, which is on students, so eliminate it.
3. Identify the reasoning, information, and/or sources that support each item on your list.	• Studies documenting the learning outcomes of online classes • Statistical data (e.g., income level, age, work status) about students who benefit from the convenience of online classes • Testimonials from students about their experiences in online classes
4. Determine whether your information, reasoning, and sources are sufficient for each item.	• Are the studies sufficient to show the impact of online classes on different kinds of students? • Do the studies and related data present a relatively comprehensive picture of online education? • Are the student testimonials representative or biased?

5

Expect to make adjustments in your claims as you learn more through your research. If necessary, revise your claims. That's part of the process of inquiry. For example, on the basis of your research into the convenience of online learning as a major factor in its popularity, as well as your investigation of learning styles, you might amend your main claim as follows:

Online classes provide learning opportunities and convenience for many students who might otherwise not have access to college, but these classes might not offer an effective learning environment for students with certain learning styles.

Do the same for each supporting claim, if necessary.

At this point you are probably ready to write a complete draft of your project. If not, move to the next step before completing your draft.

Step 6 Organize your analysis.

How you organize an analysis depends on what you determine is the most logical and effective way of presenting it to your intended audience to achieve your rhetorical purpose. One common approach is to organize your analysis according to your main claim(s) and supporting claims. The key is to arrange your claims and the evidence for each claim in a way that presents your analysis clearly and persuasively to your audience.

For example, in our hypothetical analysis of online classes, your main claim is

Online classes provide learning opportunities and convenience for many students who might otherwise not have access to college, but these classes might not offer an effective learning environment for students with certain learning styles.

Let's say you have identified the following four amended supporting claims:

- *Online classes offer flexibility and convenience for students who might not otherwise have easy access to college.*
- *Some students thrive in the self-paced learning environment of an online class.*
- *Certain learning styles make online learning less effective for some students.*
- *Face-to-face classes offer some advantages, such as instantaneous feedback from an instructor and multiple opportunities for student-to-student interactions that are not necessarily available in online classes.*

You can structure your project around these claims. Follow these steps:

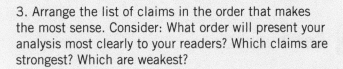

1. For each main claim, list any supporting claims.

2. Identify your evidence for each supporting claim.

3. Arrange the list of claims in the order that makes the most sense. Consider: What order will present your analysis most clearly to your readers? Which claims are strongest? Which are weakest?

4. Create an outline with each main section of your project devoted to a supporting claim.

Such an outline might look like this:

I. Introduction
    A. The growth of online classes in colleges and universities
    B. Questions about the benefits and drawbacks of online classes

II. Background
    A. Historical background on online education
    B. Background information on the recent growth of online classes
    C. The appeal of online classes for colleges, faculty, and students
    D. Concerns about online education

III. Main Claims
    A. Online classes provide greater access to college for some students.
        1. Flexibility in scheduling
        2. Convenience
    B. Some students thrive in the self-paced learning environment of an online class.
        1. Results of studies of effectiveness of online learning
        2. Student testimonials
    C. Certain learning styles make online learning less effective for some students.
        1. Studies of learning styles and online classes
        2. Student testimonials
    D. Face-to-face classes offer advantages unavailable in online classes.
        1. Studies of traditional and online classes
        2. Student and faculty testimonials

IV. Conclusion

This approach to organizing an analytical project is straightforward and flexible, but it is not the only option. Refer to your rhetorical situation to guide your decisions about form. Step #6 in Chapter 3 provides additional guidance for organizing your project.

If you have already written a rough draft, revise it according to your outline. If you have not yet written a rough draft, do so now, using your outline as a guide. Remember that as you write your draft, you might need to do additional research and adjust your claims accordingly (see Step #5 above).

Step 7   Get feedback.

Use the following sets of questions to focus the feedback you receive on the main characteristics of analytical writing:

A relevant topic worthy of analysis	• What is the main point of the analysis? Is it clear? • What makes this analysis relevant to the intended audience? • What rationale does the writer provide for examining this topic now?
Complexity	• To what extent does the analysis explain the topic? • Is the topic examined in sufficient depth? • What important factors or issues might need to be more fully examined? What alternative explanations might be explored?
Appropriate and sufficient support	• What evidence is presented to support the main claims? • How well does this evidence support the writer's claims? Is the support sufficient and persuasive? • What makes these sources appropriate for this rhetorical situation? • What evidence or support might be unnecessary?
Reasonable conclusions	• What conclusions does the writer draw from the analysis? • How do these conclusions grow out of the analysis? • Are the conclusions presented clearly and persuasively? • Do the conclusions adequately sum up the analysis and emphasize the main points of the project?

Step #7 in Chapter 3 provides additional guidance for getting helpful feedback on your draft.

Step 8 | Revise.

In analytical writing, revision is largely a matter of refining your analysis and making it understandable to your readers without sacrificing complexity. The preceding steps helped you delve more deeply into your topic to expose its complexity. Now you have to manage that complexity—for yourself and for your readers. That process might also mean clarifying for yourself what your analysis reveals and identifying more clearly the implications of your analysis in view of your rhetorical situation. At this point, then, your primary task is twofold:

1. Determine what you have learned from your analysis.

2. Sharpen the focus of your project so that your analysis is presented appropriately for your intended audience.

Address the following questions about your draft as you work through Step #8 in Chapter 3:

A relevant topic worthy of analysis	• What is the purpose of your analysis? How might you refine the main questions you are addressing to accurately reflect that purpose? • What makes your analysis relevant? What are you trying to say as a result of your analysis?
Complexity	• How does your analysis address the question(s) you pose in your project? • What are your main claims? Are they clearly presented? • How does your analysis avoid oversimplifying your topic? • Which sections of your analysis might need further explanation? Which might be unnecessary?
Appropriate and sufficient support	• What evidence do you offer to support your main claims? • Which claims might need additional evidence? • Which evidence or support, if any, can you eliminate without weakening your analysis? • What makes your sources appropriate for your topic and rhetorical situation?
Reasonable conclusions	• How do your conclusions address your main question? • Have you presented your conclusions clearly? • Which key issues might you have overlooked in your conclusions?

5

Review your draft with these sets of questions in mind and revise accordingly.

Step 9 Refine your voice.

The essay by Deborah Tannen in this chapter (page 145) illustrates the power of a writer's voice in an analysis. For example, notice how Tannen uses her own experience as a way to engage her readers, but at the same time she retains an air of authority about her subject. Your goal at this point is to revise your draft to strengthen your distinctive voice and convey a sense of authority about your topic. The advice provided in Step #9 in Chapter 3 will help you do so. Keep in mind that your voice helps establish your credibility and therefore is a factor in making your analysis persuasive to your intended audience. In addition, your voice can be strengthened by your own confidence in your analysis. If you feel confident that you have sufficiently explored the problem, trend, phenomenon, or issue you have analyzed, your voice is likely to reflect that confidence.

Step 10 Edit.

Complete Step #10 in Chapter 3. For an analysis, be especially careful about syntax problems that can result from your efforts to explain or summarize complicated ideas.

WRITING PROJECTS | ANALYSIS

1. Identify a controversial proposal in your region. Consider these examples:
   - Your governor has proposed a new tax cut that has provoked controversy among politicians and voters.
   - Your local government has proposed a ban on skateboarding in public areas such as parks and library parking lots.
   - Your college is considering a proposal for a new general education curriculum that would affect all students.

   Write an analysis of the potential impact of the proposal. Identify an appropriate audience for your analysis (e.g., students on your campus) and a medium that would best reach that audience.

2. If you have made an important decision recently, analyze the effect of that decision in your life. For example, perhaps you decided to attend a two-year college instead of a four-year college. Or you might have joined the U.S. military before attending college. For an audience of your classmates, write an essay in which you analyze the factors that led to your decision and the effects of that decision on important aspects of your life. Consider presenting your analysis in a medium other than a conventional essay that might be appropriate for your intended audience.

3. Identify a technological development that is changing the way we live. For example:
   - Social media have influenced many different aspects of our social and political lives.
   - Wireless devices such as smartphones have changed how we communicate and conduct business.
   - Online shopping has affected what goods we buy and how we buy them.

Analyze such a technological development, comparing how we do things now as a result of this development to how we did them in the past. For your project, identify a specific audience and select a medium that would most effectively reach that audience.

4. Many people use websites when planning vacations. Identify several online resources such as TripAdvisor and Lonely Planet and use them to plan a trip you would like to take. Read reviews of the place you wish to visit and develop an itinerary for a three-night/four-day trip that includes travel, sightseeing, meals, hotel/resort stay, and so on. Then write an analysis of the online resources you used to plan your trip. Evaluate the information provided on those sites and draw conclusions about their usefulness in helping you with your planning. Present your analysis in the form of a website, Prezi, or other kind of multimedia document.

5. Analyze several different television or Internet advertisements for the same kind of product, identifying which are most effective in addressing their intended audiences. For example, select several ads for different brands of cars or smartphones. On the basis of your analysis, draw conclusions about what strategies, especially visual strategies, work best in this kind of advertisement.

6. Select a popular film, TV show, or novel and analyze its appeal. What makes this work popular? What does this work have to say about a relevant or controversial topic? What insights does the author of this work present to his or her audience? Address these questions in your analysis and draw conclusions about why this work appeals to its audience.

5

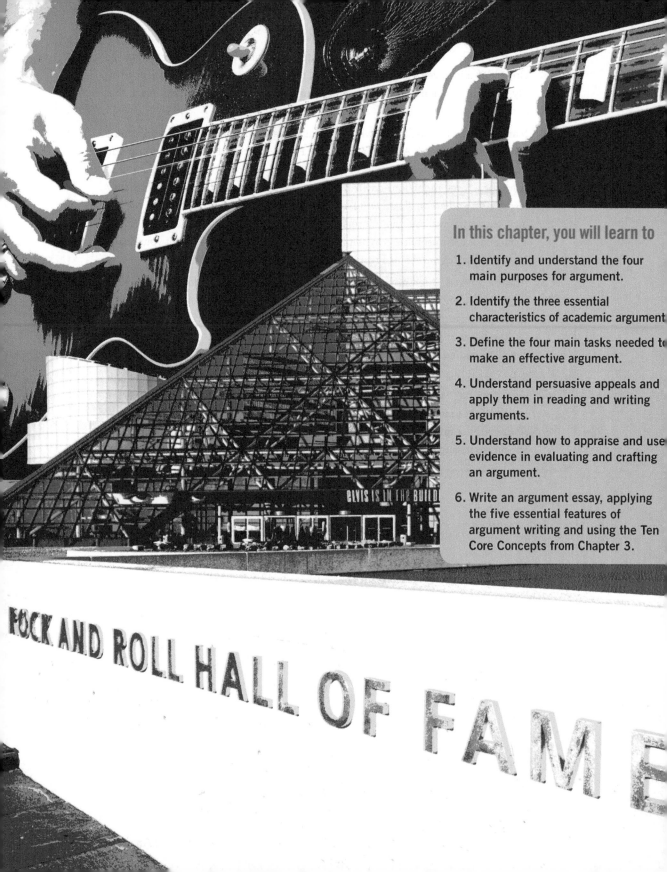

In this chapter, you will learn to

1. Identify and understand the four main purposes for argument.

2. Identify the three essential characteristics of academic argument

3. Define the four main tasks needed to make an effective argument.

4. Understand persuasive appeals and apply them in reading and writing arguments.

5. Understand how to appraise and use evidence in evaluating and crafting an argument.

6. Write an argument essay, applying the five essential features of argument writing and using the Ten Core Concepts from Chapter 3.

ELVIS IS IN THE BUILD

ROCK AND ROLL HALL OF FAME

Understanding Argument 6

I HAVE A POLICY in my classes allowing students to challenge their grades on any writing assignment. But I tell them that if they believe the grade is unfair, they must explain why and make a case for a higher grade. They must present some kind of evidence or reasoning that the grade they received does not reflect the quality of their writing for that assignment. It is not enough, I tell them, to claim that they should be rewarded for working hard on the assignment. Show me why the essay deserves a higher grade, I tell them. In other words, make a valid and convincing argument.

Even if you have never challenged a grade on an assignment, you probably make informal arguments to support a position, defend an opinion, oppose a plan, or convince someone to do something:

- to explain why a band should be honored by the Rock and Roll Hall of Fame
- to justify a decision to pursue a particular major or attend a specific college
- to express your support for a political candidate
- to convince a roommate to move to a different apartment
- to support your decision to use a certain kind of smartphone

We routinely engage in informal argumentation as we make decisions about important matters, small or large, in our lives.

You have probably also made more formal arguments that involve specific kinds of writing. In your college application essay, for example, you tried to convince the college admissions office that you deserved to be accepted into that school. Or perhaps you have posted messages to your college Facebook page in favor of a proposed new student center. In such cases, you are making an argument not only to take a stand on an issue (for example, to express support for the proposed student center because it will benefit students in a variety of ways and help create a better campus community), but also to achieve a goal or work toward a particular outcome (for example, to help make the proposed student center a reality). Argument, then, is not simply a matter of stating and supporting a position; it is also a way to participate in discussions about important issues, to address complicated situations, and to solve problems. It is a central part of how we live together.

In academic disciplines, argument is an essential means by which ideas are explored and understanding is advanced (see Focus: "Argument vs. Persuasion" on page 166). Writing effective arguments is an important component of college-level academic work.

Often, we make arguments to try to persuade someone to adopt a point of view, agree to a proposition, or take a course of action. But the goal of argumentation is not necessarily to persuade. Especially in academic contexts, argument is intended to advance understanding. Persuasion, by contrast, does not necessarily engage an audience in a dialogue about an issue; rather, persuasion is an attempt to convince the audience to think or feel a certain way. The distinction is similar to the difference between an advertisement intended to persuade consumers to purchase a specific product, such as this magazine ad for Nestlé, and one designed to present a point of view on an issue, such as this public service ad about plastic bottles. The Nestlé ad seeks to persuade consumers to purchase its brand of bottled water. By contrast, the public service ad can be seen as making an argument in favor of drinking tap water rather than bottled water, which, the ad suggests, contributes to environmental damage; if the ad seeks to persuade viewers to act in a certain way (that is, to drink tap water instead of bottled water), it does so by making a convincing argument that drinking tap water is a good idea, in part by educating the reader about the potential environmental impact of the plastic used for bottled water.

Last year, plastic bottles generated more than 2.5 million tons of carbon dioxide. Drink tap. Tappening.com.

Occasions for Argument

We engage in argument for four main reasons:

- to solve a problem
- to assert a position
- to inquire into an issue or problem
- to prevail

Arguments to Solve a Problem

In much argumentation, the parties involved address a problem in which they have a shared interest. Let's return, for example, to my course policy of allowing my students to argue for a better grade on a writing assignment. A student's purpose in making such an argument is pretty clear: he or she wants to earn a good grade and demonstrate the ability to write the kind of essay required by the assignment. By the same token, as the instructor, I have an interest in seeing that the student can complete the assignment successfully. I also want the grades I assign to motivate students to develop their writing skills. So our purposes overlap, and we both have a stake in a positive outcome to the argument. Ultimately, "winning" the argument doesn't necessarily help us achieve that outcome. The student's argument, then, is part of an effort to solve a problem: to assign a fair grade to an essay about which we seem to have different opinions. The argument for a better grade can result in our collaborative effort to reconsider how successfully the essay meets the assignment guidelines. In the process, the argument can be a way to help both of us better understand the essay so that it can be evaluated fairly.

The need to solve a problem is perhaps the most common occasion for making an argument:

- Members of a student organization decide whether to spend surplus funds on new equipment.
- Community residents debate whether to increase property taxes to build a much-needed new school building.
- Parents and school officials debate the best measures for increasing safety at their elementary school.

In each of these examples, the parties argue to solve a problem in which they all have an interest. The purpose of the argument is to achieve the best possible solution.

Arguments to Assert a Position

Some situations call for arguments in which the primary goal is to assert and justify a position:

- in a meeting of a student organization that is considering whether to boycott local stores that sell goods produced in sweatshops
- in a class discussion about legalizing same-sex marriage
- in a debate about whether to invite a controversial speaker to campus
- in a public forum to discuss whether to arm campus police

In such situations, many voices may be heard. To make an argument that asserts your position effectively can contribute to a discussion of important issues and help you gain credibility as a thoughtful participant. Your argument can enhance others' understanding of an issue and influence what they think about it.

Arguments to Inquire

In arguments about complex issues, writers often try to discover the best of many possible answers to the question or problem at hand. In such cases, the primary purpose of the argument is to understand the issue better:

- A debate about a new general education requirement enables both supporters and opponents to delve into broader questions about the purposes of a college education.
- In a controversy about whether law enforcement agencies should have access to private data on smartphones, participants examine the tension between privacy and safety.
- A proposal to moderate comments posted to a popular social media site leads to a debate about free speech and ethical behavior in online forums.

In such situations, writers make arguments as part of a careful inquiry into the issues. In this kind of argument, the writer's position emerges through that inquiry. Through the process of developing an argument, the writer discovers the most reasonable position for himself or herself. Others might reach a different conclusion, because different people can have different but reasonable positions about complex issues. Because the writer isn't trying to win the debate, he or she examines many different viewpoints before arriving at a conclusion. The goal is to understand the issue and make an effective argument to share that understanding with interested others.

Arguments to Prevail

Sometimes there is a compelling reason for trying to win an argument, and the writer's primary purpose is to prevail over opposing points of view. Such cases often involve important and controversial issues that can have a big impact on those involved:

- Students make a strong case against allowing a controversial anti-immigrant organization to demonstrate on campus.
- Members of a law enforcement organization argue against the state's adoption of "stand your ground" self-defense laws, which they believe lead to more gun violence.
- A resident strenuously opposes a town bill restricting gas drilling on the grounds that it will deprive residents of much-needed income.

In such cases, the goal is not only to oppose something but to convince others to oppose it so that it doesn't happen. The writer of an argument in such situations believes strongly that his or her position is right.

Arguments to prevail should be undertaken with a strong sense of ethical responsibility (see Focus: "The Ethics of Argument"). Trying to defeat an opponent in an argument for the sake of winning serves little purpose and could have negative consequences for all parties. In some cases, however, the writer might conclude that the issue is such that the ends justify the means and making a forceful argument meant to prevail is not only ethical but also necessary.

FOCUS   THE ETHICS OF ARGUMENT

Because argument has the power to persuade others to adopt a belief or take an action, often on matters of great importance, writers have a responsibility to engage in argumentation in an honorable manner. An argument should always be informed by a desire to seek truth or find a course of action that is morally justifiable—not to achieve self-serving, questionable, or illicit ends. A famous example of argument used for immoral purposes is Adolph Hitler's argument that anti-Jewish legislation in Germany in the 1930s was necessary to protect Germany from communism and to protect Jews from further persecution. But argument can be used for dubious purposes in much less dramatic contexts. For example, you might argue in favor of a proposed change in your major because the change will make it easier for you to graduate early, even though you believe that the change will weaken the curriculum and is probably not a good idea for most students. In such a case, you would be making an argument of questionable ethical merit. To make an ethical argument in such circumstances, you would have to acknowledge your own self-interest. In short, effective argument can be turned to honorable or questionable purposes, even in school assignments. Always consider whether the argument you are making is not only sound but also ethical.

These four purposes for argument can overlap, of course. For example, in an argument to prevail, the writer usually asserts a position, and it is often necessary to inquire before you can solve a problem. So an argument can address several purposes at once. But understanding these four main purposes can help you construct arguments that effectively meet the needs of specific rhetorical situations.

6

EXERCISE 6A   EXPLORING OCCASIONS FOR ARGUMENT

1. Identify an issue or problem that you feel strongly about. It might be a national or international issue (a human rights issue, for example) or a local issue (a controversy on your campus or in your town). Write an informal statement explaining your position on the issue. Now consider three arguments you might make about the issue. Write a brief synopsis of each argument and explain why it matters to you.

2. Find an argument on a topic you care about in a newspaper, a blog post, a magazine article, a pamphlet, something you read in a course, or a YouTube video. Summarize the main argument. Now consider what makes the argument relevant to you and others. In a brief paragraph, describe what you believe was the writer's main purpose in making the argument.

3. Take the issue you wrote about for Question #1 or #2 (or identify another issue of importance to you) and imagine a situation in which you could write an argument on that issue for each of the main purposes described in this section (to solve a problem, to inquire, to assert, to prevail). In a brief paragraph for each purpose, describe the rhetorical situation (including the audience and the form of your argument).

Understanding Argument in College

Argumentation in college is primarily about learning. As a student, you will engage in argumentative writing not only to sharpen your writing and thinking skills but also to understand your subject better. In fact, research indicates that a majority of writing assignments in college require argument of some kind. In some academic disciplines, such as economics and related social sciences, *most* writing involves argumentation, and many common forms of writing in college, such as proposals and lab reports, are actually specialized forms of argumentation.

Because argument is an essential part of the process by which scholars examine, share, debate, and promote ideas, information, and opinions about important topics or developments in their fields, it is a primary vehicle for advancing knowledge. Not surprisingly, then, academic argumentation often takes the form of arguments to inquire. An assignment in a philosophy course, for example, might ask students to take a position on a classic philosophical issue, such as the nature of reality or truth. In such an assignment, the goal isn't to prove a point but to inquire deeply into a complex question that philosophers have debated for centuries. In doing so, students learn what philosophers say about such questions as they develop their own ideas about those questions; at the same time, students learn how to engage in philosophical inquiry and argumentation.

Although the purpose of most academic argumentation is inquiry, arguments in different academic disciplines can have different characteristics. For example, a philosopher relies on logical reasoning to support a proposition about the morality of capital punishment, whereas a criminologist draws on crime statistics to make an argument about the impact of capital punishment on violent crime. Writing effective academic arguments requires understanding the conventions that govern argumentation in the discipline in which you are writing. Although a philosopher and a criminologist might each make an argument about the same subject (capital punishment), they will make different kinds of claims, use different kinds of evidence, and present their arguments in different ways.

Despite these differences, all effective argumentative writing shares **three essential characteristics**:

1. a clear main point that is relevant for the academic discipline in which the writer is writing

2. appropriate support for claims

3. shared assumptions or premises as a basis for the main argument

The following examples illustrate these essential characteristics.

In the opening paragraphs of an essay titled "Why We Won't See Any Public Universities Going Private," education scholar John D. Wiley introduces his argument by identifying a relevant problem (reduced state funding for public universities) and a solution that others have proposed (turning public universities into private ones). Wiley then clearly states his main thesis: that solution won't work.

> All around the country the story is the same: States are reducing taxpayer support for public higher education, offsetting those reductions with higher tuition. Using Wisconsin as an example, Table 15.1 illustrates the changes over the last 25 years. In some states, the changes have been even more dramatic; in others, less so. But the trend is essentially universal. Furthermore, the impacts of these changes vary, even within one

state. At UW-Madison (the flagship institution of the UW System), for example, state appropriations constituted 43.1 percent and tuition 10.5 percent of our budget in 1975. Today, those numbers are 19.5 and 15.7 percent, respectively. To make matters worse, nearly one-third of our state revenue comes to us with constraints requiring us to return it to the state for specific costs such as our share of the state utility bills, debt service, and mandatory payments to state agencies. Even if we were able to economize or find superior alternatives in any of those areas, we would not be able to reallocate the savings for other purposes. As a result, the state is providing only 13.5 percent of our base operating budget—the budget for hiring faculty and staff, and covering infrastructure and operating costs beyond debt service and utility bills. For the first time in the history of the institution, our students are contributing more to this portion of our operating budget than are the state taxpayers.

TABLE 15.1 The Changing Mix of State Funding and Tuition at the University of Wisconsin (UW) System over the Last 25 Years		
	1974–1975	2004–2005
State appropriations for UW-System per $1000 of personal income	$12.50	$5.50
State appropriations for UW-System as a share of total state spending	11.5%	3.9%
State appropriations for UW-System per FTE student (2004 dollars)	$10,600	$7,400
State appropriations for UW-System as a percent of UW-System budget	49.50%	26%
Tuition as a percent of UW-System budget	12%	21%

6

Viewing these trends, many faculty, alumni, newspaper editors, and even legislators have urged us to consider "going private." By that, they have in mind that we could agree to forego all state support in our base operating budget and rely on increased tuition, coupled with some unspecified amount of additional student financial aid (what they assume to be "the private model" of high tuition and high financial aid) for ongoing operations . These views are often expressed in terms of a comparison: "You're way underpriced at a resident tuition of $6000/year. I'm paying three times that for my daughter's tuition at (at a private school), and the education she's getting is certainly not three times better. Even if you simply doubled your tuition, you would still be a bargain, and you would replace nearly all state funds. What's the problem?" Quite aside from political considerations (unwillingness of state to "let go" of prior investments and ongoing oversight), the larger problem is that the "private model," properly understood, simply cannot be scaled up to the extent required. It's a matter of simple arithmetic, and the numbers just don't work!

Source: Wiley, John D. "Why We Won't See Any Public Universities Going Private." *What's Happening to Public Higher Education?* edited by Ronald G. Ehrenberg, American Council on Education / Praeger, 2006, pp. 327–28.

In setting up his argument, Wiley makes two important moves. First, he places his argument in the context of ongoing debates about the rising cost of college. In doing so, Wiley establishes that his topic is one that his readers (other education scholars as well as policymakers and interested citizens) are likely to find relevant. Second, he supports his claims with evidence that his readers are likely to find appropriate and persuasive. Wiley claims that public support for higher education has diminished dramatically in the past three decades, and he cites statistical evidences to show the reduction in public funding for higher education, using Wisconsin as an example of a national trend.

Wiley's argument is a good example of an academic argument whose main purpose is to inquire into a complex and important issue. The next excerpt is also an argument whose primary purpose is to inquire into a complex educational issue—in this case, whether or not raising educational standards actually improves student learning. In making their argument, the authors address a well-established problem in education: the challenge of improving learning for all students. Specifically, they examine whether formative assessment—that is, assessment designed to help students learn rather than to measure how much they have learned—can result in higher educational standards for students. Like the previous example, this argument is addressed to an academic audience (education researchers) as well as a wider audience (policymakers, politicians, and the interested public). In this excerpt, which is taken from a longer essay published in a leading education journal called the *Phi Delta Kappan*, the authors introduce their main claims, summarize their argument, and explain the evidence they will present to support their claims:

> We start from the self-evident proposition that teaching and learning must be interactive. Teachers need to know about their pupils' progress and difficulties with learning so that they can adapt their own work to meet pupils' needs--needs that are often unpredictable and that vary from one pupil to another. Teachers can find out what they need to know in a variety of ways, including observation and discussion in the classroom and the reading of pupils' written work. . . .
>
> There is nothing new about any of this. All teachers make assessments in every class they teach. But there are three important questions about this process that we seek to answer:
>
> - Is there evidence that improving formative assessment raises standards?
> - Is there evidence that there is room for improvement?
> - Is there evidence about how to improve formative assessment?

In setting out to answer these questions, we have conducted an extensive survey of the research literature. We have checked through many books and through the past nine years' worth of issues of more than 160 journals, and we have studied earlier reviews of research. This process yielded about 580 articles or chapters to study. We prepared a lengthy review, using material from 250 of these sources, that has been published in a special issue of the journal *Assessment in Education*, together with comments on our work by leading educational experts from Australia, Switzer land, Hong Kong, Lesotho, and the U.S.

The conclusion we have reached from our research review is that the answer to each of the three questions above is clearly yes. In the three main sections below, we outline the nature and force of the evidence that justifies this conclusion. However, because we are presenting a summary here, our text will appear strong on assertions and weak on the details of their justification. We maintain that these assertions are backed by evidence and that this backing is set out in full detail in the lengthy review on which this article is founded.

We believe that the three sections below establish a strong case that governments, their agencies, school authorities, and the teaching profession should study very carefully whether they are seriously interested in raising standards in education. However, we also acknowledge widespread evidence that fundamental change in education can be achieved only slowly—through programs of professional development that build on existing good practice. Thus we do not conclude that formative assessment is yet another "magic bullet" for education. The issues involved are too complex and too closely linked to both the difficulties of classroom practice and the beliefs that drive public policy. In a final section, we confront this complexity and try to sketch out a strategy for acting on our evidence.

Source: Black, Paul and Dylan Wiliam. "Inside the Black Box: Raising Standards Through Classroom Assessment." *Phi Delta Kappan*, vol. 80, no. 1, 1998, p. 138.

6

Notice that the authors rest their main argument on the "proposition that teaching and learning must be interactive," a premise that their readers are likely to accept. In effective argumentation, writers must establish clear premises from which to make their arguments, thereby identifying key assumptions or beliefs that they share with their readers as a basis for their argument.

In the following section we will examine how to construct arguments that have these three essential characteristics to meet the needs of specific rhetorical situations.

EXERCISE 6B   **EXPLORING ACADEMIC ARGUMENT**

For each of the following excerpts identify (a) the main point and (b) the evidence or support provided for the author's claims. The first excerpt is taken from an essay about gun control written soon after a gunman seriously wounded U.S. Congresswoman Gabrielle Giffords and killed others attending a political rally in Arizona in 2011. The second is from a report issued by an environmental organization about the growth of the local food movement. How well do you think the authors of each excerpt present and support their claims? Cite specific passages from the excerpts to support your answer.

(Continued)

1. Against the horrific backdrop of the Tucson, Arizona, tragedy, new gun control proposals are on the way. Some of our legislators will be tempted to apply Rahm Emanuel's aphorism, "Never let a good crisis go to waste." For example, Rep. Carolyn McCarthy, D-New York, wants to outlaw magazines with more than 10 rounds—even those already in circulation. She hasn't explained how a ban on previously sold magazines would deter anyone but law-abiding citizens.

   Still, the Supreme Court has suggested that sensible gun regulations may be constitutionally permissible. Sensible is not, however, what we have in Washington, Chicago, New York and other cities, where you can probably get a pizza delivery before a response from a 911 call. Police cannot be everywhere. . . . A regulation must be effective in promoting public safety, when weighed against reliable evidence that past restrictions have not lessened the incidence of gun-related crimes.

   Recall that Washington banned handguns for 33 years; during some of those years the city was known as the nation's murder capital. Killers not deterred by laws against murder were not deterred by laws against owning guns. Moreover, anti-gun regulations did not address the deep-rooted causes of violent crime—illegitimacy, drugs, alcohol abuse and dysfunctional schools—much less mental instability.

   In 2004, the National Academy of Sciences reviewed 253 journal articles, 99 books and 43 government publications evaluating 80 gun-control measures. Researchers could not identify a single regulation that reduced violent crime, suicide or accidents. A year earlier, the Centers for Disease Control reported on ammunition bans, restrictions on acquisition, waiting periods, registration, licensing, child access prevention and zero tolerance laws. CDC's conclusion: There was no conclusive evidence that the laws reduced gun violence.

   So much for the quasi-religious faith that more controls mean fewer murders. There are about 500,000 gun-related crimes annually in the United States. Further, Americans own roughly 250 million guns. Assuming a different gun is used in each of the 500,000 crimes, only 0.2% of guns are involved in crime each year. A ban on firearms would be 99.8% over-inclusive.

   Source: Levy, Robert A. "Gun Control Measures Don't Stop Violence." *CNN*, Cable News Network, 19 Jan. 2011, www.cnn.com/2011/OPINION/01/18/levy.anti.gun.control/.

2. The system of long-distance food supply has now become the norm in much of the United States and the rest of the world. Apples in Des Moines supermarkets are from China, even though there are apple farmers in Iowa; potatoes in Lima's supermarkets are from the United States, even though Peru boasts more varieties of potato than any other country. Today, our food travels farther than ever before, often thousands of kilometers. The value of international trade in food has tripled since 1961, while the tonnage of food shipped between countries has grown fourfold, during a time when the human population only doubled. (See Figures 1 and 2.)

FIGURE 1

Value of World Agricultural Trade, 1961–2000

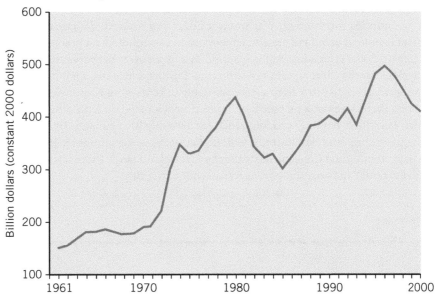

Source: Trade value and volume from United Nations Food and Agriculture Organization, FAOSTAT Statistics Database, at http://apps.fao.org, updated 4 July 2002.

FIGURE 2

Volume of World Agricultural Trade, 1961–2000

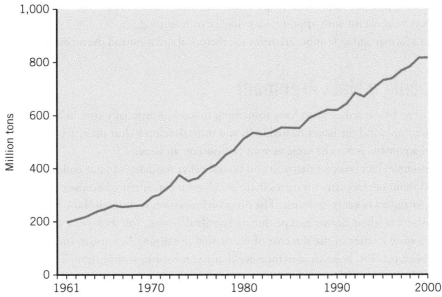

Source: Trade value and volume from United Nations Food and Agriculture Organization, FAOSTAT Statistics Database, at http://apps.fao.org, updated 4 July 2002.

(Continued)

But, as with many trends that carry serious social and ecological consequences, the long-distance food habit is slowly beginning to weaken, under the influence of a young, but surging, local foods movement in the Midatlantic and elsewhere. Politicians and voters in the counties surrounding Washington, D.C., have supported aggressive measures to protect farmland using tax credits, conservation easements, and greater emphasis on mass transit. Some of this interest is inspired by the desire to preserve the beauty of the countryside, but the campaign to preserve local farmland also rests on the assumption that farmers connected to a community are likely to farm more responsibly. Accokeek Ecosystem Farm, a seven-acre certified organic farm located on the Potomac River in southern Maryland, not only produces food for a weekly food subscription service for almost 90 families (and has started a waiting list because demand is so great), but plays a role in protecting the Chesapeake watershed (farmland holds more water than sprawling subdivisions) and keeping agrochemicals out of the Bay.

Source: Halweil, Brian. *Home Grown: The Case for Local Food in a Global Market*. World Watch Institute, 2002.

Making Arguments

To make an effective argument you must examine the issue sufficiently so that you understand it well, which often requires research. You must also complete **four main tasks**:

- Develop a main argument that is appropriate for your rhetorical situation.
- Make an appeal that is likely to be persuasive for your intended audience.
- Support your claims with appropriate evidence or reasoning.
- Adopt a format and style appropriate for the rhetorical situation and the medium you are using.

Developing a Main Argument

Core Concept #4—a writer must have something to say—is especially true in argument. As you explore your topic and the issues related to it, you must develop a clear main argument. However, your main argument is not the same as your position on an issue.

For example, let's imagine that you and several other residents of your college dormitory are concerned about new security measures that the college is considering because of recent incidents involving intruders in campus dorms. The proposed measures include prohibiting students from having visitors in their dorms except during specified hours. You and your dorm mates have decided to write a letter to the director of residential life urging her not to implement the new security measures. You hope to convince her that the measures would significantly restrict students' social activities without enhancing campus security. Your **topic**, then, is campus security. The **question** is whether the campus needs the proposed measures to improve security. You may be opposed to the proposed security measures, but that isn't your main argument; that's your **position**. You still need to identify the main argument you will make to reflect your position:

Topic
Campus security

Problem or Question
Does the campus need new security measures for dormitories to protect students?

Your Position
Opposed to proposed campus security policies

Your Main Argument
Proposed security measures will restrict students unnecessarily without improving the safety of the dorms.

Your main argument might evolve as you explore your topic and learn more about the issues at hand.

Keep in mind that your main argument is intended to help you achieve a specific goal. In arguing against proposed campus security measures, for example, you not only want to assert a clear position in opposition to the measures but you also hope to persuade the director of residential life to reconsider those measures and perhaps to make them less restrictive without compromising security. In addition, you hope your argument will win the support of other students who live in the dorms. So the argument must not only state the writer's opposition to the security measures; it must also present a persuasive case that those measures will not achieve the goal of improving security on campus, which is a goal that everyone—the students as well as the residential life director—supports.

6

EXERCISE 6C   **DEVELOPING A MAIN ARGUMENT**

1. Identify three issues that you feel strongly about. For each one, write a brief paragraph explaining your position on the issue and describing a main argument that you might make to support that position.

2. Find two or three arguments about the same topic—for example, arguments for or against gun control. Write a brief synopsis for each one that includes a statement of the writer's main argument. Compare the arguments, examining how each writer takes a stance on the issue and develops his or her main argument.

3. Think of two or three changes you would like to see on your campus or in your workplace. Now write a letter to your college president or your boss to argue in favor of these changes. Develop a main argument for each change you would like to see.

Considering the Rhetorical Situation

An effective argument must meet the needs of the rhetorical situation. In opposing the proposed security measures for the campus dormitories, for example, you would develop your main argument and supporting claims in a way that takes into account the interests and positions of the intended audience—in this case, the director of residential life and other students on campus. As you develop your argument, then, identify what you know about your audience in that situation by addressing the following questions:

- **What is your audience likely to know about this topic or situation?** Although you can't know exactly what your audience knows, you can make reasonable assumptions to help you develop an appropriate argument. For example, the residential life director will certainly understand what is involved in keeping campus dorms safe and secure. You wouldn't have to explain to her how the restrictions would work, but she might not fully appreciate what they would mean for students.

- **What is the audience's interest or stake in the issue?** Your audience might not always have the same level of interest in the issue you're addressing, but identifying why they would be interested can help you develop potentially persuasive points and find common ground. For example, the residential life director obviously has a direct stake in the situation because she is responsible for the campus dorms. Other students also have a stake in a livable, safe campus. Those interests can help you decide how to develop and present your argument so that you address shared concerns and acknowledge common ground.

- **What does your audience expect?** The residential life director would probably expect a thoughtful letter that acknowledges the importance of safe dorms. She would be less inclined to take your argument seriously if you did not show a reasonable understanding of the situation or if you dismissed her concerns. She would also likely expect a well-written letter that has a respectful tone, even if it makes a strong argument against her position.

Exploring your audience in this way can help you identify claims that are likely to be acceptable to them as well as arguments they might reject.

Sometimes, a writer knows that some readers will almost certainly reject a specific argument, especially when the topic is controversial, such as gun control or same-sex marriage. Writing about such issues requires care in considering audience, and the writer should assume that some readers will be skeptical. But rather than dismiss the views of a skeptical or even hostile audience, consider their reasons for opposing your viewpoint and try to address their concerns in your argument.

DO YOU HAVE TO WIN THE ARGUMENT?

In theory, an effective argument persuades an audience to accept a proposition, adopt a position, or take a course of action. In reality, an argument can achieve its purpose without necessarily persuading readers to adopt the writer's position, especially when it comes to issues about which people have strong views. For example, imagine that your state legislature is considering a controversial ban on certain kinds of firearms. Citizens support or oppose the ban depending on their opinions about gun control. An argument against the ban is unlikely to change the minds of those who support it, but it might influence the discussion. Because both supporters and opponents agree that lowering crime rates is desirable, an argument that the ban is likely to reduce violent crime would probably interest all parties in the debate. The goal is to contribute to the debate and influence how others think about the issue.

EXERCISE 6D **CONSIDERING THE RHETORICAL SITUATION**

1. Take the paragraphs you wrote for Exercise 11C#1 and identify an appropriate audience for each argument. Briefly describe that audience and the most important characteristics that might influence the argument you would make for that audience.

2. Find a published argument that you agree with on a topic that matters to you and imagine rewriting it for a different audience. For example, if the argument was published in your campus newspaper, imagine rewriting it for a community website in your hometown. What changes would you have to make to that argument? Why?

3. Imagine writing an argument about a controversial topic for an audience who opposes your position. First, identify a topic that interests you and summarize your position. Next, summarize opposing positions. Finally, identify two or three arguments that might appeal to that audience, trying to find common ground on the issue.

6

Making a Persuasive Appeal

Even if the main purpose of an argument is not necessarily to persuade readers, writers use persuasive appeals to strengthen an argument. Classical rhetorical theory identifies three modes of persuasion, or kinds of appeals:

- **Ethical**, or arguments based on the writer's or speaker's character
- **Emotional**, or arguments that appeal to the emotions
- **Logical**, or arguments based on reason and evidence

Most academic arguments rely on logical appeals, but even in academic arguments writers often employ all three modes of persuasion in some way.

Ethical Appeals, or Appeals Based on Character

Writers often try to strengthen their arguments by presenting themselves as reliable and trustworthy experts on the topic at hand. For example, in making an argument about a proposed mental health policy, a psychiatrist might emphasize her expertise in working with patients suffering from depression, presenting herself as someone with the appropriate knowledge and experience to understand the issue. Sometimes, a writer will rest an argument on his or her good judgment or integrity, such as when a person presents himself as a nurturing parent in making an argument about child care regulations. In ethical appeals, then, the writer's character, expertise, identity, or experience is a primary reason that the argument is persuasive.

Ethical appeals are common in advertising. Corporations use celebrities to represent them or their products—for example, former basketball star Michael Jordan for Nike shoes (see Sidebar: "Ethical Appeals in Advertising"). The suggestion is that if a world-class athlete endorses this product, it must be good. Ethical appeals are also important in law and politics. Political candidates, for example, present themselves as loving family members or successful in business as a way to make their appeal to voters more persuasive. Conversely, candidates often question their opponents' credibility, suggesting that the opponent cannot be trusted to make the right decisions on important issues.

| SIDEBAR | ETHICAL APPEALS IN ADVERTISING |

This classic ad for Nike shoes focuses on an image of basketball star Michal Jordan's athletic prowess. What argument does the ad make? How might you describe its ethical appeal?

MICHAEL JORDAN 1
ISAAC NEWTON 0

Courtesy of the Advertising Archives

In the following passage, journalist Barbara Ehrenreich uses her own first-hand experiences to support her argument that life has become more difficult for low-wage American workers. As a college professor, Ehrenreich was an expert on issues related to the working poor, but her best-selling 2001 book *Nickel and Dimed: On (Not) Getting By in America*, in which she described her experiences trying to make a living by working at low-wage jobs, helped establish her as an authority for a larger audience. In this excerpt from a 2011 essay about how the so-called Great Recession of 2008 affected America's poor, Ehrenreich refers to her experiences as a low-wage earner to supplement the statistical evidence she presents:

> At the time I wrote *Nickel and Dimed,* I wasn't sure how many people it directly applied to—only that the official definition of poverty was way off the mark, since it defined

an individual earning $7 an hour, as I did on average, as well out of poverty. But three months after the book was published, the Economic Policy Institute in Washington, D.C., issued a report entitled "Hardships in America: The Real Story of Working Families," which found an astounding 29% of American families living in what could be more reasonably defined as poverty, meaning that they earned less than a barebones budget covering housing, child care, health care, food, transportation, and taxes—though not, it should be noted, any entertainment, meals out, cable TV, Internet service, vacations, or holiday gifts. Twenty-nine percent is a minority, but not a reassuringly small one, and other studies in the early 2000s came up with similar figures.

The big question, 10 years later, is whether things have improved or worsened for those in the bottom third of the income distribution, the people who clean hotel rooms, work in warehouses, wash dishes in restaurants, care for the very young and very old, and keep the shelves stocked in our stores. The short answer is that things have gotten much worse, especially since the economic downturn that began in 2008.

Source: Ehrenreich, Barbara. "On Turning Poverty into an American Crime." *The Huffington Post*, 9 Aug. 2011, www.huffingtonpost.com/barbara-ehrenreich/nickel-and-dimed-2011-ver_b_922330.html.

Here Ehrenreich tries to strengthen her argument by invoking her credibility as an authority on the working poor. She provides statistical evidence to support her claim that "things have gotten much worse" for poor Americans in the ten years since her book was published, but she also makes an ethical appeal on the basis of her experience and knowledge about this issue.

Ethical appeals are most effective when they meet the needs of the rhetorical situation, and writers will often present themselves strategically for an intended audience. For example, in making her argument for a general audience—say, readers of a large-circulation newspaper like *USA Today*—Ehrenreich might emphasize her experience in low-wage jobs to establish her credibility, but in an argument published in a scholarly journal she might rely on her academic credentials.

6

Although ethical appeals usually rest on the *writer's* character, writers sometimes try to strengthen their arguments by relying on someone else's expertise or character. In the following excerpt from an essay about school reform, columnist David Brooks rests part of his argument on the experience and expertise of the director of a charter school called the New American Academy:

The New American Academy is led by Shimon Waronker, who grew up speaking Spanish in South America, became a U.S. Army intelligence officer, became an increasingly observant Jew, studied at yeshiva, joined the Chabad-Lubavitch movement, became a public school teacher and then studied at the New York City Leadership Academy, which Mayor Michael Bloomberg and the former New York Schools chancellor, Joel Klein, founded to train promising school principal candidates.

At first, he had trouble getting a principal's job because people weren't sure how a guy with a beard, kippa and a black suit would do in overwhelmingly minority schools. But he revitalized one of the most violent junior high schools in the South Bronx and with the strong backing of both Klein and Randi Weingarten, the president of the teachers' union, he was able to found his brainchild, The New American Academy.

He has a grand theory to transform American education, which he developed with others at the Harvard School of Education.

Source: Brooks, David. "The Relationship School." *The New York Times*, 22 March 2012, nyti.ms/19eGqt6.

In this case, Brooks argues in favor of a specific approach to school reform in part because it is endorsed by Shimon Waronker, who, Brooks suggests, has the right experience to understand what is needed to make schools work. Brooks establishes Waronker's credibility as an expert whose approach is supported by several prominent people (for example, Joel Klein, the former chancellor of New York City schools), as someone who has studied at Harvard, and as a former an intelligence officer in the U.S. Army. In this way, Brooks uses an ethical appeal to support his main argument. Writers can also call someone's credibility into question to help support their argument. For example, in arguing against a proposed school reform endorsed by a politician, a writer might point out that the politician's previous school reform efforts have failed, thus undermining the politician's credibility.

You can use ethical appeals in these same ways. For example, if you are writing an argument about the minimum wage, you might use your own work experience to help support your claims. However, for most academic assignments, you will establish your credibility primarily by demonstrating your command of the issues and knowledge of your topic.

Pathetic Appeals, or Appeals to Emotion

Appealing to readers' emotions is common in argument because it can be so effective. But because emotional appeals can be so powerful, they carry risk as well as potential reward.

Some arguments rely on emotions more than others do, but no argument is completely devoid of emotional appeal. Here is part of an essay about the disappearance of migratory songbirds in which the author's primary appeal is emotional:

Lately I have been sitting with the brooding knowledge that at least 7 million migrating songbirds were killed this spring running the gauntlet of 84,000 American communication towers that rise as high as 2,000 feet into the sky, braced by invisible guy wires that garrote the birds right out of the air.

This is actually just a fraction of the number of birds killed each year by running a collision course with human activity.

This spring has been more silent than ever. The traditional dawn chorus of birdsong has ebbed to a few lonely little souls, most belonging to non-migratory species like cardinals, bluejays, chickadees and sparrows.

They say that when Europeans first arrived on this continent, the migration of the passenger pigeons would literally darken the sky for minutes on end.

I have never seen a living passenger pigeon, and it seems that my grandchildren will not know what I mean when I talk about the dawn chorus

Vasik Olga/Shutterstock.com

of riotously busy, happy birdsong, any more than they will be able to imagine an apple orchard in full bloom buzzing with the diligent harvest of a million droning bees.

Knowledge like this makes me sick at heart. My rational side is aware that mourning is not productive, but another side of me knows that it is one of the special gifts of us humans to feel grief; to locate particular sadnesses in the larger landscape of suffering; and to use our sadness and anger at injustice as a lightening rod for change.

Other animals and birds feel grief as well, but you won't find the great community of birds gathering together to make plans to topple all the communication towers in North America.

No, the birds will go quietly, one by one, into the endless night of extinction.

Source: Browdy de Hernandez, Jennifer. "Stop the Holocaust of Migrating Birds." *Commondreams*, 29 Apr. 2012, www.commondreams.org/views/2012/04/29/stop-holocaust-migrating-birds.

In setting up her argument in favor of protecting migratory birds, many of which die in collisions with structures like towers and skyscrapers, Jennifer Browdy de Hernandez relies almost entirely on an emotional appeal. Her choice of language is intended to provoke sympathy and even outrage about the plight of migratory birds: "The traditional dawn chorus of birdsong has ebbed to a few lonely little souls"; the birds "run the gauntlet" of human construction and fly into guy wires that "garrote" them. By inciting readers' emotions with such language, Browdy de Hernandez tries to make readers more sympathetic to her argument. (Even the photograph that accompanies the essay, which depicts a beautiful bird singing its song, can evoke strong sympathies for songbirds.)

Often, emotional appeals are more subtle. In the following excerpt from an essay about the controversial Affordable Care Act that became law in 2010, U.S. Secretary of Health and Human Services Kathleen Sebelius strategically employs emotional appeals to make her argument more persuasive:

Two years ago, President Obama signed the Affordable Care Act. The President's health care law gives hard working, middle-class families security, makes Medicare stronger, and puts more money back in seniors' pockets.

Prior to 2011, people on Medicare faced paying for preventive benefits like cancer screenings and cholesterol checks out of their own pockets. Now, these benefits are offered free of charge to beneficiaries.

Over time, the health reform law also closes the gap in prescription drug coverage, known as the "donut hole." This helps seniors like Helen Rayon: "I am a grandmother who is trying to assist a grandson with his education. I take seven different medications. Getting the donut hole closed, that gives me a little more money in my pocket."

In 2010, those who hit the donut hole received a $250 rebate—with almost 4 million seniors and people with disabilities receiving a collective $1 billion. In 2011, people on Medicare automatically received a 50 percent discount on brand-name drugs in the donut hole. Over 3.6 million beneficiaries received more than $2.1 billion in savings— averaging $604 per person last year.

Source: Sebelius, Kathleen. "The Affordable Health Care Act: Strong Benefits to Seniors, Billions in Savings This Year." *The Huffington Post*, 29 April 2012, www.huffingtonpost.com/sec-kathleen-sebelius/the-affordable-care-act_b_1462694.html.

6

Here Sebelius appeals to her readers' sense of fairness by invoking sympathetic images—for example, of "hard working, middle-class families" and "a grandmother who is trying to assist a grandson with his education"—that are likely to make readers more inclined to consider her argument. Notice that Sebelius doesn't rely exclusively on emotional appeals, however; she also cites statistical evidence to support her claims. Her essay illustrates how emotional appeals can be woven effectively into an argument.

Logical Appeals, or Appeals to Reason

Because reason is often assumed to be superior to emotion when it comes to argumentation, rational arguments are often considered more valid than openly emotional ones. Of course, reason can never be completely separated from emotion, and audiences rarely react to logical arguments in a way that is devoid of emotion. Nevertheless, logic is an essential component of argumentation, and even arguments that appeal to emotion or character usually incorporate reasoning. The most common forms of logical reasoning are *inductive reasoning* and *deductive reasoning*. (Patterns of organizing an argument based on inductive or deductive reasoning are reviewed later in this chapter; here the nature of inductive and deductive reasoning is discussed.)

Inductive Reasoning

In induction, a conclusion is drawn from specific evidence. This type of reasoning is common in daily life. For example, you might have noticed more students riding bicycles and several new bicycle racks have been added to the campus. On the basis of this evidence you might reasonably conclude, or induce, that bicycles have become more popular.

Inductive reasoning is common in academic arguments, in which logical conclusions are reached on the basis of available evidence. The specific kinds of evidence and conventions governing inductive argument might differ from one academic discipline to another, but the basic approach is the same: reasoning from evidence.

Here's an example of a writer using inductive reasoning to make an argument about the value of a college education. In this excerpt from an essay titled "College Is Still Worth It," Mark Yzaguirre presents data about the impact of a college degree on a person's earnings and socio-economic status:

> Recently, the Pew Charitable Trusts came out with a report that supports what many of us have been saying to critics of higher education: While the system has its problems, by and large those with college degrees are better off than those without them, even during the recent economic turmoil.
>
> The Pew report makes several basic points that should be mentioned anytime someone claims that higher education isn't a good investment:
>
> - Although all 21–24-year-olds experienced declines in employment and wages during the recession, the decline was considerably more severe for those with only high school or associate degrees.
> - The comparatively high employment rate of recent college graduates was not driven by a sharp increase in those settling for lesser jobs or lower wages.

- The share of non-working graduates seeking further education did not change markedly during the recession.
- Out-of-work college graduates were able to find jobs during the downturn with more success than their less-educated counterparts.

These aren't trivial observations and they now have even more statistical support than before. The general economic benefits of getting a degree are still pretty clear. That doesn't mean that any college degree plan is a good one and any sensible approach to higher education, whether at the undergraduate or graduate level, should include a clear-eyed analysis of what one is likely to pay to and receive from a given school. . . .

It is simplistic and false to claim that more education always leads to more income or better job opportunities. It is also correct to point out that excessive student loan debt is a terrible burden that may not be justifiable for certain schools or fields of study. But that doesn't mean that it's good advice to tell young people who want to go to college and who are prepared to do so that they shouldn't do so because it's not worth the time or the price. Those with college degrees are still more likely to be employed than those without them and their prospects aren't bleak. While the phrase *caveat emptor* is a necessary one to consider in picking colleges and degree programs, the Great Recession shouldn't claim the idea that higher education is a ticket to a better future as one of its victims.

Source: Yzaguirre, Mark. "College Is Still Worth It." *The Huffington Post*, 16 Jan. 2013, www.huffingtonpost.com/mark-yzaguirre/college-education-worth_b_2483440.html.

Yzaguirre concludes that college is worthwhile on the basis of his evidence. He reasons inductively to arrive at that conclusion. Notice, though, that he qualifies his conclusion by saying that "it is simplistic and false to claim that more education always leads to more income or better job opportunities." In other words, the evidence allows him to conclude that, in general, college is worth the cost, but that evidence does *not* allow him to conclude that college is worth the cost for every student. Yzaguirre's care in drawing conclusions that logically follow from his evidence reminds us of one of the challenges of inductive reasoning: identifying evidence that isn't flawed, biased, or limited in some way. If the evidence is problematic, the conclusion will likely be questionable, rendering the argument weak, no matter how careful the reasoning.

Deductive Reasoning

Deductive reasoning begins with a generalization, called a **premise**, and works to a conclusion that follows logically from that generalization. The premise is the foundation for the argument. Typically, deductive reasoning is effective when the issue involves a basic principle or belief. For example, arguments against capital punishment often rest on the principle that all human life is sacred. That principle becomes the major premise, and the argument is constructed logically from that premise:

Major premise: Taking a human life is immoral.

Minor premise: Capital punishment is the willful taking of human life.

Conclusion: Capital punishment is immoral.

Evidence can still be cited in support of the argument, but the strength of the argument rests on the truth or validity of the main premise and the reasoning that leads to the conclusion.

In the following example, writer Malcolm Gladwell challenges a widespread view of media with a deductive argument. Gladwell questions the claim that social media are the key factor in recent modern uprisings against unpopular governments, such as those that occurred in eastern Europe in 2009 and (after his article was published) in Algeria, Egypt, and Libya during the "Arab Spring" of 2011. To make his argument, Gladwell compares these revolutions to other activist movements,

Robert Abbott Sengstacke/Getty Images

including the famous "Freedom Summer" protests in Mississippi in 1964, in which three volunteers—Michael Schwerner, James Chaney, and Andrew Goodman—were murdered, many black churches were set on fire, and hundreds of volunteers were beaten, shot at, and arrested. "A quarter of those in the program dropped out," Gladwell notes. "Activism that challenges the status quo—that attacks deeply rooted problems—is not for the faint of heart." What makes people capable of this kind of activism? he asks. He then gets to the basis of his argument, which is his main premise: High-risk activism "is a strong-tie phenomenon." In other words, this kind of activism depends on a strong connection to the movement. Gladwell supports this premise by referring to a study of the Freedom Summer participants indicating that what kept people involved in such dangerous movements was their "degree of personal connection to the civil-rights movement." Then he works from this premise to argue that current movements that rely on social media are not the same as previous movements like the Freedom Summer:

> The platforms of social media are built around weak ties. Twitter is a way of following (or being followed by) people you may never have met. Facebook is a tool for efficiently managing your acquaintances, for keeping up with the people you would not otherwise be able to stay in touch with. That's why you can have a thousand "friends" on Facebook, as you never could in real life.
>
> This is in many ways a wonderful thing. There is strength in weak ties, as the sociologist Mark Granovetter has observed. . . But weak ties seldom lead to high-risk activism. . . .
>
> Boycotts and sit-ins and nonviolent confrontations—which were the weapons of choice for the civil-rights movement—are high-risk strategies. They leave little room for conflict and error. The moment even one protester deviates from the script and responds to provocation, the moral legitimacy of the entire protest is compromised. Enthusiasts for social media would no doubt have us believe that King's task in Birmingham would have been made infinitely easier had he been able to communicate with his followers through Facebook, and contented himself

with tweets from a Birmingham jail. But networks are messy: think of the ceaseless pattern of correction and revision, amendment and debate, that characterizes Wikipedia. If Martin Luther King, Jr., had tried to do a wiki-boycott in Montgomery, he would have been steamrollered by the white power structure. And of what use would a digital communication tool be in a town where ninety-eight per cent of the black community could be reached every Sunday morning at church? The things that King needed in Birmingham—discipline and strategy—were things that online social media cannot provide.

Source: Gladwell, Malcolm. "Small Change: Why the Revolution Will Not be Tweeted." *The New Yorker*, 4. Oct. 2010, www.newyorker.com/magazine/2010/10/04/small-change-malcolm-gladwell.

Gladwell bases his argument on deductive reasoning:

1. He establishes his main premise: High-risk activism like the Civil Rights Movement in the U.S. requires strong social ties to succeed.

2. He examines the recent activist movements that relied on social media to show that they do not display these strong ties. (This is his minor premise.)

3. He concludes that social media cannot be the vehicle for high-risk activism.

Although deductive reasoning can be effective in arguments about issues informed by fundamental values or beliefs, it can also be used effectively in many kinds of arguments, as Gladwell's essay illustrates.

EXERCISE 6E **EXPLORING PERSUASIVE APPEALS**

6

1. Identify an issue about which you might write an argument. In a brief paragraph, summarize the main argument you would make and describe your intended audience. Now describe the appeals (ethical, emotional, or logical) that you think would strengthen your argument for that audience. For example, in an argument supporting anti-smoking laws, you might make an emotional appeal by describing the hardship caused by the death of the parent of young children from lung cancer; you might make a logical appeal on the basis of growing evidence that many serious health problems are linked to smoking.

2. Review the following passages and identify the ethical, emotional, and logical appeals in each.

   a) Today introversion and extroversion are two of the most exhaustively researched subjects in personality psychology, arousing the curiosity of hundreds of scientists.

   These researchers have made exciting discoveries aided by the latest technology, but they're part of a long and storied tradition. Poets and philosophers have been thinking about introverts and extroverts since the dawn of recorded time. Both personality types appear in the Bible and in the writings of Greek and Roman physicians, and some evolutionary

(Continued)

scientists say that the history of these types teaches back even farther than that: the animal kingdom also boasts "introverts" and "extroverts," . . . from fruit flies to pumpkinseed fish to rhesus monkeys. As with other complimentary pairings—masculinity and femininity, East and West, liberal and conservative—humanity would be unrecognizable, and vastly diminished, without both personality types.

Take the partnership of Rosa Parks and Martin Luther King, Jr.: a formidable orator refusing to give up his seat on a segregated bus wouldn't have had the same effect as a modest woman who'd clearly prefer to keep silent but for the exigencies of the situation. And Parks didn't have the stuff to thrill a crowd if she'd tried to stand up and announce that she had a dream. But with King's help, she didn't have to.

Yet today we make room for a remarkably narrow range of personality styles. We're told that to be great is to be bold, to be happy is to be sociable. We see ourselves as a nation of extroverts—which means that we've lost sight of who we really are. Depending on which study you consult, one third to one half of Americans are introverts—in other words, *one out of every two or three people you know*. . . . If you're not an introvert yourself, you are surely raising, managing, married to, or coupled with one.

Source: Cain, Susan. *Quiet: The Power of Introverts in a World That Can't Stop Talking.* Crown Publishing, 2012, pp. 3–4.

b) Wal-Mart has become the poster child for all that's wrong with American capitalism, because it replaced General Motors as the avatar of the economy. Recall that in the 1950s and the 1960s, GM earned more than any company on earth and was America's largest employer. It paid its workers solidly middle-class wages with generous benefits, totaling around $60,000 a year in today's dollars. Today Wal-Mart, America's largest company by revenue and the nation's largest employer, pays its employees about $17,500 a year on average, or just under $10 an hour, and its fringe benefits are skimpy—no guaranteed pension and few if any health benefits. And Wal-Mart does everything in its power to keep wages and benefits low. Internal memos in 2005 suggested hiring more part-time workers to lower the firm's health care enrollment and imposing wage caps on longer-term employees so they wouldn't be eligible for raises. Also, as I said earlier, Wal-Mart is aggressively anti-union.

Wal-Mart's CEO in 2007 was H. Lee Scott, Jr. Scott was no "Engine Charlie" Wilson, who as GM's top executive in the 1950s saw no difference between the fate of the nation and the fate of his company. Scott has a far less grandiose view of Wal-Mart's role. "Some well-meaning critics believe that Wal-Mart stores today, because of our size, should, in fact, play the role that is believed that General Motors played after World War II. And that is to establish this post-World War middle class that the country is proud of," he opined. "The facts are that retail does not perform that role in this economy." Scott was right. The real problem—not of his making—is that almost nothing performs that role any longer.

> The rhetorical debate over Wal-Mart is not nearly as interesting as the debate we might be having in our own heads if we acknowledge what was at stake. Millions of us shop at Wal-Mart because we like its low prices. Many of us also own Wal-Mart stock through our pension or mutual funds. Isn't Wal-Mart really being excoriated for our sins? After all, it is not as if Wal-Mart's founder, Sam Walton, and his successors created the world's largest retailer by putting a gun to our heads and forcing us to shop there or to invest any of our retirement savings in the firm.

Source: Reich, Robert. *Supercapitalism: The Transformation of Business, Democracy, and Everyday Life.* Knopf, 2007, pp. 89–90.

Appraising and Using Evidence

No matter what kind of argument you are making, identifying and using appropriate evidence is essential for effective argumentation. Almost anything can be used as evidence: statistics, opinions, observations, theories, personal experience, anecdotes. The challenge is to determine whether a particular kind of evidence is appropriate for a specific claim in a specific rhetorical situation.

Consider the debate about the state of the U.S. Social Security system. For a number of years, economists, politicians, and financial experts have been debating whether Social Security will run out of money and what, if anything, should be done to prevent that. Experts disagree about the nature of the problem, and participants in the debate routinely cite statistics and factual evidence to support their competing claims. For example, here's an excerpt from a 2012 *USA Today* editorial arguing that Congress should take steps now to avoid a default of the Social Security Trust Fund:

> Self-proclaimed defenders of Social Security maintain that, because of the retirement program's large annual surpluses, it isn't in crisis. That argument is a red herring.
>
> For one thing, those surpluses, also known as the Social Security Trust Fund, have been spent and replaced with IOUs. For another, there aren't any more surpluses. This year, Social Security will collect $507 billion in taxes and pay out $640 billion in benefits. The difference will have to be borrowed, adding to the federal deficit.
>
> Even if you believe that the trust fund is more real than the tooth fairy, the picture is gloomy. This week, the trustees who oversee Social Security reported that if the government makes good on the IOUs by borrowing, taxing or cutting elsewhere, the main trust fund will run out of money in a little more than 20 years. At that point, income from the payroll tax will only be enough to cover 75% of expected benefits. The fund for Social Security's disability program will go bust even sooner, in 2016.

Source: "Editorial: Fix Social Security." *USA Today*, 26 Apr. 2012, usatoday30.usatoday.com/news/opinion/editorials/story/2012-04-26/Social-Security-trustees-report/54562718/1.

The authors of this editorial provide what seems to be convincing evidence that Social Security will run out of money in two decades—for example, statistics showing that the Social Security Trust Fund pays out more than it takes in. They rest their argument on a report by the Fund's trustees, who express concern about the possible default of the fund. The question is whether this evidence actually supports the conclusion that the fund will run out of money. The expected deficit for one year, which they refer to in the second paragraph, does not necessarily mean continued deficits over twenty years. In addition, the trustees' prediction in the third paragraph depends upon the accuracy of their assumption about how much money the fund will need to cover benefits, which is a disputed figure.

In a rebuttal to this editorial, Max Richtman, the president and CEO of the National Committee to Preserve Social Security & Medicare, also cites the trustees' report, but he points to figures in that report that lead him to a different conclusion:

- The trust fund solvency date for Social Security has seen fluctuations many times in recent decades, from a depletion date as distant as 2048 in the 1988 report to as soon as 2029 in the 1994 and 1997 reports. This year's report is well within that range.

- Social Security will be able to pay full benefits until the year 2033. After that, there will be sufficient revenue to pay about 75% of benefits.

- There is $2.7 trillion in the Social Security Trust Fund, which is $69 billion more than last year, and it will continue to grow until 2020.

Source: Richtman, Max. "Opposing View: There is No Social Security Crisis." *USA Today*, 26 Apr. 2012, www.usatoday.com/news/opinion/story/2012-04-26/National-Committee-to-Preserve-Social-Security-Medicare/54561846/1.

Like the authors of the editorial, Richtman cites statistical evidence to support his claim but he reaches a different conclusion: "There is no Social Security crisis." Who is right?

This example illustrates that the use of evidence in arguments about complicated issues is itself complicated. In this case, the strength of the argument depends not only on the nature of the specific evidence provided but also on how that evidence is interpreted. Each side uses similar kinds of evidence but interprets the evidence differently.

In evaluating an argument, then, we have to appraise the evidence provided.

- **Is the evidence credible?** The evidence should be from a credible source. In the previous example, the source of the figures cited by the authors is a report by the trustees of the Social Security system, which lends those figures credibility. Had the authors cited figures from, say, an economist with little experience in fiscal issues related to social security, those figures could carry less weight.

- **Is the evidence appropriate for the argument?** Often, a great deal of evidence is available to support a claim, but the strength of that evidence will depend on how relevant it is to the argument. In this example, the authors could cite a wide variety of economic, financial, and historical statistics or information to support their claims about the fiscal viability of Social Security, but some evidence might be inappropriate for this argument. For example, a statement by a politician who is known to oppose Social Security as an unnecessary government program would be a weak kind of evidence to support the writers' claim that Social Security is running out of money.

- **Is the evidence applied appropriately?** Sometimes, evidence can be strong but used inappropriately. For example, the writers of the *USA Today* editorial note that "Social Security will collect $507 billion in taxes and pay out $640 billion in benefits." They use these figures appropriately to support their claim that such deficits make it more likely that the fund will run out of money. If, however, they cited these figures to argue that Social Security is already running out of money, they would be misusing these figures, since a deficit in a single year does not indicate that the fund is bankrupt.

- **Is the evidence interpreted in a reasonable way?** What a piece of evidence means is not always clear, and the same evidence can sometimes be used to support different claims. So writers must often explain what their evidence means. In this example, both Richtman and the editorial authors cite the same figure as evidence to support different claims—the date when the trustees expect Social Security to run out of money (what Richtman refers to as the "solvency date")—but they interpret this piece of evidence differently. The editorial authors assume that the date refers to a specific date when the fund will become insolvent; Richtman interprets the date as an estimate, noting that in the past the trustees have predicted different solvency dates. Part of the strength of each argument, then, rests on whether readers accept the authors' interpretation of the evidence.

- **Is important evidence missing?** Sometimes evidence that seems convincing becomes less so when other evidence is presented. Richtman, for example, notes that the Social Security Trust Fund has "$69 billion more than last year, and it will continue to grow until 2020." The authors of the editorial do not include the fund's growth in their argument, yet this figure seems to be important for estimating whether or when the fund might become insolvent. It is up to readers to decide whether that "missing" evidence weakens their argument and strengthens Richtman's claim.

Keep in mind that what counts as appropriate and persuasive evidence depends upon the rhetorical context. Personal experience might be acceptable to readers of a popular consumer magazine but not necessarily for a technical report on fuel economy for a government agency or for an essay in your Economics class. Consider your audience and purpose when determining what kinds of evidence are most appropriate and persuasive for your argument.

6

| EXERCISE 6F | APPRAISING EVIDENCE |

1. For each of the following passages, identify the claim(s) and the evidence presented in support of the claim(s). Then evaluate the strength of the evidence using the criteria discussed in this section. Excerpt A is taken from an essay by a political scientist challenging the assumption that voters act rationally when deciding which political candidates to support. Excerpt B is taken from from a book by an anthropologist examining what we can learn from traditional societies.

   a) Suppose that one scholar maintains that the average voter's belief about X is true, and another denies it. For their debate to make sense, *both* sides have to claim knowledge about (a) what the average voter believes, and (b) which belief is true. How can we get to the bottom of this sort of dispute?

   It is fairly easy to figure out what the average voter believes. High-quality surveys abound. The hard thing is figuring out how to "grade" the beliefs of the average voter—to find a yardstick against which his beliefs can be measured.

(Continued)

The most straightforward is to compare voter beliefs to known fact. We can ask voters to tell us the fraction of the federal budget that goes to foreign aid, and compare their average answer to the actual number. Studies that use this approach find that the average voter has some truly bizarre beliefs. The National Survey of Public Knowledge of Welfare Reform and the Federal Budget finds, for example, that 41% of Americans believe that foreign aid is one of the two biggest areas in the federal budget—versus 14% for Social Security. The main drawback of this approach is that many interesting questions are too complex to resolve with an almanac.

Source: Caplan, Bryan. "The Myth of the Rational Voter." *Cato Unbound*, Cato Institute, 5 Nov. 2006, www.cato-unbound.org/2006/11/05/bryan-caplan/myth-rational-voter.

b) Traditional societies are far more diverse in their cultural practices than are modern industrial societies. Within that range of diversity, many cultural norms for modern state societies are far displaced from traditional norms and lie towards the extremes of that traditional range of diversity. For example, compared to any modern industrial society, some traditional societies treat elderly people much more cruelly, while others offer elderly people much more satisfying lives; modern industrial societies are closer to the former extreme than to the latter. Yet psychologists base most of their generalizations about human nature on studies of our own narrow and atypical slice of human diversity. Among human subjects studied in a sample of papers from the top psychology journals surveyed in the year 2008, 96% were from Westernized industrial countries (North America, Europe, Australia, New Zealand, and Israel), 68% were from the U.S. in particular, and up to 80% were college undergraduates enrolled in psychology courses, i.e., not even typical of their own national societies. That is, as social scientists Joseph Henrich, Steven Heine, and Ara Norenzayan express it, most of our understanding of human psychology is based on subjects who may be described by the acronym WEIRD: from Western, educated, industrialized, rich, and democratic societies. Most subjects also appear to be literally weird by the standards of world cultural variation, because they prove to be outliers in many studies of cultural phenomena that have sampled world variation more broadly. Those sampled phenomena include visual perception, fairness, cooperation, punishment, logical reasoning, spatial orientation, analytic versus holistic reasoning, moral reasoning, motivation to conform, making choices, and concept of self. Hence if we wish to generalize about human nature, we need to broaden greatly our study sample from the usual WEIRD subjects (mainly American psychology undergraduates) to the whole range of traditional societies.

Source: Diamond, Jared. *The World Until Yesterday*. Viking Books, 2012.

2. Identify an argument you might make about an issue that matters to you. In a paragraph, state your main argument and briefly describe the audience you would address. Now list several kinds of evidence to support your argument that would be persuasive for your intended audience. Briefly explain why each kind of evidence would be appropriate for your argument.

Structuring an Argument

The most effective arguments are structured in a way that best meets the needs of the rhetorical situation, and writers generally adopt a format that presents their arguments clearly and persuasively to their intended audience:

- An argument about the influence of social media on peer groups for a communication course would likely be organized systematically around the main claims that can be made on the basis of available research.
- An essay for your campus newspaper in favor of the college's study-abroad program might be structured around your own study-abroad experience to make a case for the value of that program.
- A pamphlet supporting the legalization of medical marijuana might present several cases of patients who benefited from medicinal marijuana, with each case illustrating a main point in favor of legalization.

In each of these examples, the writer's decisions about how to structure the argument are shaped by the same basic factors:

- **Audience expectations.** Readers might be less skeptical about supporting the legalization of medicinal marijuana if the argument is presented in the form of the personal stories of patients whose lives were improved by the use of the drug.

- **Conventions governing argument in that rhetorical situation.** Academic arguments, such as a report on social media and peer groups in a communications course, usually follow accepted formats within the academic field. Other kinds of arguments, such as editorial essays for newspapers, tend to be less formally structured.

- **Purpose of the argument.** Structuring an argument around personal experiences and anecdotes, as in an essay arguing for the value of a study abroad program, might make the argument more engaging and persuasive to the intended audience (other students) and therefore be more likely to achieve the purpose of the argument (to assert a position about the issue).

As these examples illustrate, arguments can take many forms; writers should always assess the rhetorical situation carefully to determine how best to structure an argument. However, writers can also use one of four traditional ways of structuring an argument:

- classical arrangement
- Rogerian argument
- inductive reasoning
- deductive reasoning

Classical Arrangement

Classical rhetorical theory defines a standard six-part structure for an argument:

1. **Introduction:** places the main argument in context and explains why it is important or relevant.

2. **Background:** a narrative of events or statement of the facts of the case that sets the stage for the argument.

3. **Proposition:** statement of the writer's position or main argument and an indication of the key points to be made in support of the argument.

4. **Proof:** the core of the argument, in which the writer presents his or her claims and evidence to support the main argument. Often, this section is arranged so that the strongest claims and evidence are presented first.

5. **Refutation:** consideration of opposing arguments, which can be rebutted or accepted to strengthen the main argument.

6. **Conclusion:** summary of the main points of the argument. Often, the writer will make a final appeal to the audience.

The advantage of this format is that it presents the argument in a clear, straightforward way. Using this format can help writers generate ideas for their argument and insure that nothing important is left out. Although the format might seem rigid, writers have flexibility in deciding how to organize each main section.

Rogerian Argument

Based on the work of psychologist Carl Rogers, who advocated understanding and listening to resolve conflict, Rogerian argument is generally viewed as a means to negotiate differences and achieve social cooperation. Rogerian argument emphasizes resolution of the issue at hand, so writers make concessions rather than refutations. Like classically arranged arguments, Rogerian arguments have six main sections:

1. **Introduction:** presents the problem to be resolved and raises the possibility of a positive outcome.

2. **Summary of opposing views:** opposing views are stated as accurately and neutrally as possible.

3. **Statement of understanding:** the validity of opposing views is acknowledged. Without necessarily conceding that these views are always right, the writer seeks common ground with those who have opposing views.

4. **Statement of position:** the writer's position on the issue.

5. **Statement of contexts:** discussion of situations that illustrate the validity of the writer's position—in effect, providing support for that position to indicate that it can be acceptable even to those with opposing views.

6. **Statement of benefits:** an appeal to the self-interest of those with opposing views who might reconsider as a result of the writer's argument.

(Adapted from Richard Coe, *Form and Substance.* Wiley, 1981.)

Rogerian argument is most appropriate in situations in which people are deeply divided as a result of different values or perceptions and especially when conflicting parties seek a compromise. For example, an argument in favor of same-sex marriage presented in a Rogerian format would emphasize the common ground shared by those who hold strong, divergent opinions about the issue. Using a Rogerian approach in such a situation, a writer might highlight the desire for strong families, which is shared by those on either side of the debate. In such a case, pointing out the problems with opposing viewpoints is not likely to encourage those who hold such viewpoints to reconsider their position on the issue.

Inductive Reasoning

Arguments based on inductive reasoning present a conclusion drawn from available evidence. When organizing such an argument, follow these guidelines:

- **Demonstrate the relevance of the topic.** The introduction presents the topic and explains why it is relevant to the intended audience.

- **State the main argument and claims clearly.** How clearly and carefully a writer presents his or her main argument can determine how convincing that argument is to the intended audience.

- **Arrange evidence so that it best supports the main conclusion.** Because some kinds of evidence are likely to be more compelling to the audience than others, you should assess how your audience is likely to respond to specific kinds of evidence and arrange that evidence in a way that will make the argument strongest, usually presenting the most compelling evidence first.

- **Interpret and analyze the evidence for the audience.** Although your evidence might be strong, you might have to explain why it is significant. For example, if you use an anecdote about an accident involving a student who parks her car on campus, explain what that anecdote means for your argument against the new campus parking restrictions. (See "Appraising and Using Evidence" on page 189.)

Because an inductive argument relies on evidence, this approach might be used most effectively when there is strong and abundant evidence to support a main argument or position.

Deductive Reasoning

When constructing an argument on the basis of deductive reasoning, work backward from the main conclusion by following these steps:

- **Identify the conclusion.** Identify the main conclusion you want to reach in your argument. For example, let's say you support the idea of free college for all citizens and agree with politicians who advocate making public two-year colleges tuition-free for residents of the states where those colleges are located. So that's your conclusion.

- **Examine your reasons.** List your main reasons for your position, keeping in mind that some reasons will be more persuasive to an audience than others. For instance, you might believe that a college education is part of what it means to be an informed citizen and therefore strengthens democracy. That might be a valid reason for making two-year colleges tuition-free, but it might be less compelling than other reasons, such as the negative social and economic impact of the enormous debt that so many college students incur, which hurts families, communities, and the broader economy. Try to identify all the main reasons for supporting your conclusion.

- **Formulate the premise.** Your premise is the basic principle on which you will base your argument. Ideally, it should be a principle that your audience shares. Let's say your position on tuition-free college rests on your belief that all people have a right to a good education, regardless of their income level or social status. That's your premise. It will serve as the foundation for your argument:

  All people should have access to a high-quality education in their quest for a healthy, happy life. Income and social status should not determine one's access to education. Therefore, college should be free for all citizens.

You can structure your argument accordingly:

1. **Introduction:** State the problem.

2. **Main premise:** Present and explain the main premise on which the argument will be based. Also present the conclusion you will reach.

3. **Reasons:** Present the reasons for supporting the proposition. Address any counter-arguments that can weaken the main argument.

4. **Conclusion:** Restate the main conclusion in light of the evidence presented. Also remind readers of the main premise.

One benefit of structuring an argument in this way is that it encourages you to explore your subject carefully, which could lead to a stronger, more substantive essay.

Features of Argument

Like other common forms of academic writing, argument is a form of inquiry. It is a vehicle for writers to investigate and understand a complex issue or problem and make a claim about that issue or problem to others who have a stake in it.

Effective arguments have five essential features:

1. **A clear main point.** In an effective argument, the writer communicates a clear main point related to his or her position on an issue. As we saw earlier in this chapter, the main argument is not the same as the writer's position on the topic. To state that you support online privacy protection is to take a stance on that issue; to make the case that online privacy should be protected because online communication is a form of constitutionally protected speech is to make an argument in support of that stance.

2. **A relevant purpose.** The purpose of any argument should be relevant to the rhetorical situation. For instance, an argument supporting leash laws to make your campus safer and cleaner would be appropriate for your campus newspaper or a student social media site, the audience for which would likely share your concerns about campus safety. However, the same argument for an assignment in a geography and urban planning course would have to place the issue of leash laws in the context of that field—for example, how land use laws and campus ordinances are intended to create livable public spaces. Even a carefully crafted and well-supported argument is unlikely to be effective if the topic is not relevant to the intended audience.

3. **Appropriate support for claims.** Sufficient and appropriate evidence to support claims is perhaps the most obvious feature of effective argument, but supporting a claim with evidence is not always straightforward. For example, statistical data showing that the average global temperature last year was the highest in five years might be true, but such evidence would be insufficient support for an argument that the earth is getting warmer. On the other hand, data showing a rise in global temperatures over several decades would be stronger evidence for a claim that the earth's atmosphere is getting warmer. In some contexts, such as economics, statistical data might carry more weight than expert opinion, whereas in other contexts, such as art history, the views of respected scholars might be more appropriate support for a claim than statistical evidence.

4. **Complexity.** Effective arguments explore their subjects in sufficient depth to avoid oversimplifying them. For example, it might seem obvious to argue that raising student test scores will improve learning, but a closer look might reveal questions about the reliability of tests or their impact on what students learn. In an effective argument, the writer should acknowledge such questions and address them in a way that reflects the complexity of the issue. Doing so will result in an argument that is stronger and perhaps more valid. It might also foster a deeper understanding of the issue.

5. **A persuasive appeal.** An argument can be based on appeals to reason, emotion, or character, but most arguments employ whatever appeals are appropriate for the rhetorical situation. Moreover, almost all arguments employ logic in some form. Not all reasoning is valid, however. In fact, logical fallacies and flawed reasoning abound in public debates about important issues in politics, education, technology, and culture. An effective argument leads readers logically to the conclusion that the writer supports, based on evidence and sound reasoning, even when the writer is appealing to readers' emotions or invoking character.

6

The following essay illustrates these features of argumentation. In this essay, which was originally published in *The New Yorker*, a magazine devoted to culture, politics, and the arts, Law professor Ekow N. Yankah makes a case against the increasingly popular idea that college athletes should be paid. His essay appeared in late 2015, just a few weeks after a major decision by a U.S. Appeals Court regarding compensation for college scholarship athletes, which Yankah refers to in his opening paragraph. This lawsuit, which came to be known as the "O'Bannon case," was originally filed by Ed O'Bannon, who played basketball for UCLA from 1991 to 1995 on an athletic scholarship. In 2009 O'Bannon sued the National Collegiate Athletic Association, or NCAA, which sets the rules for college sports, including how and whether scholarship athletes are compensated. The NCAA has long claimed that college athletes are amateurs and therefore should not receive pay for their sports performances. O'Bannon argued that college athletes should receive compensation when the universities they play for earn millions of dollars through the use of the players' images in video games, on television broadcasts, and on merchandise such as T-shirts. The high-profile case was controversial, in part because it challenged longstanding beliefs about college sports, which by 2009 had become a multibillion-dollar enterprise. As the case made its way through the legal system, it provoked intense debate among fans as well as coaches, university officials, and legal experts such as Yankah. After several decisions in lower courts, the case ended up in the United States Court of Appeals for the Ninth

Circuit, which, as Yankah notes, handed down a mixed decision, asserting that the NCAA violated antitrust laws but also ruling that universities do not have to pay their athletes beyond the cost of attending college.

As you'll see, Yankah is not so much interested in the legal decision in the O'Bannon case as he is concerned about the broader question raised by O'Bannon's lawsuit: Should college athletes be paid? By the time Yankah wrote his essay in 2015, college sports, especially football and basketball, had become an even bigger business than when O'Bannon filed his lawsuit in 2009, and the question of whether athletes should be paid had become even more contentious. Yankah acknowledges the well-established arguments in favor of paying college athletes and concedes that athletes who play big-money sports are exploited, but he rests his own argument primarily on reason. He builds his case so that it leads logically to his conclusion that college athletes should not be paid for playing their sports. His reasoning is deductive. His main premise might be stated this way: Amateur athletics have great social and cultural value in their own right. His minor premise is that paying student athletes would undermine this value by emphasizing only the monetary worth of athletics. His conclusion, then, is that college athletes should not be paid.

Of course, in addition to his logical argument, Yankah also employs emotional appeals—for example, when he discusses his strong sense of connection to the athletic teams at the University of Michigan, which he attended. He also provides various kinds of factual evidence (inartistic proofs) to support his argument. In these ways, his essay, which was published in a popular magazine, illustrates the features of effective argument in academic contexts as well.

. . . .

Talking About This Reading

Dara Bordman (student): I had some trouble following the organization of this essay. The author's main points sometimes seemed to be all over the place, and I didn't see a direct route from the beginning to the end.

Bob Yagelski: Dara, part of the problem might be that this author is making a deductive argument, which can be challenging to follow (see the introduction to this reading above). In such cases, it helps to identify the author's main premise, which he states in paragraph 4: that sports have educational value. That premise leads to his conclusion (also stated in paragraph 4) that paying college athletes would be a mistake. Knowing that can help you see how his other points fit into his argument.

. . . .

Why N.C.A.A. Athletes Shouldn't Be Paid
by Ekow N. Yankah

1   Two weeks ago, as Americans were settling into the harvest comfort of football Saturdays, the United States Court of Appeals for the Ninth Circuit issued a ruling in the antitrust suit against the National Collegiate Athletic Association. The decision drew blood on both sides. The court sided with the players in affirming that the N.C.A.A. is not immune to antitrust regulation, but simultaneously reversed a lower-court ruling that would have granted former athletes as much as five thousand dollars a year in deferred compensation—essentially back pay—for the use of their images in video games and other commercial ventures. At the same time, the court required that the N.C.A.A. increase scholarship payouts to cover the full cost of college attendance, thus making mandatory an option that the N.C.A.A. first permitted a few years ago.

2   These legal niceties did very little to address the deeper question of fairness. The N.C.A.A. ideal of amateurism in college athletics has come to border on farce. In the highest-revenue sports—football and basketball—the argument in favor of paying players is so searingly obvious as to seem undeniable. These athletes collectively generate tens if not hundreds of millions of dollars annually for their schools. Many college coaches are the highest-paid public employees in their states—a five-million-dollar salary is no longer eye-popping—and that paycheck doesn't include gifts from boosters, who will occasionally pay for a coach's house to make sure that he stays happy.

3   But this understates the exploitation. The athletes in major football and men's basketball programs are disproportionately black, many from poor and educationally disadvantaged backgrounds. For too many of them, the N.C.A.A. is the only game in town. In some dispiriting cases, the students are so unprepared that academic failure seems inevitable. In worse cases still, their scholarships are cynically undermined by the schools themselves. Coaches steer students into empty classes (what one recent report from the University of North Carolina at Chapel Hill characterized as a "shadow curriculum" [Crouch]) or supply so-called academic support that amounts to cheating. It hardly seems coincidental, then, that sports with less African-American participation, such as baseball and hockey, maintain robust minor-league systems without the national gnashing of teeth.

> **Appropriate Support for Claims**
> In the second and third paragraphs, Yankah uses factual evidence (about coaches' salaries) and an example (of a cheating scandal involving athletes at the University of North Carolina) to support his claim that college athletes are exploited.

6

4   And yet I believe that the drive to pay college athletes is a grave mistake—not because it misdiagnoses the disease but because it suggests that the only cure is to put the patient out of his misery. It fails, first of all, to recognize the value of sports as a part of education. This value can be seen in the countless student athletes, from gymnasts to softball players, who pour hours of work into training and competing with no hope of going pro. (Similarly, many of those in even the biggest sports show dedication long after it is clear that they will never be professionals.)

5   This value is again revealed in the fact that many N.C.A.A. teams are vastly more popular than their professional counterparts. My beloved Michigan Wolverines pack the Big House with more than a hundred thousand spectators each football Saturday; the Detroit Lions, meanwhile, do not. (I know, I know—it's the Lions. That's why their stadium is smaller.) Minor-league arenas attract even fewer spectators. Fans are not only seeking athletic excellence as such—the biggest and fastest players in descending order. Our connection to the athletes is deeper. These student athletes walk the same halls, have the same professors, and sweat the same midterms that we did, however long ago. At the University of Illinois at Urbana–Champaign, where I once taught, the inscription on the statue of Alma Mater reads, "To thy happy children of the future, those of the past send greetings." It's easy to dismiss that sentiment as saccharine, but it gets at an important truth: we are embedded in our cultures and social groups, and we revel in their excellence.

6   Paying student athletes erodes that association. If a high-school football prodigy reported that he chose Michigan not for its academic quality, tradition, or beautiful campus but because it outbid all other suitors, a connection to the university's values would be lost. This is not naïve idealism. Auburn fans still bristle at accusations that Cam Newton auctioned them his services; prideful Michigan fans still smart over the sanctions surrounding Chris Webber, and over stinging comments intimating that he might just as well have attended a rival school. These episodes reveal what happens when college sports are

reduced to a market; that this occurs all too often already is no reason to surrender to it.

7   The law plays a critical role here, and the Ninth Circuit's ruling can be a constructive step. It recognizes that the N.C.A.A. is subject to antitrust regulation—unlike, say, Major League Baseball (Greenberg)—and refuses to put a monetary value on college sports. In the future, Congress could, through antitrust and commerce legislation, promote a more just landscape in college and professional sports. Professional leagues, in particular, could be encouraged to invest more seriously in their minor-league programs—the N.B.A. Development League is at least the right idea—and drop the relevant age restrictions. This would mean that the extraordinary few could go pro out of high school, and some other highfliers could enter the developmental leagues, paid whatever the market will bear. College sports might well lose some spectacular stars, but the stars alone were never really the point.

8   None of this would be easy to accomplish, of course, given the money that is at stake, and there would be casualties. Some of the players who might at least have been exposed to college would forgo it entirely. We might lose the story of the exceptional athlete, often poor and dark-skinned, who goes to school solely to play sports but then sees the world widen before him. Nor should we imagine that those who opt for the developmental leagues have made it; minor-league baseball and the lower tiers of European soccer remind us how thankless and poorly compensated (Pilon) such a life can be. But this is

6

no less true for those who skip college to pursue music or theatre, and, more to the point, there is no reason to think that we wouldn't hear stories of intellectual discovery among slightly less athletically gifted athletes from the same streets. Even if we cannot save sports (or music, or theatre) from its high-risk nature, we can go some way toward making sure that a few elite college programs are not unduly feeding off it.

9   At sports bars, when I hear people dismiss these (or other) ideas for preserving college amateurism, I realize that it's not simply a question of their being overwhelmed by the practical difficulties involved. It is, rather, another manifestation of that corrosive American belief that anything that has value must also have a price. The recent ruling, though, hints at a path ahead, a way to cheer for our student athletes without being held hostage to money, exploitation, racism, or cynicism.

> **Persuasive Appeals.**
> In the concluding paragraph, Yankah reinforces his main logical appeal by restating his belief in the value of amateur athletics as more than monetary. Notice that he also makes a subtle ethical appeal by including an image of him visiting a sports bar, which reinforces his identity as a genuine sports fan. In addition, he uses the image of fans cheering for student athletes, who should not be "held hostage to money, exploitation, racism, or cynicism." This language helps make an emotional appeal to generate sympathy among readers for the athletes, whom Yankah claims to be supporting.

Works Cited

Crouch, Ian. "The Price of Eligibility at UNC." *The New Yorker*, 24 Oct. 2014, www.newyorker.com/news/daily-comment/north-carolina-academic-scandal.

Greenberg, David. "Baseball's Con Game." *Slate*, 19 July 2002, www.slate.com/articles/news_and_politics/history_lesson/2002/07/baseballs_con_game.html.

Pilon, Mark. "Are Minor Leaguers Paid Legal Wages." *The New Yorker*, 20 Aug. 2015, www.newyorker.com/news/sporting-scene/are-minor-leaguers-paid-legal-wages.

Source: Yankah, Ekow. " Why N.C.A.A. Athletes Shouldn't Be Paid." *The New Yorker*, 14 Oct. 2015, www.newyorker.com/news/sporting-scene/why-ncaa-athletes-shouldnt-be-paid.

Questions to Consider:

1. Yankah's essay might be seen as based on deductive reasoning (see the introduction to the essay on pages 197–198). Do you think this was an effective approach to making an argument about this topic? Why or why not? What might have been different about his essay if he had approached it inductively?

2. Using the criteria for appraising evidence described in this chapter (see page 189), evaluate the evidence Yankah uses to support his claims. To what extent does his use of evidence strengthen or weaken his essay?

3. What assumptions do you think Yankah makes about his audience? (Remember that his essay was originally published in the *The New Yorker*, a large-circulation magazine that reaches an international audience.) To what extent do you think his specific persuasive appeals reflect the general nature of that audience? Do you find his appeals persuasive? Explain. What might your answer suggest about the nature of persuasive appeals?

4. In general, how convincing do you find Yankah's argument? Explain, citing specific passages that you find especially effective or ineffective. On the basis of your response to this question, what revisions would you make to his essay?

Writing Arguments

You will encounter argument throughout your academic career: in class discussions of course topics, in assigned readings, and in writing assignments. In some cases, these arguments will address important issues that go well beyond your courses. For example, in an economics class, you might read several scholarly arguments about the problem of student loan debt; at the same time, you might hear a guest on a news podcast make an argument in favor of subsidizing student loans, or perhaps you will read a blog on a newspaper website in which the writer argues against such subsidies. These examples underscore the central role argument can play in your college work as well as in your life beyond the classroom.

This section provides a framework for developing your own arguments using the Ten Core Concepts. Each step described here corresponds to a step in Chapter 3. As you develop your project, keep in mind **the five essential features of argument:**

1. **A clear main point.** Present a clear main point related to your position on an issue:
   - What is the main point you will make in this argument?
   - What purpose do you hope to achieve in making this argument?

2. **A relevant purpose.** Identify the relevance of your argument for your rhetorical situation:
   - What makes your argument relevant to your intended audience?
   - Why is your argument relevant now?

3. **Appropriate support for claims.** Support your claims with sufficient and appropriate evidence:
   - What evidence do you present to support your main claim and supporting claims?
   - What makes this evidence appropriate in the context of your rhetorical situation? Is your evidence sufficient to support your claims?

4. **Complexity.** Present your argument so that it reflects the complexity of your subject:
   - Have you explored the subject of your argument in sufficient depth and avoided oversimplifying it?
   - Which complicating factors or alternative viewpoints, if any, have you considered? How do these viewpoints help illuminate the complexity of your subject?

5. **A persuasive appeal.** Use appropriate appeals to reason, emotion, or character to make your argument persuasive:

- What persuasive appeals have you employed in your argument?
- In what ways are your persuasive appeals appropriate for your rhetorical situation?

Step 1   Identify a topic for argument.

Begin with a question about a problem or issue that matters to you:

- Should government subsidize student loans to help make college more affordable?
- Are there situations in which free speech should be restricted?
- Should Americans give up some privacy rights for greater security against terrorism?
- Should transgender people have access to the bathrooms of their choice?

Make a list of four or five such questions.

If your assignment specifies a topic, follow your instructor's guidelines. But you might still need to identify a specific topic. For example, if your instructor asks you to select from a list of approved topics, select four or five topics from that list, turn each one into a question and proceed with this exercise. Or your assignment might call for an argument about a general subject, such as gender, in which case you can list four or five questions about topics related to gender—for example, should women be allowed to serve in front-line military combat units?

Now **select the one question from your list that is most interesting to you.** Consider the following:

Your interest in the topic	The importance of the topic	Your opinion

Why does this topic interest you?
Consider what makes this topic worth exploring. It's best to make an argument about topics in which you have a strong interest.

Do you have some special connection to this topic?
For example, as a college student you might have a keen interest in student loan policy; as a mountain climber you might worry about how climate change affects regions where you climb.

Why is this topic important?
Consider whether the topic fits your assignment, is relevant to the academic field for which you are writing, or is important to a larger audience. For example, you might think hunting is fun, but is it worth making an argument about that? On the other hand, an argument about how hunting helps protect wildlife relates to significant debates about conservation, wilderness protection, and the rights of gun owners.

Do you have an opinion about this topic or a position on the issue?
Consider your feelings or attitude about the topic. What is your stance on this issue? Why do you feel the way you do?

Are you unsure?
At this point, it doesn't matter whether you have an opinion or stance. What matters is that the topic is important to you and others who might share your interests or concerns.

Exploring these questions will help you decide whether to pursue the topic. If you decide that the topic you have chosen isn't appropriate, return to your list and select a different question. Once you have a question about which you want to make an argument, develop your question using Step #1 in Chapter 3.

Step 2 Place your topic in rhetorical context.

If your assignment specifies an audience and rhetorical context, follow your instructor's guidelines. Otherwise, return to your question from Step #1 and identify an audience you would like to reach with your argument. Your question should be interesting to you but also relevant for your intended audience or your course assignment:

- Who would be interested in an argument on this topic? Why would they be interested in it?
- What makes this topic important now? What would an argument that addresses this question mean for this audience?
- What purpose would be served by making an argument about this issue, trend, phenomenon, or problem? What can be learned from such an argument? What might be accomplished?

For example, let's return to our previous question about student loans:

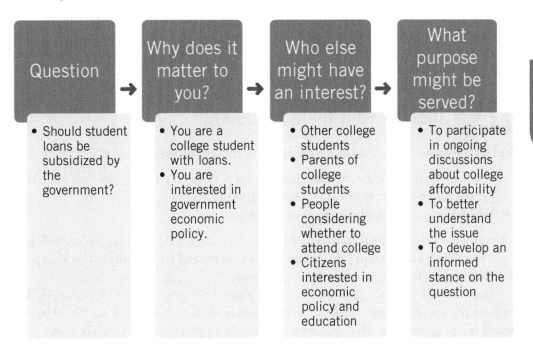

Using this procedure, explore the rhetorical context for your question, keeping notes as you go along. Then, using your notes as a guide, complete Step #2 in Chapter 3.

Step 3 Select a medium.

Most academic arguments are presented in the form of a conventional essay, but arguments in other contexts can appear in many different media. If you have a choice, consider which medium will enable you to make your argument most effectively to your intended audience.

| If your course assignment specifies a medium | Use the medium specified in the assignment guidelines. | Focus on how to present your argument effectively in this medium. |
| If you have a choice of medium | Consider which medium best addresses your intended audience. | Consider how that medium enables you to present your argument effectively. |

For example, if you are making an argument about whether the federal government should subsidize student loans and you want to reach a wider audience of college students, consider writing your argument for a blog or another social media site that is popular among college students. (Be sure that such a medium is acceptable to your instructor.)

Complete Step #3 in Chapter 3 to help you decide on an appropriate medium for your argument.

Step 4 Identify your main argument.

Your argument should grow out of the question you explored in Steps #1 and #2. Remember:

- Your main argument is not the same thing as your position on the issue, although it is related to your position. (See "Developing a Main Argument" on page 176.)
- Your main argument might evolve as you develop it.

You might not know at this point exactly what your argument will be, but as you research your topic, you will adjust and refine your argument. For now, the goal is to identify a clear main point as a starting point for developing an effective argument.

First, consider possible arguments you might make about your question. For example, here are some possible arguments to make about the question of whether student loans should be subsidized by the government. (Let's assume you generally support subsidized student loans, given your own experience trying to pay for college.)

- The president should support subsidized student loans for college.
- Student loans should be subsidized by the federal government.
- Subsidized student loans provide economic benefits for individual students and the society as a whole.

In assessing potential main arguments, consider which one best reflects your own interest and fits your rhetorical context:

Argument: The president should support subsidized student loans.

| This statement reflects unequivocal support for subsidized student loans but focuses narrowly on the president's role. | The statement does not reflect your concerns about loan debt, nor does it necessarily address the concerns of your intended audience. |

↓

Adjusted Argument: The federal government should subsidize all student loans.

| This statement reflects a position on the broader issue of student loans. | The statement still does not capture concerns about loan debt, nor does it reflect the economic complexity of the issue. |

↓

Refined Argument: Subsidized student loans provide economic benefits for individual students and for the society as a whole.

| This statement better captures the complexity of the issue and more specifically identifies the main reasons to support subsidized loans. | This statement is likely to address the concerns of your intended audience. |

6

Notice that in developing your main argument in this way, you are taking into account your rhetorical context and sense of purpose. In other words, your main argument should be shaped by your rhetorical situation.

Make a list of a few possible main arguments that grow out of your question and consider how well they fit your rhetorical situation. On the basis of that analysis, select one statement that will serve as your main argument. By following Step #4 in Chapter 3 you will develop a Guiding Thesis Statement, which is essentially a more refined statement of your main argument.

Step 5   Support your main argument.

As you develop your main argument, you will also generate supporting arguments or claims. You have four main tasks at this point:

- Identify the arguments or claims you will make in support of your main argument.
- Begin to identify evidence or reasoning to back up each claim.
- Identify opposing arguments or complicating factors.
- Rebut those opposing arguments and address complicating factors.

Usually, completing these tasks requires research. As you move through this step, you will learn more about your topic, and as a result you might need to refine your argument and adjust your claims. Remember, be open to possibilities as you proceed.

Let's return to the example of an argument in favor of subsidized student loans. Here's your main argument as you have stated it at this point:

Subsidized student loans provide economic benefits for individual students and the society as a whole.

To support this argument, you will need to show how students benefit from subsidized loans and how society benefits as well. Let's imagine that you have learned through your research that subsidized loans have lower interest rates, which means lower costs for students. You suspect that lower interest rates mean fewer loan defaults, which is good for students as well as for communities and for the banks that make the loans. One drawback to subsidized loans is that taxpayers pay for any loan defaults, but you believe that this potential drawback is outweighed by fewer defaults. Also, you consider it a benefit to society if more students are able to attend college, even though some people argue that government should not be involved in matters such as student loans.

Now you need to develop these supporting arguments and support them with evidence or reasoning; you also need to address opposing arguments. To do so, follow these steps:

State your main argument.

Subsidized student loans provide clear economic benefits for individual students and society.

List your supporting claims.

| Subsidized loans mean that more students can attend college. | Lower interest rates mean fewer defaults. | Lower default rates mean a healthier economy. |

Identify possible evidence for each supporting claim.

| Studies showing that such loans encourage more low-income students to attend college | Statistical evidence on student loan defaults | • Statements by respected economists
• Data on economic impact of loan defaults |

Identify opposing arguments or complicating factors.

| College isn't necessarily for everyone. | Lower interest rates mean lower profits on loans. | Subsidized loans amount to too much government interference in the loan market. |

Answer opposing arguments and/or complicating factors.

| True, but college should be available to those who want to attend. | Possibly, but that price is worth paying if more students attend college and fewer default on their loans. | Sometimes, strategic government interference is necessary if the potential benefits to society are worthwhile. |

Here are a few things to keep in mind as you develop support for your claims:

- **Follow the evidence.** Obviously, your evidence should support your claims, but your claims can change as you research your topic and look for evidence. You might find, for instance, that the available evidence does not support a claim. Don't make claims you can't support, which would result in a weaker (and perhaps unethical) argument.

- **Explore opposing arguments sufficiently.** Anticipating opposing arguments and identifying potential complicating factors can help you strengthen your argument. In doing so, you explore your topic more fully and make a stronger case for your position.

- **Remember that not all evidence is appropriate or persuasive.** As you find evidence to support your claims, determine whether that evidence is trustworthy, relevant to your topic, and appropriate for the rhetorical situation (see "Appraising and Using Evidence" on page 189).

Complete Step #5 in Chapter 3. You should be ready to write a complete draft of your project. Or you can move onto the next step before completing your draft.

Step 6 Organize your argument.

There are four standard ways to organize an argument (see "Structuring an Argument" on page 193); which one you select will depend upon your rhetorical situation and the nature of the argument you are making. For example, an argument against capital punishment based on the belief that all killing is wrong is probably best organized as a **deductive argument**, since the argument flows from the basic premise that killing is wrong. Keep in mind, too, that many academic disciplines have established conventions governing the form arguments take. For example, arguments in many social sciences, such as economics or sociology, are based on inductive reasoning because they rely on empirical evidence.

To decide how best to organize your argument, take into account the following considerations:

The rhetorical situation	• What structure would present your argument to your intended audience most persuasively? • What expectations, if any, will your audience likely have regarding the form of your argument? • How can you organize your essay so that your main argument is presented clearly to that audience? • What are the conventions for structuring an argument within the academic discipline in which you are writing?
The nature of your argument	• Does your argument rest on a primary belief or principle (deductive reasoning)? • Does it rely on conclusions drawn from evidence (inductive arrangement)? • Does your argument include a number of complicated supporting claims and kinds of evidence (classical arrangement)? • Is your purpose primarily to solve a problem or negotiate differences (Rogerian arrangement)?

For example, if you were writing your argument about subsidized college loans for an economics course, you would probably have to focus on the economic issues related to subsidized loans, such as how default rates might affect the financial well-being of individuals and businesses, the impact of government subsidies on interest rates, and so on; you would also be expected to present specific kinds of data to support your claims. So an **inductive argument** (in which you draw your conclusion about subsidized student loans from appropriate evidence) or **classical arrangement** (which would allow you to incorporate many supporting claims and address opposing arguments) would be good choices for structuring your argument. By contrast, if you were writing for a more general audience, you might rest your argument on a fundamental principle: governments should take certain actions for the common good. In this case, helping students attend college is in the public's interest. So you might consider making a deductive argument based on that fundamental principle. However, such an approach might make it more difficult to incorporate the supporting claims you have identified, so classical arrangement might be a better option because it would enable you to incorporate your supporting claims and evidence as well as logical reasoning on the basis of a fundamental principle.

Here's a basic outline for an argument in favor of subsidized student loans using classical arrangement:

I. *Introduction:* explanation of the relevance of the issue for intended audience

II. *Background:*
   A. Discussion of why this problem is important
   B. Brief history of the problem of student loan debt
   C. Explanation of rising college costs

III. *Proposition:* statement of main argument that government should subsidize student loans because of the potential benefits both to individual students and to society in general.

IV. *Proof:* presentation of supporting arguments and evidence to support them
   A. Subsidized loans allow more students to afford college.
   B. Lower interest rates mean fewer student loan defaults, which is better for communities, businesses, and individuals.
   C. Higher college attendance benefits individuals and communities.
   D. Lower default rates help keep the economy healthy, which benefits everyone.

V. *Refutation:* answers to opposing arguments and complicating factors
   A. College attendance might not be for everyone, but subsidized loans help make college affordable for those who wish to attend.
   B. Although subsidized loans might mean lower profits for banks, the overall benefit to the economy is worth it.
   C. Although subsidized loans require government involvement in a free market, in this case government involvement results in greater benefit to the society.

VI. *Conclusion:* emphasize benefits of college attendance and the need for government assistance in helping students avoid loan debt and defaults

You can obtain additional guidance for organizing your essay by following Step #6 in Chapter 3.

6

Feedback on your draft will be more relevant if your readers focus on the following sets of questions related to the features of effective argumentation:

A clear main point	• What is your main point? Is it clearly stated? • Is the purpose of your argument clear? • How well is the focus of your main argument maintained throughout your essay?
A relevant purpose	• What makes your topic relevant for your rhetorical situation? • In what ways does your argument contribute to ongoing discussions of this topic? • How do you address your argument to your intended audience?
Appropriate support	• What evidence or support do you provide for each of your claims? • Which claims might be strengthened with additional or different support? • Is your evidence appropriate for your topic and audience?
Complexity	• How does your argument reflect the complexity of your topic? • Do you explore your topic sufficiently? • How have you avoided oversimplifying the issues?
Persuasive appeals	• What persuasive appeals have you made? • In what ways are these appeals appropriate for your rhetorical situation? • Do these appeals weaken your argument in any way?

Follow Step #7 in Chapter 3 to analyze your feedback and help you decide which revisions to make.

Step 8 Revise.

As you consider the feedback you received for Step #7, you might find that you need to do additional research to identify evidence to support your claims or address opposing arguments or complicating factors. That's OK. Revision is an opportunity to deepen your understanding of your topic and strengthen your argument. It is also a chance to adjust and strengthen your persuasive appeals and make sure that your argument fits your rhetorical situation.

You can divide the task of revising your argument into four steps: (1) Review your draft using the questions listed in Step #7, (2) adjust your persuasive appeals, (3) review each supporting argument or claim, and (4) avoid common problems in argument.

1. **Review your draft using the questions listed in Step #7.** As you address the questions listed in Step #7, keep your audience and sense of purpose in mind.

2. **Adjust your persuasive appeals.** To make an effective argument, you must present your case in a way that is likely to be persuasive to your intended audience. That means reviewing your draft to make sure that you have used ethical, emotional, and/or logical appeals effectively (see "Making a Persuasive Appeal" on page 179). The appeals you use in making your argument depend in large part on your rhetorical situation. For example, you probably wouldn't make an exclusively emotional appeal in an argument about subsidized student loans for an economics course, but a carefully made emotional appeal might supplement an argument that is based mostly on a logical appeal.

3. **Review each supporting argument or claim.** Determine whether you have made an appropriate persuasive appeal for each supporting argument or claim. Although you should now have evidence to support each claim, you can strengthen those claims with appropriate persuasive appeals.

Let's review a few claims in our hypothetical argument in favor of subsidized student loans. For each claim, consider the kind of appeal that might be most appropriate:

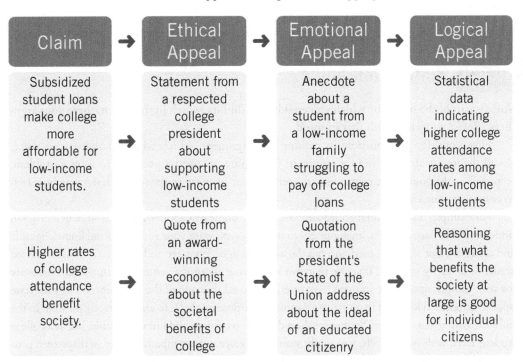

6

Use appeals that will strengthen your argument—but only if they are appropriate for your rhetorical situation.

4. **Avoid common problems in argument.** Review your draft carefully to avoid three common problems that can weaken an argument:

Missing or weak evidence	• Do you provide sufficient evidence for each claim you make? • Have you failed to support any claims? • Is the evidence presented for any of your claims weak, misleading, or inappropriate?
Flawed reasoning	• How sound is your reasoning? • Do you fall victim to any logical fallacies? • Do your conclusions follow logically from your evidence or claims?
Oversimplified or exaggerated assertions	• To what extent do you avoid oversimplifying your topic or your claims? • How does your argument do justice to the complexity of your topic? • Do you make any exaggerated claims or assertions that need to be eliminated or revised on the basis of your evidence?

Follow Step #8 in Chapter 3 to make sure you have addressed all the essential aspects of your essay.

Step 9 Refine your voice.

Voice is part of the means by which you establish credibility, which in turn strengthens your argument. Revise your draft with that in mind.

First, consider your purpose in making this argument, which will help shape your voice. Recall the four main purposes for argument (to inquire, to assert a position, to solve a problem, to prevail). Although these purposes can overlap, your primary purpose can determine how best to construct your voice.

For example, if your primary purpose in making an argument about subsidized student loans is to understand this issue—that is, an argument to inquire—you want your voice to sound knowledgeable and confident but also measured and fair. So avoid charged language and write in a straightforward academic style. By contrast, imagine that you are writing about the same topic in an editorial essay for your campus newspaper and you have recently learned that one of the U.S. senators in your state opposes subsidized loans. In that case, your primary purpose might be to assert a strong position in the public debate about the issue. Your voice should still be confident and knowledgeable, but as a college student faced with tuition bills, you might want your voice to be sympathetic and perhaps even provocative. In short, your voice should be appropriate for your purpose within your rhetorical context.

Review your draft and adjust your voice, if necessary. Step #9 in Chapter 3 will help you refine and strengthen your voice.

Complete Step #10 in Chapter 3.

WRITING PROJECTS | **ARGUMENT**

1. Identify an issue or controversy you feel strongly about. Write an argument in which you take a position on this issue. Write your argument in a way that would be appropriate for both an academic audience and a wider audience. For example, if you write about a controversy about eliminating your major at your college, you might intend your argument for readers in an academic field such as education or philosophy as well as for a wider audience interested in educational issues.

2. Rewrite the essay you wrote for Question #1 in a completely different medium. For example, if you wrote an academic argument for a course, rewrite the essay as a multimedia presentation for a different audience or as a letter to a person at the center of the issue.

   Now compare the two arguments. What changes did you make in rewriting your argument for a different medium? In what ways (if any) did you have to adjust important elements of your argument, such as your evidence or your persuasive appeals? What might a comparison of these two arguments suggest about how argument is shaped by rhetorical context and medium?

3. Think of an important experience you had that influenced your life in a significant way. Looking back on that experience, consider what larger issues the experience seems to involve. For example, if you encountered some kind of difficulty in school, you might consider your experience in light of debates about school reform or problems with education. Drawing on your experience, write an argument about an issue related to that experience. Identify an audience for whom your argument would be appropriate.

4. Review several recent tweets on a current controversy that interests you. Identify tweets that reflect a position on the issue that you support. Now develop an argument on the basis of those tweets. Write your argument for an audience similar to the audience for the original tweets and adopt a medium that would reach that audience.

5. Find an argument on a website or in a print publication about a problem that matters to you. Using that argument as a starting point, develop a proposal that would address the problem described in that argument. In your proposal, present a rationale for addressing this particular problem and make an argument in support of your solution. Write your proposal for an audience that has an interest in that problem. For example, if the problem involves safety in youth sports, you might write your proposal to the organization that sponsors youth sports in your community or to a local foundation interested in youth issues.

6

In this chapter, you will learn to

1. Identify and apply seven stylistic skills and strategies that are integral to effective academic writing.

2. Describe the four key components of academic conversations.

3. Explain four basic principles of academic inquiry.

4. Explain the purposes of summary, paraphrase, and synthesis in academic writing.

5. Understand and apply the three characteristics of effective paragraphs.

6. Understand how to frame an argument, analysis, or discussion.

7. Understand and apply strategies for effective introductions and transitions.

Working with Ideas and Information

MANY STUDENTS THINK of effective writing as a matter of crafting good sentences or using ornate language. My own students sometimes complain that they can't write well because they don't have big vocabularies. These complaints are understandable. Writing can be challenging, especially when the subject is unfamiliar to the writer. Most students genuinely want to learn to write well, and they worry about matters like word choice and punctuation. But when I hear such complaints, I always respond in the same way: Writing is ultimately about ideas. It is true that well-crafted sentences can make a piece of writing more effective, correct grammar can mean clearer prose, and having a good vocabulary can give a writer more options for choosing the right word. But those skills alone don't lead to effective writing. Without something relevant to say (Core Concept #4), a writer's well-crafted sentences, correct grammar, and impressive vocabulary mean little.

By the time they enter college, most students have developed the ability to write grammatically correct sentences, use proper punctuation, form verb tenses appropriately, spell correctly, and so on. Of course, *all* students, even the most successful writers, make mistakes and sometimes have trouble remembering certain rules of formal writing, but for the vast majority of students, learning to write effectively in college is not about learning these "basics." For most students, the main challenge is learning to write in an appropriate academic style and conveying complex ideas and information clearly in the kind of authoritative voice that college instructors expect—in other words, learning to write like a scholar. This chapter will help you do so by focusing on the stylistic skills and strategies necessary for working with complex ideas and writing the kind of prose expected in academic settings:

- developing an academic writing style
- writing effective paragraphs
- summarizing and paraphrasing
- synthesizing
- framing
- introducing
- making transitions

These skills and strategies correspond to the Ten Core Concepts described in Chapter 2. For example, developing an effective and appropriate voice in academic writing (Core Concept #9) requires understanding and applying the stylistic conventions of academic writing, which are explained in this chapter. Similarly, achieving your rhetorical purpose (Core Concept #2) requires being able to write clear, appropriate prose that conveys your ideas effectively to your intended audience. Learning to write like a scholar, then, is really a matter of understanding and applying the Ten Core Concepts. If you do that and apply the strategies described in this chapter, you are more likely to learn from your writing—and the better your writing is likely to be.

Understanding Academic Writing As Conversation

I sometimes conduct workshops to help college professors learn to work more effectively with student writers in their classes. One of my favorite activities in these workshops is to ask the professors to summarize a short text on an unfamiliar subject, such as this excerpt from a technical guide to sailing:

> No matter how good the sails look, no boat sails well when they are pulling her over at extreme angles of heel. When a boat heels excessively, she slows down, develops severe weather helm, and wallows sluggishly through the water. She must be brought back upright by depowering the sails. If powering in light and moderate winds means to make the sails full at narrow angles of attack, depowering in winds stronger than about 15 knots (apparent) means to flatten sails and trim them wider. . . .
>
> The main sheet works quickest. When a gust hits and the boat begins to flop over, quickly ease out one or more feet of main sheet and keep it eased until she rights herself. Either the helmsman or a crew can cast the sheet off—the former when he first feels the drastic weather helm through the tiller or the wheel, the latter when he sees the helmsman begin to fight the helm. Even though the wildly luffing mainsail may seem to be wasted, the boat is sailing better because she's sailing on her bottom.
>
> The jib sheet may also be eased quickly in fresh winds to spill air from the jib. The jib sheet should be moved outboard in fresh and strong winds to decrease side force and increase forward force. It may also be moved aft to increase the amount of twist in the upper part of the sail, effectively spilling wind up high, where it exerts the greatest heeling leverage over the hull.

Source: Rousmaniere, John. *The Annapolis Book of Seamanship*. Revised ed., Simon and Schuster, 1989, p. 82.

Because most of the professors in my workshops are not sailors, they usually find this text confusing and difficult to understand. Not surprisingly, they have trouble summarizing it. As experienced academic writers, they are used to summarizing difficult texts, but summarizing this excerpt stumps them. That's because, despite their expertise in their academic fields, they are unfamiliar with specialized sailing jargon (such as *jib* and *sheet*), and they don't understand the concepts (such as *heeling force* and *weather helm*) and procedures of sailing (such as *easing a sheet* or *trimming a sail*).

Like the professors in the workshop who are unfamiliar with the language and concepts of sailing, most college students are newcomers to the academic subjects they study in their courses. Students in an introductory economics class, for example, might have a basic understanding of economics, but they are likely to have little knowledge of the specialized concepts and terminology that economists use and the sophisticated way that economists think about their subject. Yet those students will probably be asked to write in ways that are similar to economists. In other words, the students will be expected to participate like experts in the conversations that economists are always having about their subject—even though the students are novices and unfamiliar with those conversations.

As a college student, you might sometimes feel frustrated (like the professors in my workshop) as you try to make sense of assigned readings or meet the professor's expectations for writing. That's understandable. You are just beginning to learn about the subject itself and the rules for writing in that discipline. If you walk into a party or a meeting that is already under way and find people engaged in intense conversation, you have to listen for a while—and maybe ask some strategic questions—in order to figure out what is going on before you can join in. Much academic writing is like that.

Learning to write effectively in college, then, is partly a matter of understanding that **most academic writing is like taking part in a conversation.** To be part of that conversation, you must develop a sense of what is going on in each discipline you study—and in academic discourse in general. In other words, you have to acquire some relevant knowledge and develop the language necessary for participating in the conversations about important subjects in that academic field. You also have to learn *how* to participate in conversations about important subjects in that discipline—that is, you have to become familiar with the conventions of writing in that discipline.

Writing effectively in college requires understanding **four key components of academic conversations:**

- **Important concepts or ideas.** Academic fields are organized around certain kinds of questions and specific bodies of knowledge. Biologists, for example, examine questions about living organisms and how they function. To address these questions, they rely on knowledge developed through research and they draw on accepted theories, such as natural selection, to help them understand that research. Similarly, psychologists explore questions about how humans think and interact with each other, drawing on various kinds of studies and theories, such as behaviorism, to understand human cognition and social interactions. To write effectively in biology or psychology requires understanding the nature of the questions that scholars in those disciplines examine and becoming familiar with key concepts in those fields. In part, students gain this understanding simply by doing the assigned work in a course and learning the subject matter. But students are unlikely to be familiar with some of the less common concepts or ideas in academic fields if they encounter them in course readings or source material. For example, if you're reading a scholarly article in psychology, you might recognize references to *behaviorism* but not to *operant conditioning*, which is an important concept in behaviorism. Without a basic understanding of operant conditioning, you might find it difficult to follow the discussion in the article.

- **Specialized terminology.** Every academic discipline has specialized words or phrases, related to key concepts in that discipline, that scholars use in their writing. In fact, most professions do, too. Like sailors, people in just about any profession or activity you can think of—engineers, lawyers, dancers, electricians, nurses—use a specialized language to do their work. Sometimes this specialized language is criticized as jargon, but it is essential to the work scholars do in their disciplines. Just as knowing specialized terms on a sailboat allows sailors to operate the boat safely and effectively, knowing the terminology in an academic field is often necessary for understanding scholarly texts in that field and can strengthen your ability to write effectively about relevant topics in that field.

- **Conventions.** Writing effectively in an academic discipline requires knowing not only what to say but *how* to say it. That means becoming familiar with some of the basic conventions of writing in that discipline. Conventions are common practices, such as how to introduce key ideas, when and how to cite sources, what is appropriate style, and how to organize a text. Some basic conventions are followed in most kinds of academic writing, but many academic disciplines have more specialized conventions that writers are expected to follow. For example, in many social science disciplines, such as psychology and economics, writers typically don't use direct quotations when citing a source; by contrast, in many fields in the humanities, such as history or English, direct quotations from sources are common and expected. In some disciplines, writers never use the first person, whereas in others, the use of first person is common. As a student who is learning new disciplines, it is essential for you to be aware that these different conventions exist and to become familiar enough with the basic conventions to be able to understand the reading and writing you are asked to do in your classes.

- **Assumptions about the audience.** Because academic writers usually write for other experts in their disciplines, they can assume that their intended audience is familiar with the key concepts, specialized language, and conventions of the discipline. They also assume their audience shares their interest in relevant topics in that discipline. For example, anthropologists usually expect their readers to have an in-depth understanding of the complexities of culture and the established theories for understanding how cultures develop and affect our lives. So they don't have to explain established concepts or theories, and they can assume that if they refer to an important study or figure in the field, their readers will not only recognize the reference but also understand its significance. As a newcomer to an academic field, you might not be part of the intended audience for specialized scholarly writing, which can make reading scholarly texts challenging. As a writer, part of your challenge is to determine what expectations you can reasonably make about your readers when it comes to the academic subject about which you're writing. For example, if you're writing an essay about ethical questions surrounding operant conditioning for a psychology class, you probably don't need to explain that concept, because you can assume your audience (your professor and other students in the psychology course) are familiar with it; however, if you're writing about the same topic for an introductory writing class, you will probably have to explain the concept and maybe even provide some history about it.

EXERCISE 7A   UNDERSTANDING ACADEMIC CONVERSATIONS

Here are the first three paragraphs of a scholarly article that was published in the *Journal of Experimental Social Psychology*. Read these paragraphs and answer the questions that follow them:

> Individualism-collectivism is perhaps the most basic dimension of cultural variability identified in cross-cultural research. Concepts related to this dimension have been employed in several social science domains (cf. Triandis, McCusker, & Hui, 1990),

---

and the individualism-collectivism dimension has come to be regarded as "central to an understanding of cultural values, of work values, of social systems, as well as in the studies of morality, the structure of constitutions, and cultural patterns" (Triandis, Brislin, & Hui, 1988). Several recent studies have suggested that individualism and collectivism are contrasting cultural syndromes that are associated with a broad pattern of differences in individuals' social perceptions and social behavior, including differences in the definition of self and its perceived relation to ingroups and outgroups (Markus & Kitayama, 1991), in the endorsement of values relevant to individual vs. group goals (Triandis et al., 1990), and in the pattern and style of social interactions (cf. Triandis, 1990).

However, little is known about the implications of these cultural differences for another social process that is fundamental to every culture: persuasion. Persuasive communications transmit and reflect the values of a culture. Persuasive messages are used to obtain the compliance that achieves the personal, political, and economic ends valued in the culture. Although social influence has always been a central arena of research in social psychology, little is understood about what differences exist in the types of persuasive appeals used in different cultures (see Burgoon, Dillard, Doran, & Miller, 1982; Glenn, Witmeyer, & Stevenson, 1977). Even less is known about the effectiveness of different appeal types in different cultures.

What types of persuasive appeals are prevalent in individualistic versus collectivistic cultures? And how do members of these different cultures differ in the extent to which they are persuaded by these appeals? This paper presents an exploration of these questions.

Source: Han, Sang-Pil, and Sharon Shavitt. "Persuasion and Culture: Advertising Appeals in Individualistic and Collectivistic Societies." *Journal of Experimental Social Psychology*, vol. 30, no. 4, July 1994, pp. 326–50.

1. Identify the key concepts or ideas discussed in this passage. (You can highlight them or make a list.)

2. What specialized terms or language do you see in this passage? Do you know what these terms mean? If not, to what extent does your lack of familiarity with these terms interfere with your understanding of the passage?

3. What conventions do these writers follow in this passage? For example, what conventions regarding writing style do they follow? How do they introduce and cite information or ideas from other sources?

4. What assumptions do you think these authors make about their audience? Who do you think their intended audience is? How do you know? Are you part of that audience? How do you know?

5. How well do you think you understand this passage? How much of your understanding of the passage is based on your knowledge of the topic and the academic discipline of social psychology? What do you think your experience with this passage suggests about participating in academic conversations as a college student?

7

Developing an Academic Writing Style

The previous section of this chapter explains the essential idea that writing well in academic contexts means understanding that you are participating in ongoing academic conversations. As you proceed through your college career, you will become more and more familiar with the important conversations in your major and you will eventually learn the specific conventions for writing in that discipline. As a new college student, however, you have to find a way into the academic conversations taking place in the courses you take. You will more easily be able to do so by following these **three guidelines for developing an academic writing style:**

- *How* **you write affects** *what* **you write.** To complete most academic writing tasks successfully requires more than having something relevant to say (Core Concept #4); it also requires saying it well. In academic writing, that means adopting an appropriate style and presenting your ideas in a way that meets the expectations of your audience. Academic audiences expect writers to know how to summarize relevant information and other points of view, to quote properly from appropriate sources, to synthesize ideas clearly, to write coherent paragraphs about complicated subject matter, and to place their arguments or analyses in the context of the larger academic subject within which they are writing. (The following sections of this chapter will help you learn these crucial skills and strategies.)

- **Good writing isn't necessarily always good writing.** Core Concept #2 ("Good writing fits the context") reminds us that what counts as good writing always depends on the rhetorical situation. In college-level academic writing, students must learn to fit into the ongoing conversations about the subjects that are the focus of the academic disciplines they are studying. But each discipline has its own specialized rules and conventions. What counts as clear and engaging prose in a history course might be considered inappropriate for an economics paper or chemistry lab report. "Good" academic writing, then, is writing that conforms to the conventions of the specific discipline in which the writer is writing. Understanding that essential principle is necessary for developing an effective academic writing style and learning to adapt your writing to different subjects.

- **Practice might make perfect, but it also means making mistakes.** As a college student, you will routinely be asked to write like a scholar without yet having mastered the skills of scholarly writing. So you will make mistakes. But those mistakes can be a sign of growth. When you try to write about a complex and unfamiliar topic while following unfamiliar conventions for academic writing, you are stretching just beyond your ability as a writer. As a result, sometimes your prose will be awkward and your ideas unclear. Ultimately, though, you can learn from such mistakes. Through practice, you will eventually acquire the skills needed to write effective academic prose. So expect some stumbling as you learn the strategies described in this chapter. If you struggle, it doesn't mean you're a "bad" writer; it probably means you're still developing the specialized skills needed to write effective academic prose.

As you work on your writing assignments, these guidelines will help you keep your mistakes in perspective, understand and build on your strengths, and identify aspects of your writing that need improvement.

Principles of Academic Inquiry

One of the main challenges students face in developing an effective academic writing style is trying to adapt to the specific conventions of different disciplines: When is it OK to use the first person? Do I always need to write an abstract? Should I cite my sources using APA or MLA style? Although these different conventions can be confusing, *all* conventions of academic writing, no matter the discipline, reflect the fact that writing is central to academic inquiry. Developing an effective academic writing style is partly a matter of learning to use language in a way that reflects **four basic principles of academic inquiry** that apply to all disciplines.

Qualify your statements

Academic writers must back up what they say (Core Concept #5). Often, that means avoiding unsupported generalizations and qualifying your statements. For example, in casual conversation or informal writing, it's acceptable to say something like this:

> Drivers just don't pay attention to speed limits.

In academic writing, which values accuracy and validity, such statements usually need to be qualified, depending on the rhetorical context:

> Drivers *often seem to* ignore speed limits.

> *Many* drivers ignore speed limits.

> Studies show that *most* drivers *sometimes* exceed speed limits.

The italicized words in these examples make the statements "more true." If you can't support a statement with evidence, then qualify it so that it is valid.

Be Specific

Academic audiences value specificity, and good writers avoid vagueness. Here's an example of a vague statement from a student essay:

> In order for education to work, things need to change.

Such a statement seems reasonable enough, but it doesn't quite hold up under scrutiny. What does it mean to say that education must "work"? What "things" must change? And what kinds of "changes" are necessary? Often, vague terms like *things* are a sign that a statement itself might be vague. Even if this statement appears in a longer paragraph explaining those "things" and "changes," such a statement is weak by the common standards of academic writing. We might revise it as follows:

> If schools are to solve the problems that prevent students from obtaining a sound education, both administrative and curricular reforms should be implemented.

Notice that in this statement the writer avoids vague terms and tries to be more specific about what it means for schools to "work." Specificity isn't always possible or even desirable, but often vagueness can weaken your writing. (By the way, you'll notice that the revised sentence employs the passive voice, which many teachers discourage. See Focus: "Active vs. Passive Voice" on page 226.)

These examples illustrate that strong academic writing is partly a result of careful word choice, which should reflect your effort to make valid, accurate, and clear statements.

Give credit

Giving credit in academic writing is not just a matter of citing sources properly (which is discussed in Chapters 11 and 12); it is also a matter of using appropriate language to signal to readers that you are using source material or referring to someone else's ideas. For example, here's a student referring to a source in a paper about education reform:

> The article states that money spent on schools can do little to improve educational outcomes.

Technically, there is nothing wrong with this sentence, but it is an awkward way of introducing information or referring to material taken from a source. For one thing, it isn't the article but the author who makes a statement. That might seem to be a minor point, but minor revisions can make this sentence stronger by bringing it into line with the conventions of academic prose:

> The author claims that money spent on schools can do little to improve educational outcomes.

> According to this author, money spent on schools can do little to improve educational outcomes.

These revised versions make it clear that the assertion being made is attributed to the author of the source, not to the writer of this sentence; they also sound as though the writer is in better command of the source material, which conveys a sense of authority.

In general, unless the assertion is yours, credit the author or source for the assertion. Because academic writing is essentially a matter of participating in ongoing conversations, crediting a source for a statement not only indicates who deserves credit for the statement but also helps place your own writing in the context of a relevant academic conversation. It shows that you are part of that conversation.

Use specialized terminology judiciously

A common complaint about academic writing is that it is full of jargon. As we saw earlier in this chapter (see page 219), however, when used properly, jargon—or specialized terminology—is not only useful but essential. All academic fields have specialized terms that refer to important ideas and concepts within those fields. The challenge for student writers is to become familiar enough with such terminology so that it becomes a tool for effective writing rather than a distraction for the reader.

In the following passage, for example, the writer discusses the increasing socio-economic inequality in higher education:

> At the same time that family income has become more predictive of children's academic achievement, so has educational attainment become more predictive of adults' earnings. The combination of these trends creates a feedback mechanism that may decrease inter-generational mobility. As children from higher socio-economic strata achieve greater

academic success, and those who succeed academically are more likely to have higher incomes, higher education contributes to an even more unequal and economically polarized society.

This passage contains terms that are widely used in academic discussions about poverty and education reform—for example, *academic achievement* and *intergenerational mobility*. These terms have specialized meaning in fields such as sociology, education, political science, and public policy and therefore can be useful for writers in those fields. Not only do these terms convey important ideas efficiently to a reader, but they also signal that the writer is knowledgeable about the subject. At the same time, such terminology can make a passage dense and difficult to follow. Some careful revisions (which are highlighted in orange the passage below) to reduce wordiness can make the same passage clearer without eliminating necessary terms:

> At the same time that family income has become more predictive of children's academic achievement, so has educational attainment become more predictive of adults' earnings. The combination of these trends could decrease intergenerational mobility. As the children of the rich do better in school, and those who do better in school are more likely to become rich, we risk producing an even more unequal and economically polarized society.

> Source: Adapted from Edsall, Thomas. "The Reproduction of Privilege." *The New York Times*, 12 Mar. 2012, campaignstops.blogs.nytimes.com/2012/03/12/the-reproduction-of-privilege/?_r=0.

In this revised version, some specialized terms ("higher socio-economic strata," "greater academic success") are replaced with more common language ("rich," "do better in school"), but key terms (*academic achievement* and *intergenerational mobility*) are preserved. Replacing those key terms with common language would result in a lengthy passage that might not be clearer. For example, *intergenerational mobility* refers to the process by which children do better economically than their parents; in other words, children attain a higher socio-economic status than their parents. Explaining that idea in a sentence or two would unnecessarily lengthen the passage. If this passage were intended for a general audience, then it might be necessary to define the term or replace it entirely; for an academic audience, however, the term enables the writer to keep the passage shorter while at the same time making an important point. It also suggests that the writer is part of the ongoing academic conversation about this topic.

The rule of thumb is to use language that communicates your ideas clearly to your intended audience:

- Use appropriate terminology to communicate specialized ideas, but make sure you understand the terminology.
- Replace confusing terms or unnecessary jargon with common words if you can do so without undermining your point or changing the meaning of the passage.

Following these guidelines will help you write prose that is both clear and sophisticated.

7

Popular writing guides, pundits, and many English teachers warn students to avoid the passive voice and use active voice in writing. The prevailing belief is that using the active voice strengthens your prose, whereas the passive voice weakens your writing by making it unnecessarily wordy and vague. Like most such "rules," that one is misleading. Remember Core Concept #2: "Good writing fits the context." Although it might be true that in many contexts the active voice makes for better writing, the passive voice is not only acceptable but also essential in academic writing. In some cases, the passive voice is actually preferable because it can change the focus of a statement to emphasize a point or idea. To illustrate, let's return to the example on page 223:

> If schools are to solve the problems that prevent students from obtaining a sound education, both administrative and curricular reforms should be implemented.

The main point of this sentence is that school reform is needed. Notice that in the main clause ("both administrative and curricular reforms should be implemented"), the use of the passive voice ("should be implemented") places the emphasis on *reforms* (which is the subject of the clause). Revising the sentence to place the main clause in the active voice changes that emphasis. Here's how that sentence might look in the active voice:

> If schools are to solve the problems that prevent students from obtaining a sound education, they should implement both administrative and curricular reforms.

Is this version clearer, more succinct, or more valid than the original sentence? Not necessarily. Notice that in the revised version the subject of the main clause is now "they" (presumably referring back to "schools"), which shifts the emphasis of the statement slightly. In this case, the passive voice enables the writer to keep the emphasis on the need for school reform—which is the main point of the sentence—not on *who* will accomplish the reform—which is an important and related topic but not the focus here. So the use of passive voice in this example does not weaken the writing; rather, it allows the writer to maintain the appropriate focus. If the writer's focus happened to be on a specific entity responsible for education reform, the active voice might be more appropriate. For example, let's assume that the writer was discussing reforms that only elected politicians could enact. In that case, the subject would be clear and the active voice more appropriate:

> If schools are to solve the problems that prevent students from obtaining a sound education, elected officials should undertake several reforms.

The passive voice should be used judiciously. Excessive or inappropriate use of the passive voice can weaken your writing. Often, active voice results in more concise prose, but as this example illustrates, writers can use the passive voice as an important tool for emphasis and clarity.

Using the advice for academic writing style in this section, revise the following statements so that they are clearer and appropriately supported or qualified. For each item, imagine an appropriate rhetorical context and indicate how that context would shape your revisions. (For example, for item (a) you might imagine that statement in an argument supporting gun control for a criminal justice course.)

a) We need better gun laws to make our communities safer. Otherwise, we'll just have more and more violence.

b) Poverty-stricken Americans of low socio-economic status will be adversely affected by legislative actions that facilitate the attainment of citizenship by undocumented residents.

c) Smartphones are convenient but they are making everyone dumber because people rely on them rather than on their own minds.

Writing Paragraphs

By the time they enter college, most students have had many hours of instruction in writing correct sentences and paragraphs. Yet new college students often struggle to write effective paragraphs that convey complex ideas clearly and coherently. Part of the problem is that the subject matter in college writing is often new and sometimes challenging, and students have to learn how to write clearly about unfamiliar ideas, concepts, and information. But students can also improve their writing by learning how to create more effective paragraphs, no matter what subject they are writing about.

Effective paragraphs in academic writing have **three key characteristics.** They are:

- **Well developed.** A paragraph should cover its topic sufficiently. Often, that means elaborating on key points, ideas, or facts and including examples. Under-developed paragraphs tend to be superficial and suggest that the writer has not explored the topic in sufficient depth.

- **Coherent.** Coherence refers to the extent to which the paragraph retains a focus on a main idea or point. In a coherent paragraph, all the sentences relate clearly to one another and communicate ideas or information relevant to the main point. Usually, but not always, a strong paragraph also has a clear topic sentence that states the main point and establishes the focus of the paragraph.

- **Cohesive.** Cohesion means that the statements, ideas, and information in a paragraph are explicitly linked together. To a great extent, cohesion is a function of the use of specific words and phrases that indicate to a reader that statements are connected. Examples are *similarly, by contrast, also, therefore, on the other hand, moreover, in addition,* and so on. Writers also achieve cohesion by repeating key words or phrases.

7

Writing Well-Developed Paragraphs

The key to writing a well-developed paragraph is making sure the topic of the paragraph is sufficiently explained or examined and the main point adequately supported. When necessary, elaborating on a point and illustrating it with examples also contributes to paragraph development. Here's an example of an under-developed paragraph from an essay about the relationship between poverty and educational achievement:

> The culture of poverty is defined by Paul Gorski as "the idea that poor people share more or less monolithic and predictable beliefs, values and behavior" (32). This is not true. Later studies show that a culture of poverty does not exist. This belief was constructed from data collected in the early 1960's showing that certain behaviors, such as increased violence and failure to foresee or plan for the future, were common among poor people. The original study portrayed stereotypes of poor students, not a culture of poverty.

In this paragraph the student tries to explain the idea of "the culture of poverty," relying on a source for information about the origins of that idea and how it has been interpreted. The author of that source, Paul Gorski, argues that the idea of a culture of poverty is actually a misunderstanding of a particular study of poverty; he cites subsequent studies that invalidate the whole idea of a culture of poverty. The student attempts to communicate Gorski's position. However, although the student defines the term *culture of poverty*, the complexity of that idea and the problems associated with it are not sufficiently explained. The student writes that the idea "is not true" and that studies show it "does not exist," but the lack of explanation makes it difficult for readers to understand the problems with the original study and how the data were interpreted. In short, the paragraph is insufficiently developed to communicate this complicated information.

In situations like this one, in which the writer is trying to convey complex ideas and information in a single paragraph, the solution is to elaborate on key ideas to make sure they are explained sufficiently to the reader. In this case, the student must provide more information about the origins of the idea of the culture of poverty, how it was misinterpreted, and how it was invalidated:

> The culture of poverty, according to Paul Gorski, is "the idea that poor people share more or less monolithic and predictable beliefs, values and behavior" (32). The idea emerged from a 1961 book by Oscar Lewis that reported on ethnographic studies of several small poor Mexican communities. Lewis's data indicated that those communities shared fifty attributes, such as frequent violence and a failure to plan for the future. From this small sample, he concluded that all poor communities share these attributes, which reflect a culture of poverty. The idea that "people in poverty share a persistent and observable 'culture'" (32–33) became popular among scholars trying to understand poverty. However, numerous later studies revealed great differences among poor communities and called the very idea of a culture of poverty into question. According to Gorski, these subsequent studies make it clear that "there is no such thing as a culture of poverty" (33). Gorski concludes that "the culture of poverty concept is constructed from a collection of smaller stereotypes which, however false, seem to have crept into mainstream thinking as unquestioned fact" (33).

In this developed version, the writer elaborates on specific points, such as how Lewis arrived at the idea of a culture of poverty and how the idea was subsequently challenged. The writer also uses quotations from the source text to provide additional information about this topic, which makes it much easier for a reader to grasp the main idea and supporting points.

Longer is not always better, of course, but when you are writing about complex ideas in academic contexts, under-developed paragraphs can result in superficial and sometimes confusing prose.

Achieving Coherence

In effective academic writing, paragraphs are not only sufficiently developed but also clearly focused and organized. A coherent paragraph has the following characteristics:

- The writer is in control of the subject matter and takes the reader deliberately from beginning to end.
- All the sentences contain relevant information.
- The discussion follows a clear and logical progression.

Often there is a topic sentence, but even without one, the main point of the paragraph is clear.

Students sometimes lose control of a paragraph when they are writing about complicated, abstract, or unfamiliar ideas and aren't sure what information to include or how to organize that information. In the following example, a student tries to explain what he believes is a basic principle of social life: competition. However, he struggles to make the main point of the paragraph clear and to present his ideas about competition in an orderly way:

> Our society is based on competition. It is natural for all of us to compete. Probably cheating is caused by our desire to succeed in competition. The first place we experience competition is at home when we cry to be held by our parents. We compete with their busy schedules to get their attention. Our next major competition is school, where we are all compared with other students. Until this time we only know that the time we spend with our parents is limited, but if we exert ourselves we get what we want. Being compared with other students is when we first realize that we compete for others' time and compliments. As children we only know that we need to get someone's attention to achieve what we need. We find that most competition is based upon being recognized.

Although the paragraph has a general focus on competition, the main idea seems to shift. The opening sentence suggests that the paragraph is about the central role competition plays in human society, but the final sentence suggests a somewhat narrower point: that competition arises from the need to be recognized. In addition, the third sentence is tangential to the main point about competition, and the paragraph isn't well organized.

To address these problems, the first task is to identify the main point of the paragraph. Stating that point in a topic sentence can help, but the topic sentence does not have to be at the beginning of the paragraph. Let's assume that the writer wants to make the point that competition arises from the human need to be recognized. That can serve as a topic sentence. We want to keep the focus of the paragraph on that main point. We also want to order the sentences so that the reader can follow the discussion easily from one supporting point to the next.

Here's a revised version of the student's paragraph:

> Our society is based on competition, and it is natural for all of us to compete. But why? Competition, it seems, arises from a basic human need to be recognized. We first experience competition very early in our lives when we cry to be held by our parents, actually competing with their busy schedules for their attention. For the first years of our lives, we learn that the time we spend with our parents is precious but limited, so we exert ourselves to get the attention we need. Our next major competition occurs in school, where we are compared with other students. We are still seeking the time and attention of others, but now we realize that we must compete with other students to be recognized. Every stage of our lives is characterized by different versions of this competition to fulfill our basic need for attention and recognition.

In this version, much of the original language is retained, but the focus on the main idea has been sharpened by adding a clear topic sentence ("Competition, it seems, arises from a basic human need to be recognized"), eliminating unnecessary material (the sentence about cheating), rewriting some sentences so that they relate more clearly to the topic sentence, and reorganizing the paragraph. The paragraph is now more coherent, which makes its main point more evident to the reader.

Coherence can be difficult to achieve, but following these three steps can help make your paragraphs more coherent and effective:

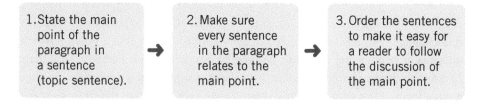

1. State the main point of the paragraph in a sentence (topic sentence).

2. Make sure every sentence in the paragraph relates to the main point.

3. Order the sentences to make it easy for a reader to follow the discussion of the main point.

Achieving Cohesion

Cohesion refers to the extent to which statements, ideas, and information in a paragraph are related and explicitly connected to one another. In concrete terms, cohesion is a measure of how well the individual sentences in a paragraph are linked together so that the reader can see the relationship between the ideas or information in one sentence to those in another sentence. If a writer does not make those relationships clear, the paragraph becomes harder for a reader to follow. Even a coherent paragraph (that is, one in which all the sentences relate clearly to the main topic of the paragraph) can lack cohesion. Fortunately, **cohesion can usually be achieved in two main ways:**

- by the strategic use of certain "linking" words and phrases (e.g., *also, similarly, by contrast, in addition, then, therefore,* etc.); and

- by the repetition of key words and phrases.

Here's a paragraph that is coherent but not cohesive. Like the example in the section on developing a paragraph (page 228), this example also addresses the idea of "the culture of poverty" and draws on the same source. In this case, the paragraph retains its focus on the main topic, which is Paul Gorski's explanation of the concept of the culture of poverty, but the paragraphs lacks cohesion that would help a reader follow the writer's discussion more easily:

> In "The Myth of the 'Culture of Poverty'" (2008), Paul Gorski examines the concept of the "culture of poverty" and how it relates to education. Numerous case studies and academic articles as well as first-hand experience are discussed. Research shows that the culture of poverty doesn't exist. Many teachers have a preconceived notion that a culture of poverty is responsible for creating unmotivated students and uninvolved parents. He goes into great detail about the bias of educators, which leads them to promote a "culture of classism" that results in an unequal education for those living in poverty. Gorski suggests several ways that teachers can better address the needs of poverty-stricken students and avoid the problems associated with bias in education.

Compare this paragraph with the following one, which has been revised to make it more cohesive. The key revisions are highlighted. Orange highlighting indicates the repetition of key words or phrases; blue highlighting indicates a linking word or phrase.

> In "The Myth of the 'Culture of Poverty'" (2008), Paul Gorski examines the concept of the "culture of poverty" and how it relates to education. Gorski draws from numerous case studies and academic articles as well as the first-hand experience of a classroom teacher to explain the origins and interpretations of this concept. In addition, he cites research to show that the culture of poverty doesn't exist. Gorski points out that many teachers have a preconceived notion that this "culture of poverty" is responsible for creating unmotivated students and uninvolved parents (2). He carefully examines this bias, which, he argues, leads educators to promote a "culture of classism" that results in an unequal education for those living in poverty (3). Gorski also suggests several ways that teachers can better address the needs of poverty stricken students and avoid this "culture of classism" and its damaging effects on poor children.

Notice how simple linking words (e.g., *also*, *this*) and careful repetition of key phrases (e.g., "culture of poverty") create connections among the sentences and enable the reader to follow the discussion more easily. Students sometimes mistakenly believe that repeating words and phrases is a mark of poor writing, but as this example illustrates, strategic repetition actually makes the passage more cohesive and therefore strengthens the writing.

7

Using the advice in this section, revise the following paragraph to make it more coherent and cohesive. Also, revise the sentences so that they reflect a more effective academic prose style:

Religion is a man-made device that has allowed people to find a meaning in life. Whether it is monotheism or polytheism, or whether it is mixes of various beliefs regarding a creator, idols, or an overall power, people revert to some form of belief for solace. Spiritualism, which is not the same as religious faith, is on the rise. Studies routinely show that Americans are much more religious than most other nations. As religions grow, cultural aspects come into play, and it is the spiritual and physical actions that tend to dictate societal and personal beliefs. Some people want to hold onto traditional values. Many traditional values and actions have faded in religions, especially in mainstream, secular society. Judaism, among other religions, has become secularized, except for some sects. The same is true of many Christian denominations.

Summarizing and Paraphrasing

Summarizing and paraphrasing are among the most important skills in academic writing. It is a rare writing task that does not include some summary or paraphrase:

- In an argument about capital punishment, the writer summarizes the main positions for and against capital punishment before defending a position on the issue.
- A chemistry lab report about campus air quality includes summaries of previous analyses of air quality.
- An analysis of housing density in a neighborhood near campus for a sociology class includes a paraphrase of a seminal study about the relationship between housing density and key socio-economic and demographic factors.
- In a literary analysis essay for an English literature course, a student summarizes the plots of several plays by Shakespeare and paraphrases a critic's evaluation of them.

These examples underscore not only how common but also how useful summary and paraphrase can be in academic writing. They also indicate that although students often need to summarize other texts, they might also need to summarize an argument, perspective, or theory that arises from multiple sources.

Usually, *summary* is distinguished from *paraphrase* (see Focus: "Summarizing vs. Paraphrasing"); in practice, however, the distinction is not always clear—or useful. For our purposes, distinguishing between summary and paraphrase is less important than understanding how to represent information and ideas from a source text accurately and how to credit the source appropriately. Accordingly, the advice in this section generally applies to both summarizing and paraphrasing.

Students are often confused by the difference between a summary and a paraphrase. That's understandable, because summary and paraphrase are very similar, and textbooks as well as online resources often contribute to the confusion.

Paraphrase. The Merriam-Webster Dictionary defines *paraphrase* as "a restatement of a text, passage, or work giving the meaning in another form." A paraphrase expresses the ideas or information from a source text in your own words. Usually, a writer paraphrases when the information and/or meaning of a source text is important but the original wording of that text is not. Sometimes writers paraphrase when the source text is specialized and difficult to understand. (When it is important to convey that original wording to readers, the writer should *quote* from the source text. See "Quoting from Sources" in Chapter 11.)

Summary. *Summary*, by contrast, is a condensed version of a source text that conveys only the main ideas or information from that text in the writer's own words. Writers summarize when they need to convey

- a key idea from a source text,
- a point of view expressed in a source text,
- the results of an analysis reported in a source text, or
- an argument made in a source text.

The main difference between a summary and a paraphrase is that a summary boils a source down into a brief passage (a sentence, a few sentences, or a paragraph), whereas a paraphrase restates the source text. Both use the writer's own words, but the purpose of each is slightly different. In a summary, the writer conveys the main point or idea of a source text; in a paraphrase, the writer restates the source text to convey the information or ideas of that source text. Typically, a writer will *paraphrase* a passage from or portion of the source text but *summarize* lengthy passages or the entire text.

Although summarizing seems to be a straightforward task, students encounter **two main problems when summarizing:**

- inaccurately representing the main point, idea, or information from the source text
- using too much of the original language from the source

For example, here's a passage from an article in which a law professor offers an analysis of the so-called "war on poverty" initiated by President Lyndon Johnson in the 1960s:

> The commitment and symbolism of the "war on poverty"—and the energy and enthu-siasm of those who fought it—were vital. For a brief period, the idea of conducting a war on poverty captured the nation's imagination. The phrase is surely one of the most evocative in our history. Yet the war's specific components were a tiny fraction even of the Great Society programs enacted between 1964 and 1968 during the administration of Lyndon Johnson, let alone those enacted during the New Deal and those added since,

7

many during the presidency of Richard Nixon. And, even considering all these, we never fought an allout war on poverty.

Source: Edelman, Peter. "The War on Poverty and Subsequent Federal Programs: What Worked, What Didn't Work, and Why? Lessons for Future Programs." *Clearinghouse Review Journal of Poverty Law and Policy*, May-June 2006, p. 8.

The following summary misses the main point of the source text:

According to Edelman, the war on poverty captured the nation's imagination.

The source text does state that the war on poverty captured the nation's imagination, but the author goes on to argue that the United States never fought an "allout war on poverty." The main point of the passage is that, despite the popularity of the idea of a war on poverty, the federal efforts intended to alleviate poverty were a small part of total government social programs. This summary, although accurate to an extent, misrepresents the point of the source passage.

Here's a summary that better represents the point of the source text:

Edelman argues that although the idea of a "war on poverty" captured the country's imagination, programs focused on addressing poverty never amounted to more than a small part of President Lyndon Johnson's Great Society programs and the social programs of other administrations.

Notice that this summary represents the source passage as a whole rather than focusing on one part of it.

It's possible that a brief summary like this would be insufficient, depending upon the nature of the writing assignment and rhetorical situation. For example, perhaps you are writing an argument in response to the source text, which means you would probably need to include a more complete representation of that source. In such a case, it's likely you would have to *paraphrase* the source passage. Here's a paraphrase that illustrates the very common problem of using too much of the original language of the source text (the passages that are taken from the source text are highlighted in orange):

The commitment and symbolism of the "war on poverty" were important. For a short time, the idea of a war on poverty captured the nation's imagination. But the specific components of the war were a tiny fraction of government programs enacted during the administration of Lyndon Johnson, not to mention those enacted before then and those added since. Even considering all these programs, an allout war on poverty was never really fought.

In this example not only are too many words and phrases taken verbatim from the source text, but also much of the sentence structure is reproduced in the paraphrase.

A more acceptable paraphrase transforms the source passage into the writer's own words while preserving the original meaning of the source text:

According to Edelman, the idea of a "war on poverty" was important for its symbolism as well as for the national commitment it reflected. But although this idea resonated with Americans for a time, the programs intended specifically to fight poverty were never more than a small part of total government social programs, whether those programs were part of Lyndon Johnson's Great Society, the earlier New Deal, or initiatives undertaken by Richard Nixon and subsequent presidents. As a result, Edelman states, a total war on poverty was never really fought.

This paraphrase borrows only essential phrases from the source text (such as "war on poverty") and restructures the passage so that the diction and syntax are the writer's own.

When summarizing or paraphrasing, follow these guidelines:

- **Accurately represent the main idea or point of the source text.** This is not simply a matter of including important information or ideas in your summary or paraphrase but also making sure that you convey the original author's intent or meaning.

- **Use your own language.** In many cases, this means finding appropriate synonyms for words in the source text, but it also means writing your own sentences rather than using the sentence structure of the source text.

- **Place quotation marks around important words or phrases from the source text.** If you reproduce key words or phrases from the source text, place them in quotation marks to indicate that the language is taken from the source text. In the previous example, the phrase *war on poverty* is placed in quotation marks not only because it is taken from the source text verbatim but also because it has become a phrase associated with a specific set of programs and a specific period in history. (See "Quoting from Sources" in Chapter 11 for advice about how to quote appropriately from a source text.)

- **Cite the source.** Whether you are summarizing, paraphrasing, or quoting directly from a source text, you must cite that source properly to indicate to your readers that you are taking ideas or information from another text. (See Chapter 12 for information about citing sources.)

EXERCISE 7D   PRACTICING SUMMARY AND PARAPHRASE

1. Write a summary and a paraphrase of the following passage:

Individualism-collectivism is perhaps the broadest and most widely used dimension of cultural variability for cultural comparison (Gudykunst and Ting-Toomey, 1988). Hofstede (1980) describes individualism-collectivism as the relationship between the individual and the collectivity that prevails in a given society. In individualistic cultures, individuals tend to prefer individualistic relationships to others and to subordinate ingroup goals to their personal goals. In collectivistic cultures, on the other hand, individuals are more likely to have interdependent relationships to their ingroups and to subordinate their personal goals to their ingroup goals. Individualistic cultures are associated with emphases on independence, achievement, freedom, high levels of competition, and pleasure. Collectivistic cultures are associated with emphases on interdependence, harmony, family security, social hierarchies, cooperation, and low levels of competition.

Source: Han, Sang-Pil, and Sharon Shavitt. "Persuasion and Culture: Advertising Appeals in Individualistic and Collectivistic Societies." *Journal of Experimental Social Psychology*, vol. 30, no. 4, July 1994, pp. 327–28.

2. Revise the summary below so that it more accurately reflects the original passage:

Original passage: Prior to the official acceptance of the low-fat-is-good-health dogma, clinical investigators, predominantly British, had proposed another hypothesis for the cause of heart disease, diabetes, colorectal and breast cancer, tooth decay, and a half-dozen or so other chronic diseases, including obesity. The hypothesis was based on decades of eyewitness testimony from missionary and colonial physicians and two consistent observations: that these "diseases of civilization" were rare to nonexistent among isolated populations that lived traditional lifestyles and ate traditional diets, and that these diseases appeared in these populations only after they were exposed to Western foods—in particular, sugar, flour, white rice, and maybe beer. These are known technically as *refined* carbohydrates, which are those carbohydrate-containing foods—usually sugars and starches—that have been machine-processed to make them more easily digestible.

Source: Taubes, Gary. *Good Calories, Bad Calories: Challenging the Conventional Wisdom on Diet, Weight Control, and Disease*. Alfred E. Knopf, 2007, pp. xix-xx.

Summary: Another hypothesis was proposed that obesity didn't occur in isolated populations until they were exposed to Western diets of refined carbohydrates. Refined carbohydrates include sugar, flour, white rice, and maybe beer.

Synthesizing

In much academic writing, writers must do more than consult sources for relevant information. They must also bring together information or ideas from a variety of sources and synthesize the material into a coherent discussion that is relevant to the task at hand. Not only is synthesizing material from several sources an essential task in most academic writing, but it also lends depth to the writing. Consider this passage from *The Young and the Digital*, an analysis of the role of media in the lives of young people:

In years past, social scientists expressed serious apprehension about the media content, especially violent and sexual imagery, that's exposed to young children and teenagers. And though violent and sexual themes in media continues to be a serious topic of debate, a growing amount of attention is shifting to the proliferation of screens in homes and in young people's lives. There is rising anxiety about the sheer amount of time children and teens spend with media and technology. According

Tyler Olson/Shutterstock.com

to a 2006 study conducted by the Kaiser Family Foundation, kids spend between six and eight-and-a-half hours a day with media. Today, playtime for many young children usually involves time with a screen. As they observe their parents' connection to mobile phones, BlackBerrys, laptops, and other electronic gadgets, many young children mimic those behaviors. We often hear, and for good reason, that young people are leading the migration to digital. But in many homes across America, parents are unwittingly teaching their kids to be digital. In the midst of the marketing and selling of the digital lifestyle, the American Academy of Pediatrics recommends that children's daily screen time be limited to one to two hours.

Source: Watkins, S. Craig. *The Young and the Digital.* Beacon Press, 2009, p. 50.

In this passage, author S. Craig Watkins draws on several sources to make his main point about the increasing amount of time young people spend using digital media. Notice that Watkins cites two specific sources (a study by the Kaiser Family Foundation and a recommendation from the American Academy of Pediatrics), but the first few sentences of the paragraph provide an overview of an important development (the shift in attention from questionable media content to the amount of time children spend with media) that Watkins likely gleaned from several additional sources. In other words, Watkins is synthesizing ideas and information not only from the two sources he cites but also from other sources that he consulted while researching his topic. As this example suggests, synthesis can be extremely useful when a writer is working with complex subject matter and many different sources.

Effective writers follow **three basic guidelines when synthesizing ideas and information**:

- Keep larger goals in mind.
- Identify a main point.
- Use only the source material you need.

Keep Larger Goals in Mind

When working with several different sources, especially in a longer project on a complicated topic, it can be easy to lose track of your reasons for consulting the specific sources you found. As you review sources and identify relevant information or ideas, remind yourself of the main goal of your project and identify how the section you are working on relates to that main goal. For example, the passage on pages 236–237 from Watkins' book *The Young and the Digital* is taken from a chapter titled "The Very Well Connected: Friending, Bonding, and Community in the Digital Age," in which Watkins examines the increasingly central role digital media play in the social lives of young people. The passage focuses on the increasing amount of time young people devote to digital media—a point that supports Watkins' analysis that digital media have become one of the most significant factors in how young people manage their social lives. Notice that in synthesizing material from his sources to make his point about the time young people devote to digital media, Watkins also connects that point to his larger point about the social impact of digital media.

7

Identify a Main Point

Source material is often varied and complicated, and when synthesizing this material you must identify what is relevant to the task at hand. In effect, you are managing information from different sources and connecting them to make a point. That task is easier if you keep focused on a main point. Here's an example in which a writer synthesizes information from several very different sources to make a point about the longstanding debates about vegetarianism:

> Debates about the efficacy of vegetarianism follow us from cradle to wheelchair. In 1998 child-care expert Dr. Benjamin Spock, who became a vegetarian late in life, stoked a stir by recommending that children over the age of 2 be raised as vegans, rejecting even milk and eggs. The American Dietetic Association says it is possible to raise kids as vegans but cautions that special care must be taken with nursing infants (who don't develop properly without the nutrients in mother's milk or fortified formula). Other researchers warn that infants breast-fed by vegans have lower levels of vitamin B12 and DHA (an omega-3 fatty acid), important to vision and growth.

Source: Corliss, Richard. "Should We All Be Vegetarians?" *Time*, 15 July 2002, p. 48+.

In this passage, the author draws on at least three separate sets of sources: (1) material about the 1998 controversy surrounding Dr. Benjamin Spock's recommendations about feeding young children a vegetarian diet; (2) the American Dietary Association's recommendations; and (3) nutritional studies of infants who were breast-fed by vegans. Although these sources all relate to the topic of the impact of vegetarianism on children, each has a different focus. The author brings them together to make a single main point, which is stated in the first sentence of the paragraph. The information from each source is clearly related to that main point. As a result, the author makes it easy for a reader to make sense of the information from these different sources.

Use Only the Source Material You Need

When working with multiple sources, you might find a great deal of relevant material that is interesting and seemingly important. But don't overwhelm your reader by trying to synthesize information from too many sources at once. In the examples in this section, the authors select information from their sources carefully and use only what they need to make their points. It is likely that in each case the author had much more information than he used. Part of your task when working with sources is to evaluate the information you have gathered and select the material that helps you achieve your rhetorical goals. Synthesis can be a powerful tool in academic writing, but if you try to squeeze too much information from too many different sources into a passage, it is likely that your prose will be less clear and your discussion more difficult for your readers to follow.

Write a brief paragraph in which you synthesize the following information about the job market for college graduates:

A Bachelor's degree is one of the best weapons a job seeker can wield in the fight for employment and earnings. And staying on campus to earn a graduate degree provides safe shelter from the immediate economic storm, and will pay off with greater employability and earnings once the graduate enters the labor market. Unemployment for students with new Bachelor's degrees is an unacceptable 8.9 percent, but it's a catastrophic 22.9 percent for job seekers with a recent high school diploma—and an almost unthinkable 31.5 percent for recent high school dropouts.

Source: Carnevale, Anthony, et al. *Hard Times: College Majors, Unemployment, and Earnings.* Georgetown University Center on Education and the Work Force, 2012, cew.georgetown.edu/wp-content/uploads/2014/11/Unemployment.Final_.update1.pdf.

More than half of all recent graduates are unemployed or in jobs that do not require a degree, and the amount of student-loan debt carried by households has more than quintupled since 1999. These graduates were told that a diploma was all they needed to succeed, but it won't even get them out of the spare bedroom at Mom and Dad's. For many, the most tangible result of their four years is the loan payments, which now average hundreds of dollars a month on loan balances in the tens of thousands.

Source: McArdle, Megan. "The Coming Burst of the College Bubble." *Newsweek*, 9 Sept. 2012, www.newsweek.com/megan-mcardle-coming-burst-college-bubble-64671.

[In 2011] about 1.5 million, or 53.6 percent, of bachelor's degree-holders under the age of 25 last year were jobless or underemployed, the highest share in at least 11 years. In 2000, the share was at a low of 41 percent, before the dot-com bust erased job gains for college graduates in the telecommunications and IT fields.

Source: Yen, Hope. "Half of New Grads are Jobless or Underemployed." Associated Press, 24 Apr. 2012. *NBCNews*, www.nbcnews.com/id/47141463/ns/business-stocks_and_economy/#.Vy-CLb7Vvf1.

Underemployment also tends to be temporary for college graduates. Even after the recession hit, Pew found that annually, about 27 percent of BA's stuck in high-school level jobs transitioned to college-level employment.... Unemployment for college graduates is higher than normal. Underemployment is more prevalent, though it's less severe than college critics portray, and perhaps no worse than during the Reagan days.

Source: Weissman, Jordan. "How Bad Is the Job Market For College Grads? Your Definitive Guide." *The Atlantic*, 4 Apr. 2013, www.theatlantic.com/business/archive/2013/04/how-bad-is-the-job-market-for-college-grads-your-definitive-guide/274580/.

Framing

You might have heard an instructor comment about "framing" an argument, analysis, or discussion:

Be sure to frame your argument clearly.

Frame your analysis of the new health care law in terms of the ongoing debates about the role of government in citizens' lives.

Try to frame your discussion in a way that makes it relevant for your readers.

In these statements, "framing" means placing your project in a context that gives it relevance or significance for your audience. It is a technique for putting into practice Core Concept #2: "Good writing fits the context." All writing must fit into a specific rhetorical situation that includes an intended audience and a context for communicating with that audience. It is part of a writer's task to show his or her audience why the topic at hand is important and meaningful. "Framing" is a term used to describe a technique for doing that.

For example, in the following passage, the authors—three biologists—frame their argument about "eusociality" in terms of an ongoing debate in their field:

For most of the past half century, much of sociobiological theory has focused on the phenomenon called eusociality, where adult members are divided into reproductive and (partially) non-reproductive castes and the latter care for the young. How can genetically prescribed selfless behavior arise by natural selection, which is seemingly its antithesis? This problem has vexed biologists since Darwin, who in *The Origin of Species* declared the paradox—in particular displayed by ants—to be the most important challenge to his theory. The solution offered by the master naturalist was to regard the sterile worker caste as a "well-flavoured vegetable," and the queen as the plant that produced it. Thus, he said, the whole colony is the unit of selection.

Modern students of collateral altruism have followed Darwin in continuing to focus on ants, honeybees and other eusocial insects, because the colonies of most of their species are divided unambiguously into different castes. Moreover, eusociality is not a marginal phenomenon in the living world. The biomass of ants alone composes more than half that of all insects and exceeds that of all terrestrial nonhuman vertebrates combined. Humans, which can be loosely characterized as eusocial, are dominant among the land vertebrates. The "superorganisms" emerging from eusociality are often bizarre in their constitution, and represent a distinct level of biological organization.

Source: Nowak, Martin A., et al. "The Evolution of Eusociality." *Nature*, vol. 466, no. 26, Aug. 2010, p. 1057.

In this passage, the authors place their specific argument in the context of a problem that evolutionary biologists have long confronted in their efforts to test Darwin's theories—a problem that they state as a question: "How can genetically prescribed selfless behavior arise by natural selection, which is seemingly its antithesis?" In this way, the authors show how their argument (which is captured in their statement in the second paragraph that "eusociality is not a marginal phenomenon in the living world") is relevant to biologists by connecting it to a recognized problem in the field—in other words, by *framing* it in terms of that recognized problem.

Here's another example, this one from a scholarly article reporting on a study of college students' use of digital media. In this passage, the author cites evidence of the increasingly important role that social media play in the lives of young Americans:

According to the Pew Internet and American Life Project, as of August 2011, 83% of 18–29 year-olds used a social network site (Madden, 2012). Their interactions on these sites were also purposeful, as Pew reports that this age group is most concerned with online identity management: 71% of them have changed the privacy settings on the sites they use (Lenhart, Purcell, Smith, & Zickuhr, 2010). Living a "literate life in the information age" (Selfe & Hawisher, 2004) increasingly means learning to navigate these spaces, managing one's identity and online data, and considering complex issues of privacy and representation. Using ethnographic case study data, this article examines how one undergraduate student integrated his use of social network sites into his everyday literacy practices to represent his identity. I approached this case study with three research questions: 1) How does this writer integrate social network sites into his everyday literacy practices? 2) How does this writer use those literacy practices to represent his identity for multiple audience groups on social network sites? 3) How does this writer negotiate site interfaces to represent his identity and communicate with others?

Source: Buck, Amber. "Examining Digital Literacy Practices on Social Network Sites." *Research in the Teaching of English*, vol. 47, no. 1, Aug. 2012, p. 10.

7

Here the author frames her own case study of a college student in terms of larger social and technological developments in contemporary society—specifically, the growing importance of social media and the emergence of practices that people of a certain age-group engage in to manage their online identities. She cites other research (from the Pew Center and by other scholars—in this case, Selfe and Hawisher) to establish the importance of social media and place her own study in the context of these important developments.

Both these examples illustrate how authors use framing not only to introduce readers to the subject matter but also to identify why their arguments or analyses are relevant. By framing their discussions, these authors explicitly connect their arguments or analyses to larger debates or conversations that matter to their readers and show how their own arguments or analyses fit into those conversations.

Framing typically happens in the introduction to a piece, but a writer might see a need to frame a segment of a piece of writing, especially in a longer essay or report that might contain several sections. For instance, in an analysis of the economic impact of a proposed tax on gasoline, the writer might include a section presenting a specific kind of cost-benefit analysis using a new economic model. In such a case, the writer might frame that section in the context of, say, an ongoing debate about whether certain kinds of taxes hurt the average consumer or benefit the economy as a whole.

When framing an argument, analysis, or discussion, use these questions to guide you:

- What makes your argument, analysis, or discussion relevant to your intended audience? Why would my audience be interested in this topic?
- To which larger debates, conversations, or arguments is your topic related? How might you connect your topic to those larger debates, conversations, or arguments?
- What makes your topic important or relevant now? How can you show your readers that your topic is important and timely?

These questions can make it easier for you to frame your discussion in a way that makes it relevant for your readers and enables them to place it in a larger context.

EXERCISE 7F PRACTICING FRAMING

1. Imagine an argument you might make about a current issue that interests you. Using the bulleted list of questions on this page, describe briefly how you would frame this argument. In your answer, identify your intended audience and a purpose for your argument.

2. Using your answer for Question #1, reframe your argument for a different audience.

3. In a brief paragraph, describe how the authors of the following passage frame their research in this introduction to their series of studies about "Millennials" (that is, people born between 1981 and 2000):

Generations, like people, have personalities. Their collective identities typically begin to reveal themselves when their oldest members move into their teens and twenties and begin to act upon their values, attitudes and worldviews. America's newest generation, the Millennials, is in the middle of this coming-of-age phase of its life cycle. Its oldest members are approaching age 30; its youngest are approaching adolescence. Who are they? How are they different from—and similar to—their parents? How is their moment in history shaping them? And how might they, in turn, reshape America in the decades ahead? The Pew Research Center will try to answer these questions through a yearlong series of original reports that explore the behaviors, values and opinions of today's teens and twenty-somethings.

Source: Keeter, Scott, and Paul Taylor. "The Millennials." *Pew Research Center*, 10 Dec. 2009, www.pewresearch.org/2009/12/10/the-millennials/.

Introductions

An introduction is a kind of roadmap to your paper: It tells your readers where you plan to go and why. In most forms of academic writing, the introduction not only presents the topic of the paper but also conveys a sense of why the topic is relevant and what the writer will say about it.

Below are four examples of introductions, each illustrating a common approach to introductions. The first three examples are from student essays: one from a paper written for an economics course, the second from a course on the history of modern China, and the third from an introductory psychology course. The fourth example is from an article by Deborah Tannen, a professor of linguistics at Georgetown University. Notice that, regardless of the approach, each introduction clearly establishes the focus of the paper and conveys a sense of the writer's main idea. Notice, too, how each introduction establishes the tone and style of the paper.

Getting Right to the Point

One of the most common mistakes students make when introducing an essay is saying too much. Often, the most effective introductions are those that get right to the point and move the reader quickly into the main body of the paper. Here's an example:

> ### The Legalization of Prostitution
>
> Prostitution is the "contractual barter of sex favors, usually sexual intercourse, for monetary considerations without any emotional attachment between the partners" (Grauerhold & Koralewski, 1991). Whenever this topic is mentioned, people usually shy away from it, because they are thinking of the actions involved in this profession. The purpose of this paper, however, is not to talk about these services, but to discuss the social, economic and legal issues behind prostitution.
>
> Source: "Comments on an Economic Analysis Paper." *WAC Student Resources*, Coe Writing Center, 2001, www.public.coe.edu/wac/legalization.htm.

7

This brief introduction quickly establishes the focus and main purpose of the paper. It also frames the topic in terms of general perceptions of prostitution and clarifies that the writer will be examining that topic from a different angle. This is a good example of a writer efficiently introducing a topic. As this writer demonstrates, sometimes the best approach is the one that uses the fewest words.

Focusing on Context

This next example, from a history paper about the impact of Mao Zedong on modern China, illustrates how an academic writer can use techniques from narrative writing to introduce a topic and at the same time establish a context for the topic. This introduction begins with a brief description of the birthplace of Mao Zedong as a way to dramatize the main point of the paper that Mao "remains the central, dominant figure in Chinese political culture today." The second paragraph provides background information so that the reader can better appreciate Mao's significance to modern China; the third paragraph establishes the focus of the paper, which examines Mao's enduring legacy in contemporary China.

Mao More Than Ever

Shaoshan is a small village found in a valley of the Hunan province, where, a little over a century ago, Mao Zedong was born. The first thing heard in Shaoshan is the music, and the music is inescapable. Suspended from posts towering over Mao's childhood home are loudspeakers from which the same tune is emitted over and over, a hit of the Cultural Revolution titled "We Love You, Mao."

The Chinese people were faced with an incredibly difficult situation in 1976 following the death of Mao Zedong. What was China to do now that the man whom millions accepted as the leader of their country's rebirth to greatness has passed away? China was in mourning within moments of the announcement. Although Mao rarely had been seen in public during the five years preceding his death, he was nevertheless the only leader that China had known since the Communist armies swept triumphantly into Peking and proclaimed the People's Republic twenty-seven years earlier. He was not only the originator of China's socialist revolution but its guide, its teacher, and its prophet.

Common sense foretold of the impossibility of erasing Communism and replacing Chairman Mao. He departed the world with his succession and China's future uncertain. With his death, historians and reporters around the world offered predictions of what was to become of China. They saw an instant end to Maoist theory. Through careful examination of Chinese life both under and after Mao, it is clear that the critics of 1976 were naïve in their prophecies and that Mao Zedong still remains the central, dominant figure in Chinese political culture today.

Source: "Comments on an Economic Analysis Paper." *WAC Student Resources,* Coe Writing Center, 2001, www.public.coe.edu/wac/Nordmann.htm.

In this example, the writer establishes the context by "telling the story" of Mao's enduring influence on China. This approach is common in the Humanities (history, literature, etc.).

Using a Reference Point

Another common approach to introductions in academic writing is to use an established idea, point of view, development, text, or study as a reference point for the topic of the paper. In this example from a paper written for a psychology course, the writers begin by referring to a study of the anxiety people experience while waiting in hospital waiting rooms.

Sitting Comfort: The Impact of Different Chairs on Anxiety

Kutash and Northrop (2007) studied the comfort of family members in the ICU waiting room. They found that no matter the situation, waiting rooms are stressful for the patients and their families, and it is the nursing staff's job to comfort both. From this emotional distress many family members judged the waiting room furniture as

"uncomfortable" and only talked about it in a negative context. From this study we have learned that there is a direct relationship between a person's emotional state and how that person perceives the physical state he or she is in, such as sitting in a chair. Is this relationship true in reverse as well? Can the way a person perceives his or her present physical state (such as sitting in a chair) affect his or her emotional state? This is the question that the present study sought to answer.

Source: Baker, Jenna, et al. "Sitting Comfort: The Impact of Different Chairs on Anxiety." *Schemata*, 2011, www.lycoming.edu/schemata/documents/Psy110GroupPaper_Final.pdf.

Here the writers use a previously published study (by Kutash and Northrop) as a reference point to raise a question that is relevant to readers interested in psychology: "Can the way a person perceives his or her present physical state (such as sitting in a chair) affect his or her emotional state?" That question clearly establishes the focus of the paper. One advantage of this approach is that the question sets up the expectation that the writer will answer the question. In this way, the writer gives the audience a clear sense of what will follow.

Telling an Anecdote

Using an anecdote to introduce a topic, which is common in many different kinds of writing, can be effective in academic writing as well. In this example, linguist Deborah Tannen shares an anecdote to illustrate the problem she will address in her article. Notice how she uses the anecdote to establish the focus of her paper and encourage the reader to continue reading.

Sex, Lies and Conversation

I was addressing a small gathering in a suburban Virginia living room—a women's group that had invited men to join them. Throughout the evening, one man had been particularly talkative, frequently offering ideas and anecdotes, while his wife sat silently beside him on the couch. Toward the end of the evening, I commented that women frequently complain that their husbands don't talk to them. This man quickly concurred. He gestured toward his wife and said, "She's the talker in our family." The room burst into laughter; the man looked puzzled and hurt. "It's true," he explained. "When I come home from work I have nothing to say. If she didn't keep the conversation going, we'd spend the whole evening in silence."

This episode crystallizes the irony that although American men tend to talk more than women in public situations, they often talk less at home. And this pattern is wreaking havoc with marriage.

Source: Tannen, Deborah. "Sex, Lies and Conversation: Why Is It So Hard for Men and Women to Talk to Each Other?" *The Washington Post*, 24 June 1990, p. C3.

Using an anecdote can be very effective, but students sometimes devote too much time to the anecdote, which can make it more difficult for readers to see where the paper might be going. If you use this approach, keep the anecdote brief and follow it up with a few sentences indicating why you're sharing the anecdote and what it means—as Tannen does in her second paragraph.

Transitions

Earlier in this chapter we noted that in effective academic writing, paragraphs must be coherent and cohesive (see pages 227–232). The same is true for an essay or other kind of document as a whole. Your sentences can be clear and your paragraphs coherent and cohesive, but if you don't connect them to one another, your essay is likely to be more difficult for your readers to follow. The main tool for keeping your essays coherent and cohesive is the transition, which is why writing effective transitions is an essential skill in academic writing. Fortunately, it is a skill that is easy to develop.

What exactly is a *transition*? It is a device to get your reader from one paragraph—or section of your document—to the next. Transitions amount to signposts that keep your readers oriented and enable them to know where they are in your text. If you have written an effective introduction that tells your readers what to expect in your text, transitions signal to your readers when they have reached each main section.

It is important to remember that you don't need a transition between every paragraph in a document. Often, the connection between paragraphs is clear because the subject matter of one paragraph clearly relates to the subject of the next. However, transitions are usually necessary

- when there is an important shift in the focus of discussion from one paragraph to the next, or
- when moving from one main section of a document to another.

The section on "Achieving Cohesion" in paragraphs (page 230) describes two strategies for writing cohesive paragraphs that can be used to write effective transitions between paragraphs to create more cohesive essays:

- using linking words or phrases (e.g., *first, second, in addition, then, therefore, that*)
- repeating key words and phrases

In addition, a third important strategy is to set up your transitions by letting a reader know what to expect in a section or in your entire document. For example, your introduction might explain that your essay will address four key questions. When making the transitions between the four main sections of your essay, you can refer back to those four questions to remind your reader what will follow.

The following passage from a student literacy narrative illustrates these common strategies for transitions between paragraphs. In this slightly humorous narrative about the student's experience in a college writing class, the writer explains the first few weeks of the class. Notice how the transitions help keep the narrative coherent and enable the reader to follow the story more easily. (Key transition strategies are highlighted in blue.)

1   Prior to college I had never had a true intensive course. My high school English classes consisted mostly of reading assigned literature, with the occasional plot summary, known as a book report, thrown in for variety. Never had a teacher of mine critiqued papers with anything more in mind than content, unless it was to point out some terrible structural flaw. That changed when I enrolled in college and found myself in a required course called Introduction to Academic Writing.

> The introductory paragraph establishes the focus of the narrative. The final sentence in particular conveys a sense of what will follow.

2   Introduction to Academic Writing was designed in part to eliminate from the writing of incoming students any weaknesses or idiosyncrasies that they might have brought with them from high school. Run-on sentences, incoherent paragraphs, and incorrect footnoting were given particular emphasis. To address these issues, the professor assigned a great deal of work. Weekly journal assignments and multiple formal essays kept us very busy indeed. And then there were the informal in-class essays.

> This paragraph begins with a repeated phrase (*Introduction to Academic Writing*) that clearly links it to the last sentence of the preceding paragraph. Also, the final sentence of this paragraph sets up the transition to the next paragraph.

3   The first such essay took place on the second day of classes so that our professor could evaluate each student's strengths and weaknesses. Before accepting our work, however, she had us exchange papers with

7

one another to see how well we could spot technical flaws. She then proceeded to walk around the room, interrupting our small-group discussions, and asked each of us what we thought of what we had read. It was not a comfortable situation, though the small size of the groups limited our embarrassment somewhat.

> The writer uses linking words (*the first such essay*) to make the transition to this paragraph. The same strategy is used for the transition to the following two paragraphs (*This unique brand; Eventually*).

4   This unique brand of academic humiliation was a palpable threat in class, which consisted mostly of students with little confidence in their writing abilities. Most of them seemed to be enrolled in majors other than English, and they viewed this remedial writing course as a painful, albeit necessary, endeavor. Our professor sympathized, I believe, and for the most part restricted her instruction to small groups and one-on-one sessions. But the in-class writing exercises were a daily hardship for the first few weeks of the semester, and I think most of us dreaded them.

5   Eventually, we were deemed ready for the first formal essay, which was a kind of expository writing in which we were to select an academic subject of interest to us and report on that subject to the rest of the class. Most of the students seemed wary of the assignment, because it was the first one in which we were given a choice of topic. All the in-class essays were on assigned topics. So the first source of anxiety was the uncertainty about which topics would be acceptable.

Although this example is narrative writing, which is less common than other forms of academic writing, its strategies for effective transitions are the same strategies used in analytical and argumentative writing. For example, here's a passage from a psychology research report published in a professional journal. The style of this passage reflects the formal writing typical of the social sciences, yet the transition strategies the authors use are the same as those in the preceding passage from the student narrative essay.

1   The Action-to-Action (ATA) model of Norman and Shallice (1986) has three subcomponents: *action schemas, contention scheduling,* and a *supervisory attentional system* (SAS).

> This paragraph establishes the expectation that the authors will discuss these three key concepts in turn, thus setting up the transitions in the following paragraphs.

2   Action schemas are specialized routines for performing individual tasks that involve well-learned perceptual-motor and cognitive skills. Each action schema has a current degree of activation that may be increased by either specific perceptual "trigger" stimuli or outputs from other related schemas. When its activation exceeds a preset threshold, an action schema may direct a person's behavior immediately and stereotypically toward performing some task. Moreover, on occasion, multiple schemas may be activated simultaneously by different trigger stimuli, creating error-prone conflicts if they entail mutually exclusive responses (e.g., typing on a keyboard and answering a telephone concurrently).

3   To help resolve such conflicts, the ATA model uses contention scheduling. It functions rapidly, automatically, and unconsciously through a network of lateral inhibitory connections among action schemas whose response outputs would interfere with each other (cf. Rumelhart & Norman, 1982). Through this network, an action schema (e.g., one for keyboard typing) that has relatively high current activation may suppress the activation of other potentially conflicting schemas (e.g., one for telephone answering). Contention scheduling allows task priorities and environmental cues to be assessed on a decentralized basis without explicit top-down executive control (Shallice, 1988). However, this may not always suffice to handle conflicts when new tasks, unusual task combinations, or complex behaviors are involved.

> In the first sentence of paragraph 3, the authors use two sets of repeated words or phrases along with a linking word (*such*). The first repeated word (*conflicts*) links this paragraph to the preceding one. The second repeated phrase (*contention scheduling*) links this paragraph to the first paragraph and reminds the reader that the discussion has moved to the second of the three main concepts mentioned in that paragraph.

4   Consequently, the ATA model also has an SAS. The SAS guides behavior slowly, flexibly, and consciously in a top-down manner. It helps organize complex actions and perform novel tasks by selectively activating or inhibiting particular action schemas, superseding the cruder bottom-up influences of contention scheduling and better accommodating a person's overall capacities and goals. For example, one might expect the SAS to play a crucial role during switches between unfamiliar incompatible tasks that are not ordinarily performed together.

> Like the previous paragraph, this one demonstrates two transition strategies: linking words (*Consequently* and *also*) and a key repeated term (*SAS*).

7

Source: Rubinstein, Joshua, et al. "Executive Control of Cognitive Processes in Task-Switching." *Journal of Experimental Psychology: Human Perception and Performance,* vol. 27, no. 4, 2001, p. 764.

The best time to strengthen the transitions in a piece of writing is during revision (Core Concept #8). Step #8 in Chapter 3 includes revising to improve your transitions. At that point in the process of revision, review your entire draft, focusing only on transitions. As you do so, keep the following **guidelines for effective transitions** in mind:

- **Set up your transitions.** An effective introduction will convey a sense of the main parts of your text. Your transitions from one main part to the next should refer to the key terms you use in your introduction. In addition, you can make transitions more effective by letting the reader know what will follow in each main section. In effect, write a brief introduction to each main section—as the authors did on the previous page.

- **Use linking words or phrases.** As the examples in this section demonstrate, there are many common words and phrases that writers use to signal a transition from one point or topic to the next or from one main section of a document to the next. Here's a brief list of some of the most common linking words and phrases:

  next

  then

  also

  in addition

  similarly

  on the other hand

  therefore

  consequently

  first, second, third, . . .

  finally

  at the same time

  sometimes

- **Repeat key words or phrases.** The examples included in this section illustrate how writers repeat key words or phrases to link one paragraph to the next and to signal to readers that they are making a transition from one point to another. Select these words and phrases carefully so that you can keep your writing cohesive without being repetitive. Repetition in itself is not a weakness in writing, but unnecessarily repeated words or phrases can make your prose tedious and distracting for readers.

Add transitions to the following passage to make it more cohesive and easier for a reader to follow:

Writing developed as a visual means of communication, and a long, continuing history of close incorporation of visual elements in many different text forms has been maintained. Illustrated manuscripts, calligraphy, and tapestries are but a few of the art forms in which distinctions between word and form are blurred to the point of meaninglessness. Olson (1992) reminds us, "The calligraphic (meaning 'words written by hand') form incorporates all the elements of a painting—line, shape, texture, unity, balance, rhythm, proportion—all within its own unique form of composition" (131).

The distance between the visual and the verbal forms of information practiced in verbal-based classrooms is highly artificial. Shuman and Wolfe (1990) draw what they see as "two pertinent conclusions": (1) Early composition that was used as a means of preserving and transmitting ideas and information through the ages took the forms of singing and drawings. (2) Early alphabetic writing was an art form that may have had less to do with composing the content of what was to be communicated than with the art form itself. "Obviously, connections between language and the arts have roots deep in antiquity" (2).

Olson explores connections between writing and art. She notes that the "Greeks chose to represent each spoken sound with a symbol (or letter). Just as speech developed out of the imitation of sound, writing developed out of the imitation of forms of real objects or beings. At the beginning of all writing stands the picture" (130).

Currently educators are interested in interdisciplinary approaches at all levels, primary through postsecondary. It is a particularly opportune moment to attempt instructional approaches that bring together art and writing.

Source: Hobson, Eric. "Seeing Writing in a Visual World." *ARTiculating: Teaching Writing in a Visual World*, edited by Pamela B. Childers et al., Boynton/Cook, 1998, pp. 3–4.

7

In this chapter, you will learn to

1. Define and analyze the audience and purpose of various document designs.

2. Identify the four key elements of document design.

3. Apply the four basic principles of document design when critiquing written documents.

4. Analyze three document design projects.

Designing Documents 8

RECENTLY a friend of mine who works as a regional planner was asked to review a proposal. The proposal had been submitted to her organization by a consulting company that manages commercial and residential projects, such as strip malls, parks, and housing developments. The consulting company was seeking to be hired to create a development plan for the rural county where my friend works. It was a big proposal for a big project, and my friend had to evaluate it to help the county decide whether to hire the company to develop its regional plan. So she carefully studied the proposal, assessing the company's ideas for regional development as well as its ability to complete a good plan on time. The document was nearly 100 pages, with detailed analyses of issues like water flow, population density, and infrastructure (roads, bridges, and so on). My friend liked many aspects of the proposal, but her biggest complaint was that the document itself looked unprofessional. Although its analysis was sophisticated, with many graphs and tables, its design, she said, was amateurish. More important, she found it difficult to locate important information in the document.

This anecdote underscores the importance of design in many documents—not only in professional settings such as my friend's workplace, but in many other contexts as well:

- A campus group that trains volunteer mentors for first-year students creates a flyer to announce a meeting for new volunteers.
- A community organization that runs a food pantry develops a brochure to advertise its services to local residents.
- A college rugby club compiles an annual report, complete with photos and charts, for the campus athletic department.

And of course many college instructors expect students to include graphs, tables, and other visual elements in print reports and to make presentations using tools such as Prezi. In each case, a well-designed document is more likely to achieve its rhetorical purpose.

Because widely available technologies make it easy to create professional-looking documents, readers often expect more than well-written content. They want the content to be presented with appropriate graphics, attractive color schemes, and pleasing layouts. Such features are much more than ornamentation. The design of a document is a rhetorical tool that helps writers communicate ideas and information effectively to their audiences and helps convince readers that a document is worth reading. Effective document design also lends credibility to the writer. Today, knowing how to design a document well is an increasingly important part of being an effective writer.

Document design includes many sophisticated elements that are beyond the scope of this textbook, but this chapter will introduce you to basic concepts to help you develop the skills you need to design documents that will achieve your rhetorical goals.

Understanding Document Design as a Rhetorical Tool

Imagine that you want to raise awareness among students on your campus about alcohol abuse. Here's a public service poster from a university health center that does just that:

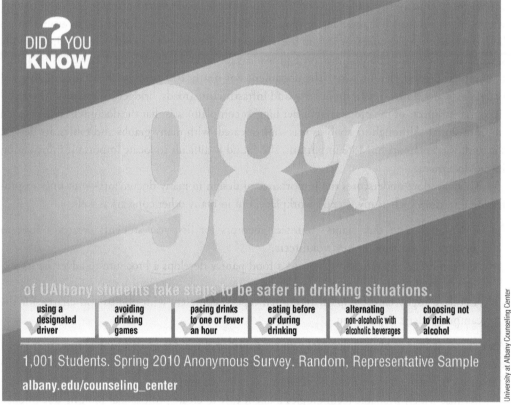

Source: Freidenberg, Brian M. *Did You Know?* Counseling Center, University at Albany, State University of New York, 2013.

What do you notice about this document? The authors certainly intend to catch your eye with the large yellow "98%" in the center of the page that contrasts with the darker background and the smaller text below it. Using color, layout, and font size strategically, they communicate a great deal of information with relatively few words. For example, they describe six different steps students can take to drink alcohol safely (using a designated driver, avoiding drinking games, and so on), and they identify the source of the information (a survey of students at that university). The layout of this information in a horizontal line of checked items at the bottom of the page sets it apart, making it more likely that you will read that information. And notice that the question in the upper left-hand corner of the document invites you into a kind of dialogue, a provocative way to entice students to read the entire document.

The authors of this poster have designed their document, first, to attract the attention of their intended audience (students at their university), and second, to communicate specific information efficiently to that audience. A more conventional document might be less effective in achieving these rhetorical goals, especially given how much information busy college students encounter in a typical day. For example, compare the poster to an email with the same information that might be sent to students as a public service announcement:

> Do you know that 98% of UAlbany students take steps to be safer in drinking situations? A random, anonymous survey of 1001 students conducted during spring, 2010, found that students take the following steps: using a designated driver, avoiding drinking games, pacing drinks to one or fewer an hour, eating before or during drinking, alternating non-alcoholic with alcoholic beverages, and choosing not to drink alcohol.

Which document is more likely to reach students? Which is more likely to grab students' attention? Which is more likely to be memorable to students?

Document design is a powerful way to make sure you reach an audience and convey ideas and information effectively. In designing your own documents, keep these points in mind:

- **Consider your audience.** The first step in designing a document is to identify the expectations of your intended audience and the rhetorical goals for your document. Who is your audience for this document? What kind of document are they likely to expect? What design features will appeal to them? A flyer announcing a campus farmer's market probably won't appeal to residents of a local retirement community if it has the flashy colors and provocative features of the public service poster on the previous page, which is intended for a much younger audience with very different tastes.

- **Consider your message.** Be clear about the ideas, information, or point you want to convey to your audience. What features will best help you convey your message? How might you use those features to emphasize key ideas and help readers find important information? For example, the large font and bright color of the figure "98%" in the poster on the facing page help emphasize the key point of the poster, which is that the vast majority of students on that campus try to use alcohol safely.

- **Avoid ornamentation.** Just as you should try to eliminate unnecessary information from a piece of writing, you should avoid design features that do little more than decorate your document. The images, graphics, font styles, colors, and layout you use should help you accomplish your rhetorical goals by communicating or emphasizing important ideas or information. If a design element doesn't help you accomplish your rhetorical goals, consider eliminating or changing it.

8

- **Make a good impression.** First impressions can influence how an audience responds to your document. If the design is effective, your audience is more likely to take your message seriously, and you are more likely to achieve your rhetorical goals. If your design is weak, you risk undermining your credibility, as happened to the authors of the poorly designed proposal in the anecdote at the beginning of this chapter.

EXERCISE 8A   **EXAMINING THE DESIGN OF DOCUMENTS**

1. Visit the websites of two or three restaurants in your town or neighborhood and review their menus. Compare the way the menus present information. How are the menus organized? How easy is it to find information about specific items that you might want to order? Which menu looks most professional? Now identify specific features that make each menu appealing or not: the colors, the layout of the pages, the use of images or graphics, and so on. Consider how these elements help you find the menu items you are looking for. What conclusions about document design might you draw from this exercise?

2. Compare the design of two or more textbooks that you are currently using for your classes (or textbooks you have used in the past). Select a representative page from each textbook and compare them. What do you notice about each page? Which pages do you find most appealing? Which are easiest to read? On the basis of this comparison, draw your own conclusions about which textbook has the most effective design.

Principles of Document Design

The public service poster on page 254 demonstrates **four basic principles of document design**:

- **Contrast:** a pronounced difference in color, size, or other design elements that can be used for emphasis or to help readers navigate a document.

- **Repetition:** strategic repeating of text, color, patterns, or other features to emphasize information or ideas and show connections between content or sections of a document.

- **Alignment:** the layout of elements of a page or document in relation to each other and to the page borders.

- **Proximity:** the positioning of information or features next to one another to show connections or emphasis.

These four principles can guide your decisions about how to design a document to meet the needs of your rhetorical situation.

Contrast

Notice how the white text stands out against this black background.

This light-colored text is more difficult to see against the yellow background.

These two examples illustrate the value of contrast—in this case, contrasting colors—to communicate or emphasize ideas and information. Contrast that is sufficiently strong, as in the top example, helps convey information more easily. Poor contrast can obscure information and make it difficult for readers to navigate a document.

Writers use contrast for three main reasons:

- **To emphasize ideas or information.** Notice, for example, that the color, size, and font of the phrase "to emphasize ideas or information" make it stand apart from the rest of this paragraph and give it greater emphasis. Contrasting images—say, of a crying baby and a smiling child—might be used to communicate an idea or point—for example, about the nature of childhood.

- **To organize a document.** Contrast is a common way to help readers navigate a document. For example, headings or subtitles that appear in sizes or colors that are different from the main text indicate to readers where different sections of a document begin and end. Icons can be used to indicate special information.

- **To establish a focus.** Contrast can be used to convey a sense of the focus or main idea of a document. In the poster on page 254, for example, the large contrasting type size for the figure "98%" helps focus the reader's attention on the point that most students use alcohol safely.

Contrast is commonly created with color and different font sizes or styles. For example, this 18-point font is immediately noticeable in a paragraph full of 12-point font. Similarly, you can use **a different font style like this** to set a title, subheading, or key sentence apart from surrounding text.

FOCUS **UNDERSTANDING TYPOGRAPHY**

8

Typography refers to letters and symbols in a document. It includes features such as *italics*, <u>underlining</u>, and **boldface** as well as the size and style of the font. You can use typography to make documents more readable, appealing, and easy to navigate. You can also use it to emphasize important ideas or information. Understanding a few basic concepts can help you use typography effectively in your documents.

(Continued)

Serif and Sans Serif. Fonts appear in two basic types: *serif*, which has small horizontal lines attached to the main lines of a letter, and *sans serif*, which does not.

serif   sans serif

Although the uses of these styles can vary, serif fonts are considered more traditional and are generally used in formal writing (such as academic assignments), whereas sans serif fonts tend to be considered more contemporary. Serif fonts are generally considered easier to read and are therefore the best choice for long passages of text (as in a traditional academic paper).

Font styles. Writers can choose from hundreds of font styles, including common styles such as `courier`, **arial**, and garamond, as well as unusual styles, such as *lucida calligraphy* and 𝔒𝔩𝔡 𝔈𝔫𝔤𝔩𝔦𝔰𝔥 𝔗𝔢𝔵𝔱. Although it is tempting to use uncommon font styles, the rule of thumb is to select fonts that make your document readable. For most academic assignments, a traditional font such as Times Roman is preferable. Also keep in mind that different font styles take up different amounts of space.

Font Size. Fonts sizes are measured in points. The standard font size for most extended text is 12-point. Sometimes, larger font sizes, such as this 14-point font or this 18-point font, are used for titles and headings or in tables and charts. However, varying the font size too often can be distracting to readers, so select font sizes strategically and be consistent in sizing the fonts you use. For example, use the same font size for all extended text and another font size for all subtitles.

Repetition

The careful repetition of specific features of a text—such as words, color, graphics, and font sizes or styles—can help make a document more readable and coherent. For example, the repetition of certain design features on the first page of each chapter of this textbook (such as color, the placement and style of images, the font size, and the layout of the page) enables you to identify the beginning of a chapter quickly and easily. In this same way, you already use repetition to help readers navigate your conventional print documents. For example, numbers in the same location on each page and subheadings separated from the main text are common features of essays or reports to help readers follow a document.

This use of repetition is so common that we might not even notice it, yet it can be used to communicate or emphasize important information very efficiently. For instance, the familiar repetition of the shape and color scheme of road signs tells motorists unequivocally that the signs contain relevant information, such as whether a traffic light or a pedestrian crossing lies ahead. (See Figure 8.1.)

FIGURE 8.1 Standard Road Signs

In the same way, a writer might use the repetition of a color or font style to indicate that certain information is important. Notice the repetition of the color blue on the web page about maintaining health in college in Figure 8.2. Blue is used to signal main ideas: the page title ("College Health: How to Stay Healthy") and the questions that represent key points ("What can I do to stay healthy?" "What should I know about nutrition and eating well?"). Blue is also used to lend a sense of cohesion to the page; notice, for example, that the bullets are blue.

8

FIGURE 8.2 Using Color to Organize Information on a Web Page

College Health:
How to Stay Healthy

▪ Knowing About My Health	▪ Eating Disorders
▪ First Aid Supplies	▪ Alcohol and Drugs
▪ Health Services	▪ Sexual Health
▪ How to Stay Healthy	▪ Sexual Assault/Rape
▪ Common Health Problems	▪ Abusive Relationships
▪ Mental Health	▪ Survival Tips
▪ Homesickness	▪ Resources

What can I do to stay healthy?

Eat nutritious food, exercise, and get plenty of rest.

What should I know about nutrition and eating well?

Eating well will keep your body strong, and help your immune system fight off germs that cause colds and other common illnesses.

Learn to:

- Eat a variety of healthy foods. Try to eat 5-7 servings of fruits and vegetables every day.
- Choose foods that are baked, steamed, or grilled, rather than fried.
- Choose fresh foods such as steamed vegetables, fresh fruits, and grilled chicken instead of fast food or processed food.
- Limit the amount of salt that you use. Check out food labels to see if the food you choose is low in sodium.
- Cut down on junk food (candy, chips, soft drinks, etc.).
- Snack on healthy foods such as popcorn, string cheese, fruits, and vegetables.
- Drink 8-10 glasses of water or non-caffeinated fluids every day.
- Remember dairy products. Dairy products such as milk, yogurt, and cheese are high in calcium, which keeps your bones healthy. Eat or drink 3 servings a day of low-fat or fat-free dairy products.
- Take a daily multivitamin (with iron and 0.4 mg folic acid) and 600 units of vitamin D each day.
- If you're a vegetarian, get all the nutrients that you need.

What do I need to know about exercise?

Another important way to stay healthy, reduce stress, and manage your weight is to exercise. Try to include aerobic exercise, muscle strengthening, and stretching exercises into your daily routine. It is recommended that you exercise approximately 60 minutes each day.

- Aerobic exercises include biking, running, fast walking, swimming, dancing, soccer, step aerobics, etc. You can tell that you are doing aerobic exercise because your heart will speed up and you will start breathing faster. However, you should still be able to talk when you are doing aerobic exercise.
- Strengthening exercises (such as sit-ups, push-ups, leg lifts, or weight training) will build up your muscles and keep your bones healthy.
- Stretching exercises (such as yoga) will make you more flexible, so you will be less likely to strain a muscle.
- You can also get exercise by doing simple things, such as walking or riding a bike (with a helmet, of course), instead of driving or taking the bus.

Source: "College Health: How to Stay Healthy." *Center for Young Women's Health*, 1 Feb. 2013, www.youngwomenshealth.org/collegehealth05.html.

Alignment

Alignment is the primary means by which writers make documents easy to read and create a sense of unity on a page or screen. When you set margins for a report or essay and keep all the paragraphs justified to the left-hand margin, you are using alignment to make your document easier to follow.

Readers depend on conventions for alignment—such as justifying paragraphs to the left or centering titles—which standardize some elements of document design to avoid confusion.

Because of these conventions, most readers find it annoying to read text that is aligned to the right-hand margin. And notice how the insertion of columns in the middle of this paragraph makes it harder to follow.

Writers can use alignment to present information efficiently and in visually appealing ways. Notice how the columns at the top of the web page in Figure 8.2 make it easy for a reader to find the right link to other pages on that website. Notice, too, that the bullet points are all aligned in the same way: indented from the left margin. Such an alignment helps set off the main questions and makes it easier for readers to follow the text.

In some kinds of documents, including brochures, newsletters, and web pages, alignment is an essential tool for designing a page or screen that is both visually appealing and easy for a reader to navigate. When aligning elements on a page, consider how the placement of elements will draw a reader's eye and enable the reader to move comfortably from one element to the next.

Proximity

Proximity creates cohesion and shows relationships among elements on a page or screen. Using this principle, you can create documents that are less cluttered and more efficiently organized, especially when you are combining text with visual elements.

Proximity can have a big impact on the appearance and effectiveness of a page. Let's imagine that you are part of a student organization that oversees all club sports on your campus, and you are creating a one-page flyer to inform students about the different club sports available to them. You might simply list all the sports:

Join a Club Sport!

Softball	Swimming
Ski Team	Badminton
Bowling	Men's Baseball
Field Hockey	Equestrian
Fencing	Women's Ultimate Frisbee
Wrestling	Men's Ultimate Frisbee
Men's Soccer	Women's Soccer
Snowboarding	Ice Hockey
Men's Volleyball	Men's Lacrosse
Mixed Martial Arts	Women's Volleyball
Women's Rugby	Tae Kwon Do

8

This unorganized list is visually aligned but tedious to read. To make it easier for students to make sense of the information, you can organize the sports by categories and place similar sports together:

Join a Club Sport!

Co-Ed Sports
- Badminton
- Bowling
- Equestrian
- Fencing
- Swimming
- Tae Kwon Do
- Ultimate Frisbee

Winter Sports
- Hockey
- Ski Team
- Snowboarding

Men's Team Sports
- Baseball
- Lacrosse
- Mixed Martial Arts
- Soccer
- Wrestling

Women's Team Sports
- Field Hockey
- Rugby
- Softball
- Soccer
- Volleyball

Simply by placing similar items together and adding space between the groups, you have organized the page in a way that makes it easier for a reader to find relevant information.

In more sophisticated documents that include images and graphics as well as text, the proximity of elements can significantly improve appearance and readability. For example, notice how many different elements catch your eye on this main web page from Yahoo.com. To make it easier for viewers to find information on a screen with so many elements, similar items are grouped together:

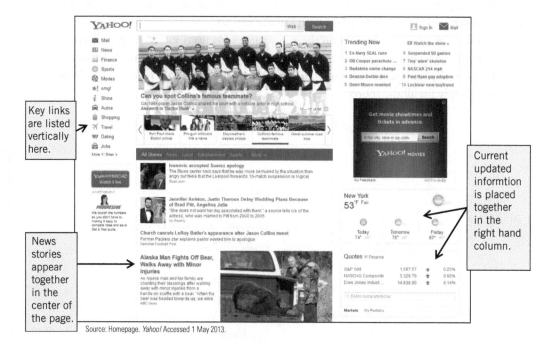

Key links are listed vertically here.

News stories appear together in the center of the page.

Current updated informtion is placed together in the right hand column.

Source: Homepage. *Yahoo!* Accessed 1 May 2013.

Strategic use of proximity can make such a complex page even more readable. Here's a web page for an organization called Cross-Cultural Solutions, which sponsors international volunteer opportunities for students:

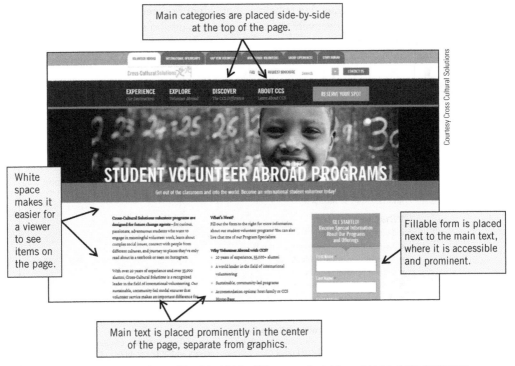

Main categories are placed side-by-side at the top of the page.

White space makes it easier for a viewer to see items on the page.

Fillable form is placed next to the main text, where it is accessible and prominent.

Main text is placed prominently in the center of the page, separate from graphics.

Source: "Student Volunteer Abroad Programs." *Cross-Cultural Solutions*, 2016, www.crossculturalsolutions.org/lp/student-volunteer-abroad-programs.

Careful grouping of similar items and the use of white space make this page appear clean and coherent, even though it contains a great deal of information. Notice, too, that repetition, contrast, and alignment make the page visually appealing and well organized. For example, the main links at the top of the page appear in similar font style and size (repetition) but in larger fonts than other text on the page (contrast), which makes them easier to find; the organization's tagline ("Get out of the classroom and into the world. Become an international student volunteer today!") appears in white font in a blue box, which makes it prominent and easy to read. In addition, all the main items are aligned vertically and horizontally, creating a balanced, cohesive, and unified page.

The most effectively designed documents, even relatively simple print texts, use all four design principles together. When deciding on the design of a document, follow three basic steps:

1. **Consider your rhetorical situation.** Who is your intended audience? What are your goals in addressing that audience with this document? What expectations might this audience have when it comes to the design of a document?

2. **Be clear about your message.** What is the central point you want to make with this document? What primary information do you hope to communicate?

3. **Apply the four principles of basic design.** How can you use contrast, repetition, alignment, and proximity to communicate your message effectively to your intended audience? How can you use these principles to make your document appealing and efficient?

Use the four basic principles of document design to evaluate this flyer from a public television station. The document is intended to help parents identify potential reading problems in their children. Assess how effectively the document uses design elements to convey its message to its intended audience.

Ed Extras

Place your school name or logo here

Helpful information about learning brought to you by Reading Rockets, Colorín Colorado, and LD OnLine

Recognizing Reading Problems

Learning to read is a challenge for many kids, but most can become good readers if they get the right help. Parents have an important job in recognizing when a child is struggling and knowing how to find help.

What to look for:

- Difficulty rhyming
- Difficulty hearing individual sounds
- Difficulty following directions
- Difficulty re-telling a story
- Struggles to sound out most words
- Avoids reading aloud

What to do:

- **Step 1: Meet with your child's teacher**
  Gather examples of your child's work that reflect your concerns. Ask the teacher for his/her observations and discuss what can be done at school and at home. Stay in touch with the teacher to monitor your child's progress.

- **Step 2: Meet with the principal and/or reading specialist**
  If your child's performance does not improve, meet with other professionals in the building to see if there are classes, services, or other interventions available.

- **Step 3: Get a referral for special education**
  If you have tried all interventions, request an evaluation. Talk to the principal to schedule this.

- **Step 4: Get an evaluation**
  A professional team—which may include a school psychologist, a speech-language pathologist, or a reading specialist—gives your child a series of tests and determines whether s/he is eligible to receive special education services.

- **Step 5: Determine eligibility**
  - If your child is found eligible for services, you and the school develop your child's Individualized Education Program (IEP), a plan that sets goals based on your child's specific learning needs and offers special services like small group instruction or assistive technology.
  - If your child is not eligible, stay involved and keep talking to the teacher about your child's progress. You can also turn to private tutoring for extra support.

Check out the *Assessment* section for more information on identifying reading problems:
www.ReadingRockets.org/article/c68

Visit our sister sites, ColorinColorado.org and LDOnLine.org, for more information about learning.

Reading Rockets, Colorín Colorado, and LD OnLine are services of public television station WETA, Washington, D.C. Reading Rockets is funded by the U.S. Department of Education, Office of Special Education Programs. Colorín Colorado, a web service to help English language learners become better readers, receives major funding from the American Federation of Teachers. Additional funding is provided by the National Institute for Literacy and the U.S. Department of Education, Office of Special Education Programs. LD OnLine is the world's leading website on learning disabilities and ADHD, with major funding from Lindamood-Bell Learning Processes.

Source: *Recognizing Reading Problems.* Reading Rockets / WETA, 2012, www.readingrockets.org/article/14541/.

Working with Visual Elements

Many documents include photographs, charts, graphics, and other visual elements. Increasingly, college instructors expect students to incorporate such elements into conventional papers. However, visual elements should never be used simply as ornamentation; rather, they should be used in a way that communicates information, conveys important ideas, and enhances the effectiveness of the document.

This section provides advice on using two common kinds of visual elements:

- tables, graphs, and charts
- images

Working with Tables, Graphs, and Charts

Many college assignments require students to work with quantitative information. For example, an analysis of the economic impact of college loan debt for an economics course will likely include various kinds of statistical data. Often, such data are most effectively presented in a table, bar graph, line graph, or pie chart. Contemporary word processing programs make it easy to create such elements in a variety of formats. However, the key to using such elements effectively is knowing what you want your readers to understand from the information you are presenting. Consider:

- **What is the nature of the information?** Numerical data can be easy to convert into a chart or table. Other kinds of information, such as directions for a procedure or a list of specific responses to a survey question, might not work as well in a graphical format. A chart or table should make the information easier for a reader to understand. Avoid using graphical formats if it makes the information more complicated or confusing.

- **What is the purpose of the information?** You present information for various reasons: to explain a concept, event, or development; to support a claim or assertion; to strengthen an argument; to illustrate a key idea or principle. The purpose can shape your decision about how best to present the information. For example, if you want to emphasize a specific set of statistics to support a central claim in an argument, using a graph or pie chart to present the data can make it more persuasive.

Tables, charts, and graphs have four basic elements:

- a title
- a vertical axis, called the *y* axis
- a horizontal axis, called the *x* axis
- the main body of data

8

Let's imagine you are writing a report on the benefits of a college education, and you wish to report the results of a survey of students who graduated in the past three years from three different departments on your campus. The survey was intended to learn about average starting salaries of graduates from your school. Numerical data such as survey results are commonly reported in the form of tables or graphs, but deciding how best to present that information depends on how you are using it in your report. If you are simply reporting the survey results to help your readers understand the average salaries of recent graduates, you might use a simple **table**. In this example, the *y* axis is used for the three different departments and the *x* axis for the three recent years; the main body of data is the starting salaries. The table would look like this:

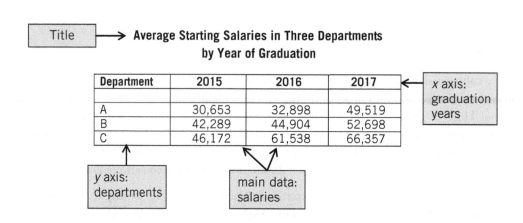

This table helps readers easily find the average salary for a specific department in a specific graduation year. Consider how much more tedious it is for readers to read an explanation of this information, which might look like this:

> The average starting salary for students who graduated from Department A in 2015 was $30,653; in 2016 it was $32,898, and in 2017 it was $49,519. For students who graduated from Department B in 2015, the average starting salary was $42,289; in 2016 it was $44,904, and in 2017 it was $52,698. Students who graduated from Department C in 2015 earned an average starting salary of $46,172; for 2016 graduates, the average starting salary was $61,538, and in 2017 it was $66,357.

Although presenting numerical information visually isn't always the most effective approach, in a case like this one, it is much more efficient than a verbal explanation.

A simple table might be too limited for presenting more complicated bodies of data, especially if you wish to compare information. Let's say that for an essay in which you argue for adjusting high school class schedules so that adolescents can get more sleep, you want to present information showing the different sleep patterns of different age groups; let's imagine you also want to show gender differences in sleep patterns to support your contention that those differences don't matter for adolescents. A **bar graph** is an effective means for comparing information. This graph shows average sleep times for people of different age groups; it also compares men and women:

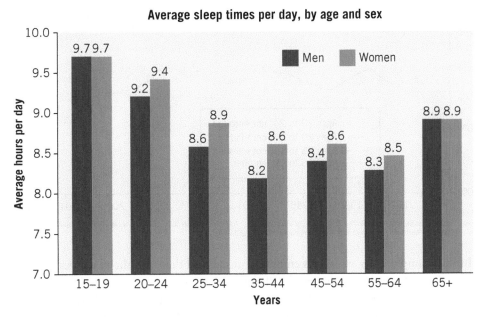

Average sleep times per day, by age and sex

Note: Data include all persons age 15 and over. Data include all days of the week and are annual averages for 2014

Source: "Charts by Topic: Sleep." *American Time Use Survey*, U.S. Bureau of Labor Statistics, 26 Oct. 2015, www.bls.gov/tus/charts/sleep.htm.

Here, the *y* axis is used for average hours of sleep per day and the *x* axis for age group.

If you wanted to show a trend or trajectory reflected in statistical information over time, a **line graph** might be a better option. For example, let's say you included in your essay about adjusting high school class schedules some data to show trends in employment rates for high school and college students over the past four decades; you want to show that employment rates for students currently in school have dropped. This line graph makes it very easy for readers to see those trends and compare the employment rates of students who are enrolled in high school or college to people of the same age who are not enrolled:

8

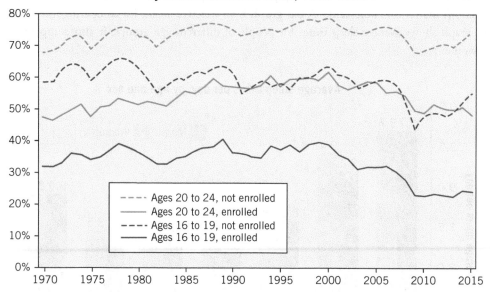

Employment-population ratios in October of young people by school enrollment status, 1970–2015

Source: "Students Less Likely to Work in October 2015 Than in the 1980s and 1990s." *TED: The Economics Daily*, U.S. Bureau of Labor Statistics, 18 May 2016, www.bls.gov/opub/ted/2016/students-less-likely-to-work-in-october-2015-than-in-the-1980s-and-1990s.htm.

In this example, the *y* axis shows employment rate and the *x* axis shows the years from 1970 to 2015. The different lines represent data from different age groups and enrollment status. For example, you can see that in 1989 approximately 40% of young people between the ages of 16 and 19 who were enrolled in school were also employed, whereas only about 23% of these students were employed in 2015. By contrast, approximately 63% of students in this age group who were not enrolled in school were employed in 1989, but only 55% were employed in 2015. This seemingly simple line graph contains a great deal of information and enables readers to see trends in the data and to compare trends among different groups as well.

Tables, graphs, and charts can present information efficiently, but they also can be misleading. For example, let's say you want to show the percentage of four items in the budget of a student organization you work for: item A (11%), item B (42%), item C (5%), and item D (42%). In addition, you want to highlight item C, which is the smallest expenditure. Your pie chart might look like this:

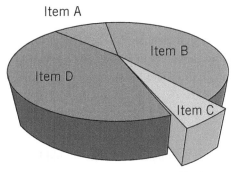

Source: "An Example of a Misleading Pie Chart." *Wikipedia*, 21 June 2012, en.wikipedia.org/wiki/Misleading_graph#/media/Misleading_Pie_Chart.png.

This three-dimensional chart, which makes it seem that you are looking at it from the side and slightly above it, is visually striking. Notice, however, that item C, which is only 5% of the budget, appears bigger than item A, which is 11% of the budget. Now here's the same information presented in a simpler, two-dimensional pie chart:

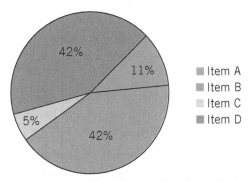

Source: "A Sample Pie Chart." *Wikipedia*, 21 June 2012, en.wikipedia.org/wiki/Misleading_graph#/media/Sample_Pie_Chart.png.

In this case, the simpler chart presents the information more accurately. Keep in mind that small changes in the design of a table, chart, or graph can dramatically affect the appearance of the information, sometimes making small differences appear much larger and thus conveying a misleading idea about that information. Although such strategies might seem effective in supporting a claim or point of view, they might also be ethically questionable. You should always use graphical elements in a way that presents information not only accurately but also ethically.

8

Working with Images

For many documents, effective design includes the use of images, but simply incorporating images into a document isn't necessarily enough to improve its design. Using images effectively is a matter of making sure the images are appropriate for your document and help address your rhetorical situation.

When using images, follow the same basic principles that apply to document design in general (see pages 256–263):

- **Consider your audience.** The images you select should be relevant to your subject matter and appropriate for your rhetorical situation. For example, a photograph of a car on a brochure about campus transportation services is probably a poor choice if the majority of students live on campus, do not drive cars to campus, and use the campus bus service. Moreover, consider whether the images you select might seem confusing or offensive to your audience. A photograph that might convey relevant information dramatically could also weaken your document if the image is considered inappropriate for some reason by your readers.

- **Consider your message.** Images in your document should reinforce important ideas or information. Ideally, images should convey information rather than just supplement written text. For example, a photograph of a specific location should enable the audience to gain an understanding of that location without a lengthy verbal description to accompany the image.

- **Avoid ornamentation.** Sometimes, images are used to enhance the appearance of a document, but too many images used only as decoration can become distracting for readers and therefore undermine the document's effectiveness.

- **Make a good impression.** Any images used in a document should contribute to the overall impression a document makes on the intended audience. A poorly selected image could weaken an otherwise effective document.

In addition to these basic principles, **consider how the content and perspective of an image fits your rhetorical situation.** For example, compare these two versions of the same photograph:

artcphotos/Shutterstock.com

artcphotos/Shutterstock.com

What is the difference between them? How does the potential impact of each differ? As this example demonstrates, simply "cropping" an image—that is, selecting a section of it and eliminating the rest—can dramatically change its impact and message. In this example, the version on the left might be appropriate for a report in a zoology class that includes descriptions of various kinds of raptors; the photograph could be used to show the size and color of a specific species of raptor. The cropped version on the right might be used to emphasize the extraordinary eyesight of raptors or to dramatize the fierce nature of a particular species. Your rhetorical purpose should dictate how you use an image and how you might alter it.

The **perspective** of an image can have a powerful effect on the message it communicates. Let's imagine you are writing an analysis of the social and economic impact of severe weather, such as a hurricane. This photograph dramatically conveys the devastating effects of the storm on property as well as the lives on local residents:

Jocelyn Augustino/FEMA

Notice that the perspective from which the photograph was taken (above and at a distance from the subjects) highlights the sense of vulnerability of the people in the photo, who appear small in comparison to the damaged homes surrounding them. This photo would be less effective in conveying these ideas if it were taken from ground level or from closer to the subjects. This photograph dramatically highlights the extent of storm-caused devastation and its impact on residents in a way that would be challenging to explain in words alone. At the same time, such an image can provoke strong emotions in readers and therefore can be used to influence readers—for example, to convince readers of the need to prepare for future storms or to contribute to a fund to help storm victims.

8

Working with Visual Elements **271**

Like any other design elements, images should be placed strategically so that they convey their messages without undermining the overall appearance of a document. Images that are too large, for example, might distract a reader from other important information on a page. Images that are too small might not communicate important information clearly.

EXERCISE 8C | **WORKING WITH VISUAL ELEMENTS**

1. Imagine you are writing an analysis of the impact of smartphone technology on college students for a general audience. For each of the following items, decide whether to present the information in a chart, table, graph, or in a written description; explain your reasons for your decision in each case:

   - The most common uses of smartphones among college students are surfing the Internet, texting, and playing games. 85% of students report using their smartphones for playing games much more often than for any other purpose.

   - In 2011 47% of college students reported owning a smartphone. In 2015 86% of college students reported owning a smartphone. In 2011, 35% of Americans owned smartphones. In 2015 64% of Americans owned smartphones.

   - Since 2008, sales of smartphones have increased by an average of 15% annually.

   - In 2015, 87% of college students reported that they used a laptop or notebook computer every week for their school work; only 64% reported using a smartphone for their school work. In 2014, 56% of college students reported using a smartphone every week for their school work.

2. Using some of the information in question #1, create a table, graph, and chart. (You can easily create these elements using a word processing program such as MS Word.) Use the same information for each graphic. Compare the table, chart, and graph. What are the differences in the way they present the same information? What advantages and disadvantages do you see to each kind of graphic?

3. Using the example from question #1, search online to find one or two images that you might use in your analysis of smartphones. Explain how you would use each image in your analysis. Justify your selection of images in terms of how they would help you accomplish specific rhetorical goals.

Designing Documents: Three Sample Projects

This section presents three common kinds of projects that illustrate how the same basic design features can make different kinds of documents effective in meeting the needs of a rhetorical situation.

Print Documents

For most college assignments you are likely to be asked to submit a conventional paper, whether in hard copy or in a digital form (such as a Microsoft Word file), but even conventional papers can be more effective when writers apply the principles of design. Whenever you submit a conventional paper for an assignment, be sure to follow the appropriate conventions for formatting, which include such elements as font size, the uses of underlining and boldface, and the format for citing sources. (See Chapter 12 for information about proper format for papers in MLA style.) You can also use the design principles in this chapter to enhance even the most traditional kind of paper by making sure that your font sizes and styles are consistent and that you use features such as underlining strategically, avoiding ornamentation.

Sometimes, however, your rhetorical situation might call for a print document that is not a conventional paper—for example, a flyer, brochure, or memo. In such cases, applying the principles of document design can enhance the document's effectiveness, even when the document is relatively simple. For example, Figure 8.3 shows a one-page flyer with information for college students about getting proper sleep. The flyer was developed by a college health and counseling center and made available in print form as well as in PDF format on the center's website. It illustrates how even a basic print document can more effectively meet the needs of a rhetorical situation when design principles are carefully applied.

1. Consider the rhetorical context. → **2. Be clear about your message.** → **3. Apply the principles of design.**

- The health and counseling center helps students deal with lifestyle and health problems common to college life. One such problem is insomnia. The center's goal is to inform students on its campus about the importance of proper sleep without overwhelming busy students with a lot of information.

- The main point is to show that college students can use several easy strategies to avoid insomnia and get proper rest. Also, knowing the common causes of poor sleep can help students avoid sleep problems.

- The one-page flyer incorporates no images and only two small graphics, but it uses the principles of contrast, alignment, and repetition to convey a great deal of information efficiently and to reinforce the main point about getting proper sleep.

8

FIGURE 8.3 College Health and Counseling Service Flyer

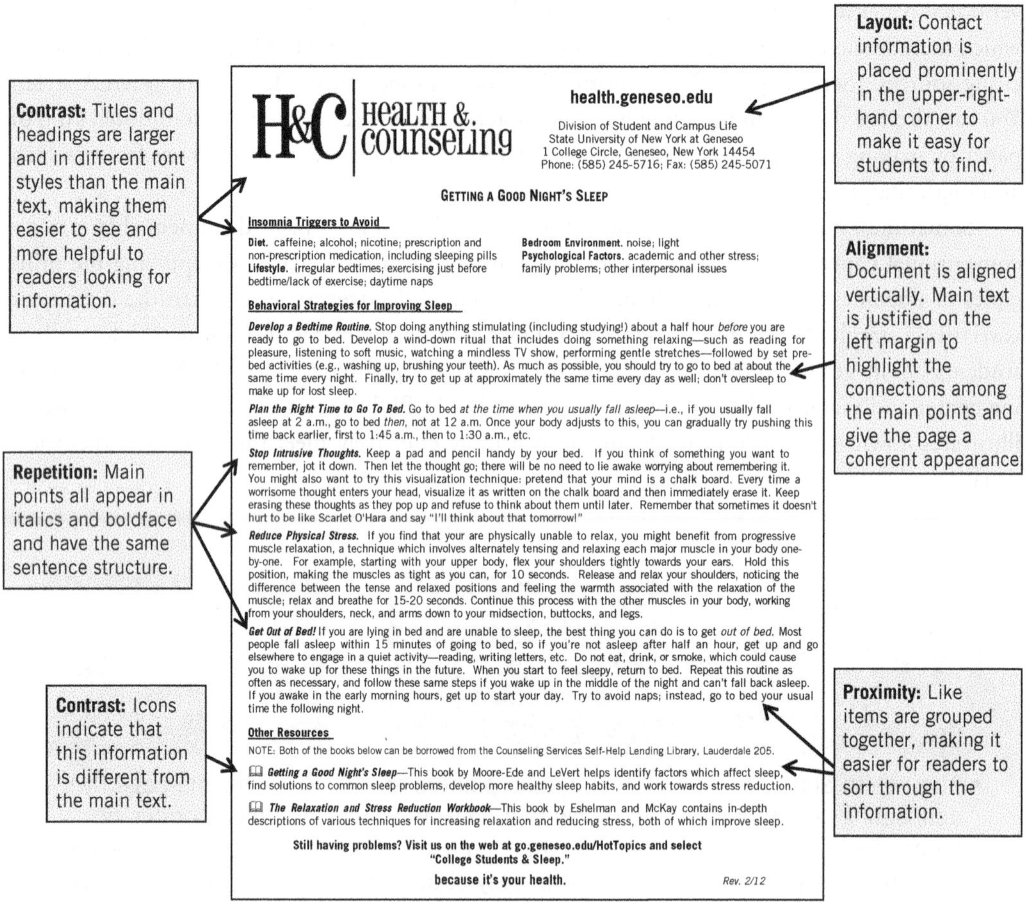

Layout: Contact information is placed prominently in the upper-right-hand corner to make it easy for students to find.

Contrast: Titles and headings are larger and in different font styles than the main text, making them easier to see and more helpful to readers looking for information.

Alignment: Document is aligned vertically. Main text is justified on the left margin to highlight the connections among the main points and give the page a coherent appearance

Repetition: Main points all appear in italics and boldface and have the same sentence structure.

Contrast: Icons indicate that this information is different from the main text.

Proximity: Like items are grouped together, making it easier for readers to sort through the information.

H&C HEALTH & COUNSELING

health.geneseo.edu

Division of Student and Campus Life
State University of New York at Geneseo
1 College Circle, Geneseo, New York 14454
Phone: (585) 245-5716; Fax: (585) 245-5071

GETTING A GOOD NIGHT'S SLEEP

Insomnia Triggers to Avoid

Diet. caffeine; alcohol; nicotine; prescription and non-prescription medication, including sleeping pills
Lifestyle. irregular bedtimes; exercising just before bedtime/lack of exercise; daytime naps

Bedroom Environment. noise; light
Psychological Factors. academic and other stress; family problems; other interpersonal issues

Behavioral Strategies for Improving Sleep

Develop a Bedtime Routine. Stop doing anything stimulating (including studying!) about a half hour *before* you are ready to go to bed. Develop a wind-down ritual that includes doing something relaxing—such as reading for pleasure, listening to soft music, watching a mindless TV show, performing gentle stretches—followed by set pre-bed activities (e.g., washing up, brushing your teeth). As much as possible, you should try to go to bed at about the same time every night. Finally, try to get up at approximately the same time every day as well; don't oversleep to make up for lost sleep.

Plan the Right Time to Go To Bed. Go to bed *at the time when you usually fall asleep*—i.e., if you usually fall asleep at 2 a.m., go to bed *then*, not at 12 a.m. Once your body adjusts to this, you can gradually try pushing this time back earlier, first to 1:45 a.m., then to 1:30 a.m., etc.

Stop Intrusive Thoughts. Keep a pad and pencil handy by your bed. If you think of something you want to remember, jot it down. Then let the thought go; there will be no need to lie awake worrying about remembering it. You might also want to try this visualization technique: pretend that your mind is a chalk board. Every time a worrisome thought enters your head, visualize it as written on the chalk board and then immediately erase it. Keep erasing these thoughts as they pop up and refuse to think about them until later. Remember that sometimes it doesn't hurt to be like Scarlet O'Hara and say "I'll think about that tomorrow!"

Reduce Physical Stress. If you find that your are physically unable to relax, you might benefit from progressive muscle relaxation, a technique which involves alternately tensing and relaxing each major muscle in your body one-by-one. For example, starting with your upper body, flex your shoulders tightly towards your ears. Hold this position, making the muscles as tight as you can, for 10 seconds. Release and relax your shoulders, noticing the difference between the tense and relaxed positions and feeling the warmth associated with the relaxation of the muscle; relax and breathe for 15-20 seconds. Continue this process with the other muscles in your body, working from your shoulders, neck, and arms down to your midsection, buttocks, and legs.

Get Out of Bed! If you are lying in bed and are unable to sleep, the best thing you can do is to get *out of bed*. Most people fall asleep within 15 minutes of going to bed, so if you're not asleep after half an hour, get up and go elsewhere to engage in a quiet activity—reading, writing letters, etc. Do not eat, drink, or smoke, which could cause you to wake up for these things in the future. When you start to feel sleepy, return to bed. Repeat this routine as often as necessary, and follow these same steps if you wake up in the middle of the night and can't fall back asleep. If you awake in the early morning hours, get up to start your day. Try to avoid naps; instead, go to bed your usual time the following night.

Other Resources

NOTE: Both of the books below can be borrowed from the Counseling Services Self-Help Lending Library, Lauderdale 205.

Getting a Good Night's Sleep—This book by Moore-Ede and LeVert helps identify factors which affect sleep, find solutions to common sleep problems, develop more healthy sleep habits, and work towards stress reduction.

The Relaxation and Stress Reduction Workbook—This book by Eshelman and McKay contains in-depth descriptions of various techniques for increasing relaxation and reducing stress, both of which improve sleep.

Still having problems? Visit us on the web at go.geneseo.edu/HotTopics and select "College Students & Sleep."

because it's your health.   *Rev. 2/12*

Source: Cholette, Beth. *Getting a Good Night's Sleep.* Division of Student and Campus Life, State University of New York at Geneseo, 2012, www.geneseo.edu/health/sleep.

Prezi Presentation

College students today are routinely asked to make presentations as part of their assignments. Often, students turn to presentation software, especially PowerPoint, which enables a speaker to present information visually to an audience. Prezi is an online tool for making presentations that is similar to PowerPoint in that it enables a writer to convey information efficiently and in visually engaging ways on screens or "slides." (See Sidebar: "Using Prezi" on page 275.) Like PowerPoint,

Prezi also allows the writer to embed images, sound, and video in a presentation. However, there are **two important differences between Prezi and PowerPoint:**

- PowerPoint presentations usually supplement the presenter's spoken words. By contrast, Prezi presentations are generally intended to be viewed online rather than presented in person by the author. However, increasingly students use Prezi in place of PowerPoint to supplement their oral presentations.
- Unlike PowerPoint, which requires you to present information sequentially from one slide to the next, Prezi is a dynamic tool that enables you to arrange text and images on a single screen according to an organizing theme or metaphor; a viewer clicks arrows to move from one place on the screen to another to follow a story or access information. Each individual screen in a Prezi presentation is therefore a section of the whole presentation rather than a discrete slide, as in PowerPoint.

Despite these differences, the same principles for designing an effective PowerPoint show apply to Prezi. The best presentations

- are well-organized,
- have a coherent visual theme,
- do not overwhelm the viewer with text,
- take advantage of the visual capabilities of the presentation tool, and
- apply the principles of design.

SIDEBAR   USING PREZI

Although there are differences between Prezi and PowerPoint, learning to use Prezi is no more difficult than learning to use PowerPoint. To use Prezi, you must create a Prezi account (visit prezi.com). The Prezi website includes a great deal of information and advice for using the tool and taking advantage of its multimedia capabilities.

Here's an example of a Prezi presentation that meets these criteria and uses design principles effectively. The author, Hayley Ashburner, created this presentation for an assignment in a writing class at the University of North Carolina at Wilmington. The assignment called for students to tell their own literacy histories and show how their experiences fit into larger cultural and historical contexts. Hayley's narrative focused on her journey from her birthplace in South Africa to a new home in Australia and the impact of that journey on her literacy and use of technology.

8

1. Consider the rhetorical context. →	2. Be clear about your message. →	3. Apply the principles of design.
• Hayley's presentation was intended for students in her writing class, but because it would be available online at prezi.com, it might also be viewed by a much broader audience. Her primary purpose was to tell her literacy history in a way that was consistent with the expectations of her course, but she also wanted her story to resonate with viewers outside her class who might simply be interested in her unique experience.	• Hayley's main idea was that her experiences growing up in two different cultures shaped her as a person and as a reader and writer. She wanted to explore how her experiences affected her sense of herself and her uses of literacy and technology in her life.	• Hayley developed her presentation so that a viewer could follow her journey as a person who grew up in two different cultures. She relied on the principles of proximity and alignment to make her presentation engaging and to organize her journey into a coherent story.

Here's the main screen of Hayley's presentation, titled "African Dreams":

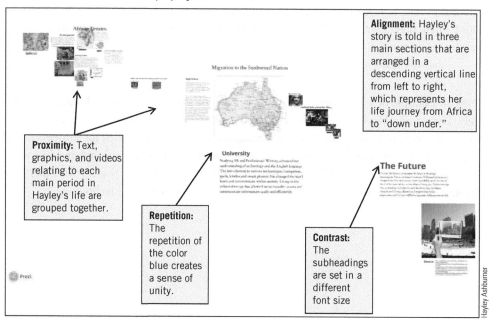

Alignment: Hayley's story is told in three main sections that are arranged in a descending vertical line from left to right, which represents her life journey from Africa to "down under."

Proximity: Text, graphics, and videos relating to each main period in Hayley's life are grouped together.

Repetition: The repetition of the color blue creates a sense of unity.

Contrast: The subheadings are set in a different font size

Hayley Ashburner

A viewer navigates the presentation by clicking arrows that appear at the bottom of the screen. Here's what a viewer sees after the first three clicks:

1. The first click emphasizes the title, "African Dreams":

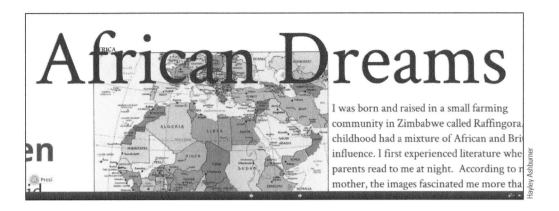

2. The next click zooms in on a map to show Hayley's birthplace:

3. The next click highlights text describing Hayley's early years:

I was born and raised in a small farming community in Zimbabwe called Raffingora. My childhood had a mixture of African and British influence. I first experienced literature when my parents read to me at night. According to my mother, the images fascinated me more than the words. My brothers and I were exposed to a variety of music by my parents and encouraged to perform in community plays.

Hayley Ashburner

Throughout her presentation, which included thirty-five separate screens, Hayley combines carefully written text with images and video clips to keep her audience engaged and to make her story coherent. Her selection of these elements also reflects her effort to communicate her main point about the influence of culture on her. The text in this screen, for example, explains how various media helped her become familiar with Australian culture:

Television, phones, radio and computers helped my family adjust to life in Australia. The internet offered a cost effective way to communicate with friends and family back in Zimbabwe. Whilst, local television and radio exposed us to Australian culture, lifestyle and events. Listening to the radio, watching television and communicating with new peers changed the way I spoke. "Ya" became "yeah", "Chum" became "Mate" and "That's tight" became "hell good!" It also advanced my taste in music.

Hayley Ashburner

The next few clicks take the viewer through two embedded videos that illustrate her evolving taste in music:

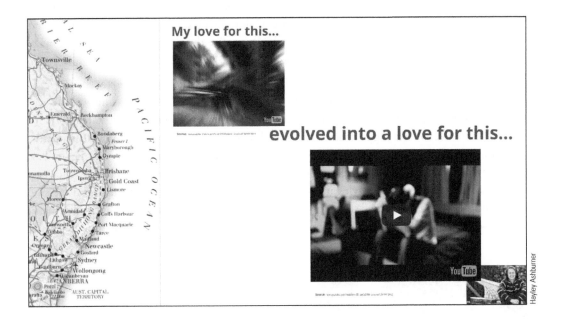

Clicking the video on the left starts a video clip with music that Hayley listened to in South Africa; clicking the right-hand video starts music that she listened to in Australia. Using sound and video in this way, she conveys to the viewer a deeper sense of her experience. The proximity of these videos and the contrast between them highlight the change in her musical tastes over time and communicates a sense of her development as a person growing up in two different cultures.

(You can view Hayley's complete presentation at http://prezi.com/c1q2bitx009e/literacy-narrative/).

Designing a Website

Websites are an invaluable means by which organizations and individuals establish a presence and communicate information to various audiences. Web authoring software (e.g., Dreamweaver) can make it easy to create a sophisticated website, but the use of basic design principles is what makes a website rhetorically effective. The most effective websites are:

- **Clean and uncluttered.** Too much text and too many images can make a website feel messy and difficult for visitors to find information. A website should not overwhelm visitors. Use relevant graphics that convey important ideas or information, and keep text limited and easy to read.

- **Easy to navigate.** Websites are tools that should be easy for visitors to use. The design should enable visitors to find information easily and quickly. Even extensive websites with many separate pages can be designed so that visitors don't get lost or confused as they seek specific information.

- **Coherent.** Appealing websites have a consistent appearance that unifies the various pages and gives the entire site a feeling of coherence. Color schemes, font styles, and graphics tend to be consistent from one page to another, which can give the site a sense of focus and make it easier for visitors to find what they are looking for.

Following these guidelines and applying the principles of design can give a website a professional appearance and enhance its ability to address its intended audience. This website was developed for the Capital District Writing Project, a non-profit organization in upstate New York that promotes effective writing instruction in schools and provides services to teachers, students, and communities to help improve writing. The main page of the website is shown in Figure 8.4. Notice how clean and uncluttered the page appears. It also has a coherent visual theme, with two main colors and consistent font styles and sizes, that is applied to all individual pages on the site. Significantly, the page is designed so that various audiences—teachers, school administrators, and parents—can get a sense of the organization's purpose and find the specific information they need.

1. Consider the rhetorical context. →	2. Be clear about your message. →	3. Apply the principles of design.
• The organization serves teachers, students, and schools in its region. Its website is intended to convey a sense of its mission to those audiences and to provide relevant information about its services. It must compete with many other organizations that are involved in education.	• The central point of the main page of the website is that the organization is an important resource for teachers and administrators interested in improving writing, teaching, and learning in their school districts.	• The main page of the website uses contrast, alignment, and proximity to convey its message and highlight important information contained on the website. It presents a clear and professional image through its strategic use of image, layout, and color.

FIGURE 8.4 Website of the Capital District Writing Project

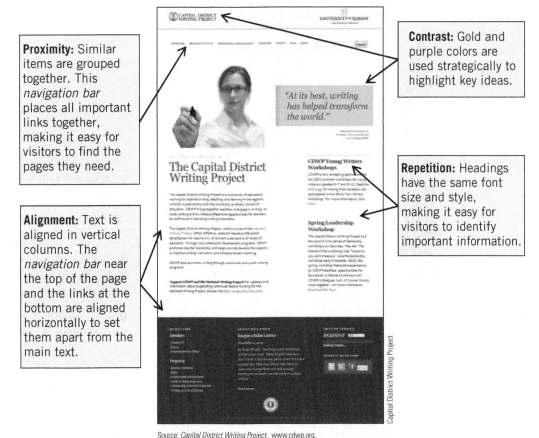

Proximity: Similar items are grouped together. This *navigation bar* places all important links together, making it easy for visitors to find the pages they need.

Alignment: Text is aligned in vertical columns. The *navigation bar* near the top of the page and the links at the bottom are aligned horizontally to set them apart from the main text.

Contrast: Gold and purple colors are used strategically to highlight key ideas.

Repetition: Headings have the same font size and style, making it easy for visitors to identify important information.

Source: *Capital District Writing Project.* www.cdwp.org.

Notice that the main elements on this page are easier to find because of the strategic use of white space between them. Also, the single image of a teacher writing reflects the organization's purpose without distracting a visitor. The navigation bar includes links for specific audiences.

In this chapter, you will learn to

1. Understand the importance of locating relevant information from a variety of sources.

2. Identify six main types of sources.

3. Explain the advantages and limitations of the three main kinds of search tools and use these tools t locate appropriate source material.

4. Develop an effective strategy for finding relevant source material.

Finding Source Material

9

RECENT STUDIES INDICATE that research-based writing, which has always been a mainstay of academic writing, is becoming ever more common in the assignments students encounter in their college courses. So being able to work effectively with sources is essential for successful college writing. This chapter will guide you in learning how to locate relevant information from a variety of sources.

Understanding Research

While I was still in college, I made a road trip with a friend that took me through the Badlands of South Dakota, a remote, sparsely populated, and starkly beautiful region of pastel-colored hills, mesas, and prairies etched with countless canyons and dry creek beds. As we drove along a desolate stretch of Interstate 90, we passed one of those large green exit signs. Under that sign someone had attached another sign: a weathered plank with hand-painted red letters that read, "Doctor wanted." The sign surprised us and made us wonder: Were the residents of that isolated area really so desperate for medical care that they took to posting hand-painted signs on the Interstate? Was their situation common in rural areas? Was medical care scarce for Americans who lived in such areas? I had never really thought about what it might be like to live in a remote area where things that I took for granted—like medical care—might not be available.

When I returned from my trip, I contacted a cousin who is a family doctor and told him about the sign. He explained that providing doctors for remote rural areas was a longstanding challenge in the U.S. that was complicated by rising health care costs and the growing use of expensive medical technology. I was intrigued and wanted to know more. I contacted a magazine editor, who expressed interest in an article on the topic. At that point, I had a topic, an interesting and relevant experience, some basic information, and a lot of additional questions. I also had a goal: to inform the readers of the magazine about a little-known problem in American health care. I was ready to learn more. I could now begin my research.

As my story suggests, research should begin with a question or problem that you want to address—one that matters not only to you but also to a potential audience. Core Concept #1 tells us that writing is a process of discovery and learning (see Chapter 2). Research is an integral component of that powerful process of inquiry. Research is not the *reason* for writing. Rather, you conduct research to explore and understand your subject. In this regard, finding sources is a purposeful activity: The sources help you achieve your rhetorical goals.

So the most important thing to remember about working with sources is that it isn't about the sources. In other words, your focus should be, first, on the purpose of your project and how it fits your rhetorical situation. So start there:

- What are you writing about and *why*?
- What are you trying to accomplish with a particular writing project?
- What do you need to know in order to accomplish your rhetorical goals?

By the time you're ready to begin consulting sources, you should already have begun exploring your subject and have a sense of your intended audience and the purpose of your project. Your rhetorical goals should guide your research—not the other way around.

SIDEBAR | **DON'T START LOOKING FOR SOURCE MATERIAL TOO SOON**

A common mistake students make in research-based writing is moving too quickly to the process of finding sources. After receiving an assignment, the first thing they do is go online to search for information about a possible topic before they have begun to develop some idea of what they will say about that topic. As a result, what they find, rather than their rhetorical purpose, guides their project. In such cases, the resulting project is often a compilation of source material rather than a genuine inquiry into the subject.

To avoid that mistake, follow the steps in Chapter 3 and don't focus on looking for source material until you have begun exploring your topic and have a good sense of your rhetorical situation. It's certainly OK to peruse source material to get ideas about a topic, but if your research is purposeful rather than haphazard, finding sources will be part of the process of inquiry that writing should be.

Doing research today is a kind of good news–bad news proposition. The good news is that students have ready access to an astonishing amount and variety of material online so that they can quickly find information on almost any conceivable topic. The bad news is that having access to so much information can be overwhelming and make it difficult to distinguish useful information from erroneous or dubious information. Following a few simple guidelines will enable you to take advantage of the wealth of material available to you and avoid the common pitfalls of finding useful and reliable sources.

The key to finding appropriate sources is threefold:

- determining what you need
- understanding available sources
- developing a search strategy

The remainder of this chapter is devoted to examining these three aspects of finding relevant source material.

Determining What You Need

To make your research efficient and successful, it's best to identify the kinds of information you need. Otherwise, your searches are likely to be haphazard and time-consuming. Follow these basic steps:

1. Consider the purpose of your project and your intended audience.
2. Generate questions you will probably need to address.
3. Identify possible sources of information to address those questions.

To illustrate, let's look at three writing assignments that call for research:

- a literacy narrative requiring you to analyze your own experiences as a young reader and writer in terms of available research on literacy development;
- an argument in favor of abolishing the electoral college in U.S. presidential elections;
- a history of your neighborhood focusing on the period since the end of World War II.

1. Consider Your Purpose and Audience

Literacy narrative	• To gain insight into your own literacy experiences • To understand literacy development in general • To share this learning with students in your writing class
Argument against electoral college	• To illuminate problems with the current election system • To propose an increasingly popular solution • To educate other students about this issue • To encourage other voting citizens to consider this solution
History of your neighborhood	• To understand important developments in your neighborhood's past • To understand how the past affects the present • To share these insights with other students of history and neighborhood residents

9

2. Generate Questions You Might Need to Address

Literacy narrative	• What important childhood experiences shaped you as reader and writer? • What role did literacy play in your life as an adolescent? • What influence did your family have on your writing and reading habits? • What does research indicate are the key factors that affect literacy ability?
Argument against electoral college	• How exactly does the electoral college work? Why was it developed? • What are the main criticisms of the electoral college? • What problems have occurred in past elections? • What solutions have others proposed? What concerns do critics have about these solutions?
History of your neighborhood	• What key economic, political, and social developments occurred in your neighborhood since WWII? What changes have taken place in that time? • How do these developments relate to broader developments in your region or the nation? • What problems does the neighborhood face today? How are those problems related to past developments?

3. Identify Possible Sources to Answer Your Questions

Literacy narrative	• Family members; former teachers • Relevant artifacts from your childhood (school papers, books, letters) • Scholarly articles and books about literacy development • Published studies of childhood literacy
Argument against electoral college	• Reference works on political science and elections • Articles in political journals, newspapers, and newsmagazines • Blog posts, public affairs websites • Materials from political watchdog groups
History of your neighborhood	• Archived newspaper articles • Documents from local historical society or state museum • Op-ed essays in local newspapers, websites, blogs • Interviews with local leaders and residents

These examples illustrate **four important points about finding sources:**

- **The kind of information you need and the possible sources for that information depend on the nature of your project and rhetorical situation.** For example, the literacy narrative assignment requires looking into your past experiences with writing and reading but also requires finding specialized information about literacy development that is most likely available only in academic publications. Moreover, because the narrative is intended for an academic audience, the instructor will probably expect you to consult scholarly sources. By contrast, the argument about the electoral college is intended for a more general, less specialized audience. It addresses a topic that has been discussed in a variety of contexts, including academic journals as well as the popular press and social media. Given that rhetorical situation and the more general appeal of the topic, some relevant sources will probably be less specialized than those for the literacy narrative assignment.

- **Identifying what you don't know will help you find the right sources for what you need to know.** By starting the research process with questions that you need to answer, you will quickly identify what you don't know about your topic, which will help you identify what you *need to know*. For example, for the argument against the electoral college, you might already have a sense of the problems with the current election system, but you might have little knowledge of the history of that system or what experts and others have said about it. Similarly, for the neighborhood history, you might know a lot about the present economic and political situation in your neighborhood but little about how it came to be that way. Posing questions about your topic helps you identify such gaps in your knowledge and point you to possible sources of information to fill those gaps.

- **Some projects call for original research.** Two of these three examples point to the possibility of students doing their own *primary research* (see Focus: "Primary vs. Secondary Research" on page 288). For the neighborhood history project, for example, students might interview residents and local leaders as well as examine archived documents in a local historical society or museum. For the literacy narrative assignments, students might interview family members and former teachers and use documents such as old school papers. These original sources will be supplemented by *secondary sources*, such as academic journals, newspapers, books, or websites.

- **Research begets research.** The more you learn about your topic, the more questions you are likely to have. That's as it should be. For example, in researching the history of your neighborhood, you might discover that the closing of a local factory after World War II left many residents out of work, which led to an exodus of young people to other towns and states. Learning about that development might lead to questions about the basis for the local economy, which in turn might lead you to look at sources (e.g., economic data) that you had not previously considered. Similarly, in reading a journal article about childhood literacy for your literacy narrative, you might encounter a reference to a study about the relationship between literacy development and social class. That study in turn might prompt you to re-examine your own literacy development in terms of your socio-economic background. As you proceed with your research, you will learn more about your topic, which will probably mean that you will begin to understand better what you need to know to complete your project.

9

Scholars usually distinguish between two kinds of research:

Primary research is firsthand investigation. It involves conducting experiments, collecting various kinds of data (such as through surveys, interviews, or observation), or examining original documents (such as manuscripts, public records, or letters) or artifacts in libraries or museums. If you interview someone, design and distribute a survey, conduct a laboratory experiment, or analyze data that have not been previously published, you are conducting primary research. Most college students do not engage in primary research, although some college assignments require such research.

Secondary research is based on the work of others. It involves investigating what other people have already published on a given subject—in other words, finding information about a topic online, in books, in magazine or journal articles, and similar sources. Most of the research college students do is secondary research. The advice in this chapter generally assumes that you are doing secondary research.

Understanding Sources

The main challenge in research-based writing is finding the right sources that have the material you need to meet the rhetorical goals for your project. Understanding the different kinds of available sources will help you meet that challenge. In this section we will examine **six main types of sources:**

- books
- scholarly journals
- magazines and newspapers
- reference materials
- websites
- social media

Some of these types of sources, such as websites, appear only online; others, however, might appear both online and in traditional print form (see Focus: "Print vs. Online" on page 291). For example, *The New York Times* is still published every day as a print newspaper, which you can find on the newsstand at a convenience store or in your library, but it also is available online at the *Times'* website, where you can access the same material that appears in the print newspaper in addition to other content, such as blogs and videos, that is not available in print form. Unless otherwise noted, the discussion in this chapter assumes that most source material you find in your research can be found both in print and online. However, given the wealth of online resources and the fact that so many traditional materials now appear in digital form, most of your source material is likely to be available online or in some digital format (such as a library database). In other words, less and less research involves traditional print sources.

Only a few years ago the difference between a traditional print source, such as a book or a magazine, and online resources, such as websites, was pretty straightforward, and searching for print materials as compared to online resources involved different search tools and procedures. However, the distinction between print and online resources has become increasingly blurred as many traditional print sources become available online or disappear altogether. Most print newspapers and magazines now have websites where online versions of print articles are available in addition to other materials, such as social media and videos, that do not appear in print form. Similarly, many scholarly journals make articles available in both print and online form, and many journals now do not appear in print format at all but are available only online. In addition, many books are now available online through services such as Google Books and Project Gutenberg, although access to many books online is partial or limited because of copyright restrictions. Moreover, the main tools for finding resources—search engines and databases (see pages 295–297)—can be accessed online with a computer, tablet, or smartphone, which means that most research required in college classes is conducted online, and students do not need to search physically for materials in a library as frequently as in the past—if at all.

As a result of these developments, students today can use various devices to gain relatively easy (and often instant) access to an astonishing variety and quantity of information and potential source material. However, although access to source material is easier today than in the past, finding the right source material is more complicated today, and much of the material available online requires more careful scrutiny than traditional print materials available in a library (see Chapter 10).

Books

In this instant-access digital age, books can seem archaic. It can be easy to find up-to-the-minute information on media websites, quickly get facts about a topic by using a search engine like Google, or instantly access information about a subject on a reference website like Wikipedia. Getting information from a book, on the other hand, requires you to go to the library (or bookstore) and physically page through the book to find what you need (unless you are using a tablet, which enables you to search the contents of a book digitally). Nevertheless, printed books continue to be stable sources of information compared to many online resources, which can change without notice or even disappear, making it difficult or impossible for readers to access or verify the information. The extensive process of producing a book requires writers and editors to consider the relevance of the content over a longer term than is necessary for much online material. Unlike websites, which can be revised and updated constantly, books are likely to remain in print for years before being revised or updated. In general, that means that if you cite information contained in a book, readers who want to track it down will likely be able to do so.

9

In addition, books—especially scholarly books—often contain the best of what is known about a subject, even when the book is several years or even decades old. That's partly because scholarly publishers generally do not publish with an eye toward what is trendy or popular; rather, they often look for material that includes well-established knowledge and important new developments in a particular field. As a result, scholarly books often reflect the state of knowledge that an academic field has generated over many years, even when the subject is current and changing. This does not mean that books are always accurate or unbiased (see Focus: "Detecting Bias" in Chapter 10); sometimes a new development in a field will significantly change or even invalidate previous thinking about an important subject in that field, and like trade books (that is, books that are published commercially and for profit), scholarly books can reflect a particular perspective or school of thought. But by and large, scholarly books and many trade books can be credible, stable sources of information.

In general, then, if you need well-established information in a field, consider searching for that information in books. For example, let's return to our earlier example of an argument about the electoral college system in United States presidential elections. You can easily find current newspaper articles and blog posts expressing various viewpoints about the electoral college, but you can gain a deep understanding of what scholars have said about this system and its development in American politics by consulting scholarly books. A quick search of your library catalog might yield several titles like this:

> Belenky, Alexander S. *Who Will Be the Next President? A Guide to the U.S. Presidential Election System*. Springer, 2013.

> Edwards, George C. *Why the Electoral College is Bad for America*. Yale University Press, 2004.

> Shaw, Daron R. *The Race to 270: The Electoral College and the Campaign Strategies of 2000 and 2004*. University of Chicago Press, 2006.

These works, all published by scholarly presses, are likely to include in-depth analyses and historical background about the electoral college that can help you understand how it works and become familiar with the questions experts have raised about it. Notice that one of these books (*Who Will Be the Next President?*) is relatively new and therefore likely to contain more recent scholarly developments. But although the other two titles are older, they are likely to reflect established scholarly thinking about this subject, which is a longstanding issue in American politics. This example illustrates the usefulness of books, even when up-to-the-minute information and opinion might be available from newspapers or social media.

Scholarly Journals

If you search your college library's periodical holdings, you will discover that there are thousands of scholarly journals devoted to every academic subject and their many subspecialties. For example, in 2016 the library of the State University of New York at Albany listed 511 scholarly journals in the field of general biology and an additional 766 journals in subspecialties such as genetics, microbiology, and immunology. Taken together, these journals reflect the most up-to-date knowledge in biology and its subfields. Every academic field, no matter how small or specialized, has its own scholarly journals. In addition, some prestigious journals publish articles from many related fields. The journal *Science*, for example, publishes articles from all fields of science.

As a general rule, scholarly journals are considered reputable, dependable, and accurate sources of information, ideas, and knowledge. Most scholarly journals are *peer-reviewed*, which means that each published article has been evaluated by several experts on the specific subject matter of the article. By contrast, articles in trade and popular magazines are usually reviewed by an editor (or sometimes by an editorial team); they are generally not evaluated by an outside panel of experts. Consequently, articles that appear in scholarly journals are generally considered to meet rigorous standards of scholarship in their respective fields. If your research leads you to material in a scholarly journal, you can usually be confident that it is credible.

The challenge facing most student writers, however, is that scholarly articles are written by experts for other experts in their respective fields. These articles can often be difficult for a novice (as almost all students are) to understand, and students can find it hard to assess whether the material in such articles fits the needs of their project. If you find yourself in such a situation (and you probably will at some point), use the following strategies to help you decide whether the material in a scholarly article is useful to you:

- **Read the abstract.** Most scholarly articles include an abstract, which is a summary of the article. Reading the abstract will give you a good idea about whether the article contains the kind of information you need.

- **Ask a librarian.** Librarians are trained to understand the characteristics and nuances of many different kinds of source material. If you're not sure about whether a specific scholarly article is relevant for your project, ask a librarian.

- **Search the internet.** Often a scholarly article is part of a larger body of work by the author(s) and others in a specific field. If you find an article that seems relevant but you're not sure whether it contains material that you need, do a quick Internet search using the subject or title of the article and/or the authors' names. Such a search might yield links to websites, such as the authors' university web pages, that are less technical and contain information that can help you decide whether the scholarly article is useful for your project.

Magazines and Newspapers

For many topics—especially topics related to current events—magazines and newspapers provide rich sources of up-to-date information. But there are many different kinds of magazines and newspapers, and their quality and dependability can vary widely. Here are the main categories:

- **Trade magazines.** Trade magazines and journals are specialized periodicals devoted to specific occupations or professions. Many are considered important sources for information and opinions relevant to those occupations or professions. *Automotive Design and Production*, for example, publishes articles about the latest technology and news related to the automobile industry. Other well-known trade journals include *Adweek*, *American Bar Association Journal*, *Business & Finance*, and *Publishers Weekly*. Although most trade publications do not peer-review the articles they publish, they nevertheless can provide reliable information and important perspectives on subjects related to their professions.

9

- **Popular magazines.** This very large category includes numerous publications on every conceivable topic, but the main feature that distinguishes popular publications from trade or public affairs journals is that popular magazines are intended for a general, non-specialist audience. *Sports Illustrated*, for example, a popular magazine, might publish an article about the top track and field athletes competing in the Olympic Games, whereas *Track & Field News*, a trade publication, might include technical articles about the latest training techniques used by world-class sprinters to prepare for the Olympics. Popular magazines tend to value the latest news and often cater to specific segments of the general population (for example, *Seventeen Magazine* targets teenage girls) in an effort to attract advertising revenue. Although they vary widely in quality and dependability, they can be an important source of information, depending upon the nature of your project. However, some college instructors consider many popular magazines less credible sources than either trade or scholarly publications, so check with your instructor to determine whether to use such magazines as sources for your project.

- **Public affairs journals.** A number of periodicals focus on politics, history, and culture and publish carefully researched articles, often by well-known scholars and other experts. Many public affairs journals have developed reputations as respected sources of the most knowledgeable perspectives on important political, economic, and social issues. Some of these journals have been publishing for many decades. Among the most well-known public affairs journals are *The Atlantic, National Review*, the *Nation*, and *Foreign Affairs*.

- **Newspapers and newsmagazines.** Daily and weekly newspapers and weekly or monthly newsmagazines are general sources for the most up-to-date information. Among the advantages of these publications for researchers is that they tend to be accessible, intended for a wide audience, and publish material on a wide variety of topics. Like popular magazines, newspapers and newsmagazines can vary significantly in quality, focus, and dependability. In general, well established newspapers, such as *The New York Times, The Washington Post, The Guardian*, and the *Los Angeles Times*, and newsmagazines, such as *Time* and *Newsweek*, tend to have rigorous editorial review and often employ fact-checkers to verify information they publish. However, like all sources, these publications are subject to bias, no matter how objective and thorough they might claim to be (see Focus: "Detecting Bias" in Chapter 10). They might be dependable and well respected, but they also represent various points of view. Don't assume that because something is published in a reputable newspaper or newsmagazine, it is free from bias.

Depending on the nature of your project, any of these kinds of publications can provide useful material, but it is important to be aware of the differences among them so that you can better judge the appropriateness of a specific source.

Reference Materials

Reference materials, such as encyclopedias, statistical abstracts, dictionaries, atlases, and almanacs, are large compilations of general or specialized information. If you need statistical information about employment rates in the U.S., for example, you can search the *Statistical Abstract of the United States*. In the past, these materials were available as large, multivolume book sets that you could usually find in a library. Today, most traditional reference materials are available online, often through your college library's website. Venerable reference resources such as *Encyclopedia Britannica* are now available online along with more recently developed resources such as *Wikipedia*. In addition, there are now many digital reference materials, such the *Gale Virtual Reference Library*, that do not appear in print form; often, you can access these resources only through paid subscriptions, but many college libraries make them available to their students.

Websites

Because the Internet contains an almost inconceivable amount of material, it can be a boon for researchers, but the sheer amount of available information online can also be overwhelming and confusing. Businesses, government agencies, media outlets, individuals, and organizations of all kinds maintain websites that can be excellent sources of information for researchers. For example, if you are looking for information about standardized testing in K–12 schools, you can search the website of the U.S. Department of Education; you can visit the websites of state education departments, school districts, and related government agencies; and you can consult the websites of the many not-for-profit organizations and advocacy groups devoted to education issues, many of which provide a wide variety of information on education-related issues. Similarly, for-profit organizations that provide education services maintain websites that can also be useful sources. In addition, the websites of media organizations devoted to education issues, such as *The Chronicle of Higher Education*, can be excellent resources. It's safe to say that with careful searching you can almost always find relevant websites that provide useful and reliable information, no matter what subject you are researching.

At the same time, all websites are not created equal when it comes to the usefulness and credibility of information they contain. We will examine how to evaluate source material in Chapter 10, but for now it is important to be able to distinguish among **five basic categories of websites:**

- **News organizations.** As noted earlier, all major newspapers and newsmagazines, such as *The New York Times* and *Newsweek*, maintain extensive websites, which are usually carefully managed and contain information that is reviewed by editors. News organizations such as NBC, PBS, and Fox also maintain extensive websites, as do smaller, lesser known news outlets such as regional newspapers. In general, these websites can be extremely useful sources of information that is generally trustworthy and up-to-date.

- **Public agencies.** Government offices, such as the U.S. Department of Labor or state departments of transportation, maintain websites that provide services to citizens but also contain relevant information. For example, the U.S. Department of Labor website offers statistical data about employment and wages; state education departments provide data about school graduation rates, testing, and funding. Often, these sites contain specialized information that is trustworthy and cannot be found elsewhere.

- **Advocacy groups.** Organizations that represent various perspectives on countless social, political, environmental, economic, education, and health issues maintain their own websites, which, like those of government agencies, can be useful sources of specialized information. Websites for well-known political advocacy groups, such as People for the American Way and the Family Research Council, as well as issue-oriented organizations, such as Greenpeace and the National Rifle Association, can be important sources as well, depending upon the subject

9

of your research, but using these websites requires understanding the organizations' purposes and perspectives and their potential biases (see Focus: "Detecting Bias" in Chapter 10). The same is true of websites maintained by organizations devoted to sports, hobbies, and leisure activities, such as dancing or hunting.

- **Business.** Today, it is a rare business that does not have an online presence. Although most websites maintained by businesses are used to advertise and sell their products and services, they can sometimes contain useful information that might not be available elsewhere. For example, the website for West Marine, a large company that sells products for boaters, includes informational web pages and videos on subjects of interest to boaters, such as repairing boats or maintaining engines.

- **Private individuals.** Anyone with access to the Internet can launch a website on any subject that interests them. These websites sometimes contain useful information and often include insights about the subject from the person who maintains the site. For example, someone with experience and expertise in photography might maintain a website that includes helpful descriptions of various techniques for taking photographs. Such sites can be worth visiting, depending upon the nature of your research project, but because most private individual websites undergo no review of their content, they require scrutiny to make sure you can trust the information you find there. Approach them with skepticism.

Social Media

Social media, such as Facebook, Twitter, and Snapchat, have become important sites for debate, discussion, and the exchange of information. Many blogs have become as important and respected as the most reputable journals as sources of ideas, opinions, and information, and services like Tumblr and Facebook can be useful sources for some kinds of information. Often, such sites contain up-to-date perspectives and information because they are constantly revised to reflect current developments. They also reflect the often overtly biased (and sometimes problematic and offensive) views of the people who use them, so carefully evaluate information and ideas you find on any social media site before using it in your research project.

As always, the nature of your project and your rhetorical situation will dictate which sources are the most relevant. For many academic writing tasks, some sources will be considered inappropriate. If you're not sure whether a specific source is appropriate for your project, check with your instructor or a reference librarian.

Locating the Right Sources

Given the wealth and variety of available resources, how do you find the information you need? There are **three primary tools for finding the right source materials** for your project:

- library catalogs
- databases
- online search engines

Library Catalogs

A library lists all the materials it holds in its online catalog, which is usually easily accessible from the library's home page. In addition to listing books held by the library, the library website typically enables you to access other resources maintained by the library, including its reference collections; periodicals (scholarly journals as well as newspapers and magazines); audio, video, and digital media holdings; government documents; and special collections (such as local historical materials or manuscripts from a well-known author). If you are searching for books on your subject, the library online catalog is the best place to start. But the library website is also a good place to start your search for other materials as well. Get to know what is available on your college library's website. It will serve you well in your research.

Databases

Databases are listings of published materials that enable you to locate articles in scholarly journals, trade journals, or popular newspapers and magazines. Some databases provide only citations or abstracts of articles in the periodicals they list; some also provide direct access to the full texts of the materials they list. The most popular databases, such as *Academic Search Complete*, are general and interdisciplinary, indexing a wide variety of materials from all subject areas. However, many databases are specialized and index only periodicals relevant to their subject. For example, *MedLine* indexes periodicals and related materials on medicine, nursing, dentistry, veterinary medicine, the health care system, and pre-clinical sciences.

Chances are that you will need to search several different databases for many of your college writing projects, so it makes sense to become familiar with the databases available through your college library. Among the most widely used databases are the following:

- **Academic Search Complete.** Multidisciplinary scholarly database, part of the *EBSCOhost* Research Databases, that includes thousands of full-text periodicals in the social sciences, humanities, science, and technology.

- **JSTOR.** Scholarly database that provides access to full-text articles from many different journals in a variety of academic disciplines.

- **Article First.** General database that indexes the content page of journals in science, technology, medicine, social science, business, the humanities, and popular culture.

- **Google Scholar.** Multidisciplinary scholarly database that lists citations for articles, papers, books, and related scholarly documents in all major academic disciplines.

- **LexisNexis Academic.** Extensive databases providing citations and full-text articles from newspapers, magazines, and many different periodicals in law, business, biography, medicine, and reference.

- **WorldCat.** General database that includes citations for any materials held by a library.

- **Scopus.** General database that indexes abstracts and provides access to the contents of thousands of international journal titles as well as conference proceedings, book series, scientific web pages, and patents, with a focus on science, technology, and medicine.

9

Keep in mind that although some databases (such as *Google Scholar*) are freely available on the Internet, others are available only through a subscription or license (e.g., *Academic Search Complete*). If your library has a subscription to these databases, you can usually access them by signing in through your library's website.

Search Engines

Search engines are websites that search the Internet for available materials. Typically, search engines return a list of links to websites and other web-based resources, which you must then visit to find the material you're looking for. Google is the most popular search engine, but there are many other search engines, including specialized search engines that focus on specific subject areas, such as automobiles, business, computers, or education. Among the most commonly used general search engines are Yahoo, Bing, and Ask.com.

Although these three kinds of resources overlap, in general you can use them as follows:

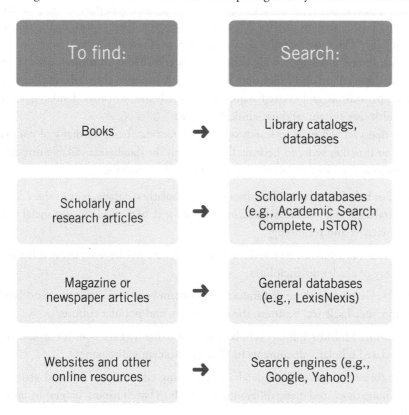

To find:	Search:
Books	Library catalogs, databases
Scholarly and research articles	Scholarly databases (e.g., Academic Search Complete, JSTOR)
Magazine or newspaper articles	General databases (e.g., LexisNexis)
Websites and other online resources	Search engines (e.g., Google, Yahoo!)

Of course, you can use an Internet search engine such as Google to find references to books, scholarly articles, and newspaper and magazine articles, but if you limit your search tools to

Internet search engines, you might miss important resources, especially if your topic is specialized and your assignment is academic in nature. (See Focus: "Databases vs. Search Engines.") It's best to use these three basic kinds of online resources in combination to be able to identify the most useful sources for your project.

Developing a Search Strategy

Understanding the many different sources available to you and knowing which search tools to use still isn't quite enough for successful research. For example, your library catalog lists thousands of book titles, but how do you even know whether searching for a book makes sense for your project? Similarly, a search engine such as Google can point you to thousands of links related to a certain topic, but what will you look for among those many links? How do you know which ones to pursue? You will more likely find what you need if you develop a general search strategy that focuses on the kinds of information you need for your project and takes advantage of all potential sources to find that information rather than limiting your search to one set of resources, such as online materials or scholarly journals.

9

To illustrate, let's return to our earlier example of an assignment to write a research-based argument in favor of abolishing the electoral college in U.S. presidential elections (see "Determining What You Need" on page 287). We identified the purpose of the project as follows:

- to illuminate problems with the current election system
- to propose an increasingly popular solution to this problem
- to encourage other voting citizens to consider this solution

Let's imagine further that you are writing this essay with several overlapping audiences in mind: classmates in your writing course, other college students, and voting citizens. So your audience is both general and academic. You have become interested in the topic because you have heard many young people of voting age express apathy about the recent presidential election, partly because the popular vote does not directly elect the president. You have also read several op-ed essays about this issue, some of which have called for abolishing the electoral college.

After reading about the electoral college online, you have decided you support the idea of replacing it with a system in which the national popular vote directly elects the president. However, you need to learn more about how the electoral college works as well as the various arguments for and against that system.

Here's the list of questions you have identified as a starting point for your research:

- How exactly does the electoral college work? Why was it developed?
- What are the main criticisms of the electoral college?
- What problems have occurred in past elections?
- What solutions have others proposed? What concerns do critics have about these solutions?

And here are some potential sources you have identified for addressing these questions:

- reference works on political science and elections
- articles in political journals, newspapers, newsmagazines
- blog posts, public affairs websites
- materials from political watchdog groups

How should you proceed?

When you have a general idea about what you might want to say about your topic (in this case, that the electoral college should be replaced with a national vote for U.S. Presidential elections) but limited knowledge of the subject, a good search strategy is to start broadly and narrow your search as you learn more about your topic and refine your main point (Core Concept #4). That means beginning with general searches of the major categories of resources—library catalogs, databases, and search engines—and then searching for more specific materials as you identify questions or subtopics that you need to explore, using the appropriate search tools at each stage. In our example the process might look like this:

1. General search for materials on your topic:
- Library catalog for books
- General database (e.g., LexisNexis)
- Search engine (e.g., Google)

2. Narrower search to explore specific issues and questions:
- Specialized databases (e.g., Worldwide Political Science Asbtracts, Google Scholar)

3. Targeted search to fill gaps and find alternative viewpoints:
- advanced search of relevant database (e.g., LexisNexis, Google Scholar) and search engine

1. Do a General Search for Materials on Your Topic

Recall your questions about the electoral college:

- How exactly does the electoral college work? Why was it developed?
- What are the main criticisms of the electoral college?
- What problems have occurred in past elections?
- What solutions have others proposed? What concerns do critics have about these solutions?

9

These should guide your general searches. You need basic information about the electoral college, its history, and the criticisms of the system. You also need information about proposed solutions. Search the three main kinds of resources for relevant materials.

Library Catalog

Libraries have different kinds of search mechanisms, but most allow users to do **keyword searches** of their catalogs for subjects or titles of books and related materials in their collections. In this case, you could use *electoral college* as a subject keyword. In 2016, a search using these keywords yielded 71 books in the library of the State University of New York at Albany. Here's what the first page of the results screen looked like:

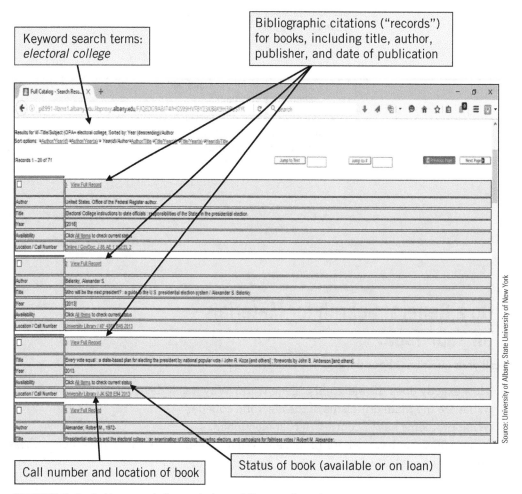

Keyword search terms: *electoral college*

Bibliographic citations ("records") for books, including title, author, publisher, and date of publication

Call number and location of book

Status of book (available or on loan)

FIGURE 9.1 A Keyword Search in a Library Catalog

This screen shows the first three of 71 total "records," which provide bibliographic information about each book as well as its call number so that you can locate it in the library. You can also click a link to check on the status of each book (whether it is out on loan, when it is due, etc.). Although search screens can differ noticeably from one library to another, they will all have these key components, including complete bibliographic information about the book (author, publisher, date of publication) and the status of the book (whether it is available for loan, where it is located in the library).

Review the search results to see which books seem most likely to contain the information you need about the electoral college. Some of the books listed in this sample search will likely provide general information about the electoral college:

Who Will Be the Next President? A Guide to the U.S. Presidential Election System (2013), by Alexander S. Belenky

After the People Vote: A Guide to the Electoral College (2004), edited by John C. Fortier

Electoral College and Presidential Elections (2001), edited by Alexandra Kura

Some specifically address the controversy about the electoral college and proposals to reform it:

Every Vote Equal: A State-Based Plan for Electing the President by National Popular Vote (2008), by John R. Koza et al.

Enlightened Democracy: The Case for the Electoral College (2004), by Tara Ross

Why the Electoral College is Bad for America (2004), by George C. Edwards

Some might be too specialized for your purposes:

Electoral Votes Based on the 1990 Census (1991), by David C. Huckabee

Based on the information in the search results, select the books that seem most useful and visit the library to review them. (You might also do an online search to find additional information about each book before visiting the library. For example, a Google search of the book's title and author will often yield descriptions of the book, reviews, and related information that can help you determine whether the book is worth borrowing from the library.)

General Databases

Search one or more general databases using the same or similar keywords. A good place to start is *LexisNexis Academic*, which indexes many different newspapers and magazines as well as other kinds of materials; it also indexes more specialized journals.

Like many databases, *LexisNexis Academic* has a basic search screen and an advanced search screen. Begin with a basic search of the news using your keywords *electoral college*. Notice that this database allows you to select categories of sources (news, legal, companies, etc.). In some cases, it might make sense to narrow your search to one such category; in this example, however, a broader search is appropriate:

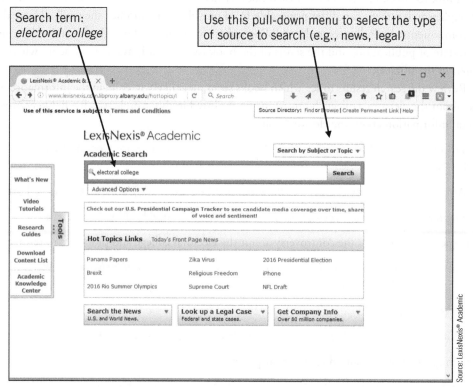

FIGURE 9.2 A Basic Search Screen in *LexisNexis Academic*

This search of "news" returned 999 entries. Here's the first screen:

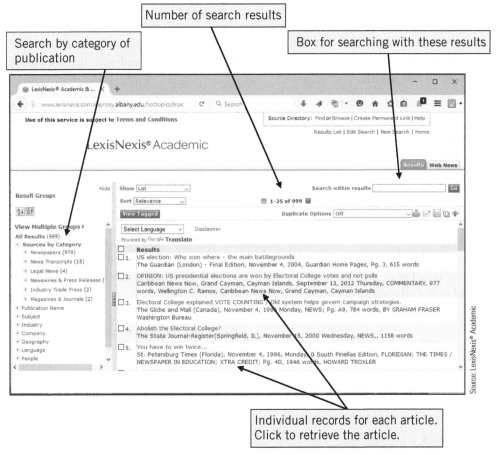

FIGURE 9.3 Search Results for "Electoral College" in *LexisNexis Academic*

Databases have very different search screens, and it might take some time to become familiar with the ones you are using. However, all major databases allow you to specify the parameters of your search (e.g., by publication type, date, author, title, keywords, and so on) so that you can search broadly or be more strategic. Moreover, they all provide the same basic information about the sources that are returned in a search, which in this example are called "records." Usually, that information includes the author, title, publication, and date of the entry. Sometimes the entry will include an abstract or summary of the source. You can use this information to review the entries and decide which ones to examine more closely.

Obviously, the 999 records returned in this sample would be too many to review, but you can **narrow your search** in several ways:

- **Search within the results.** Use more specific terms to search within the results of searches that yield too many entries. For example, you can use the keywords *presidential election* to exclude any articles about other elections. Using those keywords reduced the search in this example to 744 records.

- **Search specific publications.** Since you are interested in the American electoral college, you might search only American newspapers. You can limit your search further by searching only major newspapers (e.g., *Washington Post, The New York Times*). You can do the same for magazines and other types of publications.

- **Specify dates.** If you want to find materials related to a specific time period, you can specify the dates of the materials you want. For example, if you want articles about the 2000 Presidential Election, you might search for materials published from 1998 through 2001.

Notice that you can also search by subject. Expanding the subject list reveals a number of subtopics. The numbers in parentheses after each subtopic indicate how many of the 999 records relate to that subtopic. For example, among the 999 entries in the original search in this example, 467 are related to the subtopic "US Presidential Elections":

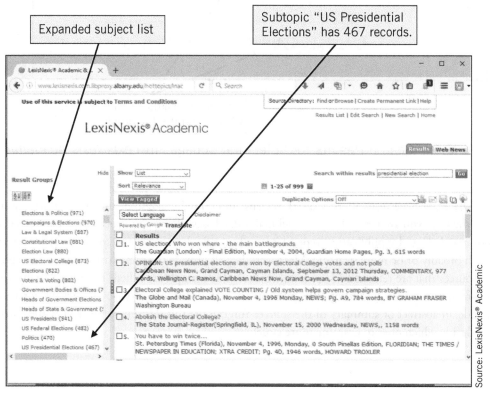

FIGURE 9.4 Using a Subject List to Search in *LexisNexis Academic*

You can use the subject categories to narrow your search further by clicking on the subject "US Presidential Elections" and search the 467 records within that category. In this way you can find sources that are more likely to be relevant to your specific topic.

As you gain experience, you will become more efficient in finding the materials you need. In the meantime, **when searching databases, follow these guidelines**:

- **Experiment with keywords.** Sometimes, it takes several different combinations of search terms before you begin to see the search results you want. In our example, the search term *electoral college* returned good results, but depending upon what you are looking for, you might have to try various other search terms: *elections, popular election, presidential elections, election controversies*, and so on.

- **Use several search strategies.** Sometimes, a basic keyword search gets you right to the materials you need. More often, you will have to try different search strategies to narrow your search to manageable numbers and to find the most relevant materials. If various keyword searches don't yield what you need, try subject searches. Try various searches within your search results. Don't rely on a single approach.

- **Use different databases.** Different databases have different search options and will return different results. Although most databases allow for refined or advanced searching, each database has its own interface with its own peculiarities. So the same keywords are likely to yield different results in different databases. In this sample search, for example, using the same keywords (electoral college) with the *Academic Search Complete* database will turn up some of the same sources but also different sources. You might also find some databases easier to use than others. Be aware that it can take some time to become familiar with the characteristics of each database, so if you have trouble finding what you need in a specific database, ask a librarian or your instructor for guidance.

Internet Search Engines

Having searched your library catalog and one or more databases, you can expand your search to include online materials using a general search engine such as Google or Yahoo!. Remember that search engines will return many more entries than a library catalog or a database, so you might have to adjust your search terms to keep the search results manageable. In our sample search you might begin with general search terms, such as *electoral college*, but be aware that such general searches will usually yield enormous numbers of results. A search of Google using those terms in 2016 yielded more than 3 million items, for instance. That kind of result isn't surprising when you remember that Google is searching the entire Internet for anything (websites, documents, etc.) that contains those two words. So try different strategies for narrowing your search. For instance, placing those terms in quotation marks (see Sidebar: "An Important Tip for Searching Databases and Search Engines" on page 306) reduced the results by half. That's still an unmanageable number, but you can review the first few pages of search results to determine whether any of the links might be useful.

9

After reviewing the first several pages of search results, narrow your search using different search terms, such as *electoral college presidential election, electoral college controversy, history of electoral college*. Each of these terms will yield different results. Review each set of results for materials that seem promising. Continue to narrow your search so that the results are not only relevant but manageable.

As you proceed with these three kinds of general searches, you will gather relevant information and gain a better understanding of your subject, which can help you search more strategically for additional materials.

---

2. Narrow Your Search to Explore Specific Issues and Questions

Your general search should yield enough information for you to begin to identify specific issues, questions, and subtopics that you need to explore further. The searches thus far in our example have yielded a lot of information about the electoral college, how it works, its history, criticisms of the system, and proposals to reform it. Although much of that information is general (e.g., books and websites explaining the electoral college), some is more specialized (e.g., analyses of specific elections in which the popular vote did not elect the president; scholarly critiques of the system). Given that your intended audience is both general and academic, you might now look more closely at what scholars and other experts have to say about the pros and cons of the electoral college.

- **Examine the references in the books you have found.** Most books contain bibliographies or works cited pages that can point you to additional sources. The references in those bibliographies often include citations of relevant scholarly articles. Make a list of citations that seem promising, and use your library catalog or a general database to track down the sources that seem most relevant.

- **Search specialized databases.** Your library website will list available databases. Find one or more that relate specifically to your subject. In this example, you could search general scholarly databases, such as *JSTOR, Academic Search Complete,* or *Google Scholar,* as well as databases specific to political science or the social sciences, such as *Worldwide Political Science Abstracts* or *Social Sciences Abstracts.* Given the nature of your project (which is intended for a general academic audience rather than a more specialized audience of readers in political science), it makes sense to search a general scholarly database, such as *JSTOR.* If you were writing your argument for a political science course, it might make more sense to search the databases specific to that field, such as *Worldwide Political Science.*

Boolean, or logical, operators are words that command a database or search engine to define a search in a specific way. The most common Boolean operators are *AND, OR,* and *NOT.* Understanding how they work can help you search the Internet and databases more efficiently:

- *AND* tells the search engine to find only sources that contain both words in your search. For example, if you entered *sports AND steroids,* your search would likely yield sources that deal with steroids in sports and would not necessarily return sources that deal with steroids or sports in general.

- *OR* broadens a search by telling the search engine to return sources for either term in your search. Entering *sports OR steroids,* for instance, would yield sources on either of those topics.

- *NOT* can narrow a search by telling the search engine to exclude sources containing a specific keyword. For example, entering *steroids NOT sports* would yield sources on steroids but not necessarily sources that deal with steroids in sports.

In addition, keep these tips in mind:

- You can use parentheses for complex searches: (*sports AND steroids*) NOT (*medicine OR law*); this entry would narrow the search to specific kinds of sources about sports and steroids that did not include medical or legal matters.

- With most search engines you can use Boolean operators in combination with quotation marks to find a specific phrase. For example, "steroid use in sports" would return sources that included that exact phrase. (See Sidebar: "An Important Tip for Using Databases and Search Engines" on page 308.) Using this strategy allows you to narrow your search further: ("*steroid in sports*") AND ("*steroid controversies*"). Such a search would find sources that include both phrases in the parentheses.

- Generally, you should capitalize Boolean operators.

9

Let's imagine that after reviewing the materials you found in your general searches, you want to know what scholars say about the implications of the electoral college for modern elections. You can search *JSTOR* for relevant scholarly articles. Here's the opening screen:

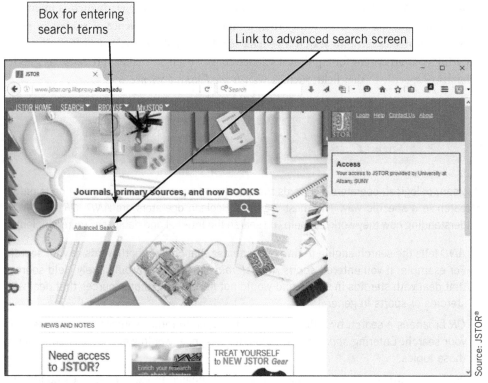

FIGURE 9.5 A Basic Search Screen for the *JSTOR* Database

A general search using the search terms *electoral college* is likely to yield too many results (in this case, such a search returned more than 33,500 articles in 2016), so an **advanced search** would make more sense. Here's part of the *JSTOR* advanced search screen:

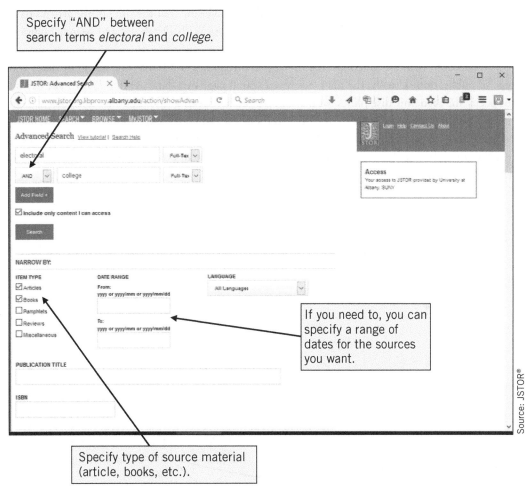

FIGURE 9.6 An Advanced Search Screen for the *JSTOR* Database

Such an advanced search screen allows you to limit your searches in various ways to increase the likelihood that the results will be useful. For example, using the drop-down menu next to each search term, you can specify that the search terms appear in the article titles rather than the body of the articles, making it more likely that the focus of the article will be relevant to your needs. Also, you can use the *Boolean operator* "and" to make sure that the titles of the articles have *both* search terms (see Sidebar: "Using Boolean Operators With Databases and Search Engines" on page 309).

In addition, you can search journals in certain disciplines and limit your search by dates and type of publication. Usually, the main advanced search page in a database like *JSTOR* allows you to specify the academic disciplines for the sources you are seeking. (Scroll down the main page to find the list of disciplines or look for a link on the advanced search page.) Doing so can dramatically narrow your search and yield much more relevant results. For example, a search of *JSTOR* in 2016 using the search terms *electoral college* only in the title of political science journals yielded 42 articles:

FIGURE 9.7 Search Results for "Electoral College" in the *JSTOR* Database

Notice that *JSTOR* search results include all relevant bibliographic information (author, title, journal, date, etc.) for each result as well as an abstract, which can help you decide whether to review the full article. If you wanted to narrow your focus to more recent elections, you could modify your search to include only articles published since 2002. Such a search returned 11 articles in 2016.

At this point, you have probably narrowed your search enough to begin reviewing specific articles. Browse these results to find articles that seem most relevant for your needs. In this example, if you scrolled through the 11 items that your final search returned, you would find an article titled "Why the Electoral College is Good for Political Science (and Public Choice)," by Nicholas R. Miller, published in 2012 in a journal called *Public Choice*. If you click the link for that entry, you'll access the article:

FIGURE 9.8 Accessing a Journal Article in a Database

A quick review of the abstract and the opening paragraph reveals that the author doesn't argue for or against the Electoral College system for presidential elections in the U.S. but instead focuses on some of the implications of that system, including its impact on the academic field of political science. That focus might not be relevant to your project, but the article seems to provide important background information and might offer an unusual perspective on the issue.

Like general databases, specialized databases can differ noticeably, and you might have to experiment with several databases to become familiar enough with their search screens to conduct effective searches. But all databases have features such as those in this example that allow you to target your searches by entering specific parameters (type of publication, dates, subject terms, and so on). No matter which databases or search engines you are using, you can apply these same basic strategies to make your searches successful. As always, consult your librarian for help, if necessary.

3. Do a Targeted Search to Fill Gaps in Your Source Information and Find Alternative Viewpoints

As you narrow your search further, more specific questions might arise or you might identify subtopics that you hadn't previously considered. For example, in reviewing scholarly articles about the role of the electoral collect in recent U.S. presidential elections, you might come across references to legal challenges to the electoral college, a topic that seems relevant to your project but one that you might not have previously encountered. At this point, if you decide you need more information about such a specialized topic, you can return to the databases that you have already searched (such as *JSTOR*) and do an additional search focused on legal challenges to the electoral college system; you can also search specialized databases, such as *Westlaw Campus*, which provides access to legal decisions. The goal at this stage is to identify any specific issues or questions you need to explore as well as gaps in the information you have already gathered.

Keep in mind that *a search is not necessarily a linear process*. The strategy described here assumes you will be continuously reviewing the materials you find. As you do, you might need to return to a general search for information on a new topic that seems important. For example, as you examine arguments in favor of using the popular vote to elect the president, you might discover that some experts have concerns about the wide variety of voting systems used by different states. If you decide that this concern is relevant to your project, return to your library catalog or a general database or search engine to find some basic information about the regulations governing the way states allow citizens to vote.

Remember that writing is a process of discovery (see Core Concept #1 in Chapter 2), and research is part of that process. You are learning about your subject matter to achieve your rhetorical goals. (The advice for Core Concepts #2 and #5 in Chapter 3 can also help you conduct more effective searches for useful source materials.)

WIKIPEDIA
The Free Encyclopedia

English
5 209 000+ articles

Русский
1 332 000+ статей

日本語
1 025 000+ 記事

Español
1 273 000+ artículos

Deutsch
1 966 000+ Artikel

Français
1 779 000+ articles

Italiano
1 293 000+ voci

Português
930 000+ artigos

中文
892 000+ 條目

In this chapter, you will learn to

1. Evaluate source material in terms of rhetorical purpose.

2. Determine the trustworthiness of a source.

3. Understand and apply the concepts of credibility, reliability, and bias when evaluating potential source material.

Evaluating Sources 10

FINDING INFORMATION for your project is one thing. Deciding whether a source is appropriate, credible, and reliable is another. Given the enormous variety of available sources, evaluating the materials you find can be challenging, but it is an integral part of research.

When evaluating sources, you need to address two main questions:

- Is the source trustworthy?
- Is the source useful for your purposes?

Answering the first question involves understanding the nature and purpose of the source itself. For example, a newspaper article about a political campaign and a campaign flyer can both be useful sources, but they are very different kinds of documents with different purposes. The purpose of a newspaper is to provide readers information about important and relevant events—in this example, a political campaign. A political campaign flyer, by contrast, is intended to present a candidate in the best possible light to persuade voters to support that candidate. Both documents can provide accurate information about the candidate, but the information they present must be considered in terms of their different purposes. The campaign flyer, for instance, might emphasize the candidate's record of voting against tax increases, whereas the newspaper article might explain that the candidate's vote against a specific tax increase resulted in reduced funding for a special program for disabled military veterans. Both sources are technically "true," but each presents information from a particular perspective and for a specific purpose.

As a writer evaluating sources for a project, you have to sort through these complexities to determine how trustworthy a source might be and whether it suits your own rhetorical purposes. The advice in this chapter will help you do so.

Determining Whether a Source Is Trustworthy

Evaluating source material requires understanding the different kinds of sources that are available to you. (Chapter 9 describes the characteristics of various kinds of sources.) It helps to develop a sense of the main similarities and differences in the general categories of sources you are likely to consult:

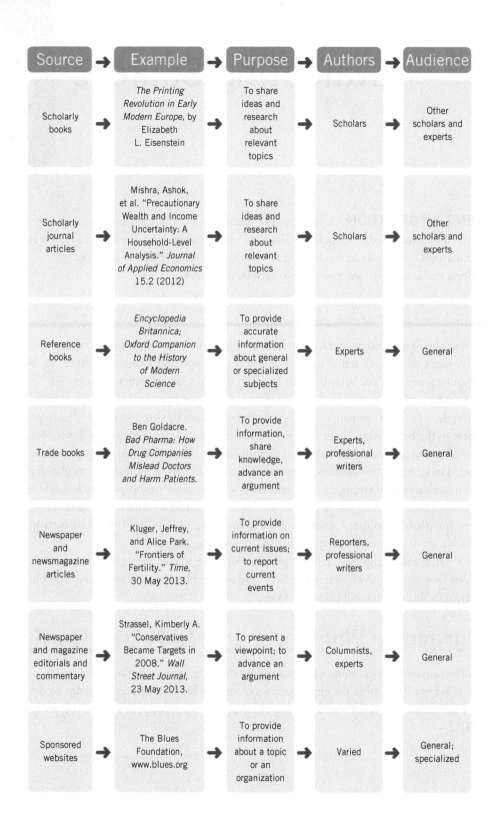

Source		Example		Purpose		Authors		Audience
Scholarly books	→	*The Printing Revolution in Early Modern Europe,* by Elizabeth L. Eisenstein	→	To share ideas and research about relevant topics	→	Scholars	→	Other scholars and experts
Scholarly journal articles	→	Mishra, Ashok, et al. "Precautionary Wealth and Income Uncertainty: A Household-Level Analysis." *Journal of Applied Economics* 15.2 (2012)	→	To share ideas and research about relevant topics	→	Scholars	→	Other scholars and experts
Reference books	→	*Encyclopedia Britannica; Oxford Companion to the History of Modern Science*	→	To provide accurate information about general or specialized subjects	→	Experts	→	General
Trade books	→	Ben Goldacre. *Bad Pharma: How Drug Companies Mislead Doctors and Harm Patients.*	→	To provide information, share knowledge, advance an argument	→	Experts, professional writers	→	General
Newspaper and newsmagazine articles	→	Kluger, Jeffrey, and Alice Park. "Frontiers of Fertility." *Time,* 30 May 2013.	→	To provide information on current issues; to report current events	→	Reporters, professional writers	→	General
Newspaper and magazine editorials and commentary	→	Strassel, Kimberly A. "Conservatives Became Targets in 2008." *Wall Street Journal,* 23 May 2013.	→	To present a viewpoint; to advance an argument	→	Columnists, experts	→	General
Sponsored websites	→	The Blues Foundation, www.blues.org	→	To provide information about a topic or an organization	→	Varied	→	General; specialized

A glance at this graphic reveals that different kinds of sources can be very similar in some respects (e.g., their intended audiences) but very different in others (e.g., their primary purpose). Having a general sense of the characteristics of these categories of sources can help you evaluate information from specific sources and determine its usefulness for your project.

Source materials within any of these general categories can also vary in terms of three important considerations when it comes to trustworthiness: credibility, reliability, and bias.

Credibility

Credibility is the extent to which a source is respected and can be trusted. It refers to your sense of whether a source is reputable and dependable and the information found there generally reliable. The credibility of a source can arise from a reputation built over time. Well-established newspapers, magazines, and publishers are usually considered credible sources because of their record of publishing certain kinds of reliable, accurate information and their demonstrated commitment to high standards of integrity. Scholarly publications, for example, are generally considered credible because they tend to be peer-reviewed and because of their commitment to holding their authors to high standards of quality and accuracy. The fact that an article published in a scholarly journal has likely been carefully evaluated by established scholars can give readers confidence that the article meets high standards for accuracy and integrity.

Credibility can also be a function of a writer's general approach to the subject matter: his or her tone, the level of fairness with which subject matter is treated, how carefully he or she seems to have examined the subject, and so on. For example, if you notice a writer making easy generalizations or drawing dubious conclusions about a complicated subject, you might be skeptical of the writer's credibility when it comes to that subject. Consider the following passage from a post on AlterNet, a website devoted to politics and culture that is well known for having a left-leaning political slant. The writer, who was an editor at AlterNet at the time, was reporting on a newspaper survey of recent Harvard graduates regarding their career choices after college. As the editor of an established news website, she might be seen as a credible professional source for information about current political, economic, and cultural issues, but the website's political perspective might also affect what information is included in the piece and how it is presented:

> Wall Street's propensity to ravage the economy, launder money, and illegally foreclose on families with no harsher punishment than a slap on the wrist seems to have irked some of the nation's brightest. Either that or the shrinkage of jobs in the finance sector is turning them off. According to a survey by the student newspaper the *Harvard Crimson*, Harvard graduates are just saying "No" to Wall Street, with some of them looking instead to put their smarts to work making America a better place.
>
> The paper reports that about a third of new graduates plan to work in finance, with 15 percent working on Wall Street and 16 percent doing consulting. In 2007, before the recession, 47 percent of

This description of Wall Street, which is at least debatable, is presented as fact, reflecting the writer's bias.

The writer provides no information about how the survey was conducted or whether its results are credible.

Harvard grads went onto work in finance and consulting, a number that fell to 39 percent in 2008, and 20 percent in 2012.

As the Huffington Post noted, it looks like the financial crisis may have triggered a change in the aspirations of the nation's brightest, prompting millennials to prefer work in industries where they can contribute to social good, like health and tech, although many of them, no doubt, want to score big in tech. At the same time, Wall Street is laying off more employees than it hires, so grads' reasons for career shifts may be more pragmatic than idealistic.

> This sentence calls into question the writer's own conclusions about the graduates' aspirations.

Source: Gwynne, Kristen. "Even Harvard Grads Don't Want to Work on Wall Street Anymore." *AlterNet*, 29 May 2013, www.alternet.org/even-harvard-grads-dont-want-work-wall-st-anymore.

This passage illustrates that inaccurate information, such as the results of the survey referred to in this passage, can be presented in a way that reflects a certain political perspective on the issue at hand. This writer seems eager to draw a specific conclusion—that the behavior of Wall Street firms has "irked some of the nation's brightest" college graduates—that isn't necessarily supported by the evidence she presents: Although the survey results, which are reported in the second paragraph of the passage, indicate a decline in the percentage of Harvard graduates seeking employment in finance, the reasons for that decline are unclear.

This example illustrates that skepticism can be healthy when evaluating source material. In this case, given the rhetorical situation (that is, the writer is writing for a left-leaning website whose readers would very likely be critical of the financial firms on Wall Street), although the writer could be considered credible as a professional journalist, the way she approaches her subject should make you look carefully and critically at the information she presents. So be judicious in deciding how you use any information from this source. You might, for example, use the figures from the student survey to show that college graduates' career decisions have changed in recent years, but you might reject the writer's conclusions about the reasons for that change.

In determining the credibility of a source, consider the following:

- **Author.** Who is the author? Do you know anything about his or her background? Is the author an expert on the subject at hand? Does he or she have an obvious agenda with respect to this subject?

- **Publication.** What is the source of the publication? Is it a scholarly book or journal? A trade magazine? A sponsored website? What do you know about this source? What reputation does it have? Is it known to have a particular slant? Is it associated with a group that espouses a particular point of view on the subject?

- **Purpose.** What is the purpose of the source? To what extent might the purpose influence your sense of the trustworthiness of the information in the source? For example, is the author presenting a carefully researched analysis of a controversial topic—say, gun control—as in a scholarly journal article, or is the writer vigorously arguing against an opposing perspective on that topic for an audience of people who share the writer's views, as in an op-ed essay on a sponsored website? Having a sense of the purpose of the source and the rhetorical situation can help you determine how skeptical to be about the information contained in the source.

- **Date.** How recent is the publication? Is it current when it comes to the subject at hand? For some kinds of information, the date of publication might not matter much, but for many topics, outdated information can be problematic.

Reliability

Reliability refers to your confidence in the accuracy of the information found in a source and the reputation of a source for consistently presenting trustworthy information. In general, credible sources gain a reputation for publishing accurate information over time. For example, major newspapers and magazines, such as the *Los Angeles Times* and the *The New Yorker*, usually employ fact checkers to verify information in articles they are preparing to publish; respected publishing houses usually edit manuscripts carefully to be sure they are accurate, and scholarly publishers employ expert reviewers to evaluate manuscripts. These practices usually mean that material published by these sources tends to be consistently accurate and trustworthy, so they gain a reputation for reliability. By contrast, many popular news outlets emphasize breaking news and sometimes publish information quickly before it can be verified. Often, such publications are not subject to the kind of rigorous editorial review that characterizes scholarly publications, which can result in inaccuracies and weaken your confidence in their reliability.

Because you are not likely to be an expert on many of the subjects you write about in college, you often won't have a sense of the reliability of a particular source, so you will have to make judgments on the basis of the nature of the source and its credibility. **Follow these guidelines:**

- **Choose credible sources.** In general, if you have a choice of sources, use those that you know or believe to be credible (see "Credibility" on page 317). Sources with reputations for credibility are more likely to supply reliable information. In general, scholarly publications, reference works (such as encyclopedias), well-established newspapers or magazines, and respected government agencies or non-governmental organizations (such as the Centers for Disease Control or the American Heart Association) tend to be safe bets as sources for your research.

- **Consult multiple sources.** Using multiple sources on the same topic can help you avoid using unreliable information. If you have information that is consistent across several sources, including sources you consider to be credible, that information is more likely to be reliable as well.

Determining whether a source is trustworthy is usually not an either-or proposition. Even credible and reliable sources might have information that isn't accurate or is inappropriate for your purposes. Your decisions about the trustworthiness of a source, then, should be guided by your rhetorical situation as well as by your own growing understanding of your subject. As you gain experience in reviewing unfamiliar sources, you will begin to develop a sense of what to look for and what to avoid when determining whether information from a source can be trusted. Such decisions about source material must also be made with an understanding of the potential bias of a source, which is discussed in the following section.

Understanding Bias

Bias is a tendency to think or feel a certain way. It is the inclination of a source to favor one point of view over others that might be equally valid—the privileging of one perspective at the expense of others. Bias is sometimes thought of as prejudice, though bias is not necessarily a negative quality. One might have a bias in favor of cats rather than dogs as pets, for example. In this textbook, bias generally refers to a source's perspective or slant.

It is important to understand that *all sources are biased in some way*. We tend to think of some kinds of source material, such as encyclopedias and other kinds of reference works, as objective or neutral. But even a venerable reference such as the *Encyclopedia Britannica* can be said to have certain biases. For example, the kind of information that is considered appropriate for inclusion in *Encyclopedia Britannica* reflects a set of beliefs about what kinds of knowledge or information are relevant and important for its purposes. Although such a reference work tries to be comprehensive, it inevitably excludes some kinds of information and privileges others. For instance, extremely technical information about the rhythms of Hip Hop music might be excluded from an encyclopedia, even though more general information about that musical form might be included. The decisions the editors make about what to include and what to exclude in the encyclopedia represent a bias, no matter how open-minded the editors might be.

Bias, then, is not necessarily a negative quality in a source, but it is essential to recognize bias in any source you consult so that you can evaluate the usefulness of information from that source. Some kinds of sources are transparent about their biases. Scholarly journals, for example, tend to make their editorial focus and purpose clear. Here is a statement of the editorial policy of a journal titled *Research in the Teaching of English*, published by a professional organization called the National Council of Teachers of English (NCTE):

> *Research in the Teaching of English* publishes scholarship that explores issues in the teaching and learning of literacy at all levels. It is the policy of NCTE in its journals and other publications to provide a forum for open discussion of ideas concerning the teaching of English and language arts.

Scholarly journals often provide such descriptions of the kinds of articles they seek to publish; they might also provide explanations of the processes by which manuscripts are reviewed. These editorial policy statements help make the biases of a journal explicit.

Many sources, even credible and reliable ones, are not so transparent about their biases. For example, although many readers consider newspapers to be trusted sources of information, many newspapers have well-established points of view. *The New York Times* is generally considered to have a liberal bias, whereas *The Washington Times* is usually thought to reflect a more conservative viewpoint. However, if you did not already have a sense of such biases, you might find it difficult to determine them. Here, for example, is the description that *The New York Times* provides of its editorial board:

The editorial board is composed of 16 journalists with wide-ranging areas of expertise. Their primary responsibility is to write *The Times's* editorials, which represent the voice of the board, its editor and the publisher. The board is part of *The Times's* editorial department, which is operated separately from *The Times's* newsroom, and includes the Letters to the Editor and Op-Ed sections.

Source: "*The New York Times* Editorial Board." *The New York Times*, 2 May 2016, www.nytimes .com/interactive/opinion/editorialboard.html.

Although this statement explains that the editorial department is separate from the newsroom at *The New York Times*, which might give readers confidence that the newspaper's reporting is not influenced by its editorial opinions, the statement does not describe a particular political slant or perspective. You would have to examine the newspaper more carefully—and probably over time—to gain a sense of its political bias.

Such examples underscore the important point that even the most credible and reliable sources will have biases; however, a bias does not mean that a source is untrustworthy. Rather, bias influences the kind of information a source might contain and how that information is presented, even when the information is trustworthy. For example, like major newspapers, major public affairs magazines are usually considered to have either a liberal bias (e.g., *The Nation*), a conservative bias (e.g., the *National Review*), or other bias (e.g., libertarian). Those biases mean that each magazine is likely to focus on some issues as opposed to others and to examine issues from a particular perspective. For instance, the *Nation* might publish an argument in favor of a proposal to increase the national minimum wage, reflecting a liberal perspective on the government's role in economic matters. The *National Review*, by contrast, might publish a critique of the same proposal, reflecting a conservative bias in favor of less government intervention in economic matters. Both articles might contain reliable and accurate information, but the information is presented in a way that reflects the political bias of the publication.

Often, the bias of a source is much more subtle and difficult to detect. For example, advocacy groups often try to appear objective in their treatment of certain issues when in fact they have a strong bias on those issues. For example, an environmental advocacy group might oppose the development of a large wind farm in a wilderness area. Its website might seem to be a neutral source of information about various kinds of energy, including wind power, but its opposition to large wind farms means that its treatment of wind power is likely to focus on the disadvantages of wind power and the harmful impact of wind turbines on wilderness areas. In such a case, even though the information on the website might be accurate, that information might also be incomplete or presented in a way that paints a negative picture of wind power. (See Focus: "Detecting Bias" on page 322.)

When evaluating a source for bias, consider these questions:

- Does this source reflect a particular perspective or point of view?
- Does this source represent a specific group, political party, business, organization, or institution?
- Does the source seem to have an agenda regarding the subject at hand?
- To what extent is the bias of this source evident? Are there blatantly slanted statements? Do you notice questionable information? To what extent does this bias seem to affect the trustworthiness of the information it presents?

Many sources that appear at first glance to be neutral or objective on a particular issue or subject might actually have a strong bias. The website shown below, for example, contains information about education reform but is sponsored by an organization that advocates a particular perspective on school reform in favor of charter schools and related movements that are controversial. Notice that nothing on the this web page conveys a sense of the organization's strong views about specific kinds of education reforms; instead, the language is neutral ("CER has created opportunities that give families choices, teachers freedom and students more pathways to achieve a great education") and seemingly nonpartisan ("Join us in our fight to make *all* schools better for *all* children"). The information on such a site can be useful, but it is important to understand that it is being presented from a particular point of view. In this case, you might find accurate information about charter schools, but you are unlikely to find studies whose results are not flattering to charter schools.

To detect bias in a source, try to identify its purpose and its perspective on the subject. Use the questions at the bottom of page 321 to evaluate the source and identify its potential bias regarding the subject. Also, read Focus: "Tips for Evaluating Online Sources" on pages 323–324.

Source: *The Center for Education Reform.* 2016, www.edreform.com.

All sources should be evaluated for trustworthiness, but different sources can present different challenges when you are trying to determine trustworthiness. **Use the following questions to guide you as you evaluate specific sources:**

Books and Articles

- **Who published this article or book?** (scholarly press, trade publisher, respected newspaper or magazine, professional organization, non-profit organization, government agency, advocacy group, business)

- **Who is the author?** (Is the author's name provided? Is the author an expert on the subject?)

- **What is the purpose?** (to share information or knowledge, to advocate for a point of view)

- **Does the source have a reputation for reliability?** (Is the source known to have a bias or slant? Is the source generally considered credible?)

- **When was it published?** (Is the date of publication indicated? Is the book or article current or outdated?)

Websites and Social Media

- **Who sponsors the site?** (a news organization, business, political organization, advocacy group, non-profit foundation, government agency)

- **What is the purpose of the site?** (to inform, to advertise or sell a product, to promote a point of view)

- **What are the contents of the site?** (Does it include relevant information? Does it have advertisements? Does it seem to contain accurate information? Are the sources of information indicated?)

- **Is the site current?** (Is the site regularly updated? Are the web pages dated? Is the information current?)

FOCUS | **TIPS FOR EVALUATING ONLINE SOURCES**

Although the advice in this chapter applies to all kinds of sources, you can follow additional steps to help you determine the trustworthiness of online sources, especially websites:

■ **Read the "About" Page.** Many websites have pages titled "About" or "About Us" that provide useful information about the authors, purpose, and sometimes the history of the site. Sites sponsored by advocacy groups and non-profit organizations often include information about their boards of directors or administrators. Such information can help you evaluate the trustworthiness of a site and determine the extent to which it might be biased. For example, a site of an organization that seems to advocate green energy but whose board of directors includes mostly business leaders from large energy companies might have a bias in favor of large business interests. By contrast, the site of a clean energy advocacy group whose directors are members of well-known environmental organizations might be less likely to support business interests when it comes to energy issues.

(Continued)

- **Look for a Date.** Most websites sponsored by legitimate organizations indicate the date when the website or individual web pages were updated. Many organizations, especially respected media organizations, update their websites daily. However, some websites are not actively maintained and can be available on the Internet many years after they cease to be updated or revised. If you cannot find dates on a website or if the only dates you find are well in the past, be wary of the material on that site.

- **Check the Links.** Many websites contain pages with various kinds of resources, including links to related websites sponsored by other organizations. Often, those links reflect a website's own biases and can help you determine whether the site is biased in a way that should concern you. If these links are not active, it indicates that the site is not well maintained—another reason to be skeptical about information you find there.

Evaluating Source Material for Your Rhetorical Purposes

Once you have determined that information from a source is trustworthy, you must still decide whether it is useful and appropriate for your project. It isn't enough to determine whether a source is credible and reliable or to identify its biases; you must also evaluate the information in terms of your own rhetorical situation and especially in light of the purpose of your project.

To illustrate, let's imagine two related but different kinds of writing assignments:

- an analysis of the ongoing debate about health care reform in the United States
- an argument about the impact of the Affordable Care Act (ACA), often called Obamacare, which became law in 2010

Suppose that the analysis is for an assignment in a writing course that requires students to examine public debates about a controversial issue; the audience includes other students in the course as well as the instructor. The argument is intended for the student newspaper on your campus. Both pieces require research. Let's imagine that for each assignment, you want to understand how the current debates about health care coverage in the United States are influenced by the controversy that occurred when the Affordable Care Act was being implemented in 2011 and 2012. In your search for information about that controversy, you found the following three sources from 2013:

- a blog post from the website of *Forbes* magazine
- a blog post from a website called California Healthline
- an article from AlterNet

Let's consider how the different rhetorical situations for these two assignments, with their different audiences and purposes, might shape your decisions about whether and how to use information from these sources:

Obamacare Will Increase Health Spending
by $7,450 for a Typical Family of Four
by Chris Conover
Forbes.com, 23 Sept. 2013

It was one of candidate Obama's most vivid and concrete campaign promises. Forget about high minded (some might say high sounding) but gauzy promises of hope and change. This candidate solemnly pledged on June 5, 2008: "In an Obama administration, we'll lower premiums by up to $2,500 for a typical family per year.... We'll do it by the end of my first term as President of the United States." Unfortunately, the experts working for Medicare's actuary have (yet again) reported that in its first 10 years, Obamacare will boost health spending by "roughly $621 billion" above the amounts Americans would have spent without this misguided law.

$621 billion is a pretty eye-glazing number. Most readers will find it easier to think about how this number translates to a typical American family—the very family candidate Obama promised would see $2,500 in annual savings as far as the eye could see. So I have taken the latest year-by-year projections, divided by the projected U.S. population to determine the added amount per person and multiplied the result by 4.

Simplistic? Maybe, but so too was the President's campaign promise. And this approach allows us to see just how badly that promise fell short of the mark. Between 2014 and 2022, the increase in national health spending (which the Medicare actuaries specifically attribute to the law) amounts to $7,450 per family of 4.

Let us hope this family hasn't already spent or borrowed the $2,500 in savings they might have expected over this same period had they taken candidate Obama's promise at face value. In truth, no well-informed American ever should have believed this absurd promise. At the time, Factcheck.org charitably deemed this claim as "overly optimistic, misleading and, to some extent, contradicted by one of his own advisers." The *Washington Post* less charitably awarded it Two Pinocchios ("Significant omissions or exaggerations"). Yet rather than learn from his mistakes, President Obama on July 16, 2012 essentially doubled-down on his promise, assuring small business owners "your premiums will go down." He made this assertion notwithstanding the fact that in three separate reports between April 2010 and June 2012, the Medicare actuaries had demonstrated that the ACA would *increase* health spending. To its credit, the *Washington Post* dutifully awarded the 2012 claim Three Pinocchios ("Significant factual error and/or obvious contradictions.")

As it turns out, the average family of 4 has only had to face a relatively modest burden from Obamacare over the past four years—a little over $125. Unfortunately, this year's average burden ($66) will be 10 times as large in 2014 when Obamacare kicks in for earnest. And it will rise for two years after that, after which it hit a steady-state level of just under $800 a year....

Obamacare will not save Americans one penny now or in the future. Perhaps the next time voters encounter a politician making such grandiose claims, they will learn to watch their wallet.

Source: Conover, Chris. "Obamacare Will Increase Health Spending by $7,450 for a Typical Family of Four." *Forbes*, 23 Sept. 2013, www.forbes.com/sites/theapothecary/2013/09/23/its-official-obamacare-will-increase-health-spending-by-7450-for-a-typical-family-of-four/#244a2e122c62.

The Premium Conundrum: Do Smokers Get a Fair Break Under Obamacare?
by Dan Diamond
California Healthline, 23 Jan. 2013

The Affordable Care Act contains a number of provisions intended to incent "personal responsibility," or the notion that health care isn't just a right—it's an obligation. None of these measures is more prominent than the law's individual mandate, designed to ensure that every American obtains health coverage or pays a fine for choosing to go uninsured.

But one provision that's gotten much less attention—until recently—relates to smoking; specifically, the ACA allows payers to treat tobacco users very differently by opening the door to much higher premiums for this population.

That measure has some health policy analysts cheering, suggesting that higher premiums are necessary to raise revenue for the law and (hopefully) deter smokers' bad habits. But other observers have warned that the ACA takes a heavy-handed stick to smokers who may be unhappily addicted to tobacco, rather than enticing them with a carrot to quit.

Possible Pain Lies Ahead for Tobacco Users

Under proposed rules, the department of Health and Human Services would allow insurers to charge a smoker seeking health coverage in the individual market as much as 50% more in premiums than a non-smoker.

That difference in premiums may rapidly add up for smokers, given the expectation that Obamacare's new medical-loss ratios already will lead to major cost hikes in the individual market. "For many people, in the years after the law, premiums aren't just going to [go] up a little," Peter Suderman predicts at Reason. "They're going to rise a lot."

Meanwhile, Ann Marie Marciarille, a law professor at the University of Missouri-Kansas City, adds that insurers have "considerable flexibility" in how to set up a potential surcharge for tobacco use. For example, insurers could apply a high surcharge for tobacco use in older smokers—perhaps several hundred dollars per month—further hitting a population that tends to be poorer.

Attitudes on Smoking Help Inform Policy

Is this cost-shifting fair? The average American tends to think so.

Nearly 60% of surveyed adults in a 2011 NPR-Thomson Reuters poll thought it was OK to charge smokers more for their health insurance than non-smokers. (That's nearly twice the number of adults who thought it would be OK to charge the obese more for their health insurance.)

And smoking does lead to health costs that tend to be borne by the broader population. Writing at the Incidental Economist in 2011, Don Taylor noted that "smoking imposes very large social costs"—essentially, about $1.50 per pack—with its increased risk of cancers and other chronic illness. CDC has found that smoking and its effects lead to more than 440,000 premature deaths in the United States per year, with more than $190 billion in annual health costs and productivity loss.

As a result, charging smokers more "makes some actuarial sense," Marciarille acknowledges. "Tobacco use has a long-term fuse for its most expensive health effects."

But Louise Norris of Colorado Health Insurance Insider takes issue with the ACA's treatment of tobacco users.

Noting that smokers represent only about 20% of Americans, Norris argues that "it's easy to point fingers and call for increased personal responsibility when we're singling out another group—one in which we are not included."

As a result, she adds, "it seems very logical to say that smokers should have to pay significantly higher premiums for their health insurance," whereas we're less inclined to treat the obese differently because so many of us are overweight.

This approach toward tobacco users also raises the risk that low-income smokers will find the cost of coverage too high and end up uninsured, Norris warns. She notes that tax credits for health coverage will be calculated prior to however insurers choose to set their banding rules, "which means that smokers would be responsible for [an] additional premium on their own."

Alternate Approach: Focus on Cessation

Nearly 70% of smokers want to quit, and about half attempt to kick the habit at least once per year. But more than 90% are unable to stop smoking, partly because of the lack of assistance; fewer than 5% of smokers appear able to quit without support.

That's why Norris and others say that if federal officials truly want to improve public health, the law should prioritize anti-smoking efforts like counseling and medication for tobacco users. And the ACA does require new health insurance plans to offer smoking cessation products and therapy.

But as Ankita Rao writes at *Kaiser Health News*, the coverage of those measures thus far is spotty. Some plans leave out nasal sprays and inhalers; others shift costs to smokers, possibly deterring them from seeking treatment.

Some anti-smoking crusaders hope that states will step into the gap and ramp up cessation opportunities, such as by including cessation therapy as an essential health benefit.

"The federal government has missed several opportunities since the enactment of the ACA to grant smokers access to more cessation treatments," the American Lung Association warned in November. "Now, as states are beginning implementation of state exchanges and Medicaid expansions, state policymakers have the opportunity to stand up for smokers in their states who want to quit."

Source: Diamond, Dan. "The Premium Conundrum: Do Smokers Get a Fair Break Under Obamacare?" *California Healthline*, 23 Jan. 2013, californiahealthline.org/news/the-premium-conundrum-do-smokers-get-a-fair-break-under-obamacare/.

How's Obamacare Turning Out? Great If You Live in a Blue State, and 'Screw You' If You Have a Republican Governor
by Steve Rosenfeld
AlterNet 25 May 2013

Obamacare implementation is becoming the latest dividing line between blue- and red-state America, with Democrat-led states making progress to expand healthcare to the uninsured and the poor—and Republican-led states saying "screw you" to millions of their most vulnerable and needy residents.

(Continued)

The latest sign of the Republican Party's increasingly secessionist tendencies comes as Obamacare passed a major milestone in California, which late last week announced lower-than-expected healthcare premiums for its 5.3 million uninsured, less than many small businesses now pay in group plans.

"Covered California's Silver Plan . . . offers premiums that can be 29 percent lower than comparable plans provided on today's small group market," the state's new insurance exchange announced Thursday, referring to the least-expensive option of four state-administered plans and posting this price comparison chart.

In contrast, the refusal by red-state America to create these health exchanges, which would be more local control—a supposed Republican value—and to accept federal funds to expand state-run Medicaid programs for the poor, means that about half the states are turning their backs on their residents, especially millions of the poorest people.

The federal government plans to step in later this summer and offer uninsured people in recalcitrant red states the option of buying plans via federally run heath care exchanges. But the poorest people can't afford that, meaning the refusal to expand Medicaid programs will leave them in the cold. They will see ads selling new federal healthcare options that will be unaffordable for them.

The New York Times reports that local healthcare advocates in red states are predicting a backlash once Obamacare is rolled out and the poor realize that they cannot take advantage of it because Republicans are blocking it. However, that does not change the bottom line in state-run Medicaid programs: the GOP is again penalizing the poor.

Progress in Blue States

Meanwhile, in blue states, there have been surprising developments in the cost of Obamacare for those people who currently are uninsured. There, the bottom line is insurance premiums are hundreds of dollars a month lower than what employers are now paying for their workers under existing group plans.

California, with 5.3 million uninsured adults, is the biggest state to release cost estimates for Obamacare. Its lower-than-expected estimates are in line with announcements in Washington, Oregon, Maryland and Vermont. The actual prices will be known after insurers file rate documents in coming weeks.

Source: Rosenfeld, Steven. "How's Obamacare Turning Out? Great If You Live in a Blue State, and 'Screw You' If You Have a Republican Governor." *AlterNet*, 25 May 2013, www.alternet.org/news-amp-politics/hows-obamacare-turning-out-great-if-you-live-blue-state-and-screw-you-if-you-have.

All three sources are relevant to both assignments, but are they useful? To answer that question, first determine whether each source is trustworthy by addressing the three main aspects of trustworthiness described in this chapter:

1. Is the source credible?

2. Is the source reliable?

3. What is the bias of the source?

Is the Source Credible?

As we saw earlier (see pages 317–319), the credibility of a source depends on several important factors: the author, the nature of the publication, the purpose of the publication, and the date. Review each source accordingly:

Is the source credible?

Blog post on Forbes.com	Blog post on California Healthline	Article on AlterNet

Who is the author?

Chris Conover: researcher at Duke University, scholar at American Enterprise Institute	Dan Diamond: managing editor of health blog, contributor to *Forbes*, a business magazine	Steve Rosenfeld: reporter for AlterNet, author of *Count My Vote: A Citizen's Guide to Voting* (2008)

What is the nature of the publication?

Blog post on the website of a major business news magazine	Blog post on the website of a non-profit foundation devoted to health care reform	Article on a website devoted to politics and culture

What is the purpose of the source?

To advocate for a position on health-related issues	To examine issues related to health care	To share information and ideas with audience interested in political issues

When was it published? Is it timely?

2013. Yes. The debate about Obamacare was intense in 2013 and continued through the 2016 presidential election.	2013. Yes. The debate about Obamacare was intense in 2013 and continued through the 2016 presidential election.	2013. Yes. The debate about Obamacare was intense in 2013 and continued through the 2016 presidential election.

Addressing these questions will help you develop a better sense of the nature of each source, which will help you determine its credibility. Evaluating these sources in comparison to each other also reveals some important differences among them. For example, AlterNet covers all kinds of newsworthy topics, whereas the California Healthline focuses only on health issues and can therefore be assumed to have more in-depth and extensive coverage of issues like the Affordable Care Act; the Apothecary, a blog on the website of *Forbes* magazine, addresses health-related issues from a business perspective.

If necessary, you can find more information to answer each of these questions about these sources. For example, you can look for more information about each author. Visiting a website like Amazon or Alibris might enable you to learn more about Steven Rosenfeld's book *Count My Vote*, which could give you insight into his background and his perspective on political issues. Similarly, you could visit the website of the American Enterprise Institute, a well-established conservative think tank, to learn more about Chris Conover's perspective. You could also find more information about the sponsor of the California Healthline to determine whether the site could be considered a credible source of information.

As noted earlier in this chapter, credibility can also be a function of a writer's tone, fairness, and general approach to the subject. With those criteria in mind, you might note that the general tone of the *Forbes* blog post toward the Affordable Care Act is negative, and the language of the AlterNet article is explicitly dismissive and disrespectful of a conservative viewpoint. These characteristics should make you a bit more skeptical about these two sources. Nevertheless, both sources seem to have accurate information about the topic of health care reform, even though they present that information from a decidedly partisan perspective.

Let's say that after examining each source in this example, you have determined that all three sources can be considered credible, despite your reservations about the AlterNet article and *Forbes* blog post. Next, try to decide whether the source is reliable.

Is the Source Reliable?

Reliability generally has to do with your confidence that a source has established a record for accuracy and credibility. In this example, both *Forbes* magazine and AlterNet represent perspectives that are consistent over time. Both sources are respected by their constituencies. You are aware of their respective political leanings, and you can judge the reliability of information from each site in the context of those perspectives (see "What Is the Bias of the Source" on page 331). For example, you expect *Forbes* magazine to be skeptical about the Affordable Care Act because it favors business and tends to oppose large government programs; by contrast, you expect articles on AlterNet to be supportive of the ACA and critical of conservative resistance to it. Neither source is surprising in this regard. In other words, each source is reliable in terms of its political perspective and generally reliable in the kinds of information it presents.

The reliability of the blog post from the California Healthline is less clear, mostly because it is a less well known and more specialized source. To gain a better sense of its reliability, you should investigate further. For one thing, you can check the "About Us" page on its website. Here's what you will find:

> California Healthline is a free, daily publication featuring health care news, opinion and original reporting, designed to meet the information needs of busy health care professionals, decision makers, media organizations and consumers. It is independently published by Kaiser Health News (KHN) for the California Health Care Foundation. California Healthline is part of the Foundation's commitment to important issues affecting health care policy, delivery and financing in California.
>
> KHN is a nonprofit news service committed to in-depth coverage of health care policy, politics, and business, reporting on how the health care system—hospitals, doctors, nurses, insurers, governments and consumers—works and doesn't work. It is responsible for the editorial content of California Healthline. KHN is an editorially independent program of the Kaiser Family Foundation, a nonprofit organization based in Menlo Park, California.

Source: "About Us." *California Healthline*, 2016, californiahealthline.org/about-us/.

This description provides the important information that the California Healthline is sponsored by an organization called California Health Care Foundation but is published independently by a national health care research and publishing organization called Kaiser Health News. That information lends credibility to the site because it suggests that the publication is nonpartisan and lacks a particular political or ideological agenda. In addition, a quick Internet search would reveal that this news service has been in existence since 1998, which strengthens your confidence in its reliability as a source of health care information. Finally, the author of this blog post seems to be an established observer of health care and business matters. Notice that, like Chris Conover, this author also writes for *Forbes* magazine, a leading and well-respected business publication. All these facts can give you confidence that this is a reliable source for information about health care issues.

This analysis enables you to conclude that all three of these sources can be considered reliable.

What Is the Bias of the Source?

You have established your sources as credible and reliable, but their usefulness to you will also depend on the extent to which they are biased.

You have already determined that *Forbes* magazine and AlterNet reflect conservative and left-leaning political biases, respectively. What about the California Healthline? Your review of its "About Us" page led you to conclude that it is credible, reliable, and probably politically nonpartisan, but even if it does not reflect a political bias, it might reflect other kinds of bias. It makes sense to look more closely at this source.

The "About Us" page indicates California Healthline is sponsored by a nonprofit organization called California Health Care Foundation. Here's how the organization describes itself on its website:

> The California Health Care Foundation (CHCF) is dedicated to advancing meaningful, measurable improvements in the way the health care delivery system provides care to the people of California, particularly those with low incomes and those whose needs are not well served by the status quo. We work to ensure that people have access to the care they need, when they need it, at a price they can afford.
>
> CHCF informs policymakers and industry leaders, invests in ideas and innovations, and connects with changemakers to create a more responsive, patient-centered health care system.
>
> CHCF supports the testing and evaluation of innovative approaches to improving care. We also commission research and analysis that policymakers, clinical leaders, payers, consumers, and the media depend on to better understand California's complex delivery system, in service of three overarching goals: improving access to coverage and care for low-income Californians, ensuring high-value care, informing decision makers.

Source: "About CHCF." *California Health Care Foundation*, 2016, www.chcf.org/about.

This explanation tells you that the foundation is not a political group and supports health care reform through research and analysis. But on the same web page you also find the following statement:

> The Affordable Care Act (ACA) has helped millions of Californians get coverage through Medi-Cal and Covered California. Yet many people struggle to get the care they need, when they need it, at a price they can afford. Drawing upon expertise in Medi-Cal, public policy, commercial and safety-net health plans and providers, and emerging service delivery and IT innovations, CHCF seeks to expand access.

From this passage you could reasonably conclude that the organization is supportive of the Affordable Care Act. That conclusion doesn't necessarily call into question the information on the California Healthline site, but it does suggest that the Healthline is likely to cover the Affordable Care Act closely and is not likely to be consistently critical of it. In other words, articles and blog posts on the site are likely to reflect a bias in favor of expanded health care reform, including the ACA.

You can examine the biases of your three sources in more depth by addressing the questions listed on page 321:

To what extent is the source biased?		
Blog post on Forbes.com	**Blog post on California Healthline**	**Article on AlterNet**

↓

Does the source reflect a particular viewpoint or perspective?		
Yes, a generally conservative viewpoint	No obvious political or ideological perspective	Yes, a left-leaning political point of view

↓

Does the source represent a specific group or organization?		
Yes, website is hosted by *Forbes* magazine.	Yes, sponsored by a nonprofit foundation that supports health care reform.	No, the site is an independent, nonprofit news entity.

↓

Does the source have an agenda regarding the subject?		
Yes, generally opposed to federal health care reform initiative	Yes, supports health care reform	Yes, generally supportive of the Obama administration's reform efforts.

↓

To what extent is the bias of the source evident?		
The critical stance toward the ACA is noticeable	Bias in favor of health care reform is implicit	Overt bias in favor of Obama administration and against its conservative opponents

At this point you should have a good sense of the biases of your three sources.

How Useful Is the Source?

Now that you have carefully evaluated your sources, you can examine their usefulness for your rhetorical purposes. Recall that both your hypothetical assignments—the analysis and the argument—are about health care reform in the United States, but their purposes and intended audiences differ, which will influence your decisions about whether and how to use the sources you have evaluated.

Let's imagine that your analysis is an effort to answer this question:

Why does the debate about the Affordable Care Act continue to be intense and confrontational so many years after it became law?

You want to understand some of the reasons for the sustained and vitriolic nature of this debate and what it might reveal about public debates in general. You are writing your analysis primarily for your instructor and other students in your class. For your argument, let's imagine that you want to make the case that the ongoing debates about the Affordable Care Act are relevant to college students. For this piece, your audience is broader than for your analysis: students and faculty who read your campus newspaper.

We can sum up the rhetorical situations for these two pieces of writing as follows:

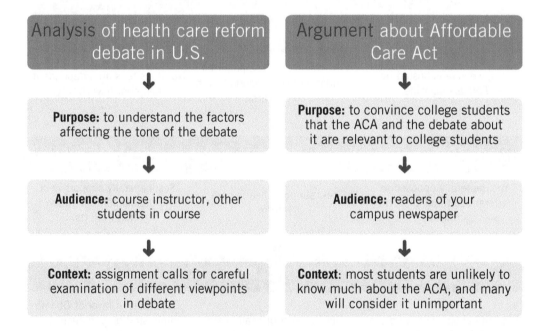

Analysis of health care reform debate in U.S.	Argument about Affordable Care Act
↓	↓
Purpose: to understand the factors affecting the tone of the debate	**Purpose:** to convince college students that the ACA and the debate about it are relevant to college students
↓	↓
Audience: course instructor, other students in course	**Audience:** readers of your campus newspaper
↓	↓
Context: assignment calls for careful examination of different viewpoints in debate	**Context:** most students are unlikely to know much about the ACA, and many will consider it unimportant

With these factors in mind you can examine how each of the three sources you found might fit into these two assignments:

- **Analysis Assignment.** For your analysis of the debate about the Affordable Care Act, you might use the article from AlterNet and the *Forbes* blog post as examples of more extreme positions in the debate. In this case, you don't need to worry much about the accuracy or reliability of the sources, because you would be using them as examples of how conservative and left-leaning viewpoints emerge in the debate about health care reform. Your analysis would require you to identify clearly the political perspectives represented by each source and how those perspectives influence the way each source represents the Affordable Care Act. For example, you might examine the numbers included in the *Forbes* blog post to show that the author presents only data that cast the ACA in a negative light. Similarly, you might evaluate the specific language used in the AlterNet article to refer to Republican or conservative positions—for example, "secessionist" and "recalcitrant"—and the unsupported claims that "the GOP is again penalizing the poor." For your purposes it would not be necessary to decide how accurate the information in each source is; you are simply analyzing *how* the sources present the information, not the information itself, so the overt biases of the sources is not a problem.

- **Argument Assignment.** For your argument, by contrast, you would likely need to present accurate information about the Affordable Care Act and the problems it is intended to address, especially in terms of how it might affect college students. You want to convince your audience that the debate about health care reform is one they should pay attention to. In this case, some of the information from the California Healthline blog post is likely to be useful in arguing that the debate matters to college students. For example, the author notes that the law is "designed to ensure that every American obtains health coverage or pays a fine for choosing to go uninsured." That fact should be important to college students, many of whom will need new health care insurance once they graduate. If you include that quotation in your argument, you will need to be confident that it is accurate. Your evaluation of this source should give you that confidence, but you can also look for other sources that could corroborate it. At the same time, the information included in the *Forbes* blog post and the AlterNet article might also be useful, but given your rhetorical purpose, you would have to take into account the obvious biases of those sources as you decide whether to use specific information. For instance, the author of the AlterNet article identifies differences in how individual states will enact the Affordable Care Act. Those differences could be important to college students because they could affect the kind of health insurance that is available to them in one state or another. However, you might be more skeptical of the author's claim that "Republican-led states [are] saying 'screw you' to millions of their most vulnerable and needy residents." Given the author's political perspective, which makes him more likely to be critical of Republican policies, it would be sensible to verify such a claim before using it in your own argument. Moreover, you would want to avoid undermining your argument by relying on sources whose political views might alienate some of your intended readers.

These examples illustrate how the rhetorical situation can influence your decisions about how to use the source material you find in your research. Obviously, you should evaluate *all* source material in terms of credibility, reliability, and bias. But how your evaluation will affect your decisions about using source material will ultimately depend upon the rhetorical goals you hope to achieve with your intended audience.

In this chapter, you will learn to

1. Understand and apply the four basic guidelines for integrating source material into your writing.

2. Identify and follow four guidelines for integrating direct quotations effectively into your writing.

3. Understand intentional and unintentional plagiarism.

4. Understand and apply six basic guidelines for avoiding plagiarism.

Using Source Material 11

STUDENT WRITERS sometimes have less trouble finding the source material they need for their projects than they do using that material effectively in their own writing. The challenge many students face is resisting the tendency to rely too heavily on source material so that it doesn't take over the student's own writing. Using source materials effectively, then, is partly a matter of keeping in mind the purpose and main point of your project. The most important guideline to follow when using any source material is to focus on your own ideas and the point *you* are making. The source material you cite should support *your* thinking and should not become the focus of your writing. (See Core Concept #4: "A writer must have something to say.") So it is important to be able *integrate* source material into your writing rather than simply reproduce information from a source. This chapter describes some basic strategies for using your source material strategically and maintaining control of your own writing.

Quoting from Sources

In academic writing, there are three main ways to integrate source material into your own prose:

- summarizing
- paraphrasing
- quoting

Summarizing and paraphrasing are discussed in Chapter 7 (see pages 232–235). In this section we will examine how to quote sources appropriately.

To integrate source material smoothly into your writing, **follow four basic guidelines:**

- Quote only what you need and when necessary.
- Reproduce the original text accurately.
- Be concise.
- Make it fit.

Quote Only What You Need and When Necessary

Writers quote from a source when the rhetorical situation dictates that it is important to include information or ideas *as stated in the original language of the source*. If you are consulting a source for specific information and don't need the exact language of the source, summarize or paraphrase the source passage. (See Chapter 7 for advice about summarizing and paraphrasing.) Sometimes, however, the original wording of the source is necessary to make or emphasize a point. In such cases, quoting can enhance your writing.

For example, imagine that you are writing an analysis of the debate about what should be done to address global climate change. One of your sources is *Field Notes From a Catastrophe*, in which author Elizabeth Kolbert reviews scientific data indicating that climate change is an increasingly serious problem. Here are two passages that you consider important and want to include in your analysis:

> All told, the Greenland ice sheet holds enough water to raise sea levels worldwide by twenty-three feet. Scientists at NASA have calculated that throughout the 1990s the ice sheet, despite some thickening at the center, was shrinking by twelve cubic miles per year. (52)

> As the effects of global warming become more and more difficult to ignore, will we react by finally fashioning a global response? Or will we retreat into ever narrower and more destructive forms of self-interest? It may seem impossible to imagine that a technologically advanced society could choose, in essence, to destroy itself, but that is what we are now in the process of doing. (189)

Source: Kolbert, Elizabeth. *Field Notes From a Catastrophe*. Bloomsbury Press, 2006.

The first passage contains important information about shrinking glaciers, which scientists consider a sign of climate change that could have a significant impact on coastal communities. The second passage is taken from Kolbert's conclusion, where she makes a plea for action to address climate change. Here's how you might use these passages in your analysis:

> Scientists have documented the decline of glaciers and arctic sea ice over the past several decades. For example, the Greenland ice sheet, which contains enough water to increase global sea levels by 23 feet, is shrinking by 12 cubic miles per year (Kolbert 52). To many scientists, the loss of glacial and sea ice is one of the most worrisome indicators that climate change is accelerating, and some argue that humans must act now to avoid potentially catastrophic impacts on human communities in the coming decades. Elizabeth Kolbert expresses the concerns of many experts: "As the effects of global warming become more and more difficult to ignore, will we react by finally fashioning a global response? Or will we retreat into ever narrower and more destructive forms of self-interest? It may seem impossible to imagine that a technologically advanced society could choose, in essence, to destroy itself, but that is what we are now in the process of doing" (189).

Notice that the first passage from the source text (p. 52) is cited but not quoted. Although the information in that passage is important, the wording of the source text is not. The second passage (p. 189), however, is quoted, because Kolbert's wording conveys her point more effectively than a summary or paraphrase would.

This example illustrates the need to be judicious in deciding whether to quote or summarize and cite your source. In making that decision, always consider the purpose of your project and the impact you wish to have on your audience.

Reproduce the Original Text Accurately

Quotation marks indicate to a reader that everything inside the quotation marks is exactly as it appears in the source text. So whenever you are using a quotation, make sure that you have accurately reproduced the passages you are quoting. Although this advice might seem obvious, misquoting is a common problem in student writing that can lead to misleading or inaccurate statements. For example, let's imagine you are writing an essay about childhood obesity and you want to use the following quotation from a study of the link between childhood obesity and cancer:

> In conclusion, overweight in 1,110,835 male adolescents, followed for 40 years, was found to be related to a 42% higher risk of developing future urothelial cancer. Our results should be viewed in terms of the growing global epidemic of obesity, especially childhood and adolescent obesity, in the last few decades as well as the increasing incidence of bladder cancer in the developed world.

Source: Leiba, Adi, et al. "Overweight in Adolescence Is Related to Increased Risk of Future Urothelial Cancer." *Obesity*, vol. 20, no. 12, Dec. 2012, pp. 2445–50.

A misplaced quotation mark or incomplete quotation could significantly change the meaning of this statement:

> According to a recent study, overweight adolescents are 42% more likely to develop urothelial cancer in their lives. The study's authors caution that their results "should be viewed in terms of the growing global epidemic of obesity, especially childhood and adolescent obesity, in the last few decades as well as the increasing incidence of bladder cancer" (Leiba et al. 2449).

In this example the writer failed to include the phrase "in the developed world" at the end of the quoted statement. Although everything else included in the quotation marks is accurate, the quoted statement is now misleading. The authors of the original study specifically noted the increase in bladder cancer *in the developed world*. Because the quotation in this example omits that phrase, a reader could misinterpret the quoted statement to mean that bladder cancer is increasing in *all* nations, not just in so-called "developed" nations.

As this example indicates, even a minor mistake in quoting from a source could result in erroneous or misleading statements.

Be Concise

One of the most common problems students have when quoting from a source is wordiness. Often, students use unnecessary words to introduce a quotation. Here's an example:

> In the article "New Teachers" by Neil Postman and Charles Weingarten, they state, "One of the largest obstacles to the establishment of a sound learning environment is the desire of teachers to get something they think they know into the heads of people who don't know it" (138).

Technically, there is nothing wrong with this sentence, but the writer could introduce the quotation more smoothly with fewer words:

> In "New Teachers," Neil Postman and Charles Weingarten state, "One of the largest obstacles to the establishment of a sound learning environment is the desire of teachers to get something they think they know into the heads of people who don't know it" (138).

> In their article, Neil Postman and Charles Weingarten state, "One of the largest obstacles to the establishment of a sound learning environment is the desire of teachers to get something they think they know into the heads of people who don't know it" (138).

> Neil Postman and Charles Weingarten state, "One of the largest obstacles to the establishment of a sound learning environment is the desire of teachers to get something they think they know into the heads of people who don't know it" ("New Teachers" 138).

Here are a few more examples:

> **Wordy:** Janet Emig, in her work "Writing as a Mode of Learning," argues that "writing serves learning uniquely because writing as process-and-product possesses a cluster of attributes that correspond uniquely to certain powerful learning strategies" (122).

> **Better:** According to Janet Emig, "Writing serves learning uniquely because writing as process-and-product possesses a cluster of attributes that correspond uniquely to certain powerful learning strategies" ("Writing as a Mode of Learning" 122).

> **Wordy:** "Nobody Mean More to Me than You and the Future Life of Willie Jordan" is an essay written by June Jordan that analyzes Black English as a language "system constructed by people constantly needing to insist that we exist, that we are present" (460).

> **Better:** In "Nobody Mean More to Me than You and the Future Life of Willie Jordan," June Jordan analyzes Black English as a language "system constructed by people constantly needing to insist that we exist, that we are present" (460).

The rule of thumb is to be concise and include only the necessary information about the source. If you're not sure how to introduce a quotation, use one of the standard approaches to introducing a quotation. (See Focus: "Four Common Ways to Introduce Quotations in Academic Writing" on page 341.) Keep in mind that if you have a bibliography or works cited page (which you should if you are using sources), you need to give your readers only enough information in your text to be able to find the citation in your bibliography or works cited page.

FOCUS · FOUR COMMON WAYS TO INTRODUCE QUOTATIONS IN ACADEMIC WRITING

If you pay attention as you read academic prose and scholarly writing in books and journals, you will notice four common patterns that writers use to introduce quotations from source materials. You can use these patterns to make your own use of source material more effective and help give your own prose a more scholarly "sound":

1. In [title of source], [name of author] states (argues, asserts, claims, suggests), "[insert quotation]."

   In *Contemporary Philosophy of Social Science*, Brian Fay argues, "Knowledge of what we are experiencing always involves an interpretation of these experiences" (19).

2. According to [name of author], "[insert quotation]."

   According to Brian Fay, "Knowledge of what we are experiencing always involves an interpretation of these experiences" (19).

3. [Name of author] states (argues, asserts, claims, suggests), "[insert quotation]."

   Brian Fay argues, "Knowledge of what we are experiencing always involves an interpretation of these experiences" (19).

4. "[Beginning of quotation]," according to [name of author], "[rest of quotation]."

   "Knowledge of what we are experiencing," Brian Fay argues, "always involves an interpretation of these experiences" (19).

You can use all four patterns to vary the way you introduce quotations and therefore avoid making your prose sound repetitive.

Make It Fit

Core Concept #9 ("There is always a voice in writing, even when there isn't an I") underscores the importance of voice in academic writing, no matter what the specific writing task might be. Many students weaken their voices by failing to integrate quotations and source material smoothly into their writing.

For example, in the following passage, the student discusses ideas for education reform proposed by the authors of a source text:

In the article "New Teachers" by Postman and Weingartner, there are several explanations as to why change is not an option for some teachers. The biggest problem is, "Where do we get the new teachers necessary to translate the new education into action? Obviously, it will be very difficult to get many of them from the old education. Most of these have a commitment to existing metaphors, procedures, and goals that would preclude their accepting a 'new education'" (133). Older teachers have no use for the "new education." This article focuses mainly on how teachers can be trained to translate this "new education" to their students.

In this example, the student relies too heavily on the source and does not allow her own voice to emerge. Part of the problem is wordiness, but also notice that the quotations from the source text tend to overpower the student's own writing style. Compare this passage to the following one, in which a student also writes about the possibility of education reform and draws on the work of a well-known education theorist. Unlike the previous example, in this case the student effectively integrates references to and quotations from the source text while maintaining her own voice:

> One of a teacher's main objectives in the classroom should be to equip students with cognitive and metacognitive skills so that they are mindful of the world around them. This process of critical thinking is an essential practice that students must not only understand but also be able to utilize in order to become knowledgeable, empowered individuals. In "The Banking Concept of Education," a chapter from the larger work entitled *Pedagogy of the Oppressed*, however, Paulo Freire discusses something *more* than providing students with critical thinking skills in school. He encourages teachers to raise students' awareness about themselves and society, so that they are able to work towards the broader idea of social change; this is what he calls "critical consciousness" (35). According to Freire, it is the responsibility of the teacher to instill in his/her students a sense of agency, fostering the potential and possibility for change. Without knowing that they have the capacity to transform society, Freire argues, students will become passive members of society; change, therefore, will never be possible. With this argument, Freire places great responsibility on the shoulders of those who work within the education system. But can educators really take on this role?

In this passage the student maintains control of the material. The paragraph includes summary, paraphrase, and quotations from the source text, but the main point of the paragraph is the student's own. (See Focus: "A Strategy for Integrating Source Material Into Your Writing" on page 343.) Moreover, the voice of the source never takes over, and the student's voice remains strong.

As you work with source material, remember that even when your assignment calls for a review or critique of a source text, the analysis and conclusions about that text are yours. So work the source material into your own writing—not the other way around.

FOCUS   **A STRATEGY FOR INTEGRATING SOURCE MATERIAL INTO YOUR WRITING**

Chapter 7 provides advice for writing clear, cohesive paragraphs. Sometimes paragraphs become incoherent because the student loses control of the source material. Use the advice provided in this chapter to avoid that problem. You can also follow a basic structure for your paragraphs when you are integrating source material into a paragraph:

1. **Topic Statement:** Introduce the subject of the paragraph and provide context for the source material to follow.
2. **Source Material:** Summarize, paraphrase, or quote from the source.
3. **Takeaway:** Comment on the source material to connect it to your topic statement.
4. **Parenthetical Citation:** Cite the source using MLA or APA format (see Chapter 12 for information about MLA style).

The sample paragraph on page 342 illustrates this structure:

One of a teacher's main objectives in the classroom should be to equip students with cognitive and metacognitive skills so that they are mindful of the world around them. This process of critical thinking is an essential practice that students must not only understand but also be able to utilize in order to become knowledgeable, empowered individuals. In "The Banking Concept of Education," a chapter from the larger work entitled *Pedagogy of the Oppressed*, however, Paolo Freire discusses something *more* than providing students with critical thinking skills in school. He encourages teachers to raise students' awareness about themselves and society, so that they are able to work towards the broader idea of social change; this is what he calls "critical consciousness" (35). According to Freire, it is the responsibility of the teacher to instill in his/her students a sense of agency, fostering the potential and possibility for change. Without knowing that they have the capacity to transform society, Freire argues, students will become passive members of society; change, therefore, will never be possible. With this argument, Freire places great responsibility on the shoulders of those who work within the education system. But can educators really take on this role?

Topic Statement: The student establishes the focus of the paragraph and provides context for the source material.

Source Material: The student paraphrases and quotes from the source.

Citation: Using MLA format, the student properly cites the source of the quoted phrase.

Takeaway: The student connects the source material to the Topic Statement and poses a question about the material to provide a transition to the next paragraph.

Additional Guidelines for Quoting from Sources
Punctuate Complete Quotations Correctly

When including a complete quotation from a source in your writing, use quotation marks and final punctuation marks as follows:

Direct Quotation:

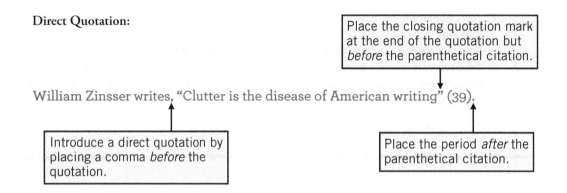

Place the closing quotation mark at the end of the quotation but *before* the parenthetical citation.

William Zinsser writes, "Clutter is the disease of American writing" (39).

Introduce a direct quotation by placing a comma *before* the quotation.

Place the period *after* the parenthetical citation.

Indirect Quotation:

In an indirect quotation, in which the word "that" follows the verb introducing the quotation, there is *no* comma after "that".

William Zinsser believes that "[c]lutter is the disease of American writing" (39).

The capital C is made lowercase because an indirect quotation does not begin with a capital letter (unless the first word of the quotation is a word that is always capitalized, such as a name or proper noun). The brackets indicate that the letter C is capitalized in the original source.

You can also introduce a quotation with a colon:

Zinsser makes a provocative point: "Clutter is the disease of American writing" (39).

However, the colon is *not* a substitute for a comma in a direct quotation. In this example, a complete sentence precedes the colon. In the example above for a direct quotation, the quotation actually completes the sentence and makes it grammatically correct.

Insert Quoted Phrases When You Don't Need an Entire Statement

Sometimes you want to quote only a word or phrase from a source rather than an entire sentence or passage. In such cases, integrate the phrase into your sentence, using quotation marks to indicate the quoted words and citing the source properly with a parenthetical citation:

The economist E. F. Schumacher argued that "work and leisure are complementary parts of the same living process" and therefore should not be considered separate from one another (55).

> In this example, there is no need for commas around the quoted phrase because it is used as part of the sentence.

> This sentence requires a comma after the quoted phrase because of the coordinating conjunction "but".

The economist E. F. Schumacher argued that "work and leisure are complementary parts of the same living process," but he also acknowledged that few people in industrialized societies understand work and leisure in this way (55).

Use Ellipses to Indicate Missing Words from a Quotation

If you quote a passage from a source but omit part of that passage, you can indicate that something is missing by using ellipses—that is, three periods, each followed by a space:

Original Passage from Source:
To my mind, voyaging through wildernesses, be they full of woods or waves, is essential to the growth and maturity of the human spirit.

Quotation with Missing Words:
Despite his ordeal at sea, in which he survived alone in a life raft for 76 days, Steven Callahan still believed in the value of wilderness experiences. "To my mind," he writes," voyaging through wildernesses . . . is essential to the growth and maturity of the human spirit" (234).

In this case, the writer decided that the phrase *be they full of woods or waves* in the original source was unnecessary and therefore omitted it; the ellipses indicate to a reader that words are missing at that point in the quoted passage.

Use Brackets to Indicate a Modified Quotation

If you have to modify a quotation in order to fit it into your sentence, use brackets to indicate changes you have made to the source material:

Original Passage from Source:

> I have focused on two people, one familiar, the other less so: Plymouth governor William Bradford and Benjamin Church, a carpenter turned Indian fighter whose maternal grandfather had sailed on the *Mayflower*.

Modified Passage in Quotation:

> In his provocative history of the Pilgrims, Nathaniel Philbrick "focuse[s] on two people, one familiar, the other less so: Plymouth governor William Bradford and Benjamin Church, a carpenter turned Indian fighter whose maternal grandfather had sailed on the Mayflower" (xvii).

In this example the writer has changed the original verb *focused* to *focuses* so that it fits grammatically into the sentence. The brackets indicate to a reader that the s at the end of "focuses" is not in the original text.

Avoiding Plagiarism

Plagiarism is the use of others' words or ideas without giving credit or presenting someone else's words or ideas as your own. It is tantamount to intellectual theft. It goes without saying that plagiarism is unethical. It is dishonest as well as unfair to your classmates, your instructor, and the plagiarized source. It is also a squandering of an opportunity to learn or make something new and useful through your academic work.

Because plagiarism is such a serious breach of ethical standards, it can have serious consequences. In the most extreme cases, plagiarism can result in lawsuits, penalties, or fines. Most colleges and universities have strict codes of student conduct that often include severe sanctions for students caught plagiarizing, including failing an assignment, failing a course, and even expulsion from school.

Plagiarism can include the following:

- **Failing to cite the source of a quotation or idea that isn't your own.** If you take information, an idea, or special language (a phrase, sentence, or lengthier passage) from a source and do not cite it properly using MLA or APA format, you are indicating to a reader that the material is your own. That's plagiarism. Any ideas, information, or quotations you use from a source must be cited properly in your own text to indicate that those ideas, information, or quotations are not yours.

- **Including a passage from a source text without using quotation marks.** Quotation marks around material that you have taken from a source indicate that the words were taken verbatim from that source and are not your own. If you use language from a source but do not place the passage in quotation marks, you are plagiarizing, *even if you cite the source.*

11

■ **Submitting someone else's work as your own.** Obviously, you are plagiarizing—and blatantly cheating—when you submit writing that someone else has done as if it is your own. This includes purchasing a paper online from so-called "paper mills" and submitting it to your instructor as if you wrote it yourself. It also includes asking a classmate or friend to write something for you and then submitting it as if it is your writing.

In most cases, these forms of plagiarism are intentional. Sometimes, however, students plagiarize unintentionally—often because they misunderstand the nature of academic research or rely too heavily on source material instead of using sources to support or extend their own ideas. To illustrate this problem, let's return to an example of a summary of a source passage from Chapter 7. This passage is taken from an article in which a law professor offers an analysis of the so-called "war on poverty" initiated by President Lyndon Johnson in the 1960s:

> The commitment and symbolism of the "war on poverty"—and the energy and enthusiasm of those who fought it—were vital. For a brief period, the idea of conducting a war on poverty captured the nation's imagination. The phrase is surely one of the most evocative in our history. Yet the war's specific components were a tiny fraction even of the Great Society programs enacted between 1964 and 1968 during the administration of Lyndon Johnson, let alone those enacted during the New Deal and those added since, many during the presidency of Richard Nixon. And, even considering all these, we never fought an allout war on poverty.

Source: Edelman, Peter. " The War on Poverty and Subsequent Federal Programs: What Worked, What Didn't Work, and Why? Lessons for Future Programs." *Clearinghouse Review Journal of Poverty Law and Policy*, May-June 2006, p 88.

Here's a summary of that passage from a student essay:

> The commitment and symbolism of the "war on poverty" were important. For a short time, the idea of a war on poverty captured the nation's imagination. But the specific components of the war were a tiny fraction of government programs enacted during the administration of Lyndon Johnson, not to mention those enacted before then and those added since. Even considering all these programs, an allout war on poverty was never really fought (Edelman 8).

The bright blue phrases in this summary indicate material that was taken verbatim from the source text. This highlighted material comprises a majority of the summary: 42 of the 72 words in this summary are taken from the source exactly as they appear in that source. That means that the summary is made up mostly of language from the source text, not the student's own words. Notice that even though the student has cited the source properly, he or she has used no quotation marks to indicate that the highlighted phrases were taken verbatim from the source text and are not the student's own words. An instructor might interpret this summary as plagiarism, because the student has not used quotation marks to indicate that most of the language is taken verbatim from the source text.

One solution in such a case is for the student simply to use quotation marks to indicate that the phrasing is taken from the original source. However, in a case like this one—in which the *ideas* from the source, *not* the original language of the source, are important—using quotation marks for all the quoted phrases would result in a cumbersome passage:

> "The commitment and symbolism of the 'war on poverty'" were important. For a short time, "the idea of a war on poverty captured the nation's imagination" (Edelman 8). But "the specific components" of the war were "a tiny fraction" of government programs "enacted during the administration of Lyndon Johnson," not to mention those enacted before then and those added since (Edelman 8). "Even considering all these" programs, "an allout war on poverty" was never really fought (Edelman 8).

There is simply no need to quote phrases like "the specific components" and "a tiny fraction," and the excessive quoting in this passage is distracting to a reader.

Avoiding plagiarism in a situation like this one (which is common in academic writing), is best accomplished by summarizing the source passage carefully so that the summary reflects the student's own words:

> According to Edelman, the idea of a "war on poverty" was important for its symbolism as well as for the national commitment it reflected (8). However, although this idea resonated with Americans for a time, the programs intended specifically to fight poverty were never more than a small part of total government social programs, whether those programs were part of Lyndon Johnson's Great Society, the earlier New Deal, or initiatives under-taken by Richard Nixon and subsequent presidents. As a result, Edelman states, a total war on poverty was never really fought (8).

Notice that the student writer's voice is strong in this passage, and although the student is drawing his or her ideas primarily from the source text, the student is using his or her *own* words and does not allow the language of the source text to take over this summary.

The best way to avoid plagiarism is to apply the Ten Core Concepts in your writing and follow the advice presented in Chapters 9, 10, and 11 for finding and using source material. If you focus on what *you* have to say in your writing, you are much less likely to plagiarize. In addition, **follow these guidelines:**

- **Use sources to support or extend your own ideas.** As noted earlier, if you focus on making and supporting your main point (Core Concepts #4 and #5), you are less likely to fall victim to unnecessarily borrowing from a source or unintentionally presenting ideas from a source as your own.

- **Summarize and paraphrase carefully.** As the example in this section illustrates, you are more likely to plagiarize inadvertently if you don't sufficiently understand the functions of summary and paraphrase, so review the advice for summarizing and paraphrasing in Chapter 7. Because academic writing so often requires you to work with source material, being able to summarize and paraphrase appropriately is essential, and developing those skills will help you avoid plagiarizing.

- **Integrate source material into your own writing.** Following the advice in this chapter will help you present source material appropriately. Apply the appropriate strategies for quoting from sources to make it clear to your readers when the material you are presenting is taken from a source and when the language is your own.

- **Credit your sources.** If using MLA style, follow the conventions for citing sources that are explained in Chapter 12. If using APA or some other format approved by your instructor, consult a library, grammar handbook, or online resources to learn how to use those citation styles correctly. Be sure to cite sources correctly so that there is no confusion about whether the material you are presenting is yours or taken from a source.

- **Take careful notes.** When you are researching a topic, keep accurate notes about the sources you have consulted so that you know where you found the material you are using and have the correct information for citing the sources. If you are using online sources, it is a good idea to bookmark the pages from which you have taken information.

- **When in doubt, cite your source.** The rule of thumb is that you must cite any material you take from a source that is not considered to be "common knowledge," which generally means facts, information, or ideas that most people might know. For example, you wouldn't need to cite Charles Darwin as the originator of the idea of natural selection, since that fact is widely known. However, determining what is common knowledge and what isn't can be difficult and subject to interpretation. If you're not sure whether to cite a source for information or an idea that you have taken from a source, cite it to be safe.

In this chapter, you will learn to

1. Identify the appropriate types of sources that require formal documentation.

2. Identify the two main components of MLA style: in-text citations and a Works Cited list.

3. Create in-text citations in MLA style for a variety of sources.

4. Create Works Cited entries in MLA style for a variety of sources.

Citing Sources Using MLA Style

12

THE PURPOSE OF CITING SOURCES is to be as clear as possible in showing where your information comes from. Citing your sources according to established style guides not only credits the source for the material you are using but also provides your readers with sufficient bibliographic information to judge or even find your sources for themselves. In general, you must document the source of

- a direct quotation,
- an idea or opinion that is not your own,
- visual materials, such as photographs, maps, or graphs, that you did not create,
- multimedia content, such as videos or audios, that you did not create, and
- information (a fact or statistic) that is not general knowledge.

In most academic writing today, writers use the Modern Language Association (MLA) style guide when they are writing in the humanities: literature, languages, performing and visual arts, history, classics, philosophy, and religion. This chapter explains how to cite sources using MLA style. The guidelines in this chapter are based on the *MLA Handbook*, 8th ed.

Two Main Components in MLA Style

MLA style uses in-text parenthetical citations to document sources. There are **two main components to in-text parenthetical citation systems:**

1. **In-text citations.** Parenthetical citations, which appear in the body of your writing, indicate to a reader that information you are presenting is taken from another source.

2. **A Works Cited List.** The Works Cited list is a separate section at the end of your document that includes bibliographic information for every source you cited in your document.

Let's imagine you are writing an essay about the cultural significance of heavy metal music and you want to refer to a specific analysis of so-called death metal music in a book by Natalie J. Purcell titled *Death Metal Music: The Passion and Politics of a Subculture*. On page 188 of that book, Purcell makes a point about the philosophical function of death metal music that you want to include in your essay. Using MLA style, you would cite your source as follows:

> Death metal music performs a genuine philosophical function by examining the dark side of human nature (Purcell 188).

If you mention the author's name in your sentence, you do not need to include it in the parenthetical citation:

> Critic Natalie Purcell considers death metal a "philosophical response, whether conscious or subconscious, to terrifying questions about nebulous human nature" (188).

The information in parentheses indicates to readers that the idea about the philosophical function of death metal is taken from page 188 of a work by Purcell. Readers can then consult your Works Cited page, where they will find the following entry:

> Purcell, Natalie J. *Death Metal Music: The Passion and Politics of a Subculture.* McFarland, 2003.

Each in-text citation in your document must have a corresponding Works Cited entry to give your readers the means to find and read the original source themselves.

FOCUS   **FOOTNOTES, ENDNOTES, AND CONTENT NOTES**

Traditionally, footnotes or endnotes were used to document sources. Strictly speaking, a **footnote** appears at the foot of the page, and an **endnote** appears at the end of the paper. However, the MLA now recommends that writers use parenthetical, or in-text, citations of the kind described in this chapter. Traditional footnotes are used not for documenting sources but for additional explanation or discussion of a point in the main text. These notes are called **content notes**.

Creating In-Text Citations in MLA Style

MLA style, which reflects the conventions of the humanities, emphasizes the author and the author's work and places less emphasis on the date of publication. When citing a work parenthetically, the author's last name is followed by a page number or range of pages. There are particular situations in which somewhat different information is given in parentheses, but *the general rule is to provide enough information to enable a reader to find the source in your Works Cited page.* You do not need to include inside the parentheses information you have already provided in the text. For instance, if you start the sentence with the author's name, you do not need to include the author's name in the parentheses.

FOCUS   **FIND THE IN-TEXT CITATION MODEL YOU NEED**

A. Work by one author (page 353)

B. Work by multiple authors (page 353)

C. Work by a corporate author (page 354)

D. More than one work by the same author (page 354)

12

A. Work by one author

If you were citing information taken from page 82 of a book called *The Printing Revolution in Early Modern Europe* by Elizabeth L. Eisenstein, the parenthetical citation would look like this:

> The widespread adoption of the printing press in the 16th century helped standardize the major European languages (Eisenstein 82).

If you used Eisenstein's name in your sentence, the citation would include only the page reference:

> Elizabeth Eisenstein examines how the widespread adoption of the printing press in the 16th century helped standardize the major European languages (82).

There is no punctuation between the author's name and the page number. Note that the parentheses are placed *inside* the period at the end of the sentence. Also, the abbreviation *p.* or *pp.* is not used before the page reference in a parenthetical citation in MLA style.

B. Work by multiple authors

When citing a work by two authors, include both authors' names in the citation (or in your sentence). For example, if you wanted to quote from page 2 of *Undead TV: Essays on Buffy the Vampire Slayer*, by Elana Levine and Lisa Parks, you could do so as follows:

> We might consider how the hit television series *Buffy the Vampire Slayer* "dramatizes the travails of its title character but uses its metaphorical representations of life and death, good and evil, comedy and tragedy to speak about the power struggles inherent in many people's everyday lives in the Western world" (Levine and Parks 2).

or

> Elana Levine and Lisa Parks assert that *Buffy the Vampire Slayer* "dramatizes the travails of its title character but uses its metaphorical representations of life and death, good and evil, comedy and tragedy to speak about the power struggles inherent in many people's everyday lives in the Western world" (2).

If you are referring to a work by more than two authors, list only the first author's name followed by the Latin phrase *et al.* (which means "and others"). For example, if you were citing information from page 79 of a journal article titled "Empirical Foundations for Writing in Prevention and Psychotherapy," by Brian A. Esterling, Luciano L'Abate, Edward J. Murray, and James W. Pennebaker, the parenthetical citation would look like this:

> Studies have shown that writing has therapeutic benefits for some patients (Esterling et al. 79).

Note that there is no comma after the name of the author.

C. Work by a corporate author

A "corporate author" is an organization, committee, or an agency (rather than an individual or group of individually named authors). When citing a corporate author, use the same format as for a single author. For example, if you were citing a study by the Center for Research on Educational Outcomes, you would do so as follows:

> According to the Center for Research on Educational Outcomes, in 37 percent of charter schools, students had math scores that were lower than their public school peers (3).

You could also include the corporate author in the parentheses; omit any initial article:

> In one recent study, 37 percent of charter schools had student math scores that were lower than in public schools (Center for Research on Educational Outcomes 3).

D. More than one work by the same author

If you cite more than one work by the same author, you need to distinguish among the works by using a shortened form of the title of each work you cite. For example, if you were quoting from two different books by Paulo Freire, *Pedagogy of Hope* and *Letters to Cristina*, your parenthetical citations might look like this:

> Freire emphasizes the crucial role of hope in the struggle for change. Acknowledging that hope "seldom exists apart from the reverses of fate" (*Letters* 14), Freire argues that the "dream of humanization . . . is always a process" (*Pedagogy* 99).

The shortened titles (*Letters* and *Pedagogy*) enable a reader to find the specific references in the Works Cited list. Also note that because it is clear from the context that both works cited are by the same author, the author's name does not need to be placed inside the parentheses. If the author's name is not included in the text itself, include it inside the parenthetical citation:

> Hope is a crucial element in the struggle for change. We should acknowledge that hope "seldom exists apart from the reverses of fate" (Freire, *Letters* 14) and remember that the "dream of humanization . . . is always a process" (Freire, *Pedagogy* 99).

Note that a comma separates the author's name from the shortened title, but no comma appears between the title and the page number.

E. Work without an author listed

If you cite a work without an author listed, include a brief version of the title in parentheses. For example, if you cited information from page 27 of an article from *The Economist* titled "Carrying the Torch," you would do so as follows:

> The sports management industry in Great Britain received a significant boost in business as a result of the 2012 Olympic Games in London ("Carrying" 27).

F. Entire work

When you refer to an entire work, include only the author's name, either in your sentence or in parentheses. No page numbers are needed.

> Cheryl Sandberg discusses the reasons women are still not adequately represented in leadership positions.

If you do not mention the author's name in your sentence, cite it in parentheses:

> For many reasons, women are still not adequately represented in leadership positions (Sandberg).

G. Quotation within a cited work

When using a quotation from one source that you have found in another source, you must show that the quotation was acquired "secondhand" and was not taken directly from the original source. In such cases, use the abbreviation *qtd. in* (for "quoted in") to indicate that you are taking the quotation from a second source rather than from the original text. For example, let's say you were reading a book called *Literary Theory* by Terry Eagleton that included a quotation by Sigmund Freud. If you wanted to use Freud's quotation in your essay, you would cite it as follows:

> Even Freud acknowledged the central importance of economics in human relations, famously stating, "The motive of human society is in the last resort an economic one" (qtd. in Eagleton 151).

In this instance, you are signaling to readers that you read Freud's statement in the book by Terry Eagleton. Your Works Cited page must include an entry for Eagleton's book but not Freud's original text.

H. Work in an anthology

Name the author of the particular work, not the editor of the entire anthology, in your citation. For example, if you were citing a story by Nathan Englander that appears in the anthology *The Best American Short Stories 2012*, edited by Tom Perrotta and Heidi Pitlor, you would not need to mention the editors of the anthology:

> Nathan Englander plays off Raymond Carver's famous story title in his short work "What We Talk About When We Talk About Anne Frank."

The entry in your Works Cited page, which would list Nathan Englander as the author of the story, would also include the editors' names.

I. Electronic sources

When citing electronic sources, follow the same principles you would use when citing other sources. However, there are many different kinds of electronic sources, which might not include the same kinds of information that are available for a print book or journal article. For example, online sources, such as websites, often do not have page numbers. If the online source has numbered paragraphs, provide the number of the paragraph in which you found the information or quotation you are citing:

(Martinez, par. 8)

Note that a comma is placed after the author's name.

If page numbers or paragraph numbers are not available, include sufficient information for readers to find the source in your Works Cited list, such as the author's last name or a brief title:

(Martinez)

J. Long quotations

In MLA style, a long prose quotation is defined as one that takes more than four lines in your paper. Quotations of more than three lines of poetry are considered long, and any amount of quoted dialogue from a play is treated as a block quotation. These quotations should be indented one-half inch from the left margin as a block quotation—*without* quotation marks. The entire block should be double-spaced, and no additional space should be used above or below the block quotation. In this example, the writer introduces a long quotation from an author named Sharon Crowley:

> Sharon Crowley offers contemporary scholars a radical inspiration from ancient times:
> I can see no reason why contemporary teachers cannot develop theories of com-
> position that are fully as rich as those developed in ancient times. Much thinking
> remains to be done, and I do not doubt that enterprising teachers of composition
> will do it—because there is a place for composition in the university, and that place
> does not depend on Freshman English. (265)

The page number for the quotation is included in parentheses at the end of the block quotation. Notice that the parenthetical citation is placed *after* the final period of the block quotation. If the author's name does not appear in the main text, include it in the parentheses.

K. Work in more than one volume

If you use more than one volume from a multivolume work in your paper, indicate the volume and page number in each citation. The volume number is followed by a colon. In this example, page 234 in volume 3 of a work by Trieste is cited:

(Trieste 3: 236)

If you cite only one volume, however, you can provide the page number only. In your Works Cited entry, list the volume number.

Creating a Works Cited List in MLA Style

Each source you cite in your text must correspond to an entry in the Works Cited list. In general, in entries that appear in a Works Cited list, MLA style emphasizes **nine core elements** that appear in some version in most entries, whether that entry refers to a traditional print text, a digital format, or another kind of nonprint source (like a work of art):

1. **Author:** The creator of the source you are citing.

2. **Title of source:** The title should be for the *specific* source (e.g., the title of a poem or article you are citing, *not* the title of the book in which the poem appeared or the magazine where the article appeared).

3. **Title of container:** The larger source that contains the specific source (e.g., the book of poems that contains the specific poem you are citing or the magazine that contains the article you are citing).

4. **Other contributors:** Others who contributed to the source, such as editors or translators.

5. **Version:** The specific version of the source, such as the revised edition of a book.

6. **Number:** The number indicates the place of the source in a sequence, such as the volume and issue numbers for scholarly journals or the episode number of a television series.

7. **Publisher:** The organization that produced the source, such as the publisher of a book or sponsor of a website.

8. **Publication date:** The date when the source was made available to a public audience.

9. **Location:** The location of the source, such as page numbers for a print source or a URL or DOI for an online source. (See Focus: "What is a DOI?" on page 358.)

Each entry in your Works Cited list should include these core elements, if available. Note that some entries might refer to containers within larger containers. For example, if you found a journal article through a database like *ArticleFirst*, the specific source you are citing is the title of the article; the journal is container #1, and the database is container #2. In such an entry, include relevant information about the larger container—such as its title and the source's location within it—and place any information about container #2 *after* all information about the source itself and container #1, separated by a period. The rule of thumb is to include information that will help your readers locate the specific source.

To create a Works Cited entry, then, follow this basic procedure:

- List core elements 1 (author) and 2 (title of source).
- List core elements 3-9 that provide information about the *first* container.
- List core elements 3-9 that provide information about the *second* container.

The examples in this chapter illustrate this procedure.

DOI stands for digital object identifier. A DOI is a unique string of numbers that identifies an electronic publication and enables you to access that publication online. It is more stable than a URL (or web address), which can change or be deleted. MLA style recommends using a DOI in a Works Cited entry, in place of a URL, if a source has a DOI assigned to it. (If there is no DOI, use the URL.)

Many scholarly journals now include DOIs for online publications. Usually, the DOI appears on the first page of the article and has the descriptor "doi." A DOI looks like a string of numbers, like this: doi: 10.1080/09243450600565795. See an example of a Works Cited entry that includes a DOI on page 364.

Your list of Works Cited should appear at the end of your project, beginning with a new page. Organize the Works Cited list alphabetically according to the authors' last names (or, if the work includes no author, the first main word of the title). In MLA style, follow these rules:

- Capitalize the first word, the last word, and every important word in titles and subtitles. Do not capitalize prepositions (such as *on* and *to*), coordinating conjunctions (such as *and* and *but*), or articles (*a, an, the*) unless they begin the title or subtitle.
- Italicize the titles of long works such as books, periodicals, and websites.
- Place the titles of shorter works, such as articles, stories, and online postings, in quotation marks.
- Italicize the titles of most containers, such as magazines, television shows, or databases.
- For sources (such as journals and magazines) that have a publication date that includes a month (Apr. 2016), abbreviate all months except May, June, and July.
- For websites or other online sources (such as databases), include a URL or a DOI (digital object identifier) if one is available for your source. Do not include *http://* or *https://* as part of the URL in your citation.
- For the publication date of online sources, list the day, month, and year, if available. If there is both an original publication date and a more recent "last modified date" mentioned on the site, then use the most recent date in your citation.
- For online sources that have no publication date listed, include the date you accessed the site at the end of your citation. Format the access date as follows: day month year (for example, Accessed 17 Oct. 2016).
- Double-space citations but do not skip spaces between entries.
- Use hanging indents for entries in the Works Cited list.

Note: The directory of in-text citation models appears on pages 352–353.

Books

Here is the general format for an entry for a book in the Works Cited page:

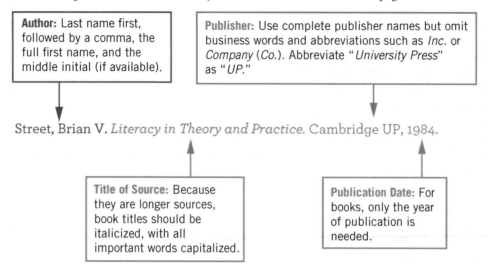

Author: Last name first, followed by a comma, the full first name, and the middle initial (if available).

Publisher: Use complete publisher names but omit business words and abbreviations such as *Inc.* or *Company* (*Co.*). Abbreviate "*University Press*" as "*UP.*"

Street, Brian V. *Literacy in Theory and Practice.* Cambridge UP, 1984.

Title of Source: Because they are longer sources, book titles should be italicized, with all important words capitalized.

Publication Date: For books, only the year of publication is needed.

Note: For online books, include the name of the site or database where the book is located and the URL.

1. Book with one author

> Fineman, Howard. *The Thirteen American Arguments: Enduring Debates That Define and Inspire Our Country.* Random House, 2008.

> Lockhart, Charles. *Gaining Ground: Tailoring Social Programs to American Values.* U of California P, 1989, ark.cdlib.org/ark:/13030/ft2p300594/.

In the second example, the URL is included at the end of the citation because the work was accessed online.

2. Book with two or more authors

> Stewart, David W., and Dennis W. Rook. *Focus Groups: Theory and Practice.* SAGE Publications, 2007.

If there are two authors, list both authors' names. Notice that only the first author is listed with the last name first.

For books with three or more authors, use the abbreviation *et al.*:

> Wysocki, Anne Frances, et al. *Writing New Media: Theory and Applications for Expanding the Teaching of Composition.* Utah State UP, 2004.

3. Two or more books by the same author

When you are listing two or more books by the same author, you do not repeat the author's name for each entry. Instead, use three hyphens and a period in place of the author's name for the second, third, and subsequent entries by the same author. Also, list the entries in alphabetical order by the book title.

Freire, Paulo. *Letters to Cristina: Reflections on My Life and Work*. Routledge, 1996.

---. *Pedagogy in Process: The Letters to Gineau-Bissau*. Seabury Press, 1978.

---. *Pedagogy of the Oppressed*. Translated by Myra Bergman Ramos, Continuum, 1970.

4. Anthology with an editor

McComiskey, Bruce, editor. *English Studies: An Introduction to the Discipline(s)*. NCTE Publications, 2006.

Hill, Charles A., and Marguerite Helmers, editors. *Defining Visual Rhetorics*. Lawrence Erlbaum Associates, 2004.

Use the description *editor* for a single editor and *editors* for multiple editors. Place the description after the editor's name, which is followed by a comma.

5. Works in an anthology

Dittrich, Luke. "The Brain That Changed Everything." *The Best American Science and Nature Writing*, edited by Mary Roach, Houghton Miffin Harcourt, 2011, pp. 46-68.

Notice that the page numbers for the article are provided, preceded by the abbreviation *pp*. Also, the description *edited by* appears before the editor's name (Mary Roach).

If you cite two or more articles (or other short works) from the same anthology, use a shortened form of the citation for each one, and then cite the entire anthology according to example #4 above. Here are two abbreviated citations as well as a citation for the complete collection that these abbreviated citations refer to:

Bhattacharjee, Yudhijit. "The Organ Dealer." Roach 1-14.

Dittrich, Luke. "The Brain That Changed Everything." Roach 46-68.

Roach, Mary, editor. *The Best American Science and Nature Writing*. Houghton Mifflin Harcourt, 2011.

In this example, readers would know that the articles by Yudhijit Bhattacharjee and Luke Dittrich are included in the anthology *The Best American Science and Nature Writing*, which is edited by Mary Roach.

6. Book with an author and an editor

Thoreau, Henry David. *Walden*. Edited by Jeffrey S. Cramer, Yale UP, 2004.

The author's name is placed first. The editor's name is placed after the title, preceded by the description *Edited by*.

7. Book with a translator

Tsunetomo, Yamamoto. *Hagakure: The Book of the Samurai*. Translated by William Scott Wilson, Kadansha International, 1979.

The description *Translated by* appears before the name of the translator (William Scott Wilson).

8. Book by a corporate author or without an author listed

> *The Condition of College and Career Readiness 2015.* ACT, 2015, forms.act.org/research/
> policymakers/cccr15/pdf/CCCR15-NationalReadinessRpt.pdf.

List the group or organization as the author. If no author or organization is listed, then omit the author and begin the entry with the title of the book. Also, if the group or organization that authored the publication is also the publisher or sponsor for the publication (as in the example above), then start the citation with the title of the work and list the group or organization (in this example, ACT) *only once*, as the publisher.

9. Introduction, preface, foreword, or afterword written by someone other than the author of the work

> Zelazny, Roger. Introduction. *Do Androids Dream of Electric Sheep?* by Philip K. Dick,
> Del Rey Books, 1968, pp. vii-x.

In this example, Roger Zelazny wrote the introduction to the book *Do Androids Dream of Electric Sheep?* by Philip K. Dick. Include the page numbers of the introduction (or preface, foreword, or afterword) after the date of publication.

10. Subsequent editions of a book

> Creswell, John W., editor. *Qualitative Research and Design: Choosing Among Five
> Approaches.* 2nd ed., SAGE Publications, 2007.

Use the abbreviation *ed.* for "edition."

11. Work in more than one volume

> Milton, John. *The Prose Works of John Milton.* John W. Moore, 1847. 2 vols.

12. Book in a series

> Pedersen, Isabel. *Ready to Wear: A Rhetoric of Wearable Computers and Reality-Shifting
> Media.* Parlor Press, 2013. New Media Theory.

This citation is similar to a citation for a book (see example #1 on page 360) except that the name of the series (New Media Theory) is placed after the date of publication and followed by a period. It is not italicized or placed in quotation marks.

13. Encyclopedia entry

The format for entries for encyclopedia articles is similar to articles in anthologies or edited collections.

> Sockett, Hugh. "The Moral and Epistemic Purposes of Teacher Education." *Handbook
> of Research on Teacher Education,* edited by Marilyn Cochran-Smith et al., 3rd ed.,
> Routledge, 2008, pp. 45-66.

This example shows an article written by Hugh Sockett that appeared in the encyclopedia *Handbook of Research on Teacher Education*, edited by Marilyn Cochran-Smith and others. If no author is listed for the specific article, then begin with the title of the article. Even when you are citing an encyclopedia or other reference work in which the entries or articles are organized alphabetically, you should include page numbers at the end of the citation.

If you accessed the encyclopedia article through an online database, include the name of the database (*Oxford Reference*, in the example below) as the second container (set in italics) followed by a comma and then the URL followed by a period:

> Lacey, Alan. "The Meaning of Life." *The Oxford Companion to Philosophy*, edited by Ted Honderich, 2nd ed., Oxford UP, 2005. *Oxford Reference*, www.oxfordreference.com/view/10.1093/acref/9780199264797.001.0001/acref-9780199264797-e-1423#.

14. Sacred text

> *The Bible*. King James Version, American Bible Society, 1980.

Insert the name of the version you are using after the title (King James Version, in this example). Include names of editors or translators, if any, before the version information.

FOCUS · **CITING WIKIPEDIA AND OTHER ONLINE REFERENCES**

Many instructors have policies regarding the use of *Wikipedia* and similar online references, so check with your instructor before using such resources in your research. In MLA Style, if you cite information taken from such sources, the format is similar to the format for citing a web page (see example #21 on page 367):

> "Ultramarathon." *Wikipedia, The Free Encyclopedia*, 9 Aug. 2016, en.wikipedia.org/w/index.php?title=Ultramarathon&oldid=733648256. Accessed 16 Aug. 2016.

In this example, because there is no author, the entry begins with the title of the article, followed by the name of the website in italics (*Wikipedia, The Free Encyclopedia*), the date when the entry was last modified, and the permanent URL for this specific entry. If the publisher or the sponsor of this site (Wikipedia, in this example) is essentially the same as the title of the website, it is not necessary to include a publisher's name in the citation.

If a site offers a permanent link or a stable URL for an article or entry or posting (as Wikipedia does), it is preferable to use that URL in your citation, rather than copying the URL from your browser. Stable URLs or permalinks are a more reliable way for readers to locate your sources.

Periodicals

Here is the general format for an article from a scholarly journal that was located in a database (in this example, *JSTOR*):

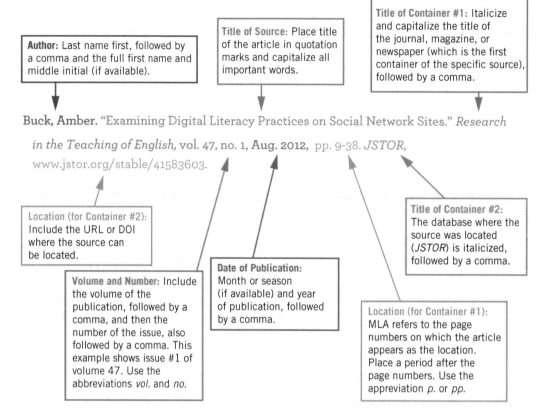

Author: Last name first, followed by a comma and the full first name and middle initial (if available).

Title of Source: Place title of the article in quotation marks and capitalize all important words.

Title of Container #1: Italicize and capitalize the title of the journal, magazine, or newspaper (which is the first container of the specific source), followed by a comma.

Buck, Amber. "Examining Digital Literacy Practices on Social Network Sites." *Research in the Teaching of English,* vol. 47, no. 1, Aug. 2012, pp. 9-38. *JSTOR,* www.jstor.org/stable/41583603.

Location (for Container #2): Include the URL or DOI where the source can be located.

Volume and Number: Include the volume of the publication, followed by a comma, and then the number of the issue, also followed by a comma. This example shows issue #1 of volume 47. Use the abbreviations *vol.* and *no.*

Date of Publication: Month or season (if available) and year of publication, followed by a comma.

Title of Container #2: The database where the source was located (*JSTOR*) is italicized, followed by a comma.

Location (for Container #1): MLA refers to the page numbers on which the article appears as the location. Place a period after the page numbers. Use the appreviation *p.* or *pp.*

If you found a print version of this source and you did not use a database, the entry would appear without the title of the database or the URL (or DOI), as follows:

> Buck, Amber. "Examining Digital Literacy Practices on Social Network Sites." *Research in the Teaching of English,* vol. 47, no. 1, Aug. 2012, pp. 9-38.

Note: If a scholarly journal article has a DOI, use that instead of a URL in your citation:

> Torres, Carlos Alberto. "Neoliberalism as a New Historical Bloc: A Gramscian Analysis of Neoliberalism's Common Sense in Education." *International Studies in Sociology of Education,* vol. 23, no. 2, 2013, doi: 10.1080/09620214.2013.790658.

This example shows a scholarly journal. **For magazines and newspapers:**

- Omit the volume and issue number.
- Include the day, month (abbreviated), and year for the date of publication, if available, and use this format: 11 Apr. 2016.

15. Article from a scholarly journal

> Mayers, Tim. "One Simple Word: From Creative Writing to Creative Writing Studies."
> *College English*, vol. 71, no. 3, Jan. 2009, pp. 217-28.

If you accessed this article online via a database such as *JSTOR, LexisNexis, InfoTrac, or Academic Search Complete*, the citation would appear as follows:

> Mayers, Tim. "One Simple Word: From Creative Writing to Creative Writing Studies."
> *College English*, vol. 71, no. 3, Jan. 2009, pp. 217-28. *JSTOR*, www.jstor.org/
> stable/25472320.

Note that this citation begins with complete print source information, including page numbers, followed by the title of the database (*JSTOR*, in this example), in italics, and a URL provided for this article in the database.

However, if you accessed this same article via the journal's website (instead of a database), the citation would appear like this:

> Mayers, Tim. "One Simple Word: From Creative Writing to Creative Writing Studies."
> *College English*, vol. 71, no. 3, Jan. 2009, www.ncte.org/library/NCTEFiles/
> Resources/Journals/CE/0713-jan09/CE0713Simple.pdf.

In this case, a URL is included *in place of* page numbers.

16. Article from a weekly or monthly magazine

> Lasdun, James. "Alone in the Alps." *The New Yorker*, 11 Apr. 2016, pp. 34-39.

If you accessed the article online through a database such as *Academic Search Complete*, include the italicized title of the database followed by a comma and then the URL provided for the article in the database (as in the example at the beginning of this section on page 366).

However, if you found the article through the magazine website, cite it as follows:

> Lasdun, James. "Alone in the Alps." *The New Yorker*, 11 Apr. 2016, www.newyorker.com/
> magazine/2016/04/11/hiking-the-via-alpina.

In this case, the URL of the magazine website replaces page numbers.

Note that this example shows a weekly magazine (*The New Yorker*). If you are citing an article in a magazine that is published monthly, use the identical format with only the month and year for the date.

17. Article from a daily newspaper

> Kepner, Tyler. "Grand Home of a Larger-Than-Life Team." *The New York Times*, national
>   ed., 21 Sept. 2008, p. N1.

Note that the page number includes the section in which the article appeared—in this example, section N, page 1. Also, if available, include the edition (in this example, *national ed.* for "national edition") before the publication date.

   If the article is accessed online through a database, include the complete print source information as listed in the database. Then list the italicized title of the database, followed by a comma and then the URL:

> Kepner, Tyler. "Grand Home of a Larger-Than-Life Team." *The New York Times*, 21 Sept.
>   2008, p. SP1. *General OneFile*, go.galegroup.com/ps/i.do?id=GALE%7CA185353770&v=
>   2.1&u=nysl_me_wls&it=r&p=GPS&sw=w&asid=fb14c17410255fa0f73229b423492e88.

If you accessed the article through the newspaper's website, cite it as follows:

> Kepner, Tyler. "Grand Home of a Larger-Than-Life Team." *The New York Times*, 20 Sept.
>   2008, nyti.ms/1SK9RCi.

List the publication date as listed on the website (this may sometimes be slightly different than the print publication date) and the URL. Some sources, such as *The New York Times*, offer a permanent URL for their articles (nyti.ms/1SK9RCi in the example above); if available, include this kind of permalink in your citation instead of copying the URL from your browser.

18. Editorial

> Kayyem, Juliette. "A Rainy Day Fund Doesn't Work if It's Always Raining." Editorial.
>   *Boston Globe*, 23 May 2013, www.bostonglobe.com/opinion/2013/05/22/another-
>   disaster-and-yet-relief-stays-same/R6DsCQCr8xhg0vZOUzlRcL/story.html.

The term "Editorial" appears after the title of the article, followed by a period. In this online example, there is no edition or page number because the article was accessed through the newspaper's website.

19. Letter to the editor

> Tamor, Sarah. Letter to the editor. *The New York Times*, 7 Apr. 2016, nyti.ms/23hYMDi.

Note that because this source was located online at the newspaper's website, there is a URL in place of page numbers.

20. Review

> Uglow, Jenny. "The Saga of the Flaming Zucchini." Review of *Consider the Fork:*
>   *A History of How We Cook and Eat*, by Bee Wilson. *The New York Review of Books*, 6
>   June 2013, www.nybooks.com/articles/2013/06/06/saga-flaming-zucchini/.

Notice that the name of the author of the review is placed first. The name of the author of the work being reviewed follows the title of the work being reviewed, preceded by the word *by* (in this example, "by Bee Wilson").

If the review does not have a separate title (like "The Saga of the Flaming Zucchini" in this example) omit that part of the citation. For publication information, use the format for the kind of source you used (e.g., newspaper website or monthly magazine).

For film reviews, include the name of the director of the film, placed after the title of the film and preceded by the description *directed by*:

> Sharkey, Betsy. "*Before Midnight* Finds Its Couple in a Dark Place." Review of *Before Midnight*, directed by Richard Linklater. *Los Angeles Times*, 24 May 2013, articles .latimes.com/2013/may/24/entertainment/la-et-mn-before-midnight-20130524.

Other Sources

21. Website

When citing an entire website, include the author, editor, or compiler of the site (if available), followed by the title of the site in italics, the name of the organization sponsoring the site, the publication date (if available), and the URL:

> *Feirstein Graduate School of Cinema*. Brooklyn College, CUNY, www.brooklyn.cuny.edu/ web/academics/schools/mediaarts/schools/feirstein.php. Accessed 30 Sept. 2016.

In this example, there is no author, so the entry begins with the title of the website (*Feirstein Graduate School of Cinema*). Also, if a site has no publication date or is revised and updated often, as in this example, include a date of access at the end of your citation.

22. Web page

For a web page, include the name of the author (if available), the title of the page in quotation marks followed by the italicized title of the website, the name of the sponsoring organization (if available), the date of publication, and the URL:

> Vandervort, Don. "Water Softener Buying Guide." *HomeTips*, 22 Apr. 2016, www.hometips.com/buying-guides/water-softener-systems.html.

If the sponsoring organization or publisher of the site is the same as the title of the overall website, then do not include the sponsoring organization in your citation. In the example above, "HomeTips" is both the name of the sponsoring organization and the name of the website, so it is listed only once in the entry (as the title of the site).

The citation for a web page by a corporate author (such as an organization or business) is similar in format:

> Writing Center at the University of Wisconsin-Madison. "Writing Cover Letters.'" *The Writer's Handbook*, U of Wisconsin-Madison, 29 Aug 2014, writing.wisc.edu/ Handbook/CoverLetters.html.

Notice that the name of the agency or organization (Writing Center at the University of Wisconsin-Madison) appears in place of an author's name. In this example, *The Writer's Handbook* is the website where the web page ("Writing Cover Letters") is located; the University of

Wisconsin-Madison is the sponsoring organization. Note that if no publication date is available, include the date when you accessed the web page at the end of the citation.

For a web page without an author, the citation appears like this:

"Dodging Bombs and Building Trust in Yemen." *UNWomen*, 24 Mar. 2016, www.unwomen.org/en/news/stories/2016/3/dodging-bombs-and-building-trust-in-yemen.

The title of the web page ("Dodging Bombs and Building Trust in Yemen") appears first, followed by the italicized title of the website (*UNWomen*), the date of publication, and the URL. In this example, because UNWomen is both the name of the website and the name of the sponsoring organization, the name of the sponsoring organization is omitted.

23. Blog

Villaespesa, Elena. "Data Stories Centralized: A Digital Analytics Dashboard." *Digital Underground*, Metropolitan Museum of Art, 29 Oct. 2015, www.metmuseum.org/blogs/digital-underground/2015/data-stories-centralized.

Include the author (if known), the title of the blog entry (in quotation marks), and the title of the blog (in italics). Next, list the sponsor of the website. Note that according to the MLA guidelines, the articles *the* and *a* are excluded from the name of a sponsoring organization or publisher in citations; so, in this example, "The" is omitted from The Metropolitan Museum of Art. Also, remember to include the date of the blog entry and the URL.

24. Podcast

Davies, Dave, narrator. "Do Voter ID Laws Prevent Fraud, or Dampen Turnout?" *Fresh Air*, National Public Radio, 15 Aug. 2012, www.npr.org/2012/08/15/158869947/do-voter-id-laws-prevent-fraud-or-dampen-turnout.

Begin with the performer's or author's name, followed by the title of the podcast in quotation marks, the italicized name of the program or series that the podcast is part of, the sponsor of the program, the date of the original broadcast, and the URL.

25. Interview

For an interview that you conduct yourself, include the name of the person you interviewed, a description (Personal interview), and the date of the interview:

Gallehr, Don. Personal interview. 19 Apr. 2010.

For a published or broadcast interview, include the name of the person who was interviewed and the title of the interview, if available, placed in quotation marks. Add the name of the interviewer if relevant. Be sure to include the publication information and the URL if it is an interview you found online. For example, in this entry, the interview was published on the website *City Pages*:

Pollan, Michael. "A Coffee Date with Michael Pollan." Interview by Keane Amdahl, *City Pages*, 7 May 2013, www.citypages.com/restaurants/a-coffee-date-with-michael-pollan-interview-6615340.

26. E-mail

> Yagelski, Robert. "A Summary of Key Revision Ideas." Received by Laura Ross,
> 28 Mar. 2016.

List the name of the person who wrote the e-mail first, followed by the subject line of the e-mail message in quotation marks, the name of the person who received the e-mail, and the date the message was sent.

27. Film

> *The Great Gatsby*. Directed by Baz Luhrmann, Warner Bros. Entertainment, 2013.

If you are discussing a film in a general way, place the title of the film first and omit the names of directors or performers. Include the company primarily responsible for distributing the film and the date of the film's original release. If you are discussing the work of a particular person connected with the film, include that person's name with a description in your citation. The example above emphasizes the work of the director of the film.

If you accessed a film online, your citation would also include the name of the site or service where you accessed the film (such as *Hulu* or *Netflix*), and a URL for the film.

28. Television or radio program

> "Second Sons." *Game of Thrones*, season 3, episode 8, Television 360, 2013.

If you are citing an episode or program in a general way (as in this first example), include the title of the episode, the series title (in italics), and the season and episode numbers. Depending on your rhetorical emphasis, you will also want to include either the production company and the year the episode was produced (as in the first example), *or* the distribution company and the date that the episode originally aired (as in the second example below).

If you are citing the work of a particular character or other person connected with the episode or program, include that person's name with a description in your citation. In this second example, the series creators and the work of a particular actor in the episode are emphasized:

> "Second Sons." *Game of Thrones*, created by David Bebioff and D. B. Weiss, performance
> by Peter Dinklage, season 3, episode 8, Home Box Office, 19 May 2013.

29. Sound recording

> Rollins, Sonny. *Saxophone Colossus*. Prestige, 1987.

When citing an entire album or collection, begin with the name of the artist(s), followed by the title of the album or collection, the recording company, and year of issue.

To cite a specific song, include the song title, in quotation marks, after the name of the artist:

> Rollins, Sonny. "You Don't Know What Love Is." *Saxophone Colossus*, Prestige, 1987.

30. Online video

> Welch, Kiera. "Useful Knots to Know: Ten Most Useful Knots." *YouTube*, 4 Dec. 2015,
> youtu.be/JGXQIrRraLA.

Include the name of the author of the video, if available. If the video was posted by someone other than the author, use the following format:

> "Led Zeppelin: Whole Lotta Love." *YouTube*, uploaded by Brian Silva, 23 Sep. 2013,
> youtu.be/uiLKT5rPHBA.

In this example, the creator of the video is not included. Begin with the title of the video in quotation marks, followed by the container (*YouTube*). Include the name of the person who uploaded the video preceded by the phrase *uploaded by*. Then list the date when the video was uploaded followed by the URL.

31. Social media

> @MalalaFund (Malala Fund). "#FACT: Increasing the number of girls completing 12yrs
> of edu by 1% could boost a country's economic growth by 0.3%." *Twitter*, 24 June
> 2016, 11:29 a.m., twitter.com/MalalaFund/status/746379764814974978.

For a short untitled message, like the tweet in this example, include the full text of the message in quotation marks as the title in your citation. Include both the date and time the message was posted, and the URL for the specific message.

> Metropolitan Museum of Art, New York. "What can be learned from unfinished films,
> from works that arrive to us as fragments?" *Facebook*, 9 May 2016, 7:48 p.m.,
> www.facebook.com/metmuseum/posts/10153693407457635.

For an online posting on a social media site (*Facebook*, in this example), include the name of the author of the post, the title of the post (or the first sentence of the post if there is no title, as in the example above), and the name of the social media site. List the date and time of the post, followed by the URL for the post.

32. Advertisement

> "Nike." Advertisement. *Adweek*, 27 Mar. 2013, www.adweek.com/adfreak/
> nikes-new-tiger-woods-ad-says-more-about-us-him-148172.

Notice that this entry includes a description of the kind of source it is (advertisement). Otherwise, the entry is similar to a web page entry.

33. Art

> Cave, Nick. *Soundsuit*. 2011, Museum of Modern Art, New York.

Cite the artist first and then the title of the work. Next, include the date when the work was created followed by the name of the institution where the art is housed and the city. If you found the art in a print source, follow the appropriate format for publication details.

34. Government publication

> United States, Department of Transportation. *Bridge Management: Practices in Idaho,
> Michigan, and Virginia*. Government Publishing Office, 2012.

For government documents, the name of the nation or state appears first, followed by the agency (Department of Transportation, in this example) and the title of the publication (*Bridge Management*). Also include the publisher (Government Publishing Office) and the date of publication (2012).

If you accessed the publication online, include the URL:

United States, Department of Transportation. *Bridge Management: Practices in Idaho, Michigan, and Virginia.* Government Publishing Office, 2012, www.fhwa.dot.gov/ asset/hif12029/hif12029.pdf.

Sample MLA-Style Research Paper

The following essay by Matt Searle, written for a writing class at Emerson College, follows MLA guidelines for formatting a research paper. Matt's essay is a causal analysis (see Chapter 5 for discussion of analysis) that explores the potential impact of digital technologies on literacy and cognition. He addresses the question, What effects are the rapidly growing uses of digital technologies having on how we read and think? As you read, notice how Matt examines this question from various angles, taking into account what different experts think and what research has shown. Notice, too, how Matt carefully documents his sources using MLA style.

For research papers, MLA recommends placing your name, the title of your paper, and other relevant information (such as the date, the course number, and the instructor's name) on the first page, as Matt has done, rather than on a separate title page. If you are required to use a title page, center this information on the page.

When formatting a paper in MLA style, remember to

- Use one-inch margins.
- Use a legible font, such as Times Roman, set at 12 points.
- Double-space the text throughout the document (including the title and Works Cited page).
- Double-space between the heading and the title and between the title and the main text on the first page.
- Indent paragraphs one-half inch.
- Number all pages, including the first page, in the upper-right-hand corner.
- Place your last name before the page number on each page. (If you are using a program such as Microsoft Word, you can use the header function to create a running head that includes your name and the page number on each page.)
- Include the Works Cited list on a separate page at the end of the document.

On the first page of his paper, Matt includes his name, his instructor's name, the course title, and the date. Include other information as required by your instructor, such as the title of the assignment. Use a separate title page only if your instructor requires it.

Matt Searle

Dr. John Dennis Anderson

Evolution of Expression

20 October 2015

The title of Matt's paper is centered and placed after his name and related information.

Anxieties Over Electracy

Over the course of the past decade, technology has shaped the way society accesses and absorbs information. In *Internet Invention: From Literacy to Electracy*, Gregory L. Ulmer argues that our culture is transitioning from traditional literacy to a type of "electracy" afforded by the digital age. However, this transition has been met with resistance by those who fear the changes it will bring. Concerns involving the superficiality of internet reading, loss of memory, and depletion of traditional literary skills have been brought to the forefront of the debate about literacy and electracy. As the internet continues to rewire our brains and becomes a ubiquitous presence in our world, we must take the time to fully understand its impact.

Because Matt mentions the name of the author of this source in his sentence, he doesn't need to include it in the in-text citation. However, because this source is one of two by the same author, Matt includes a brief title so that readers know which source by Ulmer Matt is citing. Note that he includes the page number of the source as well.

One of the primary criticisms of electracy, defined by Ulmer as being to digital media what literacy is to print, is that it causes superficial understanding (*Internet* xii). Just as Johann Gutenberg's invention of the printing press increased freedom of thought and public expression, the advent of the internet has increased the availability of information. Those who welcome this influx of data subscribe to a philosophy that Adam Gopnik has coined "Never Better-ism," a belief in the internet's potential to create a new utopia. However, there are others who are as skeptical as the "Never-Betters" are optimistic. In a well-known article titled "Is Google Making Us Stupid?," writer Nicholas Carr expresses the belief that digital literacy leads to a depletion of textual analysis and cognition. Citing his own inability to read lengthy articles without skimming and an increasing lack of patience with text, Carr claims that the internet leads to ADD-like behavior. He contends that we are no longer "scuba divers" of information—that is, we no longer critically assess what we read (57). Furthermore, internet users often feel the need to hop around to various sites rather than focus on one in particular. Though some believe this habit of "power browsing" stimulates creativity, internet critics such as Carr worry that our culture will be permanently unable to perform in-depth analysis (59). Carr cites the research of Maryanne Wolf, a developmental psychologist, to highlight this concern:

> Wolf worries that the style of reading promoted by the Net, a style that puts "efficiency" and "immediacy" above all else, may be weakening our capacity for the kind of deep reading that emerged when an earlier technology, the printing press, made long and complex works of prose commonplace. When we read online, she says, we tend to become "mere decoders of information." Our ability to interpret text, to make the rich mental connections that form when we read deeply and without distraction, remains largely disengaged. (59)

With newspapers such as *The New York Times* attracting readers by adding abstracts for every three pages and online journalists peppering their articles with hyperlinks, the medium is gradually adjusting to our changing behavior (61).

While the criticisms lodged by Carr and others towards electracy may seem extreme, some research suggests that the internet is shaping the way we think. Human brains are extremely malleable as neurons often break old connections and form new ones. Just as reading Chinese text from right to left is not a natural talent, electrate reading is very much a learned skill. Rather than following the typical linear progression of alphabetic literacy, numerous hyperlinks and a virtual cornucopia of information encourage a "zigzag" approach to reading (Rich A27). Thus, the question is not whether the internet is affecting the way we think, but whether it is modifying the brain in a positive fashion. It is possible that our neurological transition to electrate thinking is a natural progression in our mental development, but anxiety still exists over electracy's permanent effects. For example, studies have shown that the internet can have a serious impact on memory (Johnson).

According to MLA style, you must set off as a block quote any quotation that is four lines or more from your source text, as Matt does here. Indent the block quote one-half inch from the left-hand margin. Notice that the page reference is placed in parentheses *after* the period of the final sentence of the block quote.

For this citation, Matt includes the author's last name (Rich) followed by the page reference, indicating that Matt is citing information from that specific page of the source text.

For this citation, Matt includes only the author's last name (Johnson) because he is citing the entire source text rather than a specific page from that text.

Because websites such as Google easily provide the answers to our questions, some consider it no longer necessary to attempt to memorize information. In this way, we as a culture tend to "outsource" our memories to electronics rather than use our brains for retention (Johnson A7). In one study, three thousand people were asked to remember the birthdate of a relative; only forty percent of people under thirty years old were able to answer correctly as compared to eighty-seven percent of people over the age of fifty (Thompson). Even more staggering was the fact that fully a third of youths were able to recite their phone number only after checking the phone itself (Thompson).

This loss of recall seems to be directly linked to electracy, as further studies have shown that people are more likely to remember information that they believe will be deleted. According to neuroscientist Gary Small, "We're . . . [u]sing the World Wide Web as an external hard drive to augment our biological memory stores" (qtd. in Johnson A7). However, as with any neurobiological development, there are some psychological benefits. With less of our brain used for memory storage, we can free up our gray matter to be used for brainstorming and daydreaming. Some experts promote the idea that intelligence is not truly about knowing information, but instead knowing where to find it. University of Pittsburgh psychology professor Richard Moreland has labeled the perceived need to retain all information "maladaptive" (qtd. in Johnson A7). Thus, skeptics of electracy must consider both the positive and negative aspects of the transition.

The question of whether electracy will supersede traditional literacy has also become an issue in recent years. Children between the ages of eight and eighteen have increased their internet usage from an average of forty-six minutes per day in 1984 to an hour and forty-one minutes per day in the present (Rich A16). At the same time, only one-fifth of seventeen-year-olds read for fun every day, a statistic that some critics argue seems to correlate with a drastic

The abbreviation *qtd. in* (which means "quoted in") in this citation indicates that the quotation by Gary Small in this sentence was taken not from the original text by Small but from the text by Johnson.

12

drop on critical reading test scores (Rich A16). Proponents of internet reading claim that it is simply a new type of literacy that allows its users to create their own beginnings, middles, and ends. Reading online can also allow those who have learning disabilities such as dyslexia to read in a more comfortable environment and format (Rich A17).

Another argument against electrate skepticism is that the internet encourages reading amongst those who would not normally read otherwise. For example, giving internet access to low income families who may struggle to buy books has been shown to increase overall reading time (Rich A16). With ninety percent of employers listing reading comprehension as very important (Rich A16), it is essential that future generations be able to comprehend the information they take in. This means that while electracy may have a place in our culture, where it belongs is still unclear. Groups such as the Organization for Economic Cooperation and Development plan to add electronic reading sections to aptitude tests, but these actions have been scoffed at by many (Rich A17). The experts that fear our transition from literacy to electracy are aware that only the reading of traditional literate texts has been proven to cause higher comprehension and performance levels (Rich A16). Therefore, electracy opponents do not necessarily want to dissolve the medium, but simply do not want it to replace what is currently known as reading.

Ulmer does not see the internet as destroying our literate abilities, but rather building on them in what he calls a "society of the spectacle" (*Internet* xiii). In Ulmer's vision, imagination and visualization can be used in combination with critical thinking in order to solve problems: "What literacy is to the analytical mind, electracy is to the affective body: a prosthesis that enhances and augments a natural or organic human potential" ("Gregory Ulmer-Quotes"). For Ulmer, electracy is an apparatus that is to be used for future generations, which is why he labels *Internet Invention* as a new

Notice that Matt cites the source text by Rich repeatedly in these paragraphs. Normally, if you are citing the same text repeatedly, you don't need to include a citation in each sentence. However, because Matt is taking information from different pages of the same source text, he includes numerous in-text citations to indicate to readers specifically where in the source text this information appears.

Matt does not include a page number in this citation because his source is an online source without page numbers.

generation textbook (*Internet* xiii). Ulmer's convictions are reflected by others who support the movement towards electracy. These thinkers point out that when literacy first began, it also caused cynicism, but it ultimately became the widely accepted norm. Indeed, it seems that the advent of new technologies has always made people uneasy and stirred fears that the capacities of the human brain may either be replaced or diminished. However, as Ulmer sees the situation, technological progression is both a natural and welcome development. We may no longer be able to think in a purely literate and literal sense, but as Michigan State University professor Rand J. Spiro puts it, "[T]he world doesn't go in a line" (qtd. in Rich A16). If we as a culture can harness the potential of the internet, perhaps Ulmer's vision can come to fruition.

The world is constantly evolving as new technologies and philosophies begin to dominate the cultural landscape. With the internet a ubiquitous presence in the lives of almost all human beings, becoming fluent in what Greg Ulmer has dubbed electracy is integral. Fears that the internet causes superficiality, rewires our brains, and decreases literacy have been corroborated by studies, but that does not mean that the internet is without benefits. By understanding its effects and using electracy to build off our literate knowledge, we can determine where this skill fits within our society.

Works Cited

Carr, Nicholas. "Is Google Making Us Stupid?" *The Atlantic*, July-Aug. 2008, pp. 56-63.

Gopnik, Adam. "The Information: How the Internet Gets Inside Us." *The New Yorker*, 14 & 21 Feb. 2011, www.newyorker.com/magazine/2011/02/14/the-information.

Johnson, Carolyn Y. "Memory Slips Caught in the Net." *The Boston Globe*, 15 July 2011, pp. A1+.

Rich, Motoko. "Literacy Debate: Online, R U Really Reading?" *The New York Times*, late ed., 27 July 2008, pp. A1+.

Thompson, Clive. "Your Outboard Brain Knows All." *Wired*, 25 Sept. 2007, www.wired.com/2007/09/st-thompson-3/.

Ulmer, Gregory L. "Gregory Ulmer-Quotes." *European Graduate School*, 2011, www.egs.edu/faculty/gregory-ulmer/quotes/.

---. *Internet Invention: From Literacy to Electracy*. Longman, 2002.

Begin the Works Cited List on a new page after the main text of the essay. Center the term *Works Cited* at the top of the page. Note that there is no extra space between the term *Works Cited* and the first item in the list. The items are listed alphabetically by author's last name or the title (if no author is listed).

Matt follows the MLA guidelines for each item in his Works Cited list, as explained in this chapter. Notice that each item in the list is formatted with a hanging indent of one-half inch.

Index

10 Core Concepts

1 *Writing is a process of discovery and learning.*
The act of writing is rarely a straightforward, linear process, and it often takes you to places you didn't expect.

2 *Good writing fits the context.*
The writer, the subject, and the audience are the context that will determine how well a piece of writing does its work.

3 *The medium is part of the message.*
You can express your ideas in a wide variety of ways depending on the tools and technology you use.

4 *A writer must have something to say.*
Having a clear, valid main point or idea is an essential element of effective writing.

5 *A writer must support claims and assertions.*
Not only must you have something relevant to say, but you must also be able to back up what you say.

6 *Purpose determines form, style, and organization in writing.*
Every kind of text is governed by general expectations regarding its form, which helps it fulfill its purpose in a given context.

7 *Writing is a social activity.*
Writers share drafts; they write for specific audiences; and they draw on socially constructed conventions to accomplish their purposes.

8 *Revision is an essential part of writing.*
Adding, deleting, and moving material is integral to the writing process: writers keep rewriting until their message is clear to readers.

9 *There is always a voice in writing, even when there isn't an I.*
Distinctive writing results from being able to "hear" the writer's voice or personality in the word choices and sentences the writer uses.

10 *Good writing means more than good grammar.*
A perfectly correct essay can be a perfectly lousy piece of writing if it does not fulfill its purposes and meet the needs of its audience.